Org

Seventh Edition

Organized Crime

From the Mob to Transnational Organized Crime

Seventh Edition

Jay S. Albanese

Routledge
Taylor & Francis Group

LONDON AND NEW YORK

First published 1985 by Anderson Publishing

Published 2015 by Routledge
2 Park Square, Milton Park, Abingdon, Oxon OX14 4RN

and by Routledge
711 Third Avenue, New York, NY 10017

Routledge is an imprint of the Taylor & Francis Group, an informa business

Library of Congress Cataloging-in-Publication Data
Albanese, Jay S.
  [Organized crime in America]
  Organized crime: from the mob to transnational organized crime / Jay S. Albanese. – Seventh edition.
    pages cm
  ISBN 978-0-323-29606-9
1. Organized crime–United States. 2. Organized crime–United States–History–20th century. 3. Organized
crime investigation–United States. 4. Transnational crime. I. Title.
  HV6446.A34 1996
  364.1060973–dc23
                                                                                    2014019475

British Library Cataloguing in Publication Data
A catalogue record for this book is available from the British Library

ISBN-13: 978-1-138-85885-5 (hbk)
ISBN-13: 978-0-323-29606-9 (pbk)

Printed and bound in Great Britain by
TJ International Ltd, Padstow, Cornwall

Dedication

To
Leslie E. King
who also knows quite a bit about organized crime—
for her encouragement and support over many years.

Contents

About the Author

Jay S. Albanese is a professor and criminologist in the Wilder School of Government & Public Affairs at Virginia Commonwealth University. He served as Chief of the International Center at the National Institute of Justice (NIJ), the research arm of the U.S. Department of Justice. Albanese received Ph.D. and M.A. degrees from Rutgers University and a B.A. from Niagara University. He was the first Ph.D. recipient from the Rutgers School of Criminal Justice. Albanese is author or editor of 16 books, including *Criminal Justice* (5th ed., Prentice Hall, 2013), *Professional Ethics in Criminal Justice: Being Ethical When No One Is Looking* (3rd ed., Prentice Hall, 2012), *Comparative Criminal Justice Systems* (with H. Dammer) (5th ed., Wadsworth, 2014), *Transnational Crime and the 21st Century* (Oxford University Press, 2011), and *Handbook on Transnational Crime and Justice* (with P. Reichel) (2nd ed., Sage Publications, 2014). Albanese is a recipient of the Elske Smith Distinguished Lecturer Award from Virginia Commonwealth University and the Teaching Excellence Award from Niagara University. He received the Gerhard Mueller Award from the International Section of the Academy of Criminal Justice Sciences. He has served as Executive Director of the International Association for the Study of Organized Crime and is a past president and fellow of the Academy of Criminal Justice Sciences. He currently serves on the Executive Board of the American Society of Criminology.

Online Resources

Interactive resources can be accessed for free by registering at
www.routledge.com/cw/albanese

Acknowledgments

My own intellectual history regarding organized crime has contributed greatly to the composition of this book. First, several people at Rutgers served to initiate and stimulate my interest in organized crime. Richard Sparks got me interested in the subject during a graduate course, when he declared, "Organized crime is more than a bunch of uncouth Italians." Dwight Smith provided insights in both conversation and through his publications. The School of Criminal Justice at Rutgers, and the resources of the library there, continue to provide opportunities for me as an alumnus to develop professional, personal, and social relationships, some of which were first established years ago as a graduate student. Many lifelong friends were made from among the faculty and students there. Phyllis Schultze of the Don M. Gottfredson Library of Criminal Justice at Rutgers University cheerfully helped me locate many elusive sources in the course of preparing this book.

Leslie King provided a knowledgeable sounding board for ideas about organized crime for many years while serving in her role as an investigator for the New York State Organized Crime Task Force and doing subsequent work for the FBI and State Department. Judge James W. Bachman deserves special thanks for his careful review of the previous edition and his many useful suggestions. Dave Whelan also contributed good ideas for this new edition, and his background and experience in the field were a helpful sounding board. Sara Scott of Elsevier Publishing encouraged the proposal for this book and deserves thanks for seeing it through. Ellen S. Boyne, my editor, did a magnificent editorial job and is always wonderful to work with.

It is important to thank a number of my former students and friends at Virginia Commonwealth University, Niagara University, and the National Institute of Justice, where I have made many friends among colleagues, students, and alumni. Hopefully, we have influenced one another in a positive way. Although we sometimes disagreed on the path toward knowledge and experience, the premise of our pursuit never varied: at no time did we forget to have fun along the way.

Introduction

Organized crime remains one of the most fascinating manifestations of criminal behavior, yet it remains one of the least understood. There have been many important convictions of organized crime figures, new transnational links have been found, and new attention has been given to human smuggling, Internet crimes, and other modern manifestations of organized criminal activity. This book reports on these and other significant developments in organized crime in recent years.

This book conveys in a concise manner the nature, history, and theories of organized crime, together with the criminal justice response. It includes an assessment of the investigation, prosecution, defense, and sentencing of organized criminals to date. In addition, a review of alternative futures in the prevention of organized crime is presented. This book is designed, therefore, to provide a synthesis of important developments in the understanding, prevention, and criminal justice response to organized crime.

There are several features that distinguish this book from others:

- Numerous critical thinking exercises that help students apply and evaluate concepts using actual case examples. Additional exercises are available online
- A legal analysis of the offenses that underlie organized crime
- Specific attention to new forms of organized crime activity
- Application of ethics to understanding the causes of organized crime
- The nature of implications of transnational organized crime operations
- Four separate chapters on the criminal justice response to organized crime: investigation, prosecution, defense, and sentencing
- An *Organized Crime Biography* is included in each chapter, summarizing recent popular books on organized crime figures and groups
- An *Organized Crime at the Movies* special insert in every chapter, relating portrayals of organized crime in the media to organized crime in practice
- Figures in each chapter to illustrate the connections among organized crime concepts

- A glossary with definitions of key terms related to organized crime
- A time line of major events in the history of organized crime in the United States

An instructor's resource manual is available that provides answers to the critical thinking exercises, as well as several hundred questions and answers that can be used to test students' understanding of the contents of the book. Additional exercises are available online.

The careful reader of this book will come away with a clear understanding of the definition of organized crime, how it is categorized under law (as a number of distinct crimes), the individual causes of organized crime, models explaining its persistence, the history of the Mafia, Presidential investigations, nontraditional and transnational groups, and the investigation, prosecution, defense, sentencing, and prevention of organized crime. Rather than merely summarizing the existing literature in encyclopedic fashion, this book *organizes* information into a meaningful way. This will empower the student to separate the fact from fiction of organized crime. The incorporation of critical thinking exercises throughout the book will reinforce the student's ability to apply the important principles of organized crime in new fact situations and to anticipate consequences for the future.

CHAPTER 1

What Is Organized Crime?

There's something inherently more dangerous about crimes committed by two or more people.

Sammy Gravano and his son were sentenced to prison terms on charges they conspired to distribute the drug ecstasy in the New York City area. Gravano was once underboss to John Gotti and later became an informer against him, serving 5 years in prison. He ultimately moved to Arizona in the Witness Protection Program, resuming his criminal career under an assumed name. For most people, Sammy Gravano characterizes the true nature of organized crime. But is organized crime simply groups of career criminals who engage in criminal activity or are the groups and activities more systematically organized? This chapter presents the state of our knowledge regarding the nature, definition, and characteristics of organized crime.

THE FASCINATION WITH ORGANIZED CRIME

Organized crime is perhaps the most interesting form of criminal behavior. Public fascination with the "Mafia," the "Mob," the "Syndicate," and other suggestive descriptions has remained strong for more than a century. *The Godfather*, a novel, was originally published in 1969 and is the most popular book about crime ever published, and one of the best-selling novels in history.[1] More than 15 million copies have been sold. When a movie version was released in 1972, it grossed more than $200 million, making it one of the most successful movies ever made.[2]

The HBO television series "The Sopranos" first aired in the late 1990s to huge audiences. The series portrayed a fictional Italian-American organized crime family in New Jersey. The show spawned a market for video and DVD versions of old episodes and a "Sopranos Tour" that takes tourists to locations featured in the series, such as cemeteries, docks, and stores. A sporting goods store, Ramsey Outdoor, was forced into bankruptcy on the television show, but as the tour guide said, "people have trouble distinguishing between reality and fiction," especially when it comes to organized crime. The real sporting goods store never went out of business, but its business dropped off dramatically after the episode, as viewers apparently believed the television portrayal to be real. The real store had to take out ads reminding customers that it was still open and that "The Sopranos" was just a TV show.[3] In a similar way, James Gandolfini, one of the featured actors on the show, reported that people claiming to be mobsters occasionally approached him. He said, "I'd like to think that the smarter mobsters are the ones who don't come up to TV actors."[4]

This peculiar fascination with organized crime has often made it difficult to separate fact from fiction, however, and it has discouraged many criminologists from seriously studying the problem. Furthermore, its complexity, mystique, and apparent success have made reliable information difficult to come by. It has only been during the past 50 years that serious efforts to study organized crime objectively have flourished. For example, the President's Crime Commission established a task force in 1967 to investigate organized crime specifically. Its conclusions about the state of knowledge at that time were quite candid.

> Our knowledge of the structure which makes "organized crime" organized is somewhat comparable to the knowledge of Standard Oil which could be gleaned from interviews with gasoline station attendants. Detailed knowledge of the formal and informal structure of the confederation of Sicilian-Italian "families" in the United States would represent one of the greatest criminological advances ever made, even if it were universally recognized that this knowledge was not synonymous with knowledge about all organized crime in America.[5]

Investigators attempting to analyze the structure and functioning of particular organized criminal groups have pointed to the need for additional case studies, which would help confirm or deny their findings in individual circumstances.[6] Researcher Annelise Anderson has argued that there is a need for information, "about organized criminal activity itself, by which the government's new legislation and its expanding level of effort can be evaluated."[7] The U.S. Government Accountability Office, the investigative arm of Congress (formerly named the General Accounting Office), concluded that the absence of a consensus in the Justice Department about the fundamental definition of organized crime has hampered the potential success of crime control programs designed to combat it.[8] The President's Commission on Organized Crime, appointed by Ronald Reagan during the 1980s, also did not offer any clear definition of organized crime. Rather, it described a series of characteristics of "criminal groups," "protectors," and "specialist support" necessary for organized crime.[9]

This apparent confusion over what constitutes organized crime is puzzling, given the long history of interest in the subject. Key words such as "Mafia," "mob," "syndicate," "gang," and "outfit" are often used to characterize it, but the precise meaning of these terms is often lost in discussions of the "appearances" and "earmarks" of organized crime. Nevertheless, there's something inherently more dangerous about crimes committed by two or more people, in terms of the organization involved and potential for harm, so the fact that some crimes are "organized" makes them worthy of careful analysis.

DEFINING ORGANIZED CRIME

U.S. Supreme Court Justice Potter Stewart once said he did not know precisely what it is, but "I know it when I see it."[10] He was talking about obscenity, but he may as well have been speaking of organized crime. By synthesizing all the research of the past 50 years, however, it is possible to arrive at a consensus definition of organized crime.

An analysis by criminologist Frank Hagan attempted to elicit common elements of the various descriptions of organized crime. After discovering that many books failed to provide explicit definitions of organized crime, he found that definitions had been offered by 13 different authors in books and government reports about organized crime written during the previous 15 years.[11] I have updated Hagan's analysis with authors who have attempted to define organized crime more recently.[12]

The good news is that there is an emerging consensus about what actually constitutes organized crime. The bad news is that 11 different aspects of organized crime have been included in the definitions of various authors with varying levels of frequency. Table 1.1 summarizes these 11 attributes and how many authors have included them in their definition.

Table 1.1 Definitions of Organized Crime in the Literature

Characteristics	Number of Authors
Organized hierarchy continuing	16
Rational profit through crime	13
Use of force or threat	12
Corruption of public officials to maintain immunity	11
Public demand for services	7
Monopoly over particular market	6
Restricted membership	4
Nonideological	4
Specialization	3
Code of secrecy	3
Extensive planning	2

As Table 1.1 indicates, there is great consensus in the literature that organized crime functions as a continuing enterprise that rationally works to make a profit through illicit activities and that it ensures its existence through the use of threats or force and through corruption of public officials to maintain a degree of immunity from law enforcement. There also appears to be some consensus that organized crime tends to be restricted to those illegal goods and services that are in great public demand through monopoly control of an illicit market.

There is considerably less consensus, as Table 1.1 illustrates, that organized crime has exclusive membership, has ideological or political reasons behind its activities, requires specialization in planning or carrying out specific activities, or operates under a code of secrecy. As a result, it appears that a definition of organized crime, based on a consensus of writers over the course of the past 50 years, reads as follows:

> Organized crime is a continuing criminal enterprise that rationally works to profit from illicit activities that are often in great public demand. Its continuing existence is maintained through the use of force, threats, monopoly control, and/or the corruption of public officials.

SIMILARITIES AND DIFFERENCES BETWEEN ORGANIZED CRIME AND WHITE-COLLAR CRIMES

There are, of course, some confounding factors to be addressed. For example, how does an otherwise legitimate corporation that collects toxic waste, but dumps some of it illegally, fit into this definition? Is a motorcycle gang that sells drugs as a sideline part of organized crime? What about a licensed massage parlor that also offers sex for money to some customers? As many investigators have recognized, perhaps organized crime does not exist as an ideal type, but rather as a "degree" of criminal activity or as a point on the "spectrum of legitimacy."[13] Given that the product is the same, isn't the primary difference between loansharking and a legitimate loan the interest rate charged? Is not the primary difference between criminal and noncriminal distribution of a controlled substance (narcotics) whether or not the distributor is licensed (i.e., doctor or pharmacist), or unlicensed, by the state? The point to keep in mind is that organized crime is actually one type of several categories of organized criminal behavior, which are called "organizational," "corporate," "political," and "white-collar" crimes.

Crimes by corporations during the course of business, or crimes by politicians or government agencies, can also be considered part of "organized" crime. For example, official misconduct by a government official, obstruction of justice, and commercial bribery are all types of organized criminal behavior. In as much as they fulfill the requirements of the definition given earlier, they constitute a part of what is known as organized crime. As the National Advisory Committee on Criminal Justice Standards and Goals has recognized, there are more similarities than differences between organized and so-called white-collar crimes.

> Accordingly, the perpetrators of organized crime may include corrupt business executives, members of the professions, public officials, or members of any other occupational group, in addition to the conventional racketeer element.[14]

Some important differences exist between organized crime and organizational or "white-collar" crime. Perhaps the most significant distinction is the fact that organizational crimes generally occur during the course of otherwise legitimate business or governmental affairs. White-collar or organizational crime, therefore, most often occurs as criminal activity that is a *deviation from legitimate business activity*. However, organized crime, as defined earlier, occurs as a criminal activity that is a *continuing criminal enterprise* that exists to profit *primarily* from that activity.

It is important to keep in mind the fact that organized crime is not restricted to the activities of criminal syndicates. Pontell and Calavita concluded in their study of the savings and loan banking scandal that if we reserve the term "organized crime" for continuing conspiracies that include the corruption of government officials, "then much of the savings and loan scandal involved organized crime."[15] In interviews with the Federal Bureau of Investigation, Secret Service, and regulatory agencies, they found a "recurring theme" of conspiracies between savings and loan officials (insiders) and accountants, lawyers, and real estate developers (outsiders). Comparing these kinds of corrupt relationships with more traditional organized crime techniques of no-show jobs at construction sites, or payoffs for "protection," reveal they are more similar than different. Similarly, an investigation in Canada found that organized crime groups were involved in typically white-collar mortgage frauds, employing straw buyers, check fraud, and corrupted real estate insiders to carry out the fraudulent activity. In Houston, the CEO of a hospital and six others were charged in a scheme to pay cash to "patient recruiters" who sent those recruited to a partial hospitalization rehabilitation program for the mentally ill. The Medicare-eligible patients received cigarettes, food, and coupons redeemable at the hospital's store, while the scheme defrauded the Medicare program of $158 million over 7 years. Examples like these illustrate that there is, in fact, much crime that is committed by businesses, corporations, politicians, and government agencies that is as serious and harmful as the crimes of criminal enterprises, and sometimes overlaps with them.[16] An example of this overlap is provided by an indictment that charged three defendants for operating a series of fraudulent companies that sold coffee display racks as business opportunities. Buyers were told they would receive display racks and packets of coffee and assistance in establishing and maintaining a business selling the coffee. The business opportunities the defendants sold cost a minimum of $10,000. But all three defendants allegedly made numerous false statements to potential purchasers of the business opportunities to induce them to buy. These misrepresentations included statements that purchasers would earn substantial profits, that other purchasers were earning substantial profits, and that they would be given lucrative "commercial accounts." It turned out that the purchasers made little to no money on their investments, were unable to find profitable locations or accounts, and were not provided the support promised. Once purchasers began filing complaints with the Better Business Bureau or state authorities, the defendants shut down each of their companies in turn, and opened the next one. In order to evade detection, all the defendants allegedly used aliases and gave out false addresses for the company. The indictment alleges that the defendants also avoided listing their own names on corporate and promotional documents, and instead paid people who did not work at the companies to be titular presidents.[17] It can be seen in this case that the line between a generic business fraud and an ongoing criminal conspiracy can be thin indeed. In the case of the coffee business, there was no effort to sell or operate actual coffee businesses, but rather an effort to sell a bogus business opportunity to as many people as possible, so the line is crossed from simple fraud to an ongoing criminal enterprise characteristic of organized crime.

The situation overseas appears to be similar. It is reported that organized crime groups are becoming increasingly active in legal business, operating in the "gray zone" between illicit and licit markets. In Sweden, for instance, organized crime groups, including motorcycle gangs, have been found to supply legal businesses with undocumented workers and obtain fraudulent unemployment subsidies from the government. In Estonia, there is suspicion that some companies with insolvency problems have been bought by criminals, and then stripped of their assets and filing for bankruptcy, thereby defrauding the government of taxes owed.[18]

This book focuses on the activities of continuing criminal enterprises, however, in an effort to separate the myth from the reality of organized crime. This criminal activity has been shrouded in a cloak of folklore, politics, and Hollywood productions that have done little to make the causes and effects of organized crime more apparent to the public, to policy makers, and to the criminal justice system.

TERRORISM AND ORGANIZED CRIME

Terrorist attacks in the United States during the past 20 years have drawn attention to potential terrorism-organized crime links. The bombing of the World

Trade Center in 1993, the explosion at the federal building in Oklahoma City in 1995, and the airplane attacks of September 11, 2001, at the World Trade Center and the Pentagon dramatically increased concern over the questions: How did these criminals organize? Where did they obtain funds to support their criminal activity? Are there international links to these acts of domestic terrorism? These are all important questions that point to the similarities and differences between terrorism and organized crime.

Terrorism involves crimes designed to intimidate or coerce civilians or a government in order to achieve political or social objectives. Examples would include hostage-taking in order to secure freedom for those seen as imprisoned unjustly or acts of violence done in retribution for perceived past injustices. In every case, an act of terrorism has a political objective, unlike the profit motive that lies behind organized crime. Organized crime can involve violence, coercion, civilians, and governments, but the objective in organized crime is profit or corruption (needed to maintain an illegal enterprise without government interference).

Organized crime and terrorism cross paths when terrorist groups use organized crime activity to fund their political objectives. In one case, a raid of 18 houses and businesses in Charlotte, North Carolina, occurred after indictments accused 22 people of immigration violations, weapons offenses, money laundering, and illegal trafficking in cigarettes (in violation of tax laws). Several of the suspects were linked to Hezbollah, the Middle Eastern terrorist organization.[19] In another case, a South American drug trafficker agreed to allow large numbers of purported Hezbollah operatives to use Suriname as a permanent base for attacks on American targets in exchange for a multimillion-dollar payoff. He agreed to supply Surinamese passports and to assist with their applications for visas to travel from South America into the United States.[20] This case illustrates how powerful organized crime groups can use their influence to cut profitable deals with terrorists or other groups who are willing to pay for it and how organized crime activity can be employed by terrorist groups to support their larger political targets.

Figure 1.1 Illustrates the distinctions among organized crime, white-collar crime, and terrorism. It is clear that the ongoing criminal profit motive distinguishes organized crime from white-collar crime and terrorism.

TYPOLOGY OF ORGANIZED CRIME

For all the mystique that permeates discussions of organized crime, there has been relatively little attention given to establishing the precise behaviors we are talking about. That is to say, what specific types of illegal acts are we referring to when we speak of organized crime?

When one examines the descriptions and definitions of organized crime in various criminal codes and case studies, three primary categories of illicit behavior

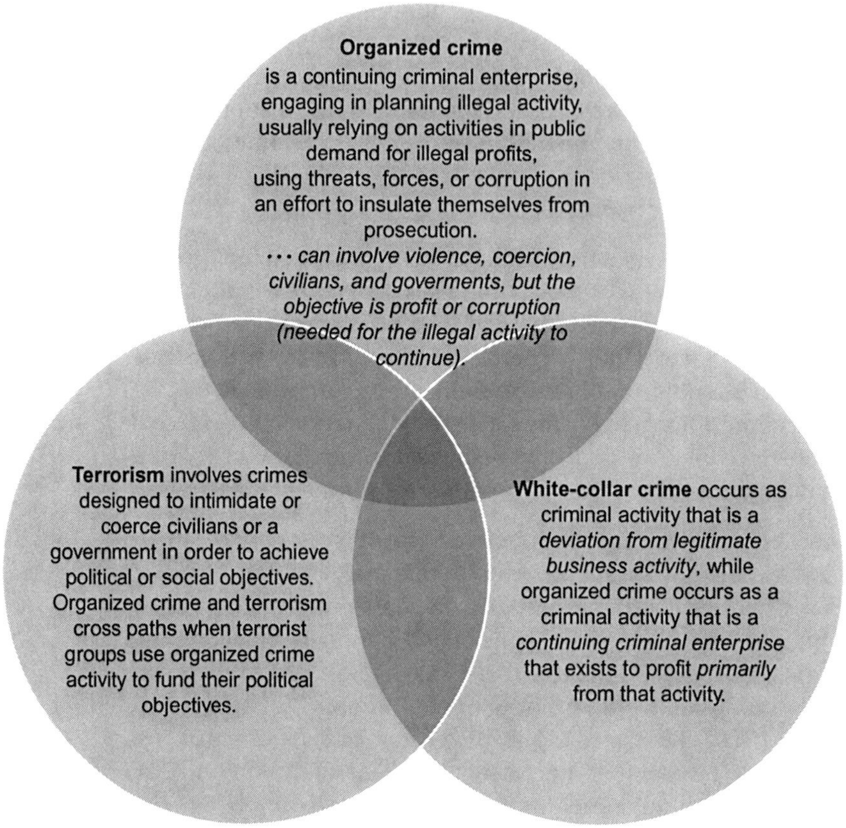

Organized crime
is a continuing criminal enterprise, engaging in planning illegal activity, usually relying on activities in public demand for illegal profits, using threats, forces, or corruption in an effort to insulate themselves from prosecution.
··· *can involve violence, coercion, civilians, and goverments, but the objective is profit or corruption (needed for the illegal activity to continue).*

Terrorism involves crimes designed to intimidate or coerce civilians or a government in order to achieve political or social objectives. Organized crime and terrorism cross paths when terrorist groups use organized crime activity to fund their political objectives.

White-collar crime occurs as criminal activity that is a *deviation from legitimate business activity*, while organized crime occurs as a criminal activity that is a *continuing criminal enterprise* that exists to profit *primarily* from that activity.

FIGURE 1.1 Distinguishing organized crime, white-collar crime, and terrorism.

emerge. These categories reflect the precise crimes that are implied when one speaks of "organized crime activity." The three categories include provision of illicit services, provision of illicit goods, and the infiltration of legitimate business or government. Within each of these categories are more specific crimes, which often draw the attention of the criminal justice system.

The provision of illicit services involves an attempt to satisfy the public demand for money, sex, and gambling that legitimate society does not fulfill. The specific crimes involved most often include loansharking, prostitution, and gambling. Loansharking is the lending of money to individuals at an interest rate in excess of that permitted by law. Organized prostitution offers sex for pay on a systematic basis. Gambling consists of games of chance that are not approved by the state. Numbers gambling, for example, is a lottery that operates without approval of the state. Each of these crimes occurs as a continuing enterprise due to the failure of a sizable portion of the public to obtain access to money, sex, or gambling in a legitimate way, such as through bank loans, marriage, or state lotteries.

The provision of illicit goods is a category of organized crime that offers particular products that a segment of the public desires, but cannot obtain through legitimate channels. The sale and distribution of drugs and the fencing (a "fence" is a person who knowingly buys and sells stolen property as an illicit business) and distribution of stolen property are examples of specific crimes in this category. There is a great demand for drugs, such as marijuana, cocaine, methamphetamine, and heroin, that are either illegal to possess or illegal to distribute outside very strict regulations imposed by the government. Needless to say, these regulations do not diminish the demand for the drugs and, as a result, some people attempt to obtain them illegally. In a similar way, a significant portion of society desires to buy products at the lowest price possible, regardless of where the seller originally obtained them. Due to this demand, organized criminals emerge who "fence" stolen merchandise (i.e., buy and sell stolen property) to customers who do not care from where it came. This stolen property might consist of automobiles, guns, jewelry, stereo equipment, cell phones, software, or any other product for which there is a high demand.

The third category of organized crime is the infiltration of legitimate business or government. Labor racketeering and the takeover of waste disposal companies are two examples of infiltration of legitimate business. Labor racketeering involves the use of force or threats to obtain money for ensuring jobs or labor peace. This often entails threatening employers or employees that if money is not paid, there will be no job for the employees or that violence, strikes, and/or vandalism will occur at the employers' companies. In a similar way, waste disposal companies in some areas have been taken over through the use of coercion to intimidate legitimate owners to sell the business or to have it operated by an outsider by means of intimidation.

Table 1.2 illustrates this three-part typology of organized crime.

Table 1.2 A Typology of Organized Crime

Type of Activity	Nature of Activity (Specific Crimes)	Harm
Provision of illicit goods and provision of illicit services	Gambling, lending, sex, narcotics, stolen property (*Examples of offenses*: illegal gambling, loansharking, prostitution, trafficking in pornography, drugs, stolen property)	• Consensual activities • No inherent violence • Economic harm
Infiltration of legitimate business or government	Coercive use of legal businesses or government agencies (from the inside or from the outside) for purposes of exploitation (*Examples of offenses*: extortion, racketeering)	• Usually nonconsensual activities • Threats, violence, extortion • Economic harm

The provision of illicit goods and the provision of illicit services are distinguished most clearly from the infiltration of legitimate business in their *consensual nature* and *lack of inherent violence*. Organized crime figures who offer illegal betting, loansharking, or drugs rely on the existing demand among the public to make money. Because they also rely heavily on return business, they want the illicit transaction to go well in order to ensure future bets, loans, and illicit sales. It is very unusual for criminal syndicates to solicit business in this fashion. Instead, those members of the public who are interested in illicit goods and services seek out the illicit opportunities. Violence plays no inherent role in the activities themselves, although bad debts cannot be collected through the courts, like they can for loans and sales in the legitimate market. Therefore, violence or threats occur when one party to the transaction feels cheated or short-changed and there is no legal alternative for resolving the dispute. Violence can also occur in an attempt to control or monopolize an illicit market. If a group wishes to corner the market on illicit gambling in a particular area, it may threaten or intimidate its illicit competitors. Once again, these threats are used as an enforcement mechanism rather than as an intrinsic part of the provision of illicit goods and services themselves.

CRITICAL THINKING EXERCISE 1.1

The Case of Selling a High School Football Player

Talented football players are in high demand at universities because winning football teams translate into increased revenues in tickets sold, games on television, bowl games, and alumni contributions. As a result, there is tremendous competition among colleges to get the best players to attend their institutions.

Two high school football coaches in Tennessee were indicted for allegedly "selling" their star player to the University of Alabama to play football. The high school team's All-American defensive lineman was 6-foot-4 and weighed 335 pounds. The coaches allegedly held discussions with representatives from several prominent football schools, beginning with demands for two vehicles, a house, and $60,000 for the rights to have their star player attend their college. The asking price ultimately climbed to $200,000. There is no evidence that the player or his single mother was offered any money, and the money allegedly was paid directly to the coaches by an alumni booster from the University of Alabama.

The player enrolled at the University of Alabama and transferred after 1 year to the University of Memphis, after the scandal broke. The National Collegiate Athletic Association found no fault with the player's conduct in this case, although there have been a number of other cases where boosters at various universities have given players, coaches, or family members money or property for the right to have a star high school player attend their college.

Critical Thinking Questions

1. Explain how any of the crimes discussed in this chapter might apply in this case.
2. If supply and demand form the basis for most organized crime, identify the supply-and-demand issues in this case. How can they be controlled more effectively?

Source: W. Smith, "The Selling of Albert Means," U.S. News & World Report (September 10, 2001), pp. 25-28.

Table 1.3 Differences between Bribery and Extortion

Extortion	1. A person obtains property from another using coercion (e.g., threats of future physical injury, property damage, or exposure to criminal charges or public humiliation) 2. There is a clear offender (the person using coercion) and victim (the threatened person) who is intimidated into turning over property to the offender
Bribery	1. A person (e.g., a public official, witness, juror) voluntarily solicits or accepts any benefit in exchange for influencing an official act 2. Unlike extortion, there is no coercion, so neither person is intimidated and both engage in the act voluntarily. Therefore, both the giver and the receiver of the bribe can be guilty of bribery

The infiltration of legitimate business or government is more predatory than the provision of illicit goods and services. Here, organized crime groups attempt to create a demand for their services rather than exploit an existing market as in the case of illicit goods and services. Demands for "protection" money or no-show jobs to avoid property damage, work stoppages, criminally motivated business or government insiders misusing their positions to exploit the business or government agency for criminal purposes, or violence are examples of the predatory nature of the infiltration of legitimate business or government. In legal terms, organized crime uses coercion or extortion in the infiltration of legitimate business, which involves implied or explicit threats to obtain a criminal objective. Coercion and extortion are not necessary to provide illicit goods or services because the demand already exists among the public. Table 1.3 illustrates the important differences between bribery and extortion and their relation to organized crime.

Bribery is a feature of organized crime in protecting illicit activities by paying or giving illicit favors to police, judges, jurors, or other public officials to "look the other way." Extortion characterizes the infiltration of legitimate business when organized crime tries to force payments from individuals or businesses using threats.

TYPOLOGY OF ORGANIZED CRIMINALS

Some typologies of organized crime attempt to classify its forms by looking at *who* is involved in the activity rather than by looking at the activity itself. For example, it is common to see discussions of traditional "street" crimes that include breakdowns by sex or race or other demographic descriptors. Such categorizations are less common in the case of organized crime, especially because estimates of its true extent are so imprecise. Typologies of organized crime focus more often on ethnicity and the nature of the structure of organized crime groups.

Ethnicity

Ethnicity (i.e., the ancestry or culture of a particular group of people) is perhaps the most common of all categorizations of organized crime, although it might be the most misleading. This is true for several important reasons:

- Organized crime is committed by a wide variety of ethnic groups, making ethnicity a poor indicator of organized crime activity.
- Evidence shows that often organized crime activities are not carried out within the boundaries of a specific ethnic group, making it interethnic.
- Other variables, such as local market conditions and criminal opportunities for certain products and services, may be much better indicators of organized crime than ethnicity.

There is a growing body of evidence that organized crime is not limited to the activities of a single ethnic group or even a few ethnic groups. The President's Commission on Organized Crime described "organized crime today" as 11 different groups that included:

- La Cosa Nostra (Italian)
- Outlaw motorcycle gangs
- Prison gangs
- Triads and tongs (Chinese)
- Vietnamese gangs
- Yakuza (Japanese)
- Marielitos (Cuban)
- Colombian cocaine rings
- Irish organized crime
- Russian organized crime
- Canadian organized crime

This curious mixture includes groups defined in terms of ethnic or national origin, those defined by the nature of their activity (cocaine rings), those defined by their geographic origin (prison gangs), and those defined by their means of transportation (motorcycle gangs).[21] Such a haphazard approach to defining and describing organized crime does little to help make sense of its causes, current events, or how policies against organized crime might be directed.

There is even evidence, as both the President's Commission and independent researchers have pointed out, that these groups and others (such as Jewish gangs) have worked with each other in the past and continue to do so in the present.[22] As a consequence, ethnicity is not a very powerful explanation for the existence of organized crime due to the large number of ethnic groups involved, their interaction with each other in criminal undertakings, and the fact that ethnicity is probably no more a causal factor than motorcycles.

Biographical attributes, such as ethnicity or methods of transportation, may help describe a particular person or group, but they do little to explain that person's or group's behavior (especially when compared to other members of that ethnic group who do not engage in organized crime activity).

A look at several investigations of ethnically based organized crime reveals why it is a weak descriptor. In addition to the fact that no single or multiple ethnic combination accounts for organized crime, ethnicity also has been found to be secondary to local criminal opportunities in explaining organized crime. A study of early twentieth century illicit cocaine trade in New York by historian Alan Block found major players with Jewish backgrounds, but also "notable is the evidence of interethnic cooperation" among New York's criminals.[23] He found evidence of Italian, Greek, Irish, and Black involvement, people who did not always work within their own ethnic group. Instead, he found these criminals to be "in reality criminal justice entrepreneurs" whose criminal careers were not within a particular organization but were involved in a "web of small but efficient organizations."[24]

A historical examination of opium smuggling networks in California by Jeffrey McIllwain concluded that the operations were "a multiethnic endeavor involving actors with various ethnic origins." Studies of contemporary drug trafficking found "numerous instances of close cooperation between Kurdish and Turkish drug trafficking groups in West Europe."[25]

An ethnography of the underground drug market by Patricia Adler in "Southwest County" found the market to be "largely competitive" rather than "visibly structured." She found participants "entered the market, transacted their deals, [and] shifted from one type of activity to another," responding to the demands of the market rather than through ethnic structures or concerns. Studies of Chinese and Greek organized crime abroad had comparable results, showing the primacy of opportunity, networks, and situational context.[26]

Similarly, a study of illegal gambling and loansharking by Peter Reuter in New York found economic considerations dictated entry and exit from the illicit marketplace. He found the criminal enterprises he studied in three areas were "not monopolies in the classic sense or subject to control by some external organization."[27] Like other investigations of organized crime groups, Reuter found that local market forces shaped the criminal behavior more so than ethnic ties or other characteristics of the criminal groups.

Organization of Crime Groups

A growing body of evidence indicates that organized crime groups revolve around specific illicit activities rather than the opposite. Desirable illicit activities, made desirable due to public demand, the local market, or other opportunity factors, appear to dictate how and what type of criminal group will emerge to exploit the opportunity. Less often, a group will attempt to "manufacture" a criminal opportunity through intimidation or extortion. This is probably due to human nature: it is easier and takes less energy to exploit the existing demand for illegal gambling, drugs, or stolen property than to "move in" forcefully on a preexisting legal or illegal business for illicit purposes.

Consider the classic ethnographic study by Francis Ianni and Elizabeth Reuss-Ianni, where Francis became a participant-observer of an organized crime group for 2 years and made observations of two other criminal groups. He found these groups to "have no structure apart from their functioning; nor do they have structure independent of their current 'personnel.'"[28] Joseph Albini's pioneering study of criminal groups in the United States and Italy drew a similar conclusion. Rather than belonging to an organization, those involved in organized crime engaged in relationships "predicated by the particular activity engaged in at any given time." The criminal "syndicate" is, in fact, "a system of loosely structured relationships functioning primarily because each participant is interested in furthering his own welfare."[29]

These studies suggest that the structure of organized crime groups derives from the activities in which they are engaged rather than by preexisting ethnic ties. Criminal-turned-informer Joseph Valachi testified before the U.S. Senate during the 1960s about his experience with a New York Italian-American crime group. He stated the function of the "family" or group was mutual protection; otherwise, "everybody operates by himself."[30] Therefore, significant attention must be given to how specific illegal activities generate particular types of criminal organizations. This is discussed further in Chapter 4.

Gender and Organized Crime

Historically, gender has played little role in the study of organized crime. Organized crime has been seen as masculine behavior with women involved only for purposes of exploitation (as in the case of prostitution) or as silent supporters of their husbands' or loved ones' questionable activities. In recent years, however, closer attention has been paid to the role of women in organized crime with some surprising results.

In an analysis of biographies, autobiographies, and case studies, James Calder attempted to understand more systematically the lives of "Mafia women."[31] These women were wives, daughters, mothers, nieces, and sisters of Mafia figures. He found these women were not receding, ignorant companions, as they often have been portrayed in fiction. Instead, he found considerable evidence that these women "have significant insight to, and awareness of criminal affiliations" of their male counterparts. These women are often not content or happy with their lives or position. They frequently feel cheated or manipulated by their men.[32] Finally, he found that these women sometimes rebel against their lifestyle, usually by way of arguments, separations, divorces, and occasionally violence.

However, there exist women involved in organized crime in their own right without dependent connections to men. An example is Arlyne Brickman, who was mistress to a number of prominent organized crime figures, including Bugsy Siegel and Joe Colombo.[33] As her biographer observed:

> Arlyne seems to feel no loyalty to anyone, an observation that, at times, caused me to suspect she might be a sociopath, cruising through life [as] a shark, simulating human emotion whenever it suited her purposes. A closer look at her history, however, led me to conclude that Arlyne does feel loyalty, however fleeting, to whomever happens to be stroking her ego.[34]

This characterization of a self-centered, emotionless person who has the appearance of a sociopath is a description that usually has characterized male organized crime figures, not females. In her role as mistress, Arlyne Brickman delivered messages between criminal figures, operated in the illegal gambling and drug markets, and eventually became a government informant when her daughter's life was threatened. In many ways, her activities parallel those of male organized crime figures.

In Italy, more than 100 women have been arrested for engaging in activities connected to organized crime from 1990-2000, whereas such arrests almost never occurred before 1990. Italy's success in prosecuting men has been offered as one reason for this change: "The more men they jail, the greater the pressure on the Mafia's women to fill the vacuum."[35] These women increasingly have been found to use their maiden names to open "clean" bank accounts, start new businesses, and collect protection money. A book based upon interviews with Mafia family members, victims, and police officials in Italy concludes that women are not innocent victims of potentially violent men, but play a vital role in supporting their husband's criminal activities in hiding fugitives, planning murders, and passing messages to incarcerated spouses from Mafia bosses.[36]

In an ethnographic study of three female gangs in the New York City area, Anne Campbell spent 6 months with each gang. The gangs were mixed racially, ethnically, and in terms of their reason for organizing. The three female gangs included a street gang, a biker gang, and a religious-cultural (Islamic) gang. As Campbell found in both her historical and empirical research,

> Girls have been part of gang life for over a hundred years, from social clubs through years of prohibition and corruption to the "bopping" gangs of the 1950s and through the civil disorders of the 1970s. ... [G]irls appear increasingly as sisters in the gang instead of molls.[37]

This growing awareness of the role of women as something more than mistresses to organized crime figures and gang members will be an interesting trend to watch in the future. Campbell found that girls still "exist as an annex to the male gang," however, and the "possibilities open to them [are] dictated and controlled by the boys."[38]

A study of 40 organized crime cases involving women in the Netherlands found ethnicity to be a spurious link among the offenders with family ties and bonds of friendship forming the basis for their participation in drug and human smuggling conspiracies. It was found that women "not only have knowledge about illegal activities but they also have crucial functions in the context of shielding illegal activities" from authorities.[39] This finding was manifested in the case of Catherine Greig who was the longtime girlfriend of crime figure and fugitive James "Whitey" Bulger. She was sentenced to 8 years in prison for her role in assisting Bulger elude capture over a period of 16 years.[40] Whether the emergence of women as independent players in organized crime becomes more common, as demonstrated in the case of Arlyne Brickman, will depend to some extent on our willingness to examine their lives more closely, and as something more than mistresses to the mob.

HOW MUCH ORGANIZED CRIME IS THERE?

The true extent of organized crime is unknown. Characteristic organized crimes, such as conspiracy, racketeering, and extortion, are not counted in any systematic way. Other offenses are known only when they result in arrests by police. Problems in relying on police arrests as a measure of criminal activity are apparent: much crime is undetected, some that is detected is not reported to police, and arrest rates go up or down depending on police activity and not necessarily on criminal activity. Keeping these reservations in mind, the Federal Bureau of Investigation tabulates arrests made by police nationwide for several offenses characteristic of organized crime. Trends in these arrests over the past 40 years are presented in Table 1.4.

As Table 1.4 illustrates, arrests for three of the four offenses have increased over the past 40 years, whereas arrests for gambling have dropped dramatically. These increases and decreases can be attributed to two primary factors:

- Change in law enforcement priorities
- Change in population base and number of police in the United States

Both the population of the United States and the number of sworn police officers have grown dramatically during the past four decades. Therefore, one would expect a "natural" increase in the number of arrests simply because there are more potential offenders and victims in the population, as well as

Table 1.4 Arrests for Crimes Related to Organized Crime

Offense	1970	1980	1990	2000	2010	40-Year Change
Drug abuse violations	65,734	351,955	785,536	1,579,566	1,273,963	19 times higher
Gambling	75,325	37,805	13,357	10,842	7,533	10 times lower
Prostitution and commercialized vice	45,803	67,920	80,888	87,620	48,281	5% higher
Stolen property (buy, receive, possess)	46,427	76,429	119,102	118,641	74,313	60% higher

Source: Federal Bureau of Investigation Uniform Crime Reports (www.fbi.gov—published annually)

more police looking for them. In a similar way, the public mood has shifted during the past four decades, especially with regard to gambling and drugs. Gambling has been legalized in many forms throughout the United States during the past 40 years because of a shift in the public perception from gambling as a "vice" to gambling as a "form of recreation."[41] Conversely, growing public concern about drugs developed over the same period. The huge increases in drug arrests (19 times higher in 2010 than in 1970) in the face of the significant drop in gambling arrests (10 times lower over the same period) clearly indicate shifting public and hence law enforcement priorities and attitudes regarding the seriousness of these forms of criminal behavior.

It is possible that the incidence of these offenses has changed over the years, but arrest statistics do not permit us to know for sure. The fact that prostitution and commercialized vice arrests have fluctuated, increasing 5% over 40 years, while arrests for stolen property have increased 60% above the 1970 level, suggests that more police, greater enforcement priority, and more actual cases have combined to produce these increases in arrests.

It is important to keep in mind, however, that not all gambling, drug, prostitution, or stolen property arrests have anything to do with organized crime. It is likely that a large number of these arrests were of individuals possessing illicit goods, or engaging in illicit services, absent organized crime connections. No effort has been made in the United States to separate organized crime versus non-organized crime cases for these offenses, but other countries have done so. In nations such as Belgium and Ukraine, for example, arrests of those who commit crimes as part of larger groups are noted at the arrest stage. The size of the group also becomes part of the official record. In this way, these countries obtain at least a general indication of individual versus organized crimes and can assess the extent to which known organized groups are involved in certain kinds of criminal activity.

THE REMAINDER OF THIS BOOK

Following this examination of the nature, definition, and typology of organized crime, the remainder of the book attempts to accomplish its objectives by answering seven specific questions:

1. What are the precise crimes we consider "organized crime"?
2. Why do people engage in organized crime as career criminals, and is it possible that what we know about various organized crime groups can be synthesized into a meaningful explanation of the continuing existence of these groups?
3. What is the history and current status of the Mafia in the United States?
4. What is the government's view of the organized crime problem and how is it changing?
5. How do transnational organized crime groups differ from locally based groups that have dominated our attention in the past?
6. Who investigates, prosecutes, and defends organized crime; what tools do they use; and how successful are they?
7. What is the best way to sentence organized crime offenders and organizations, and what are the prospects for long-term prevention?

Most books on organized crime discuss it in general terms: a list of its general characteristics, general tendencies, and names of known criminals. That approach lacks the conceptual framework required for meaningful research and investigations in the field. The term "organized crime" appears rarely in law, referring to a generic category of behaviors. Chapters 2 and 3 clearly separate these categories into specific offenses so that students of organized crime can understand the precise definitions and limits of those offenses we collectively call "organized crime."

Why people engage in organized crime, often as career criminals, is a fascinating question. Chapter 4 summarizes what is known about the causes of organized crime using past research and excerpts from the biographies of convicted organized crime members. Chapter 5 synthesizes this information into a three-part model of organized crime. This paradigm summarizes all the existing writing and research on the subject.

The history of the Mafia is shrouded in myth and folklore. Chapter 6 recounts the episodic history of the Mafia, the connection to Italy, and the distinctions between myth and reality in where the Mafia came from, how it has changed, and where it is today.

The government's perception of the nature and threat posed by organized crime fundamentally influences law, policy, and enforcement initiatives. Chapter 7 compares the two major presidential investigations of organized crime in the

United States of the past 50 years. How organized crime has changed, and the government's response to it, are clearly manifested in this comparison. Organized crime patterns and trends in "new" forms of criminal activity are also documented in Chapter 7.

CRITICAL THINKING EXERCISE 1.2

The Case of an Internet Stock Fraud

Jonathan Lebed became interested in the stock market when he and two fellow eighth graders finished fourth in a national stock-picking tournament sponsored by CNBC. He subsequently came up with a scheme to make real money, working out of his bedroom in New Jersey. Using brokerage accounts set up by his father, he bought cheap stocks traded on the Electronic Bulletin Board of the National Association of Securities Dealers. Lebed would then flood message boards on the Internet with false and misleading postings that gave the impression that these cheap stocks would soon become valuable. Messages such as "Net stock to gain 1000%," combined with false stories of who he was (a company president, rather than the 15-year-old he really was) created the illusion that he had inside knowledge about these inexpensive stocks and the companies that issued them. To prevent his identity or the source of the postings from becoming known, he used many fictitious names when posting the misleading messages about the cheap stocks he had purchased.

As soon as the stock prices rose in response to his postings, Lebed would sell his shares for a quick profit. According to the Securities and Exchange Commission (SEC), he profited from $11,000 to more than $70,000 on each trade. Lebed became the first minor ever to be charged by the SEC, accusing him of using the Internet to manipulate stocks and earning $273,000 in illegal profits. The case was settled when Lebed agreed to pay the government $285,000.

Critical Thinking Questions
1. Explain whether you would characterize this scheme as white-collar crime or organized crime.
2. Explain how any of the crimes discussed in this chapter could apply in this case.

Source: J. M. Pethokoukis, "How I Spent My Vacation: The SEC Nabs a Teen," U.S. News & World Report (October 2, 2000), p. 44.

The greatest change in organized crime over the past decade has been the transition from a focus on local crime groups and impacts to transnational organized crime. The demise of the Soviet Union and the dramatic rise in international travel and communication have formed the basis for more threatening forms of exploitation of criminal opportunities around the world. Chapter 8 provides a description and examples of the types of activities engaged in by these transnational groups.

The criminal justice response to organized crime is often given short shrift in books about organized crime. Here, four chapters are devoted to the investigation, prosecution, defense, and sentencing issues in organized crime cases. Descriptions of the types of criminal justice professionals who conduct these efforts, the nature and limits of the tools they use, and the outcomes of organized crime cases are all considered. Current "hot" issues, such as the controversy over "mob lawyers," the limits placed on undercover operations, entrapment, asset forfeiture, and sentencing options in organized crime cases, are each considered in Chapters 9-12. Chapter 12 also examines the prospects for organized crime and its reduction in the future.

ORGANIZED CRIME BIOGRAPHY

Biographies tell the life story of interesting people. In the world of criminal justice, biographies of organized crime figures offer insight into the background and motivations of the individuals who choose that lifestyle, the reasons for their choices, and their consequences. The following is a brief summary of an organized crime biography, followed by questions that ask you to reflect on the connections between that person's life and the content of this book.

Gaspipe: Confessions of a Mafia Boss
Philip Carlo (Harper, 2010)

Anthony "Gaspipe" Casso was boss of the Lucchese Mafia family in New York City. He developed a reputation for violence as he rose through the ranks and was said to be responsible for more than 50 murders. The book's author, who has written several Mafia books, was a one-time next-door neighbor of Casso.

Anthony Casso is portrayed as a loving family man, who also had the capacity to kill others when told to do so, even though some were longtime friends. Casso supported himself through drug trafficking, dealing in stolen property, and bank robbery.

Casso was ultimately caught and became a government informant. In this capacity, he provided inside information about John Gotti's planning of the murder of Gambino family crime boss Paul Castellano, among other crimes. See Figure 1.2.

FIGURE 1.2 The body of Mafia crime boss Paul Castellano lies next to a stretcher outside a New York restaurant after he and his bodyguards were gunned down in 1985 in New York. Mobster John Gotti claimed the top spot in the Gambino family following the gangland shooting. *AP Photo/Mario Suriani*

Questions
1. Why do you believe that violence, or the reputation for violence, is important to successful members of organized crime?
2. After being caught by police, what do you think would cause a longtime member of organized crime to testify against his criminal associates and friends?

ORGANIZED CRIME AT THE MOVIES

Movies seek to entertain and inform the audience about a story, incident, or person. Many good movies also hit upon important substantive themes relevant to understanding organized crime. Read the following movie summary (and watch the movie if you haven't already) and answer the questions that follow to make the organized crime subject matter connections.

The Godfather
Francis Ford Coppola, Director (1972)

Followed by The Godfather Part II (1974) and Part III (1990)

The Godfather is one of the most successful movies ever made. The film is based on a novel by Mario Puzo, and it chronicles a decade (1945-1955) in the life of a Mafia family, the Corleones. The film stars Marlon Brando, Al Pacino, Robert Duvall, Diane Keaton, and James Caan. Marlon Brando is Vito Corleone, the head ("Don" and "Godfather") of the family. Al Pacino is Michael Corleone, Vito's youngest son, who has returned from military service and does not want to be involved in the family business. His girlfriend is played by Diane Keaton. James Caan is Sonny Corleone, Vito's quick-tempered oldest son, groomed to be successor

ORGANIZED CRIME AT THE MOVIES—CONT'D

to Vito as head of the family. Robert Duvall is Tom Hagen, who is treated like a son by Vito and is the family lawyer.

The film's enduring popularity stems from its interesting depiction of the Sicilian lifestyle as much as the story itself. It opens at the wedding of Vito Corleone's daughter, and "no Sicilian can refuse a request on his daughter's wedding day," so Vito and Tom Hagen are hearing many requests from family and friends. Among the guests at the wedding is singer Johnny Fontane, Vito's godson, who asks for his help in getting a movie role to help his now struggling career. The head of the movie studio, Jack Woltz, will not give Fontane the part, but Vito Corleone says to Johnny (in what becomes one of the most recognized lines in the history of film): "I'm gonna make him an offer he can't refuse." Tom Hagen is sent to Hollywood to fix the problem, but Woltz will not budge. The next morning Woltz finds the bloody severed head of his prize stud horse lying in bed with him.

The film continues with a "war" over involvement in heroin trafficking among the five families that comprise the Mafia in the New York City area. Vito Corleone is seriously wounded, and Michael finds himself pulled into the family business in order to protect his father, engaging in murder and having to hide in Sicily. The film continues with conflict, violence, betrayal, and Sonny's murder. In the end, Michael, the reluctant youngest son, becomes head of the Corleone family.

The outstanding cast of The Godfather brings to life the characters, their personalities, and contradictions and, even though the movie and book on which it is based are both works of fiction, many people continue to believe they portray actual events. The Godfather won the Academy Award for Best Picture, Best Actor (Marlon Brando), and Best Screenplay (Francis Coppola, Mario Puzo). The film was nominated for eight additional Academy Awards.

The Godfather Part II was released 2 years later as both a sequel and a prequel. One story line involves Michael Corleone as head of the family after the events of the first movie. A second story line is told in the form of a series of flashbacks of his father's (Vito's) youth and rise to power as the original head of the Corleone family. The Godfather Part II has been ranked as perhaps the best sequel of all time, earning 11 Academy Award nominations and winning 6 (including Best Picture, Best Director [Coppola], and Best Supporting Actor [Robert De Niro]).

The Godfather Part III was released in 1990 and tells the story of Michael Corleone's efforts to make the family business legitimate. As "Michael's story," it is a departure from the other films, but Part III deals with the family's internal conflicts and tensions in a gripping way, like the earlier films. It received nominations for Best Picture, Best Director, and Best Supporting Actor (Andy Garcia).

Questions
1. Why do you believe that The Godfather is seen by many to be a real account, when it is actually a work of fiction?
2. There have been many bad "Mafia" movies over the years, so why do you think this film is not only a good Mafia movie, but also is considered one of the best films of all time?

References and Notes

1. Ferraro, T. J. (1993). *Ethnic Passages: Literary Immigrants in Twentieth Century America*. Chicago: University of Chicago Press, p. 13.

2. Pace, E. "Crime's Lingering Allure," *The New York Times* (June 6, 1982), F9.

3. Sloan, G. "Bada Bing's the Real Thing on 'Sopranos' Tour," *USA Today* (April 26, 2001), 3; Crow, K. "Neighborhood Report: Little Italy; Looking for Wiseguys in the land of checked tablecloths," *The New York Times* (December 1, 2002), 6.

4. "Family Matters," *USA Today* (January 21, 2000), 4E.

5. President's Commission on Law Enforcement and Administration of Justice (1967). *Task Force Report: Organized Crime*. Washington, DC: U.S. Government Printing Office, p. 33.

6. Ianni, F. A. J., & Reuss-Ianni, E. (1973). *A Family Business: Kinship and Social Control in Organized Crime.* New York: New American Library, p. 193.

7. Anderson, A. G. (1979). *The Business of Organized Crime: A Cosa Nostra Family.* Stanford, CA: Hoover Institution Press, p. 139.

8. U.S. Comptroller General (1977). *War on Organized Crime Faltering—Federal Strike Forces Not Getting the Job Done.* Washington, DC: U.S. General Accounting Office.

9. President's Commission on Organized Crime (1987). *The Impact: Organized Crime Today.* Washington, DC: U.S. Government Printing Office, pp. 25–32.

10. *Jacobellis v. Ohio,* 84 S. Ct. 1676 (1964).

11. Hagan, F. E. (Spring 1983). The Organized Crime Continuum: A Further Specification of a New Conceptual Model. *Criminal Justice Review, 8,* 52–57.

12. Lyman, M. D., & Potter, G. W. (2000). *Organized Crime* (2nd ed.). Upper Saddle River, NJ: Prentice Hall. Abadinsky, H. (1997). *Organized Crime* (5th ed.). Chicago, IL: Nelson-Hall; Maltz, M. (1985). On Defining Organized Crime. In H. Alexander, & G. Caiden (Eds.), *The Politics and Economics of Organized Crime.* Lexington, MA: Lexington Books.

13. Smith, D. C. (1980). Paragons, Pariahs, and Pirates: A Spectrum-Based Theory of Enterprise. *Crime & Delinquency, 26,* 358–386; Allen Martin, W. (Spring 1981). Toward Specifying a Spectrum-Based Theory of Enterprise. *Criminal Justice Review, 6,* 54–57; Albanese, J. (1982). What Lockheed and La Cosa Nostra Have in Common: The Effect of Ideology on Criminal Justice Policy. *Crime & Delinquency, 28,* 211–232; Hagan, F. E. (Spring 1983). The Organized Crime Continuum. *Criminal Justice Review, 8,* 52–57; Sacco, V. F. (1986). An Approach to the Study of Organized Crime. In R. A. Silverman, & J. J. Teevan (Eds.), *Crime in Canadian Society* (3rd ed.). Toronto: Butterworths; Kelly, R. J. (1999). *The Upperworld and the Underworld: Case Studies of Racketeering and Business Infiltrations in the United States.* New York: Kluwer Academic.

14. National Advisory Committee on Criminal Justice Standards and Goals (1976). *Report of the Task Force on Organized Crime.* Washington, DC: U.S. Government Printing Office, p. 213.

15. Pontell, H. N., & Calavita, K. (1993). White-Collar Crime in the Savings and Loan Scandal. *The Annals, 525,* 39.

16. Albanese, J. (1995). *White-Collar Crime in America.* Englewood Cliffs, NJ: Prentice Hall; Tusikov, N. (2008). Mortgage Fraud and Organized Crime in Canada. *Trends in Organized Crime, 11,* 301–308; Langford, T. "FBI Arrests Historic Houston Hospital's CEO, Son, 5 Others," *Houston Chronicle* (October 4, 2012).

17. U.S. Department of Justice (2013). *Three Florida Residents Arrested on Charges of Fraud.* Washington DC: Office of Public Affairs.

18. Kegö, W., Leijonmarck, E., & Molcean, A. (Eds.), (2011). *Organized Crime and the Financial Crisis: Recent Trends in the Baltic Sea Region.* Stockholm: Institute for Security and Development Policy.

19. "North Carolina Cigarette Sales Scheme to Aid Terror Is Busted," *The New York Daily News* (July 2, 2000); Kaplan, D. E. "Homegrown Terrorists," *U.S. News & World Report* (March 10, 2003), pp. 30–33; McConnell, M. (July–August 2007) Overhauling Intelligence. *Foreign Affairs, 86,* 49.

20. U.S. Drug Enforcement Administration (2013). *DEA and U.S. Attorney Announce Charges against Senior South American Counterterrorism Figure for Attempting to Support Hezbollah.* Washington, DC: DEA Public Affairs.

21. President's Commission on Organized Crime (1987). *The Impact: Organized Crime Today.* Washington, DC: U.S. Government Printing Office, pp. 33–128.

22. Block, A. A. (1979). The Snowman Cometh: Coke in Progressive New York. *Criminology, 17,* 75–99; President's Commission on Organized Crime, pp. 64, 81, 91; Blom, M., &

Jennissen, R. (2014). The Involvement of Different Ethnic Groups in Various Types of Crime in the Netherlands. *European Journal of Criminal Policy & Research, 20*, 51–72.

23. Block, 1979. p. 95.

24. Block, 1979. p. 95.

25. McIllwain, J. S. (Summer 1998). An Equal Opportunity Employer: Opium Smuggling Networks in and Around San Diego during the Early Twentieth Century. *Transnational Organized Crime, 4*, 31–54; Bovenkerk, F., Siegel, D., & Zaitch, D. (2003). Organized Crime and Ethnic Reputation Manipulation. *Crime, Law and Social Change, 39*, 23.

26. Adler, P. A. (1985). *Wheeling and Dealing: An Ethnography of an Upper-Level Drug Dealing and Smuggling Community.* New York: Columbia University Press, p. 80; Soudijn, M. R. J., & Kleemans, E. R. (2009). Chinese Organized Crime and Situational Context: Comparing Human Smuggling and Synthetic Drugs Trafficking. *Crime, Law and Social Change, 52*, 457–474; Antonopoulos, G. A. (2009). Are the 'Others' coming?: Evidence on Alien Conspiracy from Three Illegal Markets in Greece. *Crime, Law and Social Change, 52*, 475–493.

27. Reuter, P. (1983). *Disorganized Crime: The Economics of the Visible Hand.* Cambridge, MA: MIT Press, pp. 175–176; Reuter, P., & Rubinstein, J. (1983). Illegal Gambling and Organized Crime. *Society, 20*, 52.

28. Ianni, F. A. J., & Reuss-Ianni, E. (1973). *A Family Business: Kinship and Social Control in Organized Crime.* New York: New American Library, p. 20.

29. Albini, J. L. (1971). *The American Mafia: Genesis of a Legend.* New York: Irvington, p. 288.

30. U.S. Senate Committee on Government Operations Permanent Subcommittee on Investigations (1963). *Organized Crime and Illicit Traffic in Narcotics: Hearings Part I 88th Congress, 1st session.* Washington, DC: U.S. Government Printing Office, p. 111.

31. Calder, J. D. (1995). Mafia Women in Non-Fiction. In J. Albanese (Ed.), *Contemporary Issues in Organized Crime.* Monsey, NY: Willow Tree Press.

32. See, for example, Nina Castellano, wife of Paul Castellano, as portrayed by Joseph F. O'Brien and Andris Kurins, *Boss of Bosses* (New York: Simon and Schuster, 1991) and Rosalie Profaci's marriage to Bill Bonanno, as portrayed by Rosalie Bonanno with Beverly Donofrio, *Mafia Marriage: My Story* (New York: Avon, 1991).

33. Carpenter, T. (1993). *Mob Girl.* New York: Zebra Books.

34. *Mob Girl*, pp. 15–16.

35. Nadeau, B. "Ladies of the Mob," *Newsweek International* (June 17, 2002), 27.

36. Reski, P. (2012). *The Honored Society: The History of Italy's Most Powerful Mafia.* New York: Nation Books.

37. Campbell, A. (1984). *The Girls in the Gang.* New York: Basil Blackwell, p. 266.

38. *The Girls in the Gang*, p. 266.

39. Kleemans, E. R., & van de Bunt, H. G. (2002). The Social Embeddedness of Organized Crime. *Transnational Organized Crime, 5*, 19–36; van San, M. (2011). The Appeal of 'Dangerous' Men: On the Role of Women in Organized Crime. *Trends in Organized Crime, 14*, 281–297.

40. Bidgood, J. "Girlfriend of Crime Boss Gets 8-Year Prison Sentence," *The New York Times* (June 12, 2012), 6.

41. Albanese, J. S. (1995). Casino Gambling and Organized Crime: More Than Reshuffling the Deck. In J. Albanese (Ed.), *Contemporary Issues in Organized Crime Monsey.* NY: Willow Tree Press, pp. 25–44; McNeilly, D., & Burke, W. (2002). The Changed Culture of Gambling and Older Adults' Gambling Behaviors. *The Gerontologist, 21*, 1–15; Back, K.-J., Lee, C.-K., & Stinchfield, R. (2011). Motivation and Passion: A Comparison Study of Recreational and Pathological Gamblers. *Journal of Gambling Studies, 27*, 355–370.

CHAPTER 2

Characteristic Organized Crimes I
Conspiracy and Provision of Illicit Goods and Services

The act of preparing or organizing to commit crimes is what distinguishes organized crime from most street crimes.

The Intervale Posse (IVP) was a gang that distributed cocaine in the Dorchester neighborhood of Boston. IVP members wore Adidas clothing and used the Adidas sports insignia (three stripes) to identify themselves. Members referred to one another as "family," even though they were not related. Some older members of the group directed drugs sales by younger members. Once they were arrested, IVP members claimed they were simply a loose connection of individual drug entrepreneurs that competed with each other and that there was nothing particularly "organized" about the crimes they committed.[1] Clearly, IVP was a group committing crimes, but should this gang be considered part of organized crime?

Organized crime is often defined in sweeping terms. Comments such as "mob-linked" activity, crimes that bear the "earmarks of the Mafia," and other suggestive terms do not help us differentiate organized crimes from conventional crimes in an objective way. This chapter is designed to insert some clarity in classifying organized crimes and in distinguishing them from traditional crimes.

LEGAL DEFINITIONS OF ORGANIZED CRIMES

Organized crimes can be arranged into five categories of offenses that correspond to the typology provided in Chapter 1. Conspiracy is the most characteristic organized crime because it is the planning to commit a crime. This planning aspect of organized crime is what distinguishes it from most street crimes.

Table 2.1 Characteristic Organized Crimes

Type of Organized Crime	Nature of the Offense
Conspiracy	The planning of a criminal act
Illicit goods: Drugs and stolen property	The possession and distribution of these products under specific circumstances
Illicit services: Gambling, loansharking, and sex	The marketing and distribution of these services under certain circumstances
Extortion	Taking property through the use of threats of future harm
Racketeering	Engaging in ongoing criminal conspiracies

The provision of illicit goods or services includes conspiracy because it involves the organized or planned provision of illegal drugs, stolen property, gambling, loansharking, or sex. Each of these offenses is considered separately in this chapter.

A crime characteristic of the infiltration of legitimate business or government is extortion, which involves taking property through the use of threats of future harm. The fifth type of organized crime is racketeering, which consists of ongoing criminal conspiracies. These five types of organized crimes are summarized in Table 2.1. The latter two crimes (extortion and racketeering) are considered in Chapter 3.

This summary of characteristic organized crimes does not answer important questions. How much participation or planning is necessary to be considered conspiracy? Is one liable for the actions of others in a conspiracy? What type of harm suffices for extortion? Is a landlord liable for the actions of his tenants under the law of racketeering if his property is used to run a crack house? Can illegal gambling debts be collected lawfully? Does a sex-related product have to be legally obscene before it can be prohibited? These and many other questions arise quickly once we start asking questions about the precise limits of the crimes characteristic of organized crime. The remainder of this chapter uses actual cases to illustrate how the criminal law draws the boundaries among organized crime, conventional crimes, and otherwise lawful behavior.

CONSPIRACY

Conspiracy occurs when two or more persons agree to commit a crime—an essential feature of understanding organized crime. This is because the term "organized" connotes planned criminal activity. Indeed, the difference between an individual college student who, on the one hand, grows marijuana in his or her basement for his or her own use and who, on the other hand, develops a scheme with a roommate to sell that marijuana to pay tuition is the difference between individual crime and conspiracy to commit crime. Actual cases help illustrate where this boundary is drawn in practice.

Do Marijuana Purchases Suffice for Liability?

Two brothers, Paul and Richard Heilbrunn, established a company "Heilbrunn and Friends" (H&F) with associates Charles Stockdale and Richard Bernstein. It was begun as a food distribution warehouse, but it was actually used to import marijuana and distribute it in central Indiana. H&F threw a party on the occasion of the Indianapolis 500 race, where Stockdale and Bernstein, through a third party, approached Michael Helish about purchasing marijuana. They approached him because they believed Helish "could move a lot for us."[2] Helish was interested. Bernstein eventually shipped 5,500 pounds of marijuana to Helish through a third party in Carmel, Indiana. Helish provided $100,000 in front money and made weekly payments thereafter of several hundred thousand dollars each. In total, Helish paid approximately $1.5 million for the marijuana.

Helish was ultimately caught and charged with conspiring with the H&F organization to possess marijuana with intent to distribute. He was convicted at trial, fined, and sentenced to 14 years in prison.[3] On appeal, Helish argued that while ample evidence showed that he purchased marijuana from the H&F organization, there is no evidence of his participation in their conspiracy to distribute drugs. In essence, he claimed to be a "buyer" and not part of the H&F distribution conspiracy.

The U.S. Court of Appeals delineated how the law distinguishes mere customers of illegal goods from members of the conspiracy that provide those goods. To prove membership in a conspiracy, the government must "present sufficient evidence to demonstrate that the defendant knew of the conspiracy and that he intended to join and associate himself with its criminal design and purpose."[4] Although it is clear that "merely purchasing drugs or other property from a conspiracy, standing alone, can never establish membership in a conspiracy," a person who buys from a conspiracy "for resale is a member of the conspiracy if he at least knows its general aims."[5] The court makes it plain that a mere consumer of illegal goods does not automatically become part of a conspiracy. Participation is only inferred if there is evidence he or she knew of the conspiracy and participated voluntarily in it. As the court concluded, "Helish dealt continuously with [the H&F organization]. His purchases were not discreet transactions requiring limited contact with the conspiracy; rather they required an ongoing relationship that soured only when Helish failed to move the marijuana fast enough to satisfy Bernstein."[6] The court of appeals upheld Helish's conviction for conspiracy, pointing to two important aspects of conspiracy: no formal agreement is required among the co-conspirators and participation need be only slight for liability. Although Helish did not participate in running the H&F organization, his ongoing purchases furthered its illegal objectives, rendering him liable for conspiracy.

A question arises when the agreement required for conspiracy does not accomplish the planned crime. For example, police stopped a truck in Nevada and found a large stash of illegal drugs. The truck drivers agreed to take the truck to its destination under police surveillance so that the police could catch their co-conspirators. After the co-conspirators were caught, in what now was a police undercover sting operation, they claimed they should not be convicted because interruption of the conspiracy by police in Nevada made it impossible for the conspiracy to accomplish its goal of drug distribution. The U.S. Supreme Court held, however, that the criminal agreement inherent in conspiracy "is a distinct evil" that is punishable whether or not the crime planned ever takes place.[7]

Can a Single Cocaine Transaction Be Linked to a Conspiracy?

Another important part of the crime of conspiracy is how independent acts can be linked together as part of a single conspiracy. That is to say, a complete conspiracy need not be planned at the outset; the conspiracy can evolve through the independent activity of persons engaged toward a common criminal purpose. Links among those involved in illegal drug distribution, for example, often involve loose connections among the producers, transporters, sellers, and buyers, but they can be prosecuted together as a single conspiracy engaged in a common criminal scheme. Consider the following case.

An FBI informant, Clarence Greathouse, agreed to provide Angelo Lonardo, an alleged organized crime figure, with cocaine to be sold by "people" chosen by Lonardo. Equipped with a body recorder, Greathouse met with Lonardo to arrange the sale. Greathouse demanded one-half of the money before delivery and asked that each of Lonardo's people purchase at least one quarter-kilogram of cocaine. Lonardo agreed.

Two weeks later, when the cocaine arrived, Lonardo wanted Greathouse to speak with "his friend" on the telephone. The "friend" was William Bourjaily who asked questions about payment and the quality of the cocaine. Lonardo subsequently told Greathouse to park his car behind the Hilton Hotel in Cleveland, Ohio, and meet him in the lobby. Greathouse followed the instructions and had four quarter-kilogram bags of cocaine in a Sheraton laundry bag in the car. Greathouse entered the Hilton, while two FBI agents remained on surveillance in the parking lot.

The FBI agents spotted William Bourjaily driving around the parking lot and examining various parked cars. Inside the hotel, Greathouse gave his car keys to Lonardo, who walked to Greathouse's car. Lonardo removed the cocaine from under the seat and handed it to Bourjaily, who was still in his car.

The FBI agents immediately arrested Bourjaily and Lonardo and recovered the cocaine from Bourjaily's car. Under the passenger seat they found a leather bag containing nearly $20,000 in cash with a receipt made out to Bourjaily. They found another $2,000 in the glove compartment.[8]

Bourjaily was convicted at trial for conspiracy to distribute cocaine. He appealed, arguing the evidence was insufficient to prove his participation in a conspiracy beyond a reasonable doubt. The U.S. Court of Appeals acknowledged the government's burden of proof.

> For conviction, Bourjaily must have been shown to have agreed to participate in what he knew to be a joint venture to achieve a common goal. However, an actual agreement need not be proved. Drug distribution conspiracies are often "chain" conspiracies such that agreement can be inferred from the interdependence of the enterprise.[9]

The court found that a jury could rationally conclude that Bourjaily was a willful member of a conspiracy to distribute cocaine. This was supported by the facts that "Bourjaily took the cocaine from Lonardo" in the parking lot, Lonardo referred to Bourjaily as "his friend," and the large volume of narcotics involved "creates an inference of conspiracy." Furthermore, Bourjaily's contention that he did not know the substance in his car was cocaine "is meritless in light of the money found in his car, Lonardo's statements, and the phone call Greathouse had with Lonardo's 'friend.'"[10]

As this case makes clear, a conspiracy is an agreement (written, oral, or tacit) between two or more persons to commit a criminal act. If a person conspires with his associates to sell narcotics, for example, it is also possible to be convicted of both conspiracy (i.e., the agreement to sell narcotics) and the drug offenses (i.e., the possession and sale of them).

CRITICAL THINKING EXERCISE 2.1

The scenario that follows describes an actual situation in which the courts had to determine whether the law of conspiracy applied. Resolution of this scenario requires proper application of the legal principles discussed previously.

The Case of Babies and Cocaine Smuggling

Mothers recruited from Chicago's impoverished Englewood neighborhood were charged with "renting" their infants to women who would then fly with them on international plane trips. These women couriers made at least 34 smuggling trips to Panama and Jamaica using 20 different infants. The women were given baby formula cans that contained liquid cocaine. It is alleged that smugglers punched holes in the baby formula cans, drained the formula, and then used syringes to fill them with liquid cocaine. In some cases, cocaine also was placed in rum bottles or concealed in suitcase handles. The women with infants would then return to Chicago or New York with the drugs, which were distributed by others.

Among the 35 people charged in this smuggling scheme were the parents who "rented" their babies for short periods in exchange for money. The parents knew little of the smuggling scheme and basically saw their role merely as "loaning" their babies in an effort to get some needed money.

Critical Thinking Questions

1. Should the parents of the infants be charged as participants in the drug smuggling conspiracy? Explain.
2. What elements of conspiracy would you use to argue both for and against the parents' conviction?

Source: T. Weber, "35 Tagged in Formula Drug Scheme," *Associated Press* (December 14, 2001).

How Much Is Required Beyond a Criminal Agreement?

An interesting aspect of conspiracy is how it distinguishes between thinking about a crime and actually going through with committing a crime. If two friends sit in a room and say, "That guy should be shot!" do we have a conspiracy? The answer is no, but if one of the two friends then drew a map diagramming how such a shooting could occur, would that be sufficient for liability? What if one of them went out and bought a gun? The issue, therefore, is that conviction of conspiracy punishes a person for "planning," with another, a criminal offense, but the law cannot punish mere thought. An actual act, or *actus reus*, must occur to be held liable for any crime because the law punishes actions, not thoughts.

Virtually all conspiracy statutes on the state and federal level (an exception is a federal drug conspiracy) contain a phrase that a conspirator must perform "any act to effect the object of the conspiracy" in addition to planning.[11] The purpose of requiring an overt action, in addition to planning, is to make clear the intention of carrying out the conspiracy, even if it never occurs. This distinguishes, for the purposes of punishment, idle talk from a true criminal design.

In a landmark case, the U.S. Supreme Court assessed the validity of a drug conspiracy conviction in an Alaskan drug case. Lee Shabani entered into a drug distribution scheme with his girlfriend, her family, and others. Shabani brought cocaine from California to Anchorage, and his girlfriend and an associate sold the drugs, primarily to her relatives. An FBI agent purchased some of these drugs in an undercover operation, and Shabani's girlfriend agreed to cooperate with the prosecution.[12]

Shabani stood trial alone for conspiracy to distribute cocaine. He was convicted at trial and sentenced to 13 years in prison. He argued that an "overt act in furtherance of the conspiracy" is an essential element of the offense and that the judge failed to instruct the jury of this fact. This is significant because Shabani claimed at trial that there was no direct evidence linking him to any of the drug sales.[13]

The U.S. Court of Appeals reversed his conviction and remanded his case for a new trial, agreeing that the trial judge should have told the jury about the need to find an overt act in furtherance of the conspiracy.[14] The U.S. Supreme Court agreed to hear this case due to differences in interpretation of the federal drug conspiracy law among the circuits of the U.S. Court of Appeals.

However, the U.S. Supreme Court reinstated Shabani's conviction. In examining the federal drug conspiracy statute, it was found that

> Any person who attempts or conspires to commit any offense defined in this title is punishable by imprisonment or fine or both which may not exceed the maximum punishment prescribed for the offense, the commission of which was the object of the attempt or conspiracy.[15]

The language of this statute does not specifically require an overt act in further-ance of the conspiracy. The U.S. Supreme Court noted that other federal con-spiracy statutes, including the Organized Crime Control Act, do require an overt act for a conspiracy conviction.[16] Because Congress included the require-ment of an overt act in these other federal conspiracy statutes, the U.S. Supreme Court inferred that "Congress appears to have made the choice quite deliber-ately" in omitting the act requirement from the drug conspiracy statute.[17] In responding to Shabani's appeal, the court recognized that the law of conspiracy "does not punish mere thought; the criminal agreement itself is the *actus reus*."[18] The federal drug conspiracy statute is an exception to the law of con-spiracy and does not require an overt act as a necessary element, but most other federal and state conspiracy statutes require such an act in furtherance of the conspiracy's objectives.

Can One Withdraw from a Conspiracy by Simply Walking Away?

Organized crime poses many unique problems. One of them is when leaders of conspiracies help to plan crimes, but then lower-level figures actually carry them out. The law of conspiracy aims to punish this higher-level planning by making it difficult to "wash your hands" of involvement in a criminal scheme by simply avoiding involvement in the ultimate crime itself.

In an interesting case, William Wemette was the owner of an adult video store in Chicago. Wemette and his partner paid a "street tax" to members of the Chi-cago "Outfit," an organized crime group, for 15 years. Wemette paid this tax to protect himself and his business from harm. When he was having financial problems with his business, the "street tax" collector said "if he did not pay the tax" his business would be shut down perhaps by "an accident or a fire."[19] Wemette complained to other organized crime figures and was told to speak with Frank Schweihs, who had a reputation for violence. Schweihs arranged for a new collector, Anthony Daddino, to begin collecting the "street tax" pay-ments. Daddino collected $1,100 per month from Wemette until Wemette refused to deal with Daddino any longer.

Wemette ultimately contacted the FBI when he could no longer meet the burden of the payments and agreed to record his conversations with Daddino and Schweihs. After several months of audio and video recordings of these conversations, both Daddino and Schweihs were indicted and convicted of conspiracy and extortion.

Daddino argued on appeal that he withdrew from the conspiracy, and his con-viction should be overturned. He said that Wemette told him at one point not to come to his place anymore. Daddino responded, "Okay, buddy," and he never saw Wemette again.[20] Schweihs found someone else to collect payments after this exchange.

The legal issue is whether this action is sufficient to withdraw from the extortion conspiracy. The U.S. Court of Appeals noted that "withdrawal requires more than a mere cessation of activity on the part of the defendant; it requires some affirmative action which...defeats the purpose of the conspiracy."[21] As the court had said in an earlier case, "You do not absolve yourself of guilt by walking away from a ticking bomb."[22]

The U.S. Court of Appeals concluded in this case:

> Daddino walked away from a ticking bomb. There was no evidence to show that Daddino was no longer associated with Schweihs or the "Outfit." Without evidence of some affirmative action by Daddino, Daddino could continue silently to endorse the extortion plan although he had been relieved of the duty to participate physically by collecting the "street tax" payments.[23]

Effective withdrawal from a conspiracy requires proof of an "affirmative action" by the defendant that works to defeat the conspiracy. Absent such proof, the defendant has not effectively withdrawn. Daddino's appeal was denied.

The reason why the law is so stringent about withdrawal from a conspiracy is because the object of the conspiracy need not be completed for a conviction. Therefore, if one merely walks away, after being involved in the planning of a crime, something more is needed to absolve one of responsibility for that crime. Otherwise, lower-level criminals who carried out conspiracies would be punished, and the higher-ups involved in the planning could escape prosecution, despite their significant role.

Summarizing the Important Elements of Conspiracy

The most important elements of the crime of conspiracy are of five types. They include the nature of the agreement, extent of participation, overt acts, voluntariness, and withdrawal. These are summarized in Table 2.2.

Table 2.2 Elements of Conspiracy

Legal Aspects of Conspiracy
1. Two or more people are needed, although no formal agreement is required, and the goal of the conspiracy need not be accomplished
2. Participation need be only slight with reasonable knowledge of the conspiracy's existence, although mere presence by itself is insufficient for liability
3. An overt act in furtherance of the conspiracy is usually required for liability
4. Voluntary participation is required, and a person is liable for the acts of co-conspirators
5. Effective withdrawal from a conspiracy requires an act to defeat the purposes of the conspiracy

As Table 2.2 illustrates, liability for conspiracy generally requires a voluntary agreement between two or more people, the parties do not have to be involved extensively with the conspiracy, withdrawal is not accomplished without actions to defeat the conspiracy, and an overt act in furtherance of the conspiracy is usually required. It can be seen that the crime of conspiracy lies at the heart of organized crime because of law enforcement's goal of punishment for those who organize to commit a crime.

CRITICAL THINKING EXERCISE 2.2

The scenario that follows describes an actual situation in which the courts had to determine whether the law of conspiracy applied. Resolution of this scenario requires proper application of the legal principles discussed previously.

The Case of Murder for Hire

Garcia was a drug dealer. He was arrested by the Drug Enforcement Administration in Houston and cooperated with police officials in exchange for leniency. Information provided by Garcia led to the subsequent arrest of Antonio for cocaine distribution. Antonio believed Garcia was responsible for his arrest.

An acquaintance of Antonio, named Eugenio, called a friend who had moved to Chicago. This friend, Cabello, was given money to fly to Houston because his help was needed to solve "some problems." Once in Houston, Eugenio offered Cabello $5,000 and gave him a .357 magnum to kill Garcia. Cabello made three unsuccessful attempts to find Garcia's house, and he returned to tell Eugenio.

Eugenio told Cabello he would call his brother-in-law, Hector, to find out where Garcia lived. Eugenio obtained the directions and gave them to Cabello. Cabello left to find Garcia, but still could not find the house. Eugenio called Hector again for more precise directions.

Cabello ultimately found Garcia and shot him six times, killing him. As Cabello left the murder scene, he ran a stop sign. A sheriff's deputy pulled him over, found the gun, and realized from the smell that it had been fired recently. Cabello was ultimately indicted for murder.

Critical Thinking Questions

1. If the money and gun given to Cabello were provided by Antonio, can Eugenio be held liable for conspiracy to commit murder?
2. If Cabello did not know that Garcia was a witness in a federal case, how would this affect his liability for murder?
3. Can Cabello also be charged with conspiracy, given the facts?
4. Under what circumstances can Hector be held liable for conspiracy to murder Garcia?

PROVISION OF ILLICIT GOODS: DRUGS AND STOLEN PROPERTY

A second category of organized crimes involves the provision of illicit goods. The two most common examples are illicit drugs and stolen property. The term "provision" suggests organization and, as a result, most of the offenses in this category also involve the crime of conspiracy. A person who steals a CD player from a car possesses stolen property. Until that person sells that property, or otherwise organizes to receive or distribute it, it cannot be considered part of organized crime. Therefore, the provision of illicit goods is marked by the crime of conspiracy due to the need for two or more individuals to engage in this offense on a systematic basis. Several actual cases serve to illustrate the precise nature of these crimes.

Drugs: Liability for the Conduct of Others?

Drugs have long been associated with organized crime. To establish a complete drug trafficking case, it is necessary to identify the source (possessor and/or manufacturer), its method of distribution, and its ultimate arrival to buyers. Identifying the source and finding the method of distribution are the most significant elements in making organized crime cases, but they also are the most difficult to prove in the provision of illicit narcotics. Consider the case of Yonatan Teffera.

Teffera and Thomas Cobb disembarked from a Greyhound bus that had traveled from New York City to Washington, DC. An FBI agent and detective were working together, and they suspected Teffera and Cobb may be carrying drugs. The detective saw Teffera standing alone, approached him, and identified himself. Teffera gave a false name and said he was traveling alone. A consensual search of Teffera's person revealed no illegal substances.

After he left, the detective noticed that Cobb had joined Teffera in a cab. The detective approached the cab and identified himself. Cobb said he had not been on the bus, but had picked up his "buddy" Teffera. Cobb agreed to be searched, and the detective found a large plastic bag hidden in the crotch of Cobb's pants that contained chunks of rock cocaine.[24] Cobb was arrested and handcuffed, while Teffera argued, "I don't know him." Teffera was also arrested, and a search found two photos of Teffera and Cobb together and two consecutively numbered bus tickets (later found to be paid for in cash by one person).

Both Cobb and Teffera were tried for possession of cocaine base with intent to distribute. Expert police testimony at trial linked Cobb and Teffera together in a drug scheme, although Teffera had no drugs in his possession. According to this testimony, the person not carrying the drugs:

1. Protects the "mule" (the person carrying the drugs) from being robbed
2. Ensures the mule does not abscond with the drugs
3. Diverts police attention from the mule[25]

Cobb and Teffera were convicted at trial. Teffera appealed, arguing that there was insufficient evidence to show beyond a reasonable doubt that he was guilty of possession with intent to distribute the cocaine in Cobb's pants. The U.S. Court of Appeals delineated the standard for overturning a jury verdict for insufficient evidence:

1. Viewing the evidence in the light most favorable to the government, could any rational trier of fact have found the essential elements of the crime beyond a reasonable doubt?
2. The government's evidence need not exclude all reasonable hypotheses of innocence or lead inexorably to the conclusion that the defendant is guilty.

3. No distinction is made between direct and circumstantial evidence in evaluating the government's proof.[26]

It is clearly a "daunting" burden for a defendant to have a conviction reversed on these grounds. The question is whether Teffera, found to possess no drugs, could be found guilty of at least aiding and abetting Cobb.

To prove a person aided and abetted the possession of illegal narcotics, the government does not have to show that person ever "physically possessed" or controlled the movement of the drugs. Instead, the government must demonstrate only "sufficient knowledge and participation to indicate [the person] knowingly and willfully participated in the offense" in an effort to make it succeed.[27]

The government attempted to meet its burden of proof in this case by noting the bus tickets, photos, Teffera's use of a false name, false statements regarding whether he was alone and his destination, and the expert testimony about drug courier methods. The U.S. Court of Appeals reviewed this evidence and concluded, "the government's aiding and abetting theory runs into rough sledding from the outset."[28]

First, the government produced "no direct evidence" that Teffera knew that Cobb possessed the cocaine hidden in his clothes. Second, the government's inference that Teffera's false responses to their questions circumstantially proved his link to Cobb could also be used to argue the reverse position. Rather than lying to mislead police regarding a drug conspiracy, Teffera may have lied to disassociate himself from Cobb if he knew that Cobb was frequently in trouble and may be involved in some current illegal activity. Therefore, Teffera's lies could be used to indicate either involvement in a conspiracy or a true attempt to disassociate himself from Cobb.

The prosecution had the burden to show that Teffera not only knew about Cobb's transportation of drugs, but also *actually participated* in Cobb's avoiding detection. The court of appeals concluded, "this the government has utterly failed to do."[29] The court found that Teffera's movements in the bus station "are perfectly consistent with innocence and raise no inference that he was a lookout: He got off a bus with a friend, went to get a cab while the friend stopped to pick up a snack, and then met up with the friend again to leave."[30] Simply stated, "the government's problem" in meeting the burden of proof in this case is that Teffera's "misstatements are at least equally consistent with other plausible hypotheses."[31] Even given the expert testimony about drug "mules," the government needed more than this theory alone to link it to Teffera. Teffera's attempt to distance himself from Cobb "is just as consonant with an innocent person's fear of being associated with a guilty person as it is with an intent to help Cobb get out of the station undetected."[32]

In conclusion, the court of appeals stated:

> While we recognize that the government's proof need not be so certain as to
> exclude all inferences of innocence, in a case where the government's overall
> evidence of guilt is so thin, the alternate hypotheses consistent with
> innocence become sufficiently strong that they must be deemed to instill a
> reasonable doubt in our hypothetical juror. Even looking at the government's
> evidence in the most favorable light, we think that line has been crossed
> here.[33]

The court reversed the conviction of Teffera. Although Cobb's guilt is clear
by virtue of his transportation and possession of cocaine, the government
did not demonstrate effectively any knowledge or behaviors on Teffera's part
that made him part of the scheme directly or circumstantially. In a case like
this, the government would have to show that Teffera somehow shared in
the control of the drugs, actively took measures to protect them (more than
meeting a mule-protector profile), or had other evidence to show Teffera's role
in planning, advancing, or being aware of the illegal drug transportation.

This case demonstrates that significant drug cases can be difficult to prove.
Proving a street-level sale poses only the problem of direct observation. To
prove the existence of a drug distribution conspiracy, significantly more is
required. Evidence of planning of the scheme, movement of the drugs, and
locating their source are all difficult to do, but are required to prove organized
drug conspiracies. They often require long-term surveillance, undercover police
work, and other methods that incur large expenditures of police resources. It is
possible in the case just given, for example, that further observation of the
defendant could have linked him to an ultimate drug transaction. Ongoing
police training regarding the legal requirements for proving drug conspiracies
is as necessary as is a willingness to devote adequate time and resources to establishing the existence of significant cases.

Stolen Property: I Didn't Know It Was Stolen!

The sale, possession, and distribution of stolen property are rampant in American society and around the world. Even otherwise "law-abiding" citizens often
have no qualms in obtaining a "hot" stereo, tape player, jewelry, or other merchandise at incredibly low prices "that happened to fall off a truck." The problem, of course, is that people do not spend much time considering precisely
how the prices got so low. When the property is stolen, any price becomes a
profit, because nothing was paid to manufacture or distribute the product in
the first place. How this relates to organized crime is important. Understanding
the public's willingness to purchase merchandise with "no questions asked,"
illicit entrepreneurs emerge to cater to that market. Therefore, many people

attempt to make a living buying, trading, and, in some cases, hijacking stolen property in order to make a fast, but illegal, profit. The market for stolen property has supported a number of infamous organized crime figures.[34]

In recent times, trends in stolen property have shifted to exploit changing opportunities. Organized rings of people have been found hacking into financial databases, and then using software to recode the data onto magnetic strips on blank plastic cards. Members of the ring then serve as money mules using ATM machines to withdraw cash using the stolen financial data, Groups from Eastern Europe have been active in these kinds of stolen property schemes. In another kind of stolen property scheme, Internet copies of movies showing in theaters are distributed illegally. Either recording devices in movie theaters secretly capture copyrighted movies, or in some cases preview copies of movies are distributed illegally.[35]

In legal terms, the primary issue that arises in these organized crime cases is knowledge that the property was indeed stolen. Most stolen property statutes require "knowing" that the property is stolen as an element of the offense. This requirement prevents prosecution of those who unknowingly or mistakenly come into contact with stolen property. An interesting example is provided by the case of Peter Rosa in Brooklyn.

Rosa met with David Maniquis at a Brooklyn restaurant on several occasions. Maniquis was introduced through a third party as a source of stolen silver. Over the course of several meetings at the restaurant, Rosa agreed to buy 50 100-ounce bars of silver from Maniquis, after being told the source was a man about to retire from a silver company and being shown a sample of the merchandise. Although he expressed concern that the source, if caught, would turn them in, Rosa agreed to the sale.[36]

Rosa also discussed the possible sale of "warm" watches. Maniquis offered a list of watches he had for sale at prices about 20% of their actual value.[37] At a subsequent meeting he bought jewelry from Maniquis for 10-20% of its value. Rosa said at that time, "[T]hey're not gonna put us in jail unless [Maniquis] is wired."[38]

As it turns out, Maniquis was wired, and his conversations with Rosa were recorded. Rosa was convicted of conspiring to receive stolen property. He was sentenced to more than 4 years in prison followed by 3 years of supervised release.[39]

Rosa appealed his conviction arguing, among other things, that the government did not prove that he knew the goods were stolen. Without such knowledge, he cannot be convicted of this crime because the mental state (or *mens rea*) required under federal law is that whoever receives stolen goods must "know the same to have been stolen."[40]

The U.S. Court of Appeals found "the proof was ample" of Rosa's knowledge that he was dealing in stolen property. This proof included his remarks about the source of the silver possibly betraying them to the authorities, his statement about being in trouble if Maniquis was wired, the discussion of "warm" watches, and the price lists supplied by Maniquis that showed the property's sale price to be only 10-20% of its actual value. These statements, together with the "disparity between stated value and asking price, were so great as to create the inference that Rosa and his co-conspirators surely believed they were dealing with stolen goods."[41]

In stolen property cases, therefore, the burden is on the prosecution to show the defendant's knowledge that the property was stolen. The prices of the merchandise, remarks by the defendant, and other circumstantial evidence can be used to demonstrate this knowledge.

CRITICAL THINKING EXERCISE 2.3

The scenario that follows describes an actual situation in which the courts had to determine whether the laws involving stolen property applied. Resolution of this scenario requires proper application of the legal principles discussed in this chapter.

The Case of a Very Good Deal on Carpet

Bill Kunkle was a truck driver for a carpet company. He was assigned to transport a load of carpet from Georgia to California.

He decided during his trip that he was not being paid enough. He started drinking and resolved to sell the carpet he was carrying in the truck. He sold two rolls to the manager of a truck stop in Oklahoma City. He then stopped at Earl's Bar in Amarillo, Texas, and told some patrons that he had carpet for sale. An owner of a carpet store was in the bar and expressed interest.

Kunkle asked the carpet store owner if he was with the police, and the owner said "no." Kunkle also stated that he

was not with the police and that the carpet was not stolen. Kunkle then accepted an offer of $17,500 for the entire load.

After a gambling and cocaine-buying binge, and the report of an abandoned truck at Earl's Bar, authorities contacted Kunkle's employers and obtained numbers located on the backs of the missing carpet rolls. They were found in the carpet store in Amarillo, Texas.

Critical Thinking Questions

1. Kunkle had lawful possession of the carpet in his truck. At what point did it become "stolen" property?
2. The carpet store owner in Texas asked Kunkle if the carpet was stolen and he said it wasn't. Can the carpet store owner be held liable for receiving stolen property?
3. The carpet store owner paid $17,500 for the carpet. How does this protect him from charges of receiving stolen property?
4. Can Kunkle and the carpet store owner be held liable for conspiracy?

In a case in Harrisburg, Pennsylvania, Ben Renfro Stuart was convicted of receiving stolen government property for his involvement in the purchase of more than 100 stolen savings bonds with a face value of $1,000 each. The scheme would pay him 20 cents on the dollar.[42]

Evidence at trial determined that a codefendant gave Stuart a package of bonds wrapped in newspaper and told him to wait at the other end of a hotel parking lot. Stuart was then given instructions by radio to deliver the package and leave, earning $2,000 for this task and for another delivery. As the U.S. Court of Appeals declared, "for this minimal amount of work...a jury could well find that Stuart either knew the bonds were stolen or deliberately closed his eyes to that fact."[43]

Most states punish stolen property offenders according to the value of the property involved. In an interesting twist, Stuart argued on appeal that his participation in the scheme netted him $2,000, making that the criterion for determining his sentence. The court of appeals determined, however, that under federal sentencing guidelines (and the law in most states), "the loss is the fair market value of the particular property at issue." Therefore, Stuart was punished based on the full $129,000 face value of the bonds recovered rather than on the $2,000 he made for delivering them.

The provision of illicit goods, such as drugs and stolen property, provides income to support organized crime. This property is often obtained illegally or at incredibly low prices and then is sold to people who do not show concern about its source or legality. The range of stolen property sold continues to expand based on available opportunities, and includes everything from identification documents to rattlesnakes.[44] The huge profits that result are demonstrated in the cases just discussed. In this way, otherwise "law-abiding" citizens support organized crime activity in a direct way.

PROVISION OF ILLICIT SERVICES: GAMBLING, LOANSHARKING, AND SEX

The unlawful counterpart to the provision of illicit goods is the provision of illicit services. Like illicit goods, these offenses provide illicit products that are in public demand. In fact, it is the public demand that makes this illicit marketplace possible. Gambling, loansharking, and sex for money are the three most common forms of illicit services provided by organized crime.

The Unique Problem of Gambling: The Oldest Vice

Crimes associated with gambling pose unique problems in contemporary America, as almost every state has now legalized at least some forms of gambling. They have done so as a revenue measure, although there continues to be debate regarding its desirability as a government-sponsored enterprise. This debate is not new.

Gambling can be traced back to the beginnings of recorded history. From the very beginning, however, it has been viewed alternately as a moral weakness, a crime, or simple recreation. Given the moral repugnance associated with gambling for the bulk of its history, combined with its enduring popularity, gambling is truly the oldest vice.

Gambling can be defined as games of chance, where luck determines the outcome more than skill. The mention of gambling can be traced to very early history. For example, the Bible provides an account following the crucifixion of Jesus, where four soldiers each wanted Jesus' robe. They resolved the dispute saying, "Let's not tear it; let's throw dice to see who will get it." This story is recounted in three separate books of the New Testament.[45]

Gambling appeared to be popular among Native Americans from early historical accounts. The Onondaga Indians of New York were known to wager their possessions using dice. The Iroquois also played a version of dice.[46] The Narragansett Indians of Rhode Island and Chumash in the Northwest "often gambled for days" in games where "the worldly goods of entire tribes might change hands."[47]

Whereas Indians were known to gamble with dice or bet on the outcome of sporting contests, early American colonists were most familiar with lotteries (i.e., the sale of many lots, chances, or numbers and a few are selected for a prize). In the early 1600s, the Virginia Company of London experienced financial problems in starting a plantation in Virginia. Given the success of European lotteries, the Virginia Company was given permission to conduct lottery drawings in England (to fund plantations in Virginia). Interestingly, while the Virginia Company attempted to push lottery sales in England, it was attempting to reduce gambling back in Virginia. Reports of "gaming, idleness, and vice" were rampant, and antigambling ordinances became part of Jamestown's initial legal code.[48] The codes were ineffective in preventing the popularity of gambling.

This peculiar dichotomy where gambling was encouraged for one purpose (public funding), but seen as dissolute for another (recreation), provides an early illustration of the vacillation in attitudes toward gambling throughout history. The Puritans of Massachusetts were widely known for their opposition to gambling on moral grounds. They saw gambling as "an appearance of evil" and therefore irreligious.[49] Like Virginia, though, Massachusetts and other colonies passed laws in an effort to limit or prohibit gambling, but gambling (especially card and dice games) continued, despite the laws.[50] Nevertheless, when funds were needed for public works during the early 1700s (e.g., schools and roads), many Northeastern colonies started lotteries to raise the required funds. This provides another example of how gambling has been viewed as either a vice or a virtue, depending on how the profits are diverted (i.e., for pleasure or for public works).

Most lotteries were private enterprises, but as they grew the colonies sought to regulate them "motivated by a familiar combination of paternalism and self-interest."[51] By 1750 most states prohibited lotteries that operated without state authorization. The ability of lotteries to raise money, especially among a public outraged by taxation, increased their popularity. In fact, most of the Ivy League colleges were first endowed with funds from lotteries. By 1800, there were approximately 2,000 authorized lotteries in existence that grew in size and scope.[52] In addition, brokers were being used to run lotteries for a percentage of the profits.

Horse racing, cards, and dice games were also popular from colonial times. These games were somewhat more limiting than lotteries due to the fact that fewer people were able to participate in the same race or game by their local nature. This is in contrast to lotteries that involved entire towns, states, and the nation on several occasions. Like lotteries, these other forms of gambling were viewed with the same measure of alternating acceptance and rejection. Many early colonies and states had prohibitions against horse racing, card, and dice games, but their general popularity led to widespread disregard of the law.[53]

The allure of gambling has always attracted a disproportionate number of those who are relatively poor for obvious reasons: this is the group that most needs a change in luck, and gambling offers the possibility of an immediate and dramatic change, however slight the odds. Nevertheless, gamblers historically have come from all walks of life. Gambling among the clergy, for example, apparently resulted in a Virginia law in the 1600s that stated, "Ministers shall not give themselves to excess in drinking or yette spend their time idelie by day or by night, playing at dice, cards or any unlawful game."[54] Undergraduates at Harvard played cards unremittingly, ultimately leading to a heavy fine of five shillings if caught. Servants and minors caught gambling with cards in Massachusetts were to be "publicly whipt."[55]

Like the drinking of alcoholic beverages, gambling was widely criticized in public but enjoyed privately as a form of recreation or social intercourse. However, gambling could be employed for socially constructive purposes (e.g., lotteries to build roads), whereas drinking, prostitution, and narcotics had no redeeming social value. The fact that gambling can be used for social benefits distinguishes it from the other vices. Nevertheless, it did not prevent criticism of those who gambled for recreational purposes. Thomas Jefferson publicly argued that "gaming corrupts our disposition," but privately, he gambled. In fact, while he was composing the Declaration of Independence, he made notations in his personal log about winning and losing at backgammon, cards, and bingo.[56] In a similar vein, Benjamin Franklin manufactured playing cards.

Gambling as Vice or Recreation?

The tremendous popularity of gambling in all its forms ultimately contributed to its continuing image as a vice rather than as a form of recreation. The huge interest and participation in lotteries, cards, dice, and horse racing resulted in the commercialization of these enterprises. Gambling halls, casinos, lottery brokers, and professional gamblers resulted in a growing number of reported instances of fixed games and races, marked cards, loaded dice, and dishonest players and operators. The negative public reaction to these reports led to a series of reforms in the mid-1800s that changed the image of gambling. There was less confidence that gambling could be carried out honestly, leading to the prohibition of gambling in many places. This image of gambling as having questionable moral or legal standing continued for more than a century.[57]

There was a great deal of evidence on which the public's growing distrust of gambling was based. Lottery scandals occurred in New York, Pennsylvania, Boston, and elsewhere. In one case, $400,000 was collected and no prizes were awarded; in another, one million dollars worth of fictitious tickets were sold; in yet another, a lottery broker took $10 million in expenses for a lottery that totaled only $16 million in receipts.[58]

Horse racing suffered from similar scandals. The rise of bookmakers contributed to a concern over profit rather than thoroughbred breeding. A few documented instances of fixed races were enough to shift public opinion to believe that horse racing was a dishonest enterprise.[59] To some extent, this belief continues today.

Cards, dice, and casino games were changed in the public's eye beginning in 1835. In Vicksburg, Mississippi, several professional gamblers and saloon operators were implicated in a political conspiracy. This resulted, although circuitously, in an antigambling wave of reform that swept through many parts of the United States. Ironically, it was this reform movement that led most directly to the rise of organized crime involved in gambling. In New York, for example, the editor of the *New York Tribune*, Horace Greeley, joined with businessmen to form the New York Association for the Suppression of Gambling, the purpose of which was to "pluck the victim from the gambler's clutches." After a significant lobbying effort, New York State passed several antigambling laws in 1851, which supporters argued, "if faithfully enforced would close every gambling hall within the state."[60] Some commercial gaming enterprises were closed, but "many moved underground and operated by bribing law enforcement officials."[61] Hence, the beginnings of organized crime involvement in gambling can be characterized as the result of a successful campaign by reformers to prohibit gaming enterprises (see Figure 2.1).

Another example is provided by changes in the legal status of lotteries. By the late 1800s, most states had banned lotteries. Policy games (or "numbers") were invented to satisfy those who remained interested in the game after its

FIGURE 2.1 The popularity of gambling ultimately contributed to its continuing image as a vice rather than a form of recreation. *www.shutterstock.com*

prohibition. Numbers originally were picked by spinning a wheel, and later became more objective (and less prone to manipulation), using such numbers as the total handle for the day at the racetrack, baseball scores, cattle and customs receipts, or other combinations of numbers that appear in daily newspapers. Policy was very attractive to the poor because bets as small as five cents could be played. Tickets were sold by agents or "runners" who would canvas neighborhoods collecting bets, receiving 15% of their sales in return. During the 1880s, it was reported that New York City had more than 700 policy shops, and a cartel operated games in 20 different cities.[62] Policy games were never legalized (except in Louisiana), and they continue to stay in business by paying for "protection" from arrest. In New York City, it is estimated that more than one million people purchase illegal numbers regularly.[63]

The growing intolerance for gambling continued into the early 1900s, fueled by both pubic figures and religious leaders. Reform administrations in Buffalo, Chicago, Cleveland, Denver, Detroit, New Orleans, New York, Pittsburgh, and San Francisco all raided gambling operations. Local enforcement efforts prompted a number of states to go further in prohibiting gambling. By 1910, Arizona, New Mexico, and Nevada passed laws that even banned card playing at home. Other states passed laws making it easier to prosecute illegal gaming operators.[64] In fact, the message back then was strikingly similar to the antidrug messages of today. Consider this statement in a Methodist church in Texas in 1909: "Don't gamble. Don't play cards. Don't bet on race horses. Don't speculate on wheat. Don't speculate on the stock exchange. Don't throw dice. Don't shirk honest labor. Don't be a gambler; once a gambler, always a gambler."[65]

By the 1930s, though, gambling was making a return as a legal form of recreation (or vice). Horse racing returned through a parimutuel betting system regulated by the state. Although lotteries were still prohibited, they were reemerging from one of the same sources of their initial prohibition: churches. During the Depression era, churches turned to bingo and other lottery games as a way to raise funds. Remarkably, Florida legalized slot machines during this same period but church groups successfully lobbied against them, arguing that the slot machines were taking the "nickels and dimes of common laborers."[66] The church groups were eventually able to pressure the state legislature to repeal the law and prohibit slot machines in 1937. By 1940, it was estimated that nearly 25% of all Americans gambled on church lotteries.[67] As New York Mayor Fiorello LaGuardia observed, "if bingo is unlawful in one place, it cannot be lawful in another."[68] LaGuardia's observation regarding the inherent ironies of legal versus illegal gambling remains unresolved today. The shifting legal status of gambling today, and the confusion it causes, becomes clearer if one examines some recent cases.

Is Legal Gambling a Constitutionally Protected Right?

By the early 1990s, most states had legalized some form of gambling. Lotteries are the most popular manifestation of legal gaming, although casino gambling and betting on sporting contests are legal in more jurisdictions than ever before.

As legal gaming grows, spurred largely by its ability to generate large revenues with little investment risk, conflict has arisen between jurisdictions with and without legal games. A classic case was that between North Carolina and Virginia. North Carolina did not have a state-sponsored lottery, but Virginia did. Edge Broadcasting owned and operated a radio station in North Carolina, but was very near the Virginia-North Carolina border. In fact, more than 90% of the radio station's listeners were in Virginia with the remainder living in nine North Carolina counties.

The radio station wanted to broadcast Virginia lottery advertisements due to its large Virginia audience. However, the radio station was located in North Carolina where such lotteries were illegal. Should the radio station be permitted to broadcast the lottery ads?

This debate ended in the U.S. Supreme Court, which considered the case in light of the First Amendment guarantee of freedom of speech. The court concluded that "the Government has a substantial interest in supporting the policy of non-lottery States, as well as not interfering with the policy of States that permit lotteries."[69] With regard to the First Amendment, the court held that "gambling implicates no constitutionally protected right; rather, it falls into a category of 'vice' activity that could be, and frequently has been, banned altogether."[70]

Despite the growing legalization of gambling in a variety of forms, therefore, there is no constitutional right to gamble, nor do radio stations have a right to broadcast advertisements that feature legal gambling to nongambling states. The U.S. Supreme Court noted that the constitution "affords a lesser protection to commercial speech" than to other forms of expression under the First Amendment, and that federal laws that prohibit lottery advertising in non-lottery states "directly" serve the governmental interest in "balancing the interests of lottery and non-lottery States."[71] Therefore, legalized gambling continues to be a state prerogative and not a constitutional right. States without legal gaming are protected from the advertisements of other states so inclined in "balancing" the mutual interests of these states.

What Are the Elements of an Illegal Gambling Business?

Given the dramatic increase in both the forms and the number of states now involved in legal gaming, it is not always clear what constitutes illegal gambling under current law. An illustrative case is that of John Murray at the Willow Bar in Somerville, Massachusetts.

The case arose out of an internal investigation of a customs inspector, who was believed to own a bar without permission of the U.S. Customs Service. The customs service placed an undercover agent, Janet Durham, in the bar as a waitress for about 4 months. Agent Durham observed that a telephone near a corner bar stool at the rear of the Willow Bar was used to accept bets on dog and horse races. While in her undercover role as a waitress, agent Durham observed several people sit or stand near the corner bar stool, answer the telephone, accept money from customers, and make notations on small pieces of paper. These people included John Murray.

Murray was convicted at trial of conducting and conspiring to conduct a gambling business. Under federal law, it is necessary that a person "conduct, finance, manage, supervise, direct, or own all or part of an illegal gambling business."[72] First, an illegal business is one that violates state law. Second, the illegal gambling business must involve five or more persons. Third, the illegal gambling business must remain "in substantially continuous operation" for more than 30 days or gross more than $2,000 in a single day.[73] These are the three elements that must be proven to convict someone of involvement in an illegal gambling business under federal law.

On appeal, the U.S. Court of Appeals reversed Murray's conviction. It found that evidence "shows that, at most, four persons operated a gambling business out of the corner bar stool of the Willow Bar for a period in excess of 30 days, and that the identity of those involved frequently changed."[74] The prosecution argued that others participated in the illegal gambling business, increasing the total to five or more as required by law. The U.S. Court of Appeals disagreed, however, noting that agent Durham was inside the Willow Bar for 56 days, and persons answering the telephone and making notes on paper four or fewer times during a 56-day period cannot "be said to have participated in a manner that was necessary or helpful to the gambling business for a period in excess of 30 days," as required by law.[75]

An illegal gambling business is distinguished from a legal gambling business, therefore, in its violation of state law where it operates, the need for meaningful involvement by five or more persons, and the requirement that it last for more than 30 days or gross more than $2,000 per day. This federal statute helps distinguish gambling as a form of organized crime from gambling that is recreational in nature. This purpose is made clear in the legislative history of this law where Congress intended it to address "illegal gambling activities of major proportions" in order "to reach only those persons who prey systematically upon our citizens and whose syndicated operations are so continuous and so substantial as to be of national concern."[76] Figure 2.2 illustrates the three elements required for an illegal gambling business under federal law.

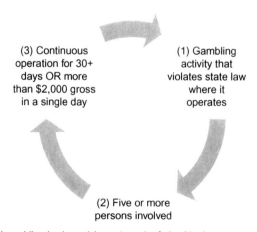

(3) Continuous operation for 30+ days OR more than $2,000 gross in a single day

(1) Gambling activity that violates state law where it operates

(2) Five or more persons involved

FIGURE 2.2 Illegal gambling business (elements under federal law).

Is Placing a Bet Sufficient for Involvement in an Illegal Gambling Enterprise?

The case of John Murray, as discussed above, raises the issue, but does not answer the question, of how much participation is required for one to be legally culpable for participation in an illegal gambling enterprise. Does a single bet suffice? Multiple bets? Is other activity supportive of the enterprise needed?

Consider the case of Karin Follin. She and four others were convicted of operating an illegal casino at the Stewart Lodge in Canton, Mississippi. A police investigator visited the casino eight times in 5 weeks and observed Follin serving drinks, cooking steaks, wiping off kitchen counters, examining dice, and, on several occasions, taking and placing bets.[77] As noted in the previous section, at least five persons are necessary to constitute an illegal gambling business under federal law. Follin appealed her conviction arguing that she was only a bettor and, in that capacity, cannot be held to be part of the illegal business.

The U.S. Court of Appeals agreed that the law prohibits "any degree of participation in a gambling operation except participation as a mere bettor."[78] The reason for the exclusion of "mere bettors" from liability under federal law is "to bring within federal criminal legislation not all gambling, but only that above a certain minimum level."[79] The court also admitted there is "no bright line" that can be drawn to establish what is "necessary or helpful" to a gambling enterprise as compared to mere betting. It noted that the extent of participation "depends on the facts in a given situation."[80] The court concluded that Follin's activities "went beyond the realm of a mere bettor" because of her assistance in managing the illegal gambling business, and her conviction was affirmed.[81]

Even though gambling is now permitted in nearly all states in some form, there are many who violate the restrictions placed on legal gambling and fulfill the elements of operating an illegal gambling enterprise. For example, instances of lottery scams continue (in which no prize is paid out or winnings are skimmed), organized poker games, sports betting operations, illegal lotteries, kickbacks involving video poker machines, and protection of illegal gambling.[82] It is clear that gambling remains a popular activity and vigilance is required to insure that it is conducted in accordance with the law so as not to cheat bettors or taxpayers.

LOANSHARKING

Loansharking, or usury, is lending money at an interest rate that exceeds the legal limit. Its connection with organized crime is linked closely to gambling.

CRITICAL THINKING EXERCISE 2.4

The scenario that follows describes an actual situation in which the courts had to determine whether the laws involving illegal gambling applied. Resolution of this scenario requires proper application of the legal principles discussed in this chapter.

The Case of Poker for Profit

Undercover police officer Russo attempted to conduct a gambling investigation in Erie, Pennsylvania. In his undercover role, he attempted to enter what he believed to be an illegal gambling operation on the second floor of Dominick's Restaurant.

He was stopped by Lou and told to wait. Some time later, Billy approached Russo and questioned him about his background and past poker playing, apparently in an effort to see if he was a police officer. Billy permitted Russo to observe the game that night, taking him to the second floor of the restaurant through three locked doors, protected by buzzers, a surveillance camera, and a lookout.

Once inside, undercover officer Russo observed about 10 people playing poker. Twenty to twenty-five hands were played each hour, and the "pot" (i.e., total amount wagered)

averaged $300 per hand. Two men served drinks and cigarettes, and Lou, Billy, and two others served as "cut men." The cut men took the "rake" from each pot (i.e., a percentage given to the person who runs the game for overhead and profit). Officer Russo left the game at 4:40 a.m., and 15 people were still playing.

Officer Russo returned and played poker at that location five times over the next 6 months. He noticed that several of the same people acted as doormen or cut men during these games.

Ultimately, Billy admitted that he had been operating the game for 2 years and that he earned $200–$300 a night. He also stated that Lou worked for him.

Critical Thinking Questions

1. Can Billy be convicted of running an illegal gambling enterprise under federal law?
2. How does the fact that Billy made only $200–$300 per game affect his liability?
3. Federal law requires involvement by at least five people. If at no time were five of the people at any given game, how would this affect Billy's liability?

Profits reaped from illegal gambling enterprises often have been used to make even more money by lending it to customers at usurious rates. The interest rate is set by law to ensure that customers are not exploited by banks or other lenders. The law of usury also deters individuals from incurring unlawful debts, such as those resulting from illegal gambling losses.

Sometimes the profits from lawful businesses are used for loansharking. In a typical case, Robert Panaro, Joseph DeLuca, and 14 codefendants were convicted on loansharking charges in Nevada. It was revealed at trial that Herbie Blitzstein, a person with ties to Chicago organized crime, gave DeLuca $25,000 to set up an auto repair and used car business in Las Vegas. DeLuca then split all the proceeds from the business with Blitzstein, who would in turn lend the money to people on the street at very high interest rates. In another case, nine men in Philadelphia used several businesses, including a pizza parlor, cafe, and bars to conduct illegal gambling and then make loans to betting customers at usurious rates of interest. The suspects threatened customers with weapons and told them that if they did not pay their debts someone would kill them, break their legs, or physically harm their family members.[83] In this way, legitimate businesses were used to support an unlawful loansharking enterprise.

Usury: Are Threats Needed for Liability?

An important case that involved charges of loansharking was that of Mario "Murph" Eufrasio, Santo "Sam" Idone, and Gary Iacona. These persons were alleged to have been part of the Scarfo "Family," a Philadelphia- and New Jersey-based group of the Cosa Nostra or Mafia. Idone, a "capo" in the Scarfo organization, supervised a group of soldiers and associates that included Eufrasio and Iacona. As the U.S. Court of Appeals noted later, "the function of soldiers and associates, and of the mob generally, was to make money by illegal means."[84]

At trial, intercepted conversations and expert testimony were used to prove that Eufrasio, Idone, and Iacona collected unlawful debts on usurious loans. An "unlawful debt" under federal law is one that is incurred during illegal gambling activity.[85] Therefore, any debts incurred from illegal gambling are unlawful because the activity itself is unlawful. Because these debts have no legal standing, banks cannot lend money to repay these debts, and these debts cannot be collected lawfully either. As a result, loansharks may lend or offer to lend money to those who have no other way to repay gambling losses. The defendants in this case were found to collect debts on "numerous" loans with effective annual interest rates from 78% to 293%. One witness testified he borrowed $4,500 from Iacona for 12 weeks and paid $540 in interest. Idone and Iacona supplied the money and authorized the illegal loans, while Eufrasio was their agent who reported on his crew's loansharking activities to Scarfo.[86] All the defendants were convicted.

On appeal, it was argued that the government must prove the defendants were in the "continuous" business of usury to find them guilty on this charge. The U.S. Court of Appeals held that federal law requires an unlawful debt to be collected as part of "the business of lending money or a thing of value" at usurious rates; "a 'continuous' business is not required."[87] Only a single act is necessary for liability. Furthermore, an exchange of cash is not required, as long as there exists "a single act which would tend to induce another to repay on an unlawful debt incurred in the business of lending money."[88]

Iacona also appealed on grounds that the government did not prove he threatened people for failure to repay these usurious loans. Such a claim "has no merit" because threats are not an element of the crime of collecting unlawful debts.[89] All that is required is the attempt to collect the debt itself. In fact, the accused's ignorance of the specific interest rate charged on a usurious loan is not a defense either because it is not an element of the offense. Collecting an unlawful debt is all that is required. Threats incur liability for another crime (extortion) and ignorance of the defendant is not an excuse for any crime.

Loansharking is important in understanding the nature of organized crime activity because it shows how illicit profits can be used to generate even more illicit money and, thereby, maintain growing criminal enterprises.[90] It is also related to money laundering, discussed in Chapter 10, in that loansharking provides a means to move illicit profits away from their initial source, making them difficult to trace.

CRITICAL THINKING EXERCISE 2.5

The scenario that follows describes an actual situation in which the courts had to determine whether the laws involving usury applied. Resolution of this scenario requires proper application of the legal principles discussed in this chapter.

The Case of Collecting a Debt

Cunningham was an associate of the Genovese crime family. Ferris was a licensed electrician and longtime friend of Cunningham. He was well aware of Cunningham's reputation as a collector of loanshark debts who used threats and violence in the process. Ferris had several customers who had contracted for electrical work but had not paid in full. The customers had been charged an exorbitant price for the work and disputed the amount they were billed.

Ferris asked Cunningham to send his collectors to visit several of these customers to collect the full amount owed, and Cunningham added a 25% surcharge for his collection efforts. Conversations between Ferris and Cunningham clearly showed Ferris's understanding and support of the use of fear, threats, and intimidation to collect the money.

Critical Thinking Questions

1. How would you determine whether Ferris's efforts constitute simple debt collection or something that is illegal?
2. How is Cunningham's reputation as a debt collector for loansharks relevant in this case?

SEX AND ORGANIZED CRIME

Sex and organized crime are linked in two distinct ways: prostitution and pornography. Organized prostitution has been used to profit from the money made by individual prostitutes from sex acts in exchange for "protection" or other services offered to prostitutes. Pornography is manufacturing and marketing illicit depictions of sex in the form of photographs, films, and videos to a segment of the public that desires them. As in the case of illicit goods and the other illicit services, organized crime involvement in the sex industry is made possible entirely through a continuing public demand for these services. A decreased demand for these services would undoubtedly result in a smaller market for organized crime involvement.

Prostitution: It Was Only a Modeling and Escort Service

Engaging in prostitution is not an organized crime in itself because it fails to fulfill the definition presented in Chapter 1. Simply stated, prostitution often involves little planning or organization in its commission. It becomes a part of organized crime when it is planned or organized in a systematic way. In the United States, there has been a history of criminal entrepreneurs who "organize" prostitutes and take a percentage of their income as a "commission."

The question that arises in these situations is: Why would a prostitute agree to pay a commission to a "pimp" or "madam" when these people are not necessary to the act? There are two answers to this question. First, there have been instances where prostitutes have been coerced into joining such "prostitution rings" under threat of bodily harm. Second and more often, however, the "pimp" or "madam" provides useful services to the prostitute. These services might include renting a "safe" hotel or rooms for the prostitutes to ply their trade and screening of customers so that the threat of dangerous, unhealthy, or suspected undercover police officers is reduced. Without these services, street prostitution is a much more dangerous and threatening business.

Actual cases of organized prostitution frequently involve problems in proving that the "pimp," "madam," or other organizer knew of the nature of the enterprise. People simply don't put an advertisement in the newspaper soliciting customers for prostitutes. These organizers often develop clever ways to disguise their prostitution business as something legitimate.[91] The prostitution enterprises sometimes involve coercion, threats, and movement of the victims, qualifying them as human trafficking enterprises which are discussed in Chapter 7.[92] Nevertheless, proving in court that the operators *knew* it was an illegal enterprise can be difficult.

An actual case illustrates the difficulty of proving the existence of a prostitution business. Penelope Hatteras (see Figure 2.3) operated several businesses in Houston, Dallas, Atlanta, and Denver. These businesses were advertised as "nude modeling and escort services." Customers would call these businesses, and "models" would be dispatched directly to the customer's location. The customer paid by cash or credit card. What was actually occurring was organized prostitution. Once the "model" reached the customer, she would negotiate a monetary agreement in exchange for sex acts.[93]

Hatteras, her accountant Charles Holcomb, and others were eventually arrested and charged with violating the *Mann Act* (1910). This federal law prohibits anyone who "knowingly persuades, induces, entices, or coerces any woman or girl" to travel between states or countries "for the purpose of prostitution or debauchery, or for any other immoral purpose...with or without her consent."[94]

Holcomb, the accountant, appealed his conviction, arguing that the evidence against him was insufficient for violation of the Mann Act. As the U.S. Court of Appeals stated, the government cannot establish his guilt under the Mann Act "by simply showing his awareness of prostitution." The government "must also produce some evidence suggesting that Holcomb knowingly agreed with

FIGURE 2.3 Penelope Hatteras served 26 months in prison after she was convicted of running a prostitution ring. *AP Photo/Houston Chronicle, Larry Reese*

Hatteras that her operation would entice women to cross state lines for the purpose of prostitution."[95]

The government demonstrated at trial that Holcomb set up Hatteras's books, distributed pay to the "models," and that he suspected Hatteras was operating a prostitution ring. But there was no evidence that Holcomb was aware "that the models were crossing state lines" (a requirement of the Mann Act).[96] As a result, Holcomb's conviction was reversed.

It is important to keep in mind that Holcomb's actions would be sufficient to convict him for conspiracy to engage in prostitution under most state laws. A reasonable person would have been aware of what was going on under these circumstances, and Holcomb admitted he had suspicions. The point here is that the federal Mann Act requires *interstate* movement of women for the purposes of prostitution, knowledge of which Holcomb did not possess. Hatteras and others involved in the enterprise were convicted in this case, however, because the facts demonstrated their knowledge of interstate movement of women for the purposes of prostitution.

As in all criminal law, *reasonable knowledge* is required for liability for nearly all crimes. In prostitution cases, for instance, *actual knowledge* that prostitution occurred is not necessary, as long as there is evidence that a *reasonable person* should have drawn that conclusion.

In a similar case, Alvin Sigalow was general manager for two massage parlors in New York City. The massage parlors "engaged in the prostitution business" and actually were owned by others who used Sigalow as a "front man."[97] The business advertised through mailings to potential customers in New York, New Jersey, and Connecticut and also through advertisements in *The Village Voice* newspaper and *Screw* magazine.

Sigalow was convicted of aiding and abetting "the promotion, management, establishment, or carrying on" of a prostitution enterprise in violation of the federal *Travel Act* (1961). This act prohibits using interstate or foreign commerce in the promotion of an illegal activity (including prostitution).[98] In affirming his conviction, the U.S. Court of Appeals held that a person can be convicted "so long as he knows that nature of the substantive offense he furthers or promotes."[99] Similar to the "nude modeling" case given earlier, reasonable knowledge of the elements of the crime suffices for liability. Actual knowledge need not be proven, as long as a reasonable person would have drawn that conclusion about the nature of the activity.

Distinguishing the Risqué from the Obscene

Some people get their sexual gratification vicariously through pornography. Interestingly, the term *pornography* has no legal meaning. It is a generic term that refers to sexually explicit material. Such material is illegal only when it is also "obscene" under law. Therefore, state and federal laws are directed at "obscene" material rather than at pornography.

A problem arises when one attempts to define obscenity in an objective manner. The courts have wrestled with this problem for many years, deciding on the current legal definition in 1973. The definition of obscenity is a central issue, of course, in establishing criminal liability.

The U.S. Supreme Court set the current legal standard for obscenity in the case of *Miller v. California*.[100] Marvin Miller conducted a mass mailing to advertise the sale of illustrated books. The brochures advertised four books titled *Intercourse, Man-Woman, Sex Orgies Illustrated*, and *An Illustrated History of Pornography*. The brochure also featured a film titled *Marital Intercourse*. The brochures consisted primarily of pictures and drawings "very explicitly depicting men and women in groups of two or more engaging in a variety of sexual activities, with genitals often prominently displayed."[101] The case resulted from a complaint to the police from a person who had been sent five of these unsolicited brochures. The legal issue was whether these materials were legally obscene and, hence, in violation of the law.

The U.S. Supreme Court admitted that there had been a "somewhat tortured history of the court's obscenity decisions," but it was able to reach a five-justice majority.[102] The definition of obscenity agreed upon by the court consisted of three parts. Obscenity was said to exist when the average person, applying contemporary community standards, would find that the work:

1. Taken as a whole, appeals to the prurient interest in sex
2. Portrays sexual conduct (as specifically defined by state law) in a patently offensive way
3. Taken as a whole, lacks serious literary, artistic, political, or scientific value[103]

The majority emphasized that it was not their function to usurp the state prerogative to define obscenity. It did, however, provide examples of what state laws could include as obscenity. The court felt that "patently offensive representations of ultimate sexual acts, normal or perverted, actual or simulated" as well as "masturbation, excretory functions, and lewd exhibition of the genitals" could be included as obscene "hard-core" sexual conduct.[104] Nevertheless, the U.S. Supreme Court ruled that a requirement forcing obscenity proceedings "around evidence of a national 'community standard' would be an exercise in futility."[105] It held

> It is neither realistic nor constitutionally sound to read the First Amendment as requiring that the people of Maine or Mississippi accept public depiction of conduct found tolerable in Las Vegas, or New York City.[106]

Although this definition of obscenity contains several objective elements, it remains difficult to apply in practice. This has made both the prosecution and the defense of obscenity cases problematic. Observe how the U.S. Supreme Court has subsequently carved conditions and exceptions to its own definition set forth in *Miller.*

In *Paris Adult Theatre I v. Slaton,*[107] the U.S. Supreme Court ruled that the exhibition of obscene films is not protected from prosecution even when viewing is limited to consenting adults. Two films shown in an adult theater were found to be obscene, despite the fact that minors were excluded and adult patrons were warned of the nature of the material. The court also held that states have the power to determine whether the exhibition or sale of obscene material "has a tendency to injure the community as a whole, [or] to endanger the public safety," even though the scientific evidence on this point is unsettled.[108]

In another case, Billy Jenkins, a theater manager in Albany, Georgia, exhibited the film *Carnal Knowledge.* The critically acclaimed film was directed by Mike Nichols and starred Jack Nicholson, Candice Bergen, and Art Garfunkel. Jenkins was convicted for violating Georgia's obscenity law by showing this film. A jury found it to exceed the "community standards" of Albany, Georgia.

Therefore, the film failed a crucial part of the obscenity test set forth in *Miller*. The U.S. Supreme Court reversed the conviction.[109] The court was put in the precarious position of having to interfere, only 1 year after *Miller*, with a state's interpretation of its own community standards. Therefore, the U.S. Supreme Court made it clear that the locality does not necessarily have the last word in setting its own "community standards."[110]

The U.S. Supreme Court added another caveat to the law of obscenity when a New York City radio station played a recording of comedian George Carlin's monologue titled, "Filthy Words." The monologue dealt with various uses of "seven dirty words" that cannot be said over the airwaves. A man who heard the broadcast while driving with his son complained to the Federal Communications Commission (FCC). Although the FCC did not find the monologue obscene, it was found to be "patently offensive" and not in the "public interest." It was banned from broadcast.

In a five-to-four decision, the U.S. Supreme Court upheld the FCC ruling. It found that the broadcast of "indecent material" was not protected by the First Amendment because it "confronts the citizen not only in public, but in the privacy of the home, where the individual's right to be left alone plainly outweighs the First Amendment rights of an intruder."[111] Also, the majority found that the broadcast media is "uniquely accessible" to children. Interestingly, indecent speech in a nonobscene book would still be protected by the First Amendment unless it was broadcast over the airwaves. As the majority declared, "of all forms of communication, it is broadcasting that has received the most limited First Amendment protection," due to its intrusiveness and accessibility to children.[112]

The U.S. Supreme Court ruled in *New York v. Ferber*[113] that states may prohibit the distribution of material that is not obscene if it depicts sexual conduct by a juvenile. In its decision, the court made yet another exception to the *Miller* standard:

> The test for child pornography is separate from the obscenity standard enunciated in *Miller*... A trier of fact need not find that the material appeals to the prurient interest of the average person; it is not required that sexual conduct portrayed be done so in a patently offensive manner; and the material at issue need not be considered as a whole.[114]

Therefore, the portrayal of children in any type of material dealing with sexual conduct can be defined by the states as obscene, regardless of the *Miller* guidelines.

Finally, the U.S. Supreme Court invalidated a portion of a Washington State obscenity statute in *Brockett v. Spokane Arcades* and its companion case *Eikenberry v. J-R Distributors*.[115] The law included, as part of its definition of obscenity, material that incites "lust or lasciviousness." It was held that "lust" connotes a "normal interest in sex." Therefore, that part of the statute was struck down because it did not appeal to the "prurient interest."

It can be seen that, once again, a state's interpretation of obscenity law according to "community standards" is ultimately subject to concurrence by the U.S. Supreme Court. As one analysis concluded,

> [a] major myth fostered by the Court is that obscenity can be constitutionally controlled at the local level using local standards... Try as it might, the Supreme Court, under the present approach, cannot escape the need to impose national standards to measure national rights and protections and, in the end, to act as a national censorship board.[116]

The inability of the court to refrain from continually altering the application of such terms as "serious value," "prurient interest," and "community standards" set forth in *Miller* illustrates the inadequacy of that definition of obscenity. The uncertainty and continuing flux in determining the legal limits of obscenity undoubtedly has affected prosecutions for violations of these laws.

The Attorney General's Commission on Pornography found a "lack of effective enforcement of obscenity laws throughout most parts of the country."[117] This "striking underenforcement" was illustrated by the fact that only 100 individuals were indicted (and 71 convicted) for violation of federal obscenity laws in the 8 years preceding the commission's report.[118] Some of the blame for this lackluster record was placed on the low priority given obscenity cases in comparison to other crimes, although the commission "reject[ed] the view" that a new legal definition of obscenity is needed.[119] Efforts in recent years have been focused on protecting minors from involvement in obscenity and pornography.

Pornography: I Didn't Know the Model Was a Minor

While legislatures and courts continue to struggle with legal definitions of obscenity, people are making a profit from manufacturing and distributing explicit depictions of sex in books, magazines, videos, and computer software. These people are part of organized crime to the extent that they fulfill the definition in Chapter 1, that is, as part of a continuing criminal enterprise.

A common defense to charges of obscenity is failure to know the depictions are obscene or failure to know the models or performers used are minors. Keep in mind that when minors are used, it does not matter if the pornography falls outside the definition of obscenity; a person may still be held criminally liable (see the case in the previous section).

In 1994, the U.S. Supreme Court heard a landmark case involving an alleged violation of the Protection of Children Against Sexual Exploitation Act of 1977. This federal law prohibits "knowingly" manufacturing, distributing, or receiving" a visual depiction of "a minor engaging in sexually explicit conduct."[120]

In this case, Rubin Gottesman owned and operated X-Citement Video. Undercover police posed as pornography retailers in a sting operation. During the course of this investigation, media revealed that actress Traci Lords appeared in pornographic films before she was 18 years old. An undercover police officer asked X-Citement Video for these videos, and Gottesman sold the officer 49 videotapes featuring Lords before her 18th birthday. Two months later, Gottesman shipped 8 more tapes of Lords to the undercover officer in Hawaii.[121]

The two transactions resulted in federal charges against Gottesman and X-Citement Video for violating the child pornography act. The defendants argued that the child pornography act is unconstitutional because it does not require that a person know a model or performer is a minor. The U.S. Supreme Court held that the law is constitutional. It "rejects the most natural grammatical reading" of the law, and the court concluded that a person may be held liable under this law as long as he or she *both* knowingly manufactures, distributes, or receives a depiction of explicit sexual conduct *and* knows that depiction is of a minor.[122] Without such knowledge, the court stated, a drugstore that develops film could be held liable for returning photos or for delivering them. However, proving such knowledge makes it harder to enforce the law. In this case, however, Gottesman knew Traci Lords was underage so his conviction was affirmed.[123] The courts also have given states and localities wide latitude in regulating nude and seminude dancing and other "borderline" sex-related activity through liquor law restrictions, business zoning laws to certain areas of town, and strict monitoring to protect against obscenity or organized crime activity.[124]

The priority given to either prostitution or pornography cases has not been high, especially in terms of their relationship to organized crime. The President's Crime Commission Task Force on Organized Crime, reporting 50 years ago, concluded prostitution plays "a small and declining role in organized crime's operations." This was because prostitution is "difficult to organize and discipline is hard to maintain."[125] In addition, a few important convictions of organized crime figures in prostitution cases in the 1930s and 1940s were believed to have a deterrent effect. In recent years, the situation appears to have changed little. The President's Commission on Organized Crime, reporting 30 years ago, gave little explicit attention to prostitution and pornography. A report on "The Income of Organized Crime" completed for the commission concluded that approximately 20% of illegal income from prostitution is related to organized crime.[126] No estimates were made for pornography.

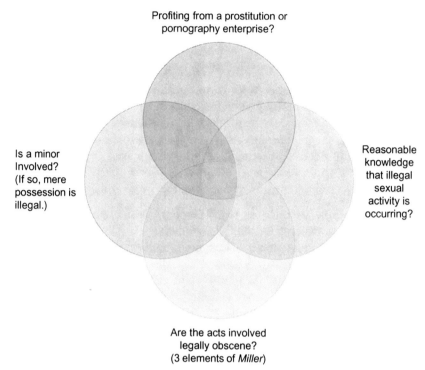

Profiting from a prostitution or
pornography enterprise?

Is a minor
Involved?
(If so, mere
possession is
illegal.)

Reasonable
knowledge
that illegal
sexual
activity is
occurring?

Are the acts involved
legally obscene?
(3 elements of *Miller*)

FIGURE 2.4 Major issues in sex and organized crime.

The Attorney General's Commission on Pornography concluded that organized crime "exerts substantial influence and control over the obscenity industry," although it also found that "a number of significant producers and distributors are not members" of organized crime groups.[127] These rather contradictory findings summarize the confused state of knowledge in this area. While no one rejects the idea that organized crime is involved in prostitution and pornography businesses, there is little evidence or consensus regarding precisely how much of it is produced or controlled by organized crime groups.

Figure 2.4 illustrates the four major issues when discussing sex and organized crime. It shows the overlapping concerns about the nature of the conduct, knowledge of the nature of the activity, the age of those involved, and whether profiting from a prostitution or pornography business is occurring.

The Internet and Pornography

Expansion of the Internet and dramatic increases in its accessibility around the world have resulted in concern about its content. Pornography used to be confined largely to magazines, theaters, and videos for which the buyer has to make an overt effort to obtain. The Internet allows people to load, download, and distribute obscene material inside their own homes with very little time or effort.

The role of the Internet in distributing pornographic text and images led to the passage by Congress of Title V of the Telecommunications Act of 1996. Titled the "Communications Decency Act," Title V contains two provisions that prohibit "the knowing transmission of obscene or indecent messages to any person under 18 years of age" or sending or displaying "patently offensive messages in a manner available to a person under 18 years of age."[128] The intent of the law was to protect minors from pornographic images and messages on the Internet. The law was challenged in court immediately after it was passed.

The U.S. Supreme Court held that the terms "indecent transmission" and "patently offensive display" violate the First Amendment's protection of freedom of speech. The court ruled that the terminology used in the Communications Decency Act was too vague, imprecise, and would "provoke uncertainty among speakers" regarding its applicability. The act was held to be unconstitutional, although the U.S. Supreme Court ruled in 2003 that libraries that receive federal funding could be forced to use a software filter to block Internet pornography from library users (see Figure 2.5).[129]

FIGURE 2.5 Internet users view computer screens at a public library. The U.S. Supreme Court ruled in 2003 that libraries that receive federal funding could be forced to use a software filter to block Internet pornography. *Ellen S. Boyne*

The problem of imprecision again arose when the court evaluated dial-a-porn operators who offer sexually suggestive telephone messages for a fee. The court held there, as it did in the Internet case, that obscene messages are illegal, but "indecent" ones are not.[130] Unlike radio and television, where one can be "taken by surprise by an indecent message," both dial-a-porn and the Internet "require the listener to take affirmative steps to receive the communication." As a result, both indecent and obscene messages are prohibited on television and radio broadcasts, but only obscene messages are prohibited on the Internet or in dial-a-porn. Quoting itself from an earlier case, the court remarked, "the level of discourse reaching a mailbox simply cannot be limited to that which would be suitable for a sandbox."[131]

Congress responded to this U.S. Supreme Court ruling in 2000 by passing another law, the Child Online Protection Act (COPA).[132] The intent of the law was to prohibit transmission of objectionable material to minors via the Internet. Courts have found this law impossible to enforce because current technology does not permit a Web publisher to restrict content based on the geographic location of the user in order to determine whether material is "harmful to minors" according to "contemporary community standards" as the law mandates.[133] Because the legal definition of obscenity is determined by states and localities, Internet content that is unlawful in one location may not be unlawful in another. Technology to regulate content for a worldwide audience may ultimately help solve this problem: The U.S. Supreme Court upheld a temporary injunction to prevent COPA from taking effect and a federal judge issued a permanent injunction in 2007. The basis for the court's rejection of the law was that software filters that block access to pornographic sites work well and do not pose the problems that COPA creates.[134] Congress passed still another law (18 U.S.C. § 2252A(a)(3)(B)), which was challenged immediately and heard in a 2008 U.S. Supreme Court case. The court held that a statute is facially invalid if it prohibits a substantial amount of protected speech, but this new law was found to avoid this by prohibiting obscene material depicting (actual or virtual) children engaged in sexually explicit conduct and any other material depicting actual children engaged in sexually explicit conduct. The statute's important feature included that the defendant must "intend" that the listener believe the material to be child pornography. The statute's requirements were found to be clear, and the Supreme Court upheld the law's constitutionality under the First Amendment.[135]

Congress and the various state legislatures are free to write new laws that define objectionable speech and images according to the accepted legal definition of obscenity set forth in *Miller v. California*. It is likely that such legislative efforts will continue, as concern about offensive material grows in proportion to increases in computer availability, Internet usage, and the threat of organized crime around the nation and the world.[136] A problem that remains is that greater effort is needed to determine the extent to which organized crime is involved in pornography, and how demand reduction, better technology, and other crime prevention methods can be employed to reduce the profitability of this illicit marketplace.

CRITICAL THINKING EXERCISE 2.6

The scenario that follows describes an actual situation in which the courts had to determine whether the laws involving obscenity applied. Resolution of this scenario requires proper application of the legal principles discussed in this chapter.

The Case of Child Pornography on the Computer

Muck was an employee of Glenayre Electronics. His employer discovered that he had downloaded child pornography from the Internet to his computer at work. The company seized the laptop computer that it had furnished him for use at work and would not turn it over to police until a warrant was obtained because the computer also contained confidential corporate information.

Muck was fired from his job and prosecuted for receiving and possession of child pornography. He later sued his employer for seizing the contents of his computer, violating his right to privacy.

Critical Thinking Questions

1. Does Muck's employer have any right to seize the contents of his computer? Explain your reasoning.
2. How would you rule if Muck had purchased his own small safe, brought it to work, and placed his laptop computer in it each night and the company opened the safe to examine the contents of the computer?

SUMMARY

Conspiracy is the characteristic organized crime. The act of preparing or organizing to commit crimes is what distinguishes organized crime from most street crimes, and conviction of conspiracy punishes this organization as a separate crime.

The provision of illicit goods and services has been the primary source of revenue for organized crime groups over the years. Gambling, loansharking, sex, drugs, and stolen property remain popular due to strong public demand. Important elements in establishing the legal limits of these crimes were described in this chapter, using actual cases as illustrations.

The case of the IVP drug gang that opened this chapter has been shown to be part of organized crime because it was ongoing, identifiable, had members who identified themselves as such, the gang made decisions about how to handle rival drug dealers, and, in the words of the U.S. Court of Appeals, "the IVP was no innocent group of teenagers, but rather was sophisticated and experienced in its own way in the rough, violent business of drug dealing."[137] The IVP fulfilled the requirements for criminal conspiracy.

The next chapter considers the remaining two categories of organized crime: extortion and racketeering. Their fundamental difference from the provision of illicit goods and services is highlighted.

ORGANIZED CRIME BIOGRAPHY

Biographies tell the life story of interesting people. In the world of criminal justice, biographies of organized crime figures offer insight into the background and motivations of the individuals who choose that lifestyle, the reasons for their choices, and the consequences. The following is a brief summary of an organized crime biography, followed by questions that ask you to reflect on the connections between that person's life and the content of this book.

Paddy Whacked: The Untold Story of the Irish American Gangster
T. J. English (Harper, 2006)

The author takes a revisionist view of the rise of the American mob, arguing that Irish figures, rather than Italians, were responsible for establishing organized crime in the United States. Following their immigration to America after the Irish famine of the 1840s, the unique Irish personality (containing resentment, suspicion, rebellion, Catholic background, and clans) combined with impoverished conditions to develop Irish organized crime groups. Prohibition provided a means out of poverty, but infighting and a propensity toward violence were ultimately their undoing. The book describes operations involving well-known criminal and political figures from the 20th century, pointing to the broad reach of Irish-American organized crime.

The author makes reference to Joseph Kennedy and liquor smuggling, crime figures Jack "Legs" Diamond, Dean O'Banion, James "Whitey" Bulger, corruptible first-generation Irish cops, an Irish madam, connections to corrupt politics, excessive alcohol consumption, and unpredictable behavior. Although this era of organized crime has ended, the author attempts to show how the Irish were the first to establish organized crime in the United States in a significant way.

Questions
1. It has been argued that use of a specific racial, ethnic, or national group to describe organized crime is misleading. Why?
2. Why do you think Irish organized crime did not continue to dominate the American scene like Italian-American organized crime?

ORGANIZED CRIME AT THE MOVIES

Movies seek to entertain and inform the audience about a story, incident, or person. Many good movies also hit upon important substantive themes relevant to understanding organized crime. Read the following movie summary (and watch the movie if you haven't already) and answer the questions that follow to make the organized crime subject matter connections.

Blow
Ted Demme, Director (2001)

Blow, a slang term for cocaine, is based on a true story of an American cocaine smuggler, George Jung. George (Johnny Depp) moves to California with a friend, "Tuna" (Ethan Suplee), after being raised in a financially struggling family in Massachusetts. George and Tuna rent a beachfront apartment, but they are lazy and come up with the idea of selling marijuana.

They meet the primary marijuana dealer in the area and make a lot of money selling marijuana. Another friend moves back to Boston so they supply him as well. As the customer demand increases, they decide to start buying drugs directly from Mexico and import them using small planes; they also buy a large house in Acapulco.

George eventually gets arrested and is sentenced to 2 years in prison. He jumps bail to be with his dying girlfriend and his drug smuggling group dissolves. As a wanted man, George

ORGANIZED CRIME AT THE MOVIES—CONT'D

visits his parents in Massachusetts, who realize his fugitive status, and the police catch him there after his mother calls the police (to the chagrin of his father).

George is sentenced to 3 years in prison where he meets a Colombian drug smuggler who introduces him to cocaine smuggling. Upon his release, George meets up with his former fellow inmate, who introduces him to drug lord Pablo Escobar (Cliff Curtis) in Colombia. George immediately becomes a major importer for Escobar and hides his money in a bank in Panama.

George soon becomes wealthy and marries a beautiful Colombian woman, Mirtha (Penelope Cruz). He brings his parents to his new mansion in California. His father knows how George made his money, but does not disapprove, apparently overwhelmed by the extent of his wealth.

George is later shot in the shoulder during a drug deal, the result of his friend becoming a paranoid cocaine user who double-crosses him. George decides to get out of the drug smuggling business, but when he tries to withdraw his money from the Panama bank, he discovers the government has seized it all.

George and Mirtha have a daughter, but George has trouble breaking his cocaine habit. They argue about money in front of their child, just as George's parents did in front of him years earlier. They throw a birthday party, inviting many of their old drug smuggling friends. When they bring out cocaine, however, it turns out the waiters are federal agents, and everyone is arrested. George goes to prison in return for the freedom of his wife and daughter. A year later, he is released, Mirtha has divorced him, and he tries to resurrect his relationship with his daughter.

Without money, George tries to set up one last big drug deal, but he is double-crossed again and sent away for a long prison term. The film ends with George still in prison, dreaming about his now-grown daughter and the relationship they will never have.

Questions

1. George was involved in a series of drug conspiracies over many years. Why do you believe he didn't get out of the drug business after being caught the first time?
2. Conspiracy is the characteristic organized crime, but the police caught George several times. How were the police able to accomplish this?

References and Notes

1. *United States v. Patrick and Arthur*, 248 F.3d 11 (1st Cir. 2001).
2. *United States v. Auerbach and Helish*, 913 F.2d 407 (7th Cir. 1990) at 409.
3. at 409–410.
4. *United States v. Auerbach and Helish*, 913 F.2d 407 (7th Cir. 1990) at 414–415 and *United States v. Anderson*, 896 F.2d 1076 (7th Cir. 1990). For more on the importance of reasonable knowledge of the conspiracy for liability, see *United States v. Grasso*, 724 F.3d 1077 (9th Cir. 2013) and *United States v. Surtain*, 519 Fed. Appx. 266 (5th Cir. 2013).
5. *United States v. Douglas*, 818 F.2d 1317 (7th Cir. 1987) and *United States v. Marks*, 816 F.2d 1207 (7th Cir. 1987).
6. *United States v. Auerbach and Helish*, at 415.
7. *United States v. Jimenez Recio*, 71 U.S.L.W. 4076 (2003).
8. *United States v. Bourjaily*, 781 F.2d 539 (6th Cir. 1986), 197 S. Ct. 2775 (1987).
9. at 544.
10. at 545; for more on the importance of the requisite specific intent to distribute drugs for liability for conspiracy, see *United States v. Cortes-Caban*, 691 F.3d 1 (1st. Cir 2012).
11. From the general conspiracy statute, 18 U.S.C. 371.
12. *United States v. Shabani*, 993 F.2d 1419 (9th Cir. 1993).

13. at 1420.

14. at 1422.

15. Comprehensive Drug Abuse Prevention and Control Act of 1970, Pub. L. 91–513, 84 Stat. 1236, at 1265. This act was amended by the Anti-Drug Abuse Act of 1988, Pub. L. 100–690, 102 Stat. 4377, 21 U.S.C. 846, but the drug conspiracy elements were not altered.

16. Organized Crime Control Act of 1970, Pub. L. 91–452, 84 Stat. 922, 18 U.S.C. 1511.

17. *United States v. Shabani*, 114 S. Ct. 1048.

18. at 1052.

19. *United States v. Schweihs and Daddino*, 971 F.2d 1302 (7th Cir. 1992) at 1309.

20. at 1323.

21. at 1323; For more on the elements required for effective withdrawal from a conspiracy, see *United States v. Schiro*, 679 F.3d 521 (7th Cir. 2012).

22. *United States v. Patel*, 879 F.2d 294 (7th Cir. 1989), cert. denied, 110 S. Ct. 1318.

23. *United States v. Schweihs and Daddino*, 971 F.2d 1302 (7th Cir. 1992) at 1323.

24. *United States v. Teffera*, 985 F.2d 1082 (D.C. Cir. 1993).

25. at 1085.

26. *United States v. Lam Kwong-Wah*, 924 F.2d 298 (D.C. Cir. 1991).

27. *United States v. Raper*, 676 F.2d 841 (D.C. Cir. 1982).

28. *United States v. Teffera*, 985 F.2d 1086 (D.C. Cir. 1993).

29. at 1087.

30. at 1087.

31. at 1088.

32. at 1088.

33. at 1088; for more on the conduct required to establish participation in a conspiracy, see *United States v. Herrera*, 466 Fed. Appx. 409 (5th Cir. 2012).

34. See, for example, the biography of Henry Hill, whose life was depicted in the film *Goodfellas*. Pileggi, T. (1985). *Wiseguys*. New York: Simon and Schuster.

35. Bjorhus, J. "Fraud Alert: Bold New ATM Schemes Prompt Warnings," *Minneapolis Star Tribune* (January 23, 2013); U.S. Department of Justice (2013). *Leader of Internet Piracy Group "IMA-GiNE" Sentenced in Virginia to 60 Months in Prison for Criminal Copyright Conspiracy*. Washington, DC: Office of Public Affairs, p. 5.

36. *United States v. Rosa*, 17 F.3d 1531 (2d Cir. 1994).

37. *United States v. Rosa*, 17 F.2d 1538 (2d Cir. 1994).

38. *United States v. Rosa*, 17 F.2d 1538 (2d Cir. 1994).

39. at 1537.

40. 18 U.S.C. Sec. 2315.

41. at 1547.

42. *United States v. Stuar t*, 22 F.3d 76 (3d Cir. 1994).

43. at 81.

44. U.S. Department of Justice (2013). *Two Florida Men Convicted in Philadelphia of Conspiring and Trafficking in Protected Reptiles*. Washington, DC: Office of Public Affairs; Fenoff, R., & Spink, J. (2014). Counterfeiting. In J. Albanese (Ed.), *Encyclopedia of Criminology & Criminal Justice*. Malden, MA: Wiley-Blackwell.

45. Mark 15:24, Luke 23:34, John 19:24.

46. Chafetz, H. (1960). *Play the Devil.* New York: Potter Publishing, p. 8.

47. Rosecrance, J. (1988). *Gambling without Guilt: The Legitimation of an American Pastime.* Belmont, CA: Brooks/Cole, p. 12.

48. *Gambling without Guilt: The Legitimation of an American Pastime,* pp. 12–13.

49. Geis, G. (1979). *Not the Law's Business.* New York: Schocken, p. 223.

50. *Play the Devil,* p. 17.

51. *Gambling without Guilt: The Legitimation of an American Pastime,* p. 13.

52. Ashbury, H. (1969). *Sucker's Progress: An Informal History of Gambling from the Colonies to Canfield* (first Published in 1938). Montclair, NJ: Patterson Smith, pp. 76–78.

53. Robertson, W. H. P. (1964). *The History of Thoroughbred Racing in America.* Englewood Cliffs, NJ: Prentice Hall, p. 8; Longstreet, S. (1977). *Win or Lose: A Social History of Gambling.* Indianapolis: Bobbs-Merrill.

54. *Play the Devil,* p. 13.

55. *Win or Lose,* p. 37.

56. *Win or Lose,* p. 37.

57. Skolnick, J. (1978). *House of Cards.* Boston: Little, Brown.

58. Ezell, J. S. (1960). *Fortune's Merry Wheel.* Cambridge, MA: Harvard University Press.

59. Findlay, J. M. (1986). *People of Chance.* New York: Oxford University Press.

60. *Play the Devil,* p. 94.

61. *Gambling without Guilt: The Legitimation of an American Pastime,* p. 23.

62. *Sucker's Progress,* pp. 88–106.

63. *Gambling without Guilt: The Legitimation of an American Pastime,* pp. 24–25.

64. *Gambling without Guilt: The Legitimation of an American Pastime,* pp. 36–37.

65. *Sucker's Progress,* p. 451.

66. *Gambling without Guilt: The Legitimation of an American Pastime,* p. 41.

67. *Gambling without Guilt: The Legitimation of an American Pastime,* p. 38.

68. *Fortune's Merry Wheel,* p. 279.

69. *United States v. Edge Broadcasting Co.,* 113 S. Ct. 2696 (1993) at 2703.

70. *United States v. Edge Broadcasting Co.,* 113 S. Ct. 2696 (1993) at 2703.

71. *United States v. Edge Broadcasting Co.,* 113 S. Ct. 2696 (1993), pp. 2703–2704.

72. U.S.C. Sec. 1955(b)(1).

73. U.S.C. Sec. 1955(b)(1)(iii).

74. *United States v. Murray,* 928 F.2d 1242 (1st Cir. 1991) at 1246.

75. *United States v. Murray,* 928 F.2d 1242 (1st Cir. 1991) at 1249.

76. H.R. Rep. No. 91-1549, 91st Congress, 2d Session (1970) and 1970 U.S.C. Congressional and Administrative News, at 4007, 4029.

77. *United States v. Follin,* 979 F.2d 369 (5th Cir. 1992) at 372.

78. *United States v. Follin,* 979 F.2d 369 (5th Cir. 1992) at 373.

79. *United States v. Bridges,* 493 F.2d 918 (5th Cir. 1974) at 922.

80. *United States v. Follin,* 979 F.2d (5th Cir. 1992) at 373.

81. *United States v. Follin,* 979 F.2d (5th Cir. 1992) at 373.

82. U.S. Department of Justice (2013). *Jamaican Citizen Pleads Guilty in Connection with International Lottery Scheme Based in Jamaica.* Washington, DC: Office of Public Affairs;

Rashbaum, W. K. "Scion of Art Family, in Court, Admits Role with a Gambling Ring," *The New York Times* (November 12, 2013); U.S. Department of Justice (2013). *Six Charged in Ohio with Operating an Illegal Gambling Business and Other Related Offenses.* Washington, DC: Office of Public Affairs; U.S. Department of Justice (2013). *Former South Pittsburg, Tenn., Mayor and Co-conspirator Plead Guilty to Conducting Illegal Gambling Business.* Washington, DC: Office of Public Affairs.

83. *United States v. Panaro,* 241 F.3d 1104 (9th Cir. 2001); U.S. Department of Justice (2013). *Alleged Members of Violent Loan Sharking and Illegal Gambling Organization Charged in Philadelphia.* Washington, DC: Office of Public Affairs.

84. *United States v. Eufrasio,* 935 F.2d 553 (3d Cir. 1991) at 559.

85. 18 U.S.C. Sec. 1961(6).

86. *United States v. Eufrasio,* 935 F.2d 553 (3d Cir. 1991) at 562.

87. *United States v. Eufrasio,* 935 F.2d 553 (3d Cir. 1991) at 576.

88. *United States v. Eufrasio,* 935 F.2d 553 (3d Cir. 1991) at 576.

89. *United States v. Eufrasio,* 935 F.2d 553 (3d Cir. 1991) at 577.

90. MacDonald, A., & Whalen, J. (September 1, 2009). Loan Sharks Circle Credit-Starved Consumers. *Wall Street Journal, 254,* A13; Mayer, R. (2010). *Quick Cash: The Story of the Loan Shark.* DeKalb, IL: Northern Illinois University Press.

91. Schmidt, M. S. "F.B.I. Charges 159 Men with Forcing Teenage Girls into Prostitution," *The New York Times* (July 29, 2013), 6.

92. U.S. Department of Justice (2013). *Fairborn, Ohio, Man Pleads Guilty to Sex Trafficking.* Washington, DC: Office of Public Affairs.

93. *United States v. Holcomb,* 797 F.2d 1320 (5th Cir. 1986).

94. 18 U.S.C. Sec. 2422.

95. *United States v. Holcomb,* 797 F.2d 1327.

96. *United States v. Holcomb,* 797 F.2d 1327.

97. *United States v. Sigalow,* 812 F.2d 783 (2d Cir. 1987).

98. 18 U.S.C. Sec. 1952.

99. *United States v. Sigalow,* 812 F.2d 786.

100. 93 S. Ct. 2607.

101. at 2611–2612.

102. at 2612–2613.

103. at 2615.

104. at 2615.

105. at 2618.

106. at 2619.

107. 93 S. Ct. 2628 (1973).

108. at 2621. For a review of this evidence, see Donnerstein, E., Linz, D., & Penrod, S. (1987). *The Question of Pornography: Research Findings and Policy Implications.* New York: The Free Press.

109. *Jenkins v. Georgia,* 94 S. Ct. 2750.

110. Zuckman, H. L., & Gaynes, M. J. (1983). *Mass Communications Law* (2nd ed.). St. Paul, MN: West Publishing.

111. *FCC v. Pacifica Foundation,* 98 S. Ct. 3026, at 3040.

112. *FCC v. Pacifica Foundation,* 98 S. Ct. 3026, at 3040.

113. 102 S. Ct. 3348.

114. at 3358.

115. 105 S. Ct. 2794.

116. *Mass Communications Law*, p. 141.

117. U.S. Attorney General's Commission on Pornography (1986). *Final Report*. Washington, DC: U.S. Government Printing, Office, p. 366.

118. U.S. Attorney General's Commission on Pornography (1986). *Final Report*. Washington, DC: U.S. Government Printing, Office, p. 367.

119. at 366.

120. 18 U.S.C. 2252.

121. *United States v. X-Citement Video*, 114 S. Ct. 8061 (1994).

122. at 8061 (1994).

123. Mauro, T. "Burden of Proof Made More Difficult in Child-Porn Cases," *USA Today* (November 30, 1994), 3.

124. *Bar v. Village of Somerset*, U.S. App. Lexis 704 (2003).

125. President's Commission on Law Enforcement and Administration of Justice (1967). *Task Force Report: Organized Crime*. Washington, DC: U.S. Government Printing Office, p. 4.

126. Fishman, S., Rodenrys, K., & Schink, G. (1987). The Income of Organized Crime. In *President's Commission on Organized Crime, Organized Crime Today*. Washington, DC: U.S. Government Printing Office, p. 463.

127. U.S. Attorney General's Commission on Pornography (1986). *Final Report*. Washington, DC: U.S. Government Printing, Office, p. 1053.

128. 47 U.S.C.A. Sec 223.

129. *Reno v. American Civil Liberties Union*, 117 S. Ct. 2329 (1997); *United States v. American Library Association*, 123 S. Ct. 2297 (2003).

130. *Sable Communications v. FCC*, 109 S. Ct. 2829 (1989).

131. *Bolger v. Drug Products Corp.*, 103 S. Ct. 2875 (1983).

132. 47 U.S.C.A. Sec. 231.

133. *American Civil Liberties Union v. Reno*, 217 F.3d 163 (3d Cir. 2000); Kim, G. H., & Paddon, A. R. (1999). Cybercommunity versus Geographical Community Standing on Online Pornography. *Rutgers Computer and Technology Law Journal*, 25(Fall), 63; Miller, H. L. (1999). Strike Two: Analysis of the Child Online Protection Act's Constitutional Failure. *Federal Communications Law Journal*, 52, 155.

134. *United Sates v. Williams*, 128 S.Ct. 1830 (2008).

135. *ACLU v. Gonzales*, 2007 U.S. Dist. Lexis 20008 (2007); *Ashcroft v. American Civil Liberties Union*, 122 S. Ct. 1700 (2002); Russo, R. (2006). *Ashcroft v. ACLU: Congress' Latest Attempt to Get COPA Passed Depends on the Effectiveness and Restrictiveness of Filtering Software*. Loyola University New Orleans School of Law: Law and Technology Annual. Vol. 6 (Spring), 83.

136. Holden, M. "Police Make Global Swoop on Internet Child Porn," *Reuters* (November 28, 2001); Albanese, J. (2009). Looking for a New Approach to an Old Problem: The Future of Obscenity and Pornography. In R. Muraskin, & A. Roberts (Eds.), *Visions for Change: Crime and Justice in the 21st Century* (5th ed.). Upper Saddle River, NJ: Prentice Hall.

137. *United Sates v. Patrick and Arthur*, 248 F.3d 11 (1st Cir. 2001).

CHAPTER 3

Characteristic Organized Crimes II
Infiltration of Business, Extortion, and Racketeering

Extortion characterizes the infiltration of legitimate business by organized crime in the same way that conspiracy characterizes the systematic provision of illicit goods and services.

A pair of brothers, Joseph and Fred Scalamandre, operated several construction companies on Long Island. They were charged with racketeering and conspiracy to commit fraud for directing their subcontractors to create nearly $1 million in false invoices, submit them for payment by check from the Scalamandres, and then cash the checks, returning the money to the Scalamandres—who later charged the invoices to public and private construction contracts. They later pleaded guilty to conspiring to pay members of organized crime in New York City $40,000 per year to influence trade unions in favor of their construction projects. Lawyers for the Scalamandres said the money was paid to mob figures only under duress; they "dreaded having to make the payments to organized crime members and did so unwillingly over a several-year period." The false invoices, they claimed, merely reflected the way they generated cash in order to make the payments.[1]

INFILTRATION OF BUSINESS AND GOVERNMENT

This case illustrates the problem of infiltration of business by organized crime. Is it the product of conspiracy, businesses paying money for preferential treatment so they can make even more money, or is it extortion, businesses paying money under threat of future personal or financial harm? Businesses and government agencies tend to be influenced and/or infiltrated by organized crime interests in one of two situations:

1. Circumstances in which corruption is common. This may take the form of local government corruption, union corruption, or police corruption, which permits criminal groups to operate with a degree of immunity. In these situations, businesses do not believe that turning to authorities for help will afford them protection from criminal threats.

2. Circumstances in which the nature of the business or its clientele is considered questionable or undesirable. Clubs that feature nude dancing, massage parlors, and bars are examples of businesses that are sometimes infiltrated by organized crime because they do not want close police scrutiny of their business operations or customers or they want protection from competition in their neighborhood.

In these situations, businesses pay money to organized crime figures or government agencies in order to avoid legitimate competition or regulations in their area of business or in exchange for protection from harm to their property, workers, or customers. Therefore, infiltration of business can be either predatory toward business or provide assistance to marginal businesses. In most cases, however, the infiltration of business constitutes extortion, which is a distinct crime. This chapter examines extortion and racketeering in organized crime. These two offenses help distinguish victims from offenders in understanding organized crime activities.

EXTORTION

Blackmail is obtaining property from another because of threats of future physical injury, property damage, or exposure to ridicule or criminal charges. Blackmail has become synonymous with extortion, and most jurisdictions have replaced the older term, "blackmail," with "extortion."

Some jurisdictions require that the property actually be obtained in order to complete the crime of extortion. Other jurisdictions require only the threat and proof that the defendant intended to carry out the threat, placing the victim in fear. The act required for blackmail or extortion, therefore, is the threat of future harm. The nature of the threatened harm varies somewhat by jurisdiction, but it includes bodily harm, damage to property, damage to reputation, criminal accusations, or abuse of public office. The threat, of course, must be serious enough to place a reasonable person in fear. Joking or insincere threats are judged according to a reasonableness standard.

An example of blackmail is provided by the former chief judge of New York State's highest court who made threats to a woman. The woman ended an affair with the judge, and he claimed he would sell sexually explicit photos of the woman and her new boyfriend if she did not give money to the judge.[2] In this case, it was the threat of damage to reputation, rather than the abuse of a public office, that formed the basis for the threat of future harm. In a similar case of "sextortion," a man anonymously sent multiple email messages to a New Hampshire woman identified as "Jane Doe." He told Jane Doe that he had "x-rated" photos of her and, as proof, sent her private photos that had been stored on Jane Doe's laptop computer, which had been stolen. He directed her to take new photographs and videos of herself engaging in various sexually explicit scenarios and to email the files to him. When she refused, he threatened to "leak" the photographs and other personal information about her on the Internet. He also threatened to send the photographs he already had to her exhusband, boyfriend, and a recent former employer.[3]

Although now considered synonymous, blackmail and extortion have different origins. Blackmail is derived from European terms for money or payment (e.g., French *maille*, Gaelic *mal*, German *Mahl*). The "black" is believed to reflect the illegal nature of the payments and also may refer to the metal in which the payment was made. Copper or an other base metal was usually used, rather than silver (a "white" metal). With the advent of paper currency, metals are now used infrequently as a form of payment, but the term "blackmail" continues to be used today.

Extortion was originally limited to unlawful taking of property by abuse of a public office or an official position. The U.S. federal extortion law, called the *Hobbs Act* (1946), defines extortion as a crime that takes place "under color of official right." Under this law, it must be shown that a government official improperly induced a payment from another in return for the official's explicit act or promise. An example of this type of extortion is a former city mayor in New Jersey, who was convicted of extortion for obtaining $150,000 from contractors seeking to do business with the city in exchange for the mayor seeing that they got the business. In other cases, the governors of Rhode Island and Louisiana were convicted of extortion for taking kickbacks (i.e., monetary payments) from companies looking to secure state contracts in exchange for them being awarded those contracts.[4] Courts have also held that private citizens can be prosecuted for extortion under the "color of official right" when the defendant aids or conspires with public officials to commit extortion.

Extortion necessarily involves some form of fear, threat, or coercion that is used to extract the property or benefit sought. Extortion is also distinguished from the crime of robbery in that robbery is a form of theft using threats of immediate harm, whereas extortion involves threats of future harm. Blackmail and extortion usually involve verbal threats, but nonverbal threats suffice as long as their meaning is clear and unambiguous.

Protection Rackets

Extortion has long been associated with organized crime. It is used as a source of income for organized crime groups. "Protection rackets," by which money is extracted from a victim in exchange for not doing damage to a business, construction site, or their employees, has occurred many times. When a victim refuses to pay, damage occurs and the victim often relents and pays under duress. There are numerous documented accounts of organized crime groups that have infiltrated construction unions, hotels, and restaurants, as well as the garment, meat, and waste disposal industries.[5] Crime groups in New York City, for example, have gained control of unions in various industries and thereby were able to engage systematically in extortion by demanding kickbacks on contracts or guaranteeing labor peace or an uninterrupted shipment of supplies. Members of powerful organized crime groups have drawn salaries from various companies but performed no work. For example, organized crime figure John Gotti was a salesman for ARC Plumbing and Sammy "the Bull" Gravano was president of JJS Construction Company, although there was little evidence ever produced that they did any work for these companies. Instead, they held "on the books" job titles as a sham, when they really made money through extortionate threats and other criminal enterprises.

There is no precise estimate of the extent to which extortion of this type occurs, but interviews conducted with business owners in Chinatown communities in New York City found that nearly 70% admitted to being approached by gangs for money, goods, or services—most of these businesses paid what was asked. In Russia, it has been estimated that as many as four-fifths of all businesses pay some form of extortion. In Indonesia, small businesses are reported to pay up to 20% of their gross annual income on unofficial payments necessary to obtain licenses and avoid government interference.[6] It is difficult to know the true extent of blackmail and extortion because victims are under duress and are not likely to report their situation.

A study of the New York City construction industry found that a very thin line often separates bribery from extortion. For example, sometimes the construction contractors voluntarily made payoffs to building inspectors to get construction approvals (thus, bribery by the contractors), but other times the inspectors made threats of withholding or denying those approvals in order to receive payoffs from the contractor (thus, extortion by the inspectors). It was not always clear whether payments like these or others made to public officials as kickbacks or to union officials for labor peace were made in response to threats or given by the victim voluntarily in order to speed the construction process. In an analogous fashion, a business victimization survey conducted in three high-crime neighborhoods in English cities found that invitations to participate in organized crime are common and that businesses often engaged with organized crime voluntarily.[7] It has been found in some cases that victims are willing to pay extortion money to powerful organized crime groups for protection in order to prevent themselves from being extorted by a continuing series of individual criminals or local gangs. A similar situation has been found in Asia, where countries including Japan, Korea, Thailand, and Indonesia have all faced problems of organized crime infiltration of the legitimate business sector by threats, force, or corruption. A study in Sweden also found networks of "fixers" and criminal entrepreneurs who link clients with the black market for labor.[8]

An actual case helps illustrate the scope of the crime of extortion.

Jobs for Sale

One extortion case involved a scheme to sell jobs at Eastman Kodak Company in Rochester, NY. When production needs increased, a Kodak employment counselor, John Baron, began hiring new employees. Because the standard hiring procedure was "laborious and time-consuming," Baron began accepting lists of prospective employees, as well as applications, from supervisors, managers, and other Kodak employees. This practice of hiring from this "referral list" was "apparently known to Baron's superiors, and tacitly approved by them." At trial, it became known that prospective employees paid $500-$1,000 to be hired.[9]

Defendant Robert Capo, for example, was a barber in the area who told friends and customers he could help them get jobs at Kodak for $1,000. On several occasions he received these payments, which were passed through intermediaries to John Baron. Each of these applicants was hired.

An inquiry by the FBI was begun, and a grand jury convened to investigate allegations concerning the selling of jobs. In testimony before the grand jury, defendants attempted to deny the allegations or to cast the blame at one another. At one point, "Baron threw several of the gifts he had received, including a stereo and two [video] recorders, into a dumpster" to escape the attention of the investigators.

The conspiracy to extort money for jobs ultimately collapsed when several people, some of whom had paid for jobs but were not hired, testified before the grand jury. For example, FBI agents interviewed one of the codefendants about three $500 checks from two job applicants. The defendant (Walter) told them he had worked on the car of one, charging $1,000, and the other $500 was payment for winning the Super Bowl pool. When it was pointed out that the $500 check was written prior to the Super Bowl, Walter stated, "Well, maybe she knew I was going to win." When the FBI later questioned the two job applicants, they denied any involvement in a Super Bowl pool or that Walter had worked on one of their cars.

During their appeal, one of the claims made by the defendants was that their conduct did not amount to extortion. The U.S. Court of Appeals disagreed, saying, "The essence of extortion ... is the extraction of property from another through the wrongful use of fear. The victim's fear need not be fear of bodily harm but may be fear of a loss that is purely economic."[10]

Furthermore, the court held that the federal extortion law (the Hobbs Act) "has been held [in prior cases] to reach conduct threatening the loss of a status that would produce future assets." The court explained the application of the law in this case:

> The loss of an opportunity to obtain employment as a wage or salary earner constitutes no less an "economic loss" than does the loss of an opportunity to

> obtain a one-time contract for the supply of materials or services. The
> amounts at stake for the victim may differ; the time periods during which the
> victims would receive benefits may differ. But the nature of the loss is the
> same. We conclude that the fear that a job opportunity will be lost is the type of
> fear whose extortionate exploitation is within the reach of the Hobbs Act.[11]

As a result, the U.S. Court of Appeals upheld the convictions for extortion in
this job-selling scheme at Kodak. Extortion occurs, therefore, when money
or property is obtained from wrongful use of fear of a lost job opportunity.
It is clear that the crime of extortion characterizes the infiltration of legitimate
business by organized crime in the same way that conspiracy characterizes the
systematic provision of illicit goods and services.

Under Color of Official Right

Under the Hobbs Act (1946), extortion by a government official affecting interstate or foreign commerce is prohibited "in any way or degree." Extortion
"under color of official right" involves misconduct by government officials,
where payments or favors are solicited to influence his or her exercise of duties.
Property is "extorted" under the Hobbs Act when a public official "asserts that
his or her official conduct will be controlled" due to an action or promise. These
actions or promises might include a favorable vote, failure to write a ticket, or
other miscarriage of official responsibility.[12] For example, a county commissioner in Georgia was sentenced to 3 years in prison for soliciting and accepting
illicit payments in exchange for his official efforts to secure government contracts for a private contractor.[13]

In a Louisiana case, a bail bondsman and local police department were charged
with extorting money from travelers who passed through town in exchange for
reducing or dismissing DWI charges.[14] In New York, inspectors for the New
York City Taxi and Limousine Commission pleaded guilty to extortion for taking bribes for overlooking defects and certifying inspections for taxicabs that
were never inspected. Most were sentenced to 2 or 3 years in prison.[15] A
New Jersey police officer was convicted for extorting money from bar owners
in exchange for influencing the town council and mayor in deciding whether
the bars should be fined for various liquor law violations.[16]

In another case, two Puerto Rico police officers arrested eight people for illegally possessing firearms and marijuana. The officers then solicited a bribe payment of $50,000 from one of those charged to have the case dismissed. Both
officers spoke with the defendant multiple times over the telephone, discussing
payment details and strategies for dismissing the case. In exchange for the bribe,
the officers misidentified a codefendant in court, leading to the dismissal of the
defendant's case. However, the defendant was cooperating with federal law
enforcement all along, and the two officers were fired, convicted, and sentenced

to 5 years in prison.[17] Clearly, the law of extortion applies to a variety of behaviors, all of which involve obtaining property by way of coercion or threats, implied or explicit, of some future harm.

CRITICAL THINKING EXERCISE 3.1

The scenario that follows describes an actual situation in which the courts had to determine whether the laws involving extortion applied. Resolution of this scenario requires proper application of the legal principles discussed in this chapter.

The Case of Repaying a Loan

Isaac loaned money to Melvin several times over the course of 2 years. The amounts usually ranged from $5,000 to $30,000, and the total amount loaned was approximately $100,000 over the span. At the time of each loan, Melvin agreed to repay the loan amount plus 20% interest within 10 weeks.

Melvin made periodic payments, but had difficulty meeting his commitments to Isaac. Isaac confronted him on several occasions and stated he would use physical force if Melvin

failed to repay the loans, even if Isaac had to "do 20 years." Isaac's threats caused Melvin to make out a will, buy a gun for protection, and carry it when he met with Isaac. A third party recorded some of Isaac's threats during a collection attempt.

Critical Thinking Questions

1. Considering the facts given here, can Isaac be found liable for extortion?
2. Assume that Isaac only intimidated Melvin, but never struck him. How would that affect his liability?
3. Assume that the interest rate charged by Isaac was within the legal limit allowed by law. How does that affect his liability?

RACKETEERING

Racketeering is covered by a federal law that provides for extended penalties for crimes committed as part of an ongoing criminal enterprise. The crime of racketeering was established as part of the Organized Crime Control Act (1970). The Racketeer Influenced and Corrupt Organizations (RICO) section of that act makes it unlawful to acquire, operate, or receive income from an enterprise through a pattern of racketeering activity. An enterprise is any legal or illegal ongoing business or group that is used as a base for criminal activity. Racketeering activity is defined very broadly, and most felonies are included under the law, if conducted as part of an enterprise and pattern. An enterprise can be any individual or group (legal or illegal organization) that commits these crimes. The pattern is two or more felonies committed within a 10-year period (excluding any periods of imprisonment of the defendants).

An actual case illustrates how the RICO law is applied in practice. Ronald Trucchio was charged as a "captain" (i.e., held a leadership position) in the New York Gambino crime family who worked with a criminal group operating in both Florida and New York called the "Young Guns." A government witness, Michael Ciaccio, was a member of a New York-based Young Guns operation and testified that Trucchio was indeed a member of the Gambino crime family who accepted tribute payments from the Young Guns' drug sales and other criminal activities. According to Ciaccio, Trucchio was concerned with escalating violence in South Florida by the Young Guns, and he directed Ciaccio to monitor their activities and locate potential witnesses against them for possible retribution. A second witness, Joseph Kondrotos, was a member of the Young Guns and testified that Trucchio was a captain in the Gambino crime family. He corroborated Ciaccio's testimony that Young Guns leaders regularly paid tribute to Trucchio and described many crimes committed by the Young Guns in Florida. According to Kondrotos, Young Guns' members discussed killing potential witnesses against them, including prosecutors and a potential witness residing with them in jail, as well as the witness' mother. A third witness, Frank Scarabino, was an associate of the DeCavalcante crime family of New Jersey and provided a general description of the structure of organized crime families and testified that Trucchio was a captain in the Gambino crime family. A fourth witness was an FBI special agent who testified as an expert on the Gambino crime family. He described the structure of the American Mafia and stated that Trucchio was at least an acting captain in the Gambino crime family, according to informants' statements, cooperating witnesses, and surveillance.

In making the RICO case against Trucchio, the government had to prove beyond a reasonable doubt

1. That *an enterprise* existed that affected interstate commerce (e.g., the ongoing Gambino crime family and Young Guns with documented criminal activities in two states)
2. That the *defendant was connected* with (i.e., associated or employed by) the enterprise (e.g., testimony that he was a "captain" in the Gambino family with supervisory responsibility for criminal operations)
3. That the defendant conducted or engaged in *racketeering activity* through the commission of at least two acts of racketeering (e.g., testimony regarding more than two racketeering offenses, including operating a gambling business, extortion, drug distribution, etc.)
4. That the defendant engaged in a *pattern* of racketeering activity (testimony that he directed and engaged in multiple felonies in his role in the Gambino family)

Through the testimony of the government's four witnesses (three organized crime members and an FBI agent), the government proved the racketeering charges against Trucchio.[18]

In another manifestation of this kind of criminal activity, members of the Aryan Brotherhood of Texas (ABT) gang pleaded guilty to racketeering charges related to ABT's criminal enterprise. Members agreed to commit multiple acts of murder, robbery, arson, kidnapping, and narcotics trafficking on behalf of the ABT gang. They collected dues, committed disciplinary assaults against fellow gang members, and discussed acts of violence against rival gang members. The ABT was established in the early 1980s within the Texas prison system and was modeled after the Aryan Brotherhood, a gang that was formed in the California prison system during the 1960s. Originally concerned with the protection of white inmates and white supremacy/ separatism, the ABT expanded its criminal enterprise to include illegal activities for profit.[19]

A similar kind of ongoing organized gang activity took place in Buffalo. Members of the 10th Street gang admitted knowing that rival drug dealers were making a substantial amount of money selling crack cocaine in the area controlled by the 10th Street gang. One gang member dressed in old, dirty clothes and pretended to be a crack cocaine user. He purchased crack cocaine from the rival drug dealers and returned to a 10th Street gang drug house, telling fellow gang members that he did not see any guns inside the house. The 10th Street gang members then armed themselves, went to the location, and shot the rival drug dealers using an AK-47 in an effort to force the rival drug dealers out of the neighborhood. A total of 35 10th Street gang members and associates were charged with racketeering in this case.[20] The RICO law attaches extended penalties (up to 20 years' imprisonment) for crimes committed in "racketeering" fashion, that is, specified felonies committed as part of a criminal enterprise and as part of a pattern. These RICO provisions were established to attack organized crime groups and their operations. Chapter 10 provides information on the use of RICO as a prosecution tool.

Hidden Ownership and Skimming Profits

The precise scope and meaning of "enterprise," "pattern," and activities that suffice for "racketeering activity" have been developed through a series of court challenges and interpretations. Although passed in 1970, the RICO law was used infrequently until the 1980s, probably due to its complexity and the need to develop complicated and detailed cases to prosecute under these provisions. Court challenges to the law have upheld its provisions and have further broadened its scope. A few examples illustrate this trend.

Matthew Ianniello and Benjamin Cohen were part of a group that skimmed profits from bars and restaurants they owned in New York City. These bars and restaurants were ostensibly owned by others, and liquor licenses were obtained in the names of others, but they were really "fronts" for Ianniello and Cohen. The skimming involved Ianniello and Cohen taking cash paid by customers and keeping it for themselves. This entailed keeping false accounting records (that undercounted the true income of the bars and restaurants) and filing false income and sales tax returns that also failed to reflect the actual income of these enterprises.[21]

Ianniello, Cohen, and their associates were convicted of racketeering, violating the RICO provisions in using the bars and restaurants as fronts to engage in tax evasion and mail fraud (mail fraud is any attempt to unlawfully obtain money or valuables in which the postal system is used in the commission of the crime; mailing a false tax return is an example of mail fraud). They appealed, arguing that there must be "a combination of relationship and continuity between separate acts" in order to establish a "pattern" necessary for a RICO conviction. The U.S. Court of Appeals held (and the U.S. Supreme Court denied review) that when a person commits two felonies "that have the common purpose of furthering a continuing criminal enterprise with which that person is associated," the elements of "relatedness and continuity" are satisfied.[22] The convictions of Ianniello and Cohen were affirmed, showing that the "pattern" of crimes under RICO do not need to be directly related to each other as long as they are related to and continue the ongoing criminal scheme.

This court finding helps make clear the distinction between felonies committed as part of an ongoing criminal enterprise and those isolated crimes that may be committed by a repeat offender. These cases show how the terms "enterprise," "pattern," and "racketeering activity" must be interrelated for a RICO conviction. It is necessary to show that a person was associated with an individual or group (the "enterprise"), that the group's member(s) committed two or more offenses within a 10-year period (the "pattern"), and that those offenses were any of the felonies specified in the statute ("racketeering activity"). This illustrates the distinction between "street" crimes and organized crime. A habitual offender is not necessarily a RICO offender if his or her offenses are not associated with each other or are not associated with an ongoing criminal enterprise. Therefore, many organized crime figures are also career criminals, but not all career criminals are members of organized crime because their acts do not constitute racketeering activity.

The overlap that sometimes exists between legal and illegal enterprises can be difficult to detect. An investigation by the New Jersey Commission of Investigation found that state regulations had successfully rid the garbage collection and disposal industry of organized crime involvement. However, the lack of regulations in the growing recycling industry led organized crime figures to become involved through real estate ownership, equipment leasing, and hiding behind seemingly legitimate front companies. In addition, 30 individuals who had been barred from the New York State garbage industry due to organized crime ties were later found to be operating in New Jersey (see Figure 3.1).[23]

It can be seen that racketeers are criminal opportunists looking to profit systematically from ongoing criminal enterprises and that continuing vigilance is required to prevent and detect their presence. Figure 3.2 illustrates the important aspects of proving involvement in a racketeering enterprise.

FIGURE 3.1 The garbage collection and disposal industry has been tainted by organized crime involvement in some jurisdictions. *www.shutterstock.com*

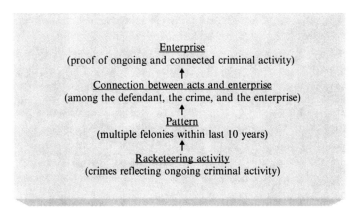

FIGURE 3.2 Elements of racketeering.

I Didn't Know My Property Was a Crackhouse

Growing concern about drugs has led to an attack on all its manifestations, including the places where people actually ingest the drugs. Congress passed what is commonly known as the "crackhouse statute" (1986) in response to negligent landlords who ignored or abandoned their property, allowing it to become a place where drug users stayed, sold, bought, and ingested illegal narcotics.

The crackhouse statute prohibits "knowingly" maintaining "any place" for the purpose of manufacturing, distributing, or using controlled drugs. It also prohibits not only the managing or controlling in any way of a building or room, but also knowingly and intentionally renting, leasing, or making available for use a building or room for the purpose of manufacturing, distributing, or using drugs.[24]

Consider the case of Randolph Lancaster who owned a house in Washington, DC. Over the course of 6 months, the house was searched a number of times by several different law enforcement agencies. On each occasion, police found "large groups of individuals" inside with drugs and drug paraphernalia. Lancaster was aware of the searches but did nothing to remedy the problem. Prosecuted under the "crackhouse" law, Lancaster was convicted of maintaining a crackhouse. He was sentenced to prison, and his house was seized by the government. His appeal unsuccessfully challenged the constitutionality of the crackhouse law.[25]

In a similar case, Mei-Fen Chen owned the Della Motel in Houston. She claimed she was unaware that drug transactions were taking place there, although four former tenants testified that she had witnessed drug transactions, alerted tenants when police were coming, and encouraged drug sales by providing storage and loaning them money. Chen admitted seeing syringes in the parking lot of the motel, but claimed "she believed they came from a nearby hospital." Prosecuted under the crackhouse law, she claimed she was unaware of drug transactions at her motel. The U.S. Court of Appeals held, however, "all the circumstances ... support either a finding of actual knowledge or willful blindness on the part of Chen."[26]

These cases illustrate that the crackhouse law holds landlords and owners liable for what they know, or failed to know due to deliberate ignorance, about illegal activities occurring on their properties. In essence, the crackhouse law extends the concept of racketeering to those who provide the forum for criminal activity in addition to those who actually carry it out. This extension of complicity in ongoing criminal activity is designed to curtail that activity by reducing the number of "safe havens" that exist for it.

THE SECRETIVE NATURE OF CRIMINAL ENTERPRISES

Unlike legitimate businesses, criminal enterprises are secretive by nature. It is sometimes possible to arrest a criminal for multiple crimes, but it is more difficult to link each of them as part of a pattern connected to a particular ongoing enterprise.

Consider the case of Albert Tocco, the alleged "boss" of Chicago Heights. He and others extorted money from people who were engaged in criminal activity, such as "chop shops" that disassembled stolen cars, illegal gambling operations, and houses of prostitution. In some ways, these are desirable targets for extortion because the victims are unwilling to go to the police for fear of exposing their own criminal activity. Based on the testimony of informants, Tocco was implicated in numerous acts of extortion and also in four murders. He was ultimately located after fleeing to Greece, returned to the United States, convicted of 34 crimes, and sentenced to 200 years' imprisonment.[27]

Given this plethora of criminal activity, it is still difficult to put it all together. Even with the testimony of former "insiders," electronic surveillance, and even undercover officers, the evidence of an ongoing enterprise is often fragmentary. The RICO provisions have increased the possible penalties, as noted earlier, which offers an incentive for prosecutors to attempt to connect individual crimes to something larger. In the case of Tocco given earlier, the U.S. Court of Appeals held that "the government is entitled to try to prove all the racketeering acts making up the pattern of racketeering activity, so that it may obtain a conviction even if the jury rejects some of its theories."[28] Therefore, even if a jury ultimately rejects the existence of an ongoing criminal enterprise, it may still convict on the individual crimes charged.

In a similar case, Joseph Massaro was charged with racketeering as a member of the Lucchese organized crime group in New York City. He ran an organization called the Entertainment Plus Agency, which booked topless dancers in clubs on Long Island. He tried to force his services on club owners through intimidation (i.e., extortion). When he found that one of his associates was stealing from him, he shot him in the head. In order to prove racketeering, the prosecution must provide evidence to show how these crimes (extortion and murder) are each linked to his ongoing criminal enterprise. In this case, the evidence connecting Massaro to all these crimes and to the large criminal group was persuasive, given the fact that the murder occurred because of a theft of funds earned from his ongoing extortion enterprise. He was convicted on all counts and sentenced to life imprisonment.[29]

The U.S. Supreme Court became involved in a racketeering case involving a series of bank thefts that were allegedly conducted by a group that was loosely organized and did not appear to have had a leader or hierarchy. The defendant argued that the government must prove the RICO enterprise had an ascertainable structural hierarchy distinct from the charged predicate acts. The U.S. Supreme Court held that only three structural features were necessary: a purpose, relationships among those associated with the enterprise, and sufficient longevity to permit pursuit of the purpose. However, additional structural features, such as hierarchy or a chain of command, were not required to be convicted of racketeering.[30]

RICO is a sweeping law with far-reaching consequences for the defendant. However, it is a tool for the government to fight the "organizations" that maintain organized crime rather than prosecution of individuals for isolated acts. It was observed more than 70 years ago that "racketeering cannot exist without protection."[31] The RICO provisions attempt to remove some of the protection that surrounds criminal enterprises by exposing those involved to extended penalties beyond that entailed by the crimes themselves. The RICO law provides civil remedies as well. These remedies are discussed in Chapter 10.

CRITICAL THINKING EXERCISE 3.2

The scenario that follows describes an actual situation in which the courts had to determine whether the laws involving racketeering applied. Resolution of this scenario requires proper application of the legal principles discussed in this chapter.

The Case of the Avengers Motorcycle Club

Michael Khalil was national president of the Avengers Motorcycle Club (AMC), an organization with local chapters in Michigan, Ohio, Indiana, Illinois, and West Virginia. Avengers identified themselves by wearing clothing that bears the insignia of the club. The AMC has a constitution and bylaws, elected officers, and a requirement that members follow the rules of the club. There was evidence produced that at Kahlil's direction the club planned violence against a rival motorcycle club, the Iron Coffins, which frequented locals bars in a county where AMC also had a chapter.

One member of the Avengers became an informant for the FBI after nine pounds of marijuana was found in his home. Subsequently, an undercover agent also joined the AMC. They implicated club president Khalil in drug sales, although he only sold drugs to them on two occasions.

Critical Thinking Questions

1. Is there enough evidence to convict Kahlil under RICO? Explain.
2. What argument should Kahlil make in his defense against a racketeering charge?

SUMMARY

This chapter has defined the scope of organized crime activity as it relates to predatory crimes. Based on the typology of organized crime presented in Chapter 1, it can be seen that the provision of illicit goods, the provision of illicit services, and the infiltration of legitimate business can be characterized by the crimes of conspiracy, extortion, and racketeering.

Organized crime engenders a plethora of activity, but this chapter has shown that it can be categorized and defined in explicit terms. The nature of the offenses discussed here provides the groundwork for the remainder of the book. The causes, investigation, prosecution, defense, and sentencing of organized crime, explained in subsequent chapters, rely on a specific understanding of the nature of organized criminal activity itself.

ORGANIZED CRIME BIOGRAPHY

Biographies tell the life story of interesting people. In the world of criminal justice, biographies of organized crime figures offer insight into the background and motivations of the individuals who choose that lifestyle, the reasons for their choices, and the consequences. The following is a brief summary of an organized crime biography, followed by questions that ask you to reflect on the connections between that person's life and the content of this book.

Gomorrah: A Personal Journey into the Violent International Empire of Naples' Organized Crime System
Robert Saviano (Picador, 2009)

Using trial transcripts and investigative reporting, the author describes organized crime (the Camorra) in the Naples region of Italy. He explains the battles between rival factions for control of the region's drug trade, as well as toxic waste disposal, weapons trafficking, arrangements with South American and Nigerian drug cartels, and money laundering using diamonds and legal businesses throughout Europe.

There is also a high level of violence involved in both the protection and the expansion of criminal operations in various criminal markets. Murders are particularly brutal, and the author travels to numerous crime scenes to document the circumstances. He also worked at a Chinese textile factory in Naples, at a construction site, and even as a waiter at a Camorra family wedding to gather information. Therefore, the book contains undercover reporting, economic analysis, and a social history of the Naples area, which as a port city controls clothing distribution, art collecting, construction trades, toxic waste disposal, and the underworld market of drug trafficking.

The ability of the Camorra to maintain control of these markets is documented, with businesses and government officials out to protect their own interests rather than the common good. Interestingly, given occasional successful prosecutions, women, especially widows, are often promoted to high-ranking positions to provide ongoing protection to criminal enterprises.

Questions
1. Why do you believe that some particular areas, such as Naples, have had notable difficulty in removing organized crime influence from their communities?
2. The author of this book undertook some reporting under dangerous circumstances to gather his information. What do you see as the cost-benefit of such risky reporting?

ORGANIZED CRIME AT THE MOVIES

Movies seek to entertain and inform the audience about a story, incident, or person. Many good movies also hit upon important substantive themes relevant to understanding organized crime. Read the following movie summary (and watch the movie if you haven't already) and answer the questions that follow to make the organized crime subject matter connections.

Casino
Martin Scorsese, Director (1995)

Based on the book by Nicholas Pileggi, *Casino* is loosely based on the life of Frank "Lefty" Rosenthal who ran the Stardust and other casinos for the mob during the 1970s into the 1980s. The names and events in the movie are fictitious, so the film and book are a novelization of the facts. Robert De Niro plays Sam "Ace" Rothstein (based on the life of Lefty Rosenthal), who is called in by the mob to run the fictitious Tangiers Casino in Las Vegas (based on the Stardust).

Joe Pesci plays Nicky Santoro, a character based on the life of Anthony Spilotro, an enforcer for the Chicago Outfit. Santoro is sent to Las Vegas by the Chicago Outfit to make sure that money is skimmed off the top from casino earnings and sent back to Chicago, given that the casino was financed with the teamsters' pension fund.

Rothstein is a competent, rational operator who understands how to run a casino and the nefarious kinds of people with whom he associates. Santoro is the exact opposite: short-tempered, amoral, and extremely violent. When

Continued

ORGANIZED CRIME AT THE MOVIES—CONT'D

Santoro is asked to protect Rothstein, he shows unprovoked brutality in carrying out his task.

Major problems arise when Ginger (Sharon Stone) enters Rothstein's life (based on the real Geraldine McGee). Ginger is addicted to substances, unstable, and unpredictable. She and Rothstein have a child and get married, but Rothstein catches her with her old boyfriend, Lester, a pimp. Lester is beaten by Rothstein's men, but Ginger and Lester kidnap the daughter and flee to Los Angeles. Rothstein ultimately convinces Ginger to come back home with the daughter, but he throws her out again when she is caught on the phone planning his assassination.

Ginger returns again, but her relationship with Rothstein is beyond repair. Ginger seduces Nicky as a ploy to secure her fair share of Rothstein's money. This begins a dangerous affair between two very unstable people, which ends in a violent confrontation. Ginger returns to Rothstein and demands her share of the money and jewelry. She manages to steal Rothstein's key to his safe deposit box and collects a large amount of cash and drives off, only to be arrested by federal agents.

Ginger's arrest precipitates a wave of violence among mob members fearing prosecution and snitches; Rothstein is nearly killed in a car bomb, and he suspects Nicky is behind it. Nicky is betrayed by his own crew and is killed before Rothstein can find him, and Ginger dies of a drug overdose. The film ends with a voiceover explaining that the Tangiers casino is leveled and that next-generation casinos are being run by corporations rather than by the mob. An interesting fact is that Rothstein's lawyer in the film is played by Oscar Goodman, Lefty Rosenthal's actual lawyer and current mayor of Las Vegas. Sharon Stone received an Academy Award nomination for Best Actress.

Questions

1. What offenses were involved with the systematic skimming of profits from casino earnings?
2. Most casinos are now operated by large corporations, and their connection to organized crime is largely a thing of the past. Why do you believe the mob was ultimately unsuccessful as casino managers?

References and Notes

1. Gootman, E. "Brothers Plead Guilty in Mob Payoffs for Construction Businesses," *The New York Times* (November 15, 2001).

2. Wolfe, L. (1994). *Double Life.* New York: Pocket Books.

3. U.S. Department of Justice (2013). *Maine Resident Pleads Guilty to Engaging in Cyber "Sextortion" of New Hampshire Victim.* Washington, DC: Office of Public Affairs, September 18.

4. *United States v. Addonizio*, 451 F.2d 49, cert. denied, 92 S. Ct. 949 (1972); Deslatte, M. "Ex-Louisiana Governor Edwards Sentenced to 10 Years in Prison," *The Charleston Gazette* (January 9, 2001); "Ex-R.I. Governor Humbled by 11-Month Jail Sentence," *The Charleston Gazette* (January 22, 2000).

5. *United States v. International Brotherhood of Teamsters*, 247 F.2d 370 (2d Cir. 2001); Jacobs, J. B., Friel, C., & Radick, R. (1999). *Gotham Unbound.* New York: New York University Press.

6. Chin, K. -l. (1996). *Chinatown Gangs: Extortion, Enterprise, and Ethnicity.* New York: Oxford University Press; Finckenauer, J. O., & Waring, E. J. (2001). *Russian Mafia in America.* Boston, MA: Northeastern University Press; Sjaifudian, H. (1997). Graft and the Small Business. *Far Eastern Economic Review, 160*(October 16), 32; Tilley, N., & Hopkins, M. (2008). Organized Crime and Local Businesses. *Criminology and Criminal Justice: An International Journal, 8*, 443–459; Transcrime (2012). *Study on Extortion and Racketeering: the Need for an Instrument to Combat Activities.* Brussels: European Commission.

7. New York State Organized Crime Task Force (1990). *Corruption and Racketeering in the New York City Construction Industry*. New York: New York University Press.

8. McFarlane, J. (2001). Corruption and the Financial Sector: The Strategic Impact. *Journal of Financial Crime, 9,* 8–21; Heber, A. (2009). Networks of Organised Black Market Labour in the Building Trade. *Trends in Organized Crime, 12,* 122–144.

9. *United States v. Capo,* 791 F.2d 1054 (2d Cir. 1986).

10. at 1061.

11. at 1062.

12. 18 U.S.C.A. Sec. 1951; *McCormick v. United States,* 111 S. Ct. 2807 (1991).

13. U.S. Department of Justice (2013). *County Commissioner Sentenced for Attempted Extortion and Bribery*. Washington, DC: Office of Public Affairs, June 12.

14. *United States v. Stephens,* 964 F.2d 424 (5th Cir. 1992).

15. *United States v. Abbadessa,* 848 F. Supp. 369 (E.D.N.Y. 1994).

16. *United States v. DeLaurentis,* 47 Fed. App. 170 (2002).

17. U.S. Department of Justice (2013). *Former Puerto Rico Police Officers Sentenced for Roles in Scheme to Extort a State Defendant for $50,000*. Washington, DC: Office of Public Affairs, November 18.

18. *United States v. Trucchio,* 2007 U.S. App. LEXIS 1968 (11th Cir. 2007).

19. U.S. Department of Justice (2013). *Aryan Brotherhood of Texas Gang Members Plead Guilty to Federal Racketeering Charges*. Washington, DC: Office of Public Affairs, January 31 and March 1.

20. Federal Bureau of Investigation (2013). *Member of 10th Street Gang Pleads Guilty to RICO Conspiracy*. Buffalo Office, January 18.

21. *United States v. Ianniello and Cohen,* 808 F.2d 184 (2d Cir. 1986), cert. denied, 107 S. Ct. 3229.

22. at 192.

23. State of New Jersey Commission of Investigation (2011). *Industrious Subversion: Circumvention of Oversight in Solid Waste and Recycling in New Jersey*. December, www.state.nj.us/sci/pdf/Solid %20Waste%20Report.pdf.

24. 21 U.S.C. Sec. 856.

25. *United States v. Lancaster,* 968 F.2d 1250 (D.C. Cir. 1992).

26. *United States v. Chen,* 913 F.2d 183 (5th Cir. 1990) at 186.

27. *United States v. Crockett and Tocco,* 979 F.2d 1204 (7th Cir. 1992).

28. at 1211.

29. *Massaro v. United States,* 2001 U.S. App. LEXIS 24266, (S.D.N.Y., November 29, 2000).

30. *Boyle v. United States,* 129 S.Ct. 2237 (2009).

31. Chamberlin, H. B. (January 1932). Some Observations Concerning Organized Crime. *Journal of Criminal Law and Criminology, 22*(5), 667.

CHAPTER 4

Causes of Organized Crime
Influences on Individuals

Unfortunately, very little attention has been paid to the causes of organized crime as a special kind of criminal behavior.

Bill Bonanno (see Figure 4.1) is the son of Joe Bonanno, who was a Sicilian immigrant and the alleged boss of one of New York's five large mafia "families" (a group not necessarily related by blood or family ties). The Bonanno family had oversight of an array of legal and illegal businesses that were run by people associated with them. The illegal activities included gambling, loansharking, and extortion, among others. Joe Bonanno was not an educated man, but was a successful leader, although his life was marred with gang violence, police surveillance, answering subpoenas, government prosecutions, and the betrayal of friends. Given this background, why would his son choose to continue in his father's footsteps? Unlike his father, Bill Bonanno was college educated, articulate, and served in the military. He could have been successful at any number of legitimate professions, but he chose instead to run the "family business" as his father did. The result was a life much like his father's, in which he became known as an "organized crime figure" rather than a "successful businessman."[1] Why?

The reason why people engage in crime is perhaps the fundamental issue in the study of criminal justice. Over centuries, a large body of literature has been developed that attempts to explain the existence of crime. The bad news is that crime exists in societies of all types. As Emile Durkheim pointed out a century ago, "Crime is not present only in the majority of societies of one particular species but in all societies of all types. There is no society that is not confronted with the problem of criminality."[2] The good news is that levels of crime vary dramatically both within and among nations. Therefore, there is both room for improvement and many examples within the United States and around the world to study.

FIGURE 4.1 Joseph Bonanno Jr., left, and Salvatore "Bill" Bonanno, sons of mobster Joe Bonanno, appeared before the grand jury in New York. As one of New York's original five Mafia families, the Bonannos were implicated in bookmaking, protection, and loansharking operations. *AP Photo File*

IS ORGANIZED CRIME UNIQUE?

Unfortunately, very little attention has been paid to the causes of organized crime as a special kind of criminal behavior. As we shall see, some have argued that explanations of crime should be universal, whereas others argue that different manifestations of crime may require different explanations. In either case, it is obvious that different people commit different crimes for different reasons. Therefore, more than one explanation is likely needed to explain the crimes of many diverse people.

Organized crime is distinguished from most other forms of crime in that it is usually a career pattern. Most organized criminals engage in persistent criminal activity over a long period of time. This is not the case with most crime. Studies of delinquency have found (and common experience suggests), for example, that most juveniles engage in some acts of delinquency but very few become frequent or serious offenders.[3] Furthermore, the vast majority do not go on to become adult offenders.

Organized crime is also distinguished from other kinds of criminal behavior in its organization. As explained in Chapter 1, most criminal behavior is spontaneous or involves very little planning. Organized crime, however, requires organization in order for it to be effective and successful over the long-term.

The long-term, continuing nature of organized crime activity, together with the organization required for the acts themselves, suggests that organized crime is unique as a criminal choice. White-collar crime requires organization, but it is almost never a career pattern—instead, it is a deviation from otherwise legitimate business activity. In a similar way, some street crimes are committed by career criminals, but these offenses usually require little organization (e.g., muggings, burglary, robbery, theft). These examples point to important distinctions between organized crime and other forms of criminal behavior.

The question remains, however, as to whether the causes of organized crime are different from the causes of other types of crime. This chapter offers a four-part typology of existing explanations of crime: positivist, classical, structural, and ethical. Actual case studies are used in an effort to show how these explanations of crime might apply to individual instances of organized crime.

POSITIVIST: SOCIAL AND ECONOMIC INFLUENCES

The positivist perspective in criminology corresponds with the rise of social science and the scientific method in the late 1800s. Positivism looks to internal or external influences as the cause of criminal behavior. Many attempts to explain crime and delinquency have been attempted over the last century, employing some combination of psychological, social, economic, and biological factors, although most rely on social factors.[4] All these theories have in common the assumption that changes in these conditions will reduce or prevent criminal behavior.

None of these theories specifically addressed the two features unique to organized crime: a career criminal pattern and organization in the crimes themselves. The theory that comes closest, however, is that of Richard Cloward and Lloyd Ohlin. Their book, *Delinquency and Opportunity*, attempts to formulate a theory of delinquent gangs.[5] Although they focus on juvenile delinquency, their theory has direct implications for organized crime. The authors argue, as Robert Merton did before them, that crime results from a lack of access to legitimate means (i.e., "blocked opportunity") for achieving social goals (e.g., make a good living, have a family).[6] They also believe, however, that even illegitimate means for obtaining social goals are not available to everyone. As a result, some lower-class neighborhoods provide greater opportunity for illegal gain than others.

Cloward and Ohlin conclude that three types of criminal subcultures develop when young people withdraw legitimacy from middle-class standards (i.e., social goals) because they lack the means to achieve them (e.g., unequal employment opportunities or the inability to go to college). The three subcultures they identify are criminal, conflict, and retreatist. The criminal subculture is the result when these young people associate with, and go on to become, adult criminals. The conflict subculture is where fighting gangs develop and status is obtained by violence and coercion. The retreatist subculture is composed of those who lack opportunity or the ability to gain status in the criminal or conflict subcultures. These people drop out and may become drug addicts.[7]

Most relevant to the causes of organized crime is the criminal subculture. Cloward and Ohlin provide the example of the "fence," a dealer in stolen property, who exists in many lower-class neighborhoods. The fence often "encourages delinquent activities" by leading young people to steal "in the most lucrative and least risky directions." They believe the same point "may be made of junk dealers in some areas" and "racketeers who permit minors to run errands."[8] Therefore, the "apprentice criminal" moves from one status to another in the "illegitimate opportunity system," developing "an ever-widening set of relationships with members of the semi-legitimate and legitimate world." In this way, the young person becomes socialized into the criminal subculture, a process made possible, according to Cloward and Ohlin, by blocked opportunities for success in legitimate society.

If a person cannot successfully gain access or status in the criminal subculture, "the possibility of a stable, protected criminal style of life is effectively precluded."[9] Therefore, blocked opportunity does not lead directly to a life of crime, according to this theory. Instead, there must exist opportunities to form relationships with the criminal subculture, as well as the personal ability to gain status in this milieu. This merging of age groups and "value integration" is necessary for young people to become part of the adult criminal subculture. James O'Kane found this theory of "blocked opportunity" useful in explaining the organized crime involvement of ethnic minorities in the United States.[10] A study of Vietnamese-American youth gangs in southern California found that exposure to gangs in the neighborhood and pro-gang attitudes (developed by negative school attitudes, alienation, family conflict, and perceived benefits of gang membership) were the best predictors of gang involvement.[11]

Other sociological theories of crime use similar techniques to explain how a young person becomes an adult criminal. One theory places emphasis on the "delinquent traditions" found in lower-class neighborhoods.[12] Another theory gives most importance to "learning," through personal associations, that crime is acceptable behavior.[13] Still another points to peer group pressure and how young people attempt to "neutralize" the guilt they feel about their criminal behavior by rationalizing it.[14] Cloward and Ohlin's theory makes an effort to address each of these factors at least implicitly, and therefore is the most complete as a positivistic explanation for emergence of an organized criminal.

The life histories of organized crime figures often show a pattern similar to that described by Cloward and Ohlin. Henry Hill, whose life has been the subject of a best-selling biography (*Wiseguy*) and film (*Goodfellas*), is illustrative. Henry came from a large, working-class family in a poor neighborhood in Brooklyn. He took his first job at age 12 at a cab stand across the street. It was there that he was socialized into the criminal subculture. He was taught how to pass counterfeit $20 bills, deal in stolen property, illegal gambling, and a host of other illegal activities.

> At Christmas, Tuddy [Vito Vario] taught me how to drill holes in the trunks of junk Christmas trees he'd get for nothing, and then I'd stuff the holes with loose branches. I'd stuff so many branches into those holes that even those miserable spindly trees looked full. Then we'd sell them for premium prices, usually at night and mostly around the Euclid Avenue subway stop. It took a day or two before the branches came loose and began to fall apart. The trees would collapse even faster once they were weighed down with decorations.[15]

Scams ranged from small to large, but they had common elements: he was taught by adult criminals and his acceptance grew as he performed small errands pleasingly for these people. From the perspective of Cloward and Ohlin's positivistic approach, Henry's ultimate entrance into the criminal subculture of organized crime grew directly from the limited opportunities he faced in his neighborhood and the countervailing possibility for success in the criminal subculture just across the street. In the words of Henry Hill

> To me being a wiseguy was better than being President of the United States. It meant power among people [who] had no privileges. To be a wiseguy was to own the world. I dreamed about being a wiseguy the way other kids dreamed about being doctors or movie stars, or firemen or ballplayers.[16]

The problem with Cloward and Ohlin's explanation, and all positivistic explanations of criminal behavior, is that they place too much emphasis on external (or internal) influences on behavior and give too little consideration to the criminal decision. That is to say, despite all influences in one's life, a person must still make a decision to violate the law. Poor neighborhoods, bad associates, and improper supervision of a young person certainly make it difficult to become a law-abiding adult, yet it happens all the time. So in some ways, positivistic explanations of crime beg the question. There is a long list of influences that help us to understand why a person may have chosen to commit crimes, but this does not determine that decision. Therefore, positivistic explanations point to conditions that make a criminal lifestyle an easy choice, but they do not explain why or how that choice is made in the face of competing choices, such as redoubling one's energies in a noncriminal direction.

CLASSICIST: HEDONISM AND THE ODDS OF APPREHENSION

In many ways, the classical perspective is the converse of positivism. Instead of focusing on influential factors that contribute to crime, as positivism does, classicists see crime as the result of a free-will decision to choose it. This free-will decision is guided by the pain-pleasure principle: that is, people always will act in a way that maximizes pleasure and minimizes pain.

Classicists believe that people are hedonistic and will naturally seek pleasure at every opportunity and avoid pain. The way to prevent crime in this view is through deterrence. Criminal behavior is prevented, therefore, when the pain associated with criminal conduct (i.e., likelihood of apprehension and punishment) is greater than the pleasure derived from the crime (usually economic gain).

A different type of classical approach focuses on "routine activities" or "situational crime prevention." This perspective concentrates on "criminal settings" (environments conducive to organized crime activity) rather than on the motivations of individuals or groups of people. By focusing on the circumstances of crime, this perspective examines the availability of opportunities to commit specific crimes using the principle of routine activities. Routine activities assume that levels of organized crime are determined by facilitating factors: availability of attractive targets, a low level of supervision, and low risk of apprehension.

Rather than focusing on distant causes of crime (e.g., poverty, poor education, peer groups), the focus is shifted to practical ways to reduce the opportunities for crime or to minimize their harm.[17] Situational crime prevention has been used primarily in addressing high volume traditional crimes, such as burglary and theft. Nevertheless, there is emerging evidence that this approach can be useful in reducing organized crimes by limiting criminal opportunities and minimizing harm.[18] Efforts have been made to apply the situational crime prevention perspective to organized crime, including the manufacture of methamphetamine, automobile theft, open-air drug markets, prostitution, and crime displacement.[19] All these empirical efforts have shown at least partial support for the situational perspective in preventing organized illicit activity.

A limitation of the situational crime prevention perspective is that the precise strategies needed for reducing criminal opportunities are not always evident. The theory requires that crime prevention techniques be directed at five areas:

1. Increasing the effort for offenders (e.g., target hardening, controlling crime facilitators),
2. Increasing the risks (e.g., surveillance of offenders and victims, screening entrances and exits),

3. Reducing the rewards (e.g., removing targets, controlling markets),
4. Reducing provocations (e.g., reducing temptations, avoiding disputes), and
5. Removing excuses (e.g., setting rules, alerting conscience).[20]

The precise methods to be taken to achieve these goals depends on the specific crime to be prevented and its underlying preparatory behaviors (called "scripts"), but empirical efforts have shown that it is not always clear which specific methods can be expected to have an impact on organized crime activity.[21]

Michael Gottfredson and Travis Hirschi offer a classical explanation that they intend to explain "all crime," including organized crime.[22] They believe that crime results from "the tendency of individuals to pursue short-term gratification in the most direct way with little consideration for the long-term consequences of their acts." This tendency is associated with impulsiveness, aggression, and lack of empathy. They base this theory on the classical assumption that "human behavior is motivated by the self-interested pursuit of pleasure and avoidance of pain."[23] Following the classical view, the only effective way to prevent criminal behavior is through the threat of apprehension and punishment that will outweigh (at least in the mind of the offender) the pleasure derived from the criminal conduct.

The problem with the general theory of crime, and the classical viewpoint in general, is an overemphasis on the impact of penalties for crime prevention. First, deterrence is not very effective in criminal justice because the odds of apprehension are quite low and uncertain. Second, the hedonism, or "tendencies" toward short-term gratification, must come from somewhere. If they are innate, what prevents the majority of us from engaging in a life of crime? If only some of us have these tendencies, where do they come from? Classical explanations have difficulty with these questions. A study of several hundred organized crime offenders in Europe found that "internal drives are the hardest element to capture, particularly when offenders seem to be motivated internally (i.e. they were not talked into it by others)." So the motivation for short-term gratification requires other explanations of crime.[24]

Another example drawn from the biography of Henry Hill illustrates these points. It can be argued that, despite his social surroundings, Henry Hill made a free-will choice to engage in a life of crime that was guided by the pain-pleasure principle. Before he worked at the cab stand in Brooklyn, Henry had made observations and drawn conclusions about the advantages of a criminal lifestyle.

> The men at the cabstand were not like anyone else from the neighborhood. They wore silk suits in the morning and would drape the fenders of their cars with handkerchiefs before leaning back for a talk. He had watched them double-park their cars and never get tickets, even when they parked smack in front of a fire

hydrant. . . . And the men at the cabstand were rich. They flashed wads of $20 bills as round as softballs and they sported diamond pinky rings the size of walnuts. The sight of all that wealth, and power, and girth was intoxicating.[25]

This suggests that Henry Hill was making a conscious choice to join the organized crime group due to the benefits (pleasure) it would bring. When his father objected to his employment at the cab stand the following year, Henry "wouldn't listen to what he said." His father "worked hard his whole life" as an electrical worker, but could never get ahead. Henry said, "we could never move out of our crummy three-bedroom house jammed with seven kids," and he decided, "my old man's life wasn't going to be my life."[26] He chose the criminal lifestyle available at the cab stand. It can be seen that positivists focus on what factors might have influenced his decision-making, whereas classicists focus on the decision itself.

Classicists would also argue that Henry Hill's life of crime may never have gotten started, or would have been quite brief, if the odds of apprehension and punishment had been greater. This may be true, although the odds of criminal apprehension for unplanned street crimes reported to police, such as burglary and larceny, is only about 15%. Given the fact that most of these crimes are never reported to police, the true odds are less than 10%.[27] It is reasonable to surmise that the odds of apprehension for planned crimes, such as those Henry Hill was committing, are even lower. Compounding this is the volume of criminal activity committed by career criminals. At one time, Henry Hill saw several police cars outside a lounge he frequented so he went instead to his girlfriend's house. It wasn't until he turned on the radio that he knew what crime he was wanted for.[28] Because the odds of apprehension were so low, he had engaged in a great deal of criminal activity without ever being caught. When people like him are ultimately caught, the penalty or prison time is seen as a long-term cost of doing business rather than a penalty for a specific act. Classicism places much importance on the free-will decision to engage in crime, but its solution (deterrence) is untenable, given the low odds of apprehension.

STRUCTURAL: CAPITALISM AND ARBITRARY LAWS

From the structural perspective, "It remains a matter of controversy whether it is the criminal structure that creates the need for illicit goods and services or whether, on the contrary, it is a widespread demand for these things that stimulates and nourishes the illegal activities of organized crime groups."[29] It is this challenge of cause and effect that forms the basis for the structural view of crime causation. This approach focuses less on individual behavior and more on how acts come to be defined as criminal. Social, economic, and political circumstances cause certain behaviors to be defined as criminal, resulting in a great deal of "marginal" criminal behavior, according to the structuralists. Examples would include gambling, prostitution, loansharking, and pornography. Structuralists would argue that we create some of our own organized crime problems by prohibiting gambling unless the state is running the game, disallowing prostitution unless it is sanctioned by the state, or forbidding lending at high interest rates, unless the interest rate is approved by the state. These inconsistencies are viewed by structuralists as a mechanism by which we create illicit markets and then prosecute people for catering to the demand that the state has manufactured.

CRITICAL THINKING EXERCISE 4.1

The scenario that follows describes a situation that shows the actual circumstances of people who became organized crime figures. Respond to the questions that follow, employing the principles from this chapter.

The Case of the Making of "Sammy the Bull" and Ivankov

Sammy Gravano was born and raised in Brooklyn, New York. He was held back twice in school to repeat grades in both elementary and middle school due to learning problems. He reacted to these setbacks by becoming tough. He fought like a "little bull" and earned the nickname "Sammy the Bull." He dropped out of high school and called the kids in school "nerds" who were doing it the "easy way" instead of living by their wits through thefts and scams as Sammy and his gang members did. Sammy only robbed from commercial establishments because "they had insurance" and did not steal from private homes. He was caught and imprisoned on several occasions, but this experience appeared to improve his reputation among the criminal elements. His propensity toward violence and ability to carry out a variety of illegal scams, such as illegal gambling, loansharking, and theft, helped bring him to the attention of established organized crime groups in New York City that involved him in organized crime on a larger scale.

Vyacheslav Ivankov was raised in a poor section of Moscow, Russia. By the time he was 15 years old, he was a street brawler "who beat up people for the fun of it." His "toughness" brought him to the attention of known gangsters who taught Ivankov to carry out more sophisticated extortion schemes against businesses. Once caught and imprisoned, his reputation and connections in the criminal world expanded further, and he became involved with criminals at an international level.

Critical Thinking Questions

1. Given the parallels in the lives of Sammy Gravano and Vyacheslav Ivankov, how might you explain the progression of their criminal conduct using a positivist or classical approach?
2. Explain why you believe positivist or classical approaches do a better job in explaining their criminal conduct.

Sources: Peter Maas, Underboss (New York: Pocket Books, 1997); Robert I. Friedman, Red Mafiya (Boston: Little, Brown, 2000), pp. 108–110.

Structuralists also argue that the American capitalist ideology, which equates success with income accumulation, encourages people to disregard the rights of others who stand in their way. The line between a successful business person, a white-collar criminal, and an organized crime figure, according to this view, is narrow indeed, distinguished only by the method (legal or illegal) by which the money was obtained, not by who may have been exploited in garnering it.[30]

As Alan Block and William Chambliss explain, the structuralist perspective links capitalism and crime to class conflict:

> The structure of capitalism creates both the desire to consume and—for a large mass of people—an inability to earn the money necessary to purchase the items they have been taught to want. . . . Another fundamental contradiction of capitalism derives from the fact that the division of a society into a ruling class that owns the means of production and a subservient class that works for wages leads to conflict between the two classes. . . . It follows that as capitalism develops and conflicts between social classes continue . . . more and more acts will be defined as criminal and the amount of crime will increase.[31]

In this view, capitalism promotes organized crime by placing a premium on income generation and the ensuing conflict between the working class and those who control the legitimate market. Crimes are created to control the working class, according to the structuralists.

If the capitalist ideology lies at the root of organized crime, it can be argued that socialist economies would have less organized crime because of less pronounced disparities in income and opportunities within society. However, this does not appear to be the case. Organized crime, corruption, and smuggling have been reported to be widespread in many different kinds of socialist countries.[32]

Organized crime also has flourished in circumstances characterized by either strong or weak government structures. In his study of the Neapolitan Camorra crime group in Italy, for example, Vincenzo Ruggiero argues that "one cannot assert that organized crime prospers where there is little sense of a state; on the contrary, it prospers where there is too much state, or at least where the state is present in formal bureaucratic details, routine, hypertrophied and predatory."[33] This may be true of organized crime that involves corruption of government processes, but the emergence of "La Cosa Nostra" in Sicily argues the reverse: entrenched organized crime groups arose from the weak central government in Italy that was unable to enforce contracts, creating the opportunity for private enforcers called "gambellotto" or "mafioso" (see Chapter 6). This was also the case with the Camorra in Italy at the time of unification of the Italian peninsula in 1860. The Camorra was entrusted with the task of maintaining order when regular police had been sent to back up the army.[34] The Camorra played the "role of Broker," mediating disputes as private individuals assumed a government role. Therefore, organized crime has emerged both in situations where the political and economic control exercised by the government is strong, and also where it has been weak.

On the one hand, the structural view helps in understanding the inconsistencies in our laws regulating gambling, sex, and other consensual "vices." On the other hand, it offers little help in understanding the behavior of individuals who violate the law. Our case study of Henry Hill shows that he cared most about self-enrichment. He and his associates "wanted money, they wanted power, and they were willing to do anything necessary to achieve their ends."[35] How does this differ from the motivations of a legitimate businessperson who wants the same things and will do anything necessary and legal to achieve those ends? The structuralists do not provide an explanation other than the economic inequalities faced by Hill from an early age (already addressed by the positivists) and the fact that many (but not all) of the crimes committed by Hill involved the vices, where the law is inconsistent across jurisdictions.

ETHICAL: WHEN CRIME BRINGS PLEASURE, NOT GUILT

The ethical perspective sees crime as a moral failure in decision-making. In this view, crime occurs when a person makes a criminal choice because of a failure to appreciate the act's wrongfulness and its impact on the victim. The ethical explanation of criminal conduct recognizes that external factors play a role in influencing some people to engage in crime, but these factors do not cause the crime by themselves as positivists suggest. In a similar way, the ethical perspective sees a freely willed decision that lies at the base of virtually all criminal behavior, but there is no hedonistic "tendency" to engage in crime controlled only by the risk of apprehension as the classicists suggest.

Instead, crime occurs when criminal acts bring pleasure rather than guilt or shame, according to the ethical perspective on crime. Ethicists argue that people are often incapable of thinking through decisions in ethical terms because ethical principles and decision-making are rarely part of the educational process and often not modeled by parents. Lacking education and experience with ethical decisions, people often do what comes naturally: they make decisions based on their own self-interest, and they fail to understand or appreciate the legitimate interests of others or of the community at large.

First, classicists are correct in emphasizing the free-will choice that underlies all behavior. If behavior was determined by internal or external influences, we would be no different than the lower animals. Yet pain versus pleasure does not determine behavior either. If it did, most of us would be criminals. If the low odds of apprehension and punishment were the only obstacles that stood in our way for committing a crime, we would all be career criminals. As noted earlier, the odds of apprehension and punishment are quite low. Over the years, they have fallen further.[36] Therefore, there is more at work in law-abiding behavior than the threat of police and criminal penalties.

Second and likewise, the positivists get only part of the picture. There is no doubt that bad economic and social conditions affect opportunities for success in legitimate society. Indeed, a society should be evaluated by the number and quality of opportunities it provides for legitimate success. However, if a person's behavior was determined by his opportunities, there would be no successful people from disadvantaged backgrounds, and everyone in prison would be from socially or economically deprived areas. This is clearly not the case. Many people emerge successfully from disadvantaged backgrounds, and a number of people in prison are "white-collar" offenders who had every advantage in life. Therefore, more is at work in explaining crime than social and economic conditions.

Third, the structuralists point to the inconsistencies in American criminal law, by which we criminalize and decriminalize behaviors for political and economic reasons, often unrelated to social harm. This should be avoided to the extent possible because consistency in law helps promote consistency in expectations for the behavior of citizens. In addition, laws implemented for symbolic reasons, rather than for reasons of public safety, can result in the creation of illicit markets and criminal opportunities that outweigh any benefit intended by the law. Nevertheless, structuralists do not help us explain why some individuals choose to exploit an illicit market created by gambling laws, for example, while most of us do not.

The ethical view sees crime as placing one's own self-interest above the interests of others. Any short-term gain for the offender obtained from a crime is far outweighed by understanding the wrongfulness of the conduct and the harm it causes to the victim or community. From an ethical standpoint, therefore, a person refrains from criminal behavior because it does not bring pleasure. Ethical decision-making and reinforcement from an early age would help inculcate the notion of personal and social responsibility for one's own behavior. This is something that is lacking today in government, business, and, not surprisingly, organized crime.

Figure 4.2 illustrates how criminal conduct can be seen as emanating from kinds of casual influences including ethical, classical, positive, and structural. It can be seen how these different kinds of influences can be present for different individuals in different situations.

FIGURE 4.2 Potential influences on criminal conduct.

The scenario that follows describes the actual circumstances of an organized crime figure. Respond to the questions that follow, employing the principles from this chapter.

The Case of the Irish Mob

The so-called "Westies" was an Irish organized crime group in the Hell's Kitchen neighborhood on the West side of Manhattan. They were prosecuted into near extinction during the 1980s.

The group that formed the nucleus of the Westies were high school dropouts from working-class homes. They were known "more for their nerve than their brains," emulating existing gangs, such as that of Mickey Spillane, which grew out of the same neighborhood culture. The Westies were different, however, in that they were motivated almost entirely by profit rather than respect for their neighborhood or heritage. Incidents of fighting and violence were common among the Westies, and they often fought among themselves. A reputation for violence served to enhance a person's standing in the neighborhood.

On a "typical" day, two of the group's leaders, Jimmy Coonan (the leader) and Mickey Featherstone (the enforcer), would pick up money for numbers gambling, loansharking debts, and extortion payments from the union at the piers. They were known in the neighborhood for using violence to intimidate their victims.

Ultimately, the Westies self-destructed due to greed and reckless violence. After a trial for racketeering and murder, Coonan was sentenced to 75 years in prison without parole, based in part on the testimony of Featherstone, who had become a government informant to reduce his own sentence.

Critical Thinking Questions

1. Explain the criminal behavior of the Westies using a positivistic explanation.
2. Explain the crimes of the Westies using a classical approach.
3. Explain the crimes of the Westies using an ethical explanation.
4. Which of these explanations appears to explain the Westies' crimes most adequately?

Source: T. J. English, The Westies: The Irish Mob (New York: St. Martin's, 1991).

The biography of Henry Hill illustrates how the failure to possess an ethical outlook results in a twisted, and often self-centered, world view:

> Anyone who stood waiting his turn on the American pay line was beneath contempt. . . . They were the timid, law-abiding, pension-plan creatures neutered by compliance and awaiting their turn to die. To wiseguys, "working guys" were already dead. Henry and his pals had long ago dismissed the idea of security and the relative tranquility that went with obeying the law.[37]

This contempt for law-abiding citizens is made possible by the failure to feel guilt when it is appropriate. Similar to many other criminals, Hill and his associates felt pleasure when most people properly feel guilt.

> It was just that stuff that was stolen always tasted better than anything bought. . . . Paulie [Vario] was always asking me for stolen credit cards whenever he and his wife, Phyllis, were going out for the night. . . . The fact that a guy like Paul Vario, a capo in the Lucchese crime family, would even consider going out on a social occasion with his wife and run the risk of getting caught using a stolen credit card might surprise some people. But if you knew wiseguys you would know right away that the best part of the night for Paulie came from the fact that he was getting over on somebody. . . . The real thrill of the night for Paulie, his biggest pleasure, was that he was robbing someone and getting away with it.[38]

In this case, crime brought pleasure, not guilt. The value system was upside-down. Ethics focuses on inculcation of moral values that would re-emphasize the responsibility every person has for his or her own decisions and insists that objective ethical guidelines exist by which these decisions should be made and prioritized.[39] The failure of individuals to comprehend, feel guilty about, and gauge their actions by the long-term consequences of their conduct lies at the heart of the ethical view of criminal behavior (Table 4.1).

SUMMARY

This chapter presented a four-part typology of explanations of organized crime: positivistic, classical, structural, and ethical. Table 4.1 summarizes this four-part typology of explanations. The biography of Henry Hill, an organized crime figure, was used in each section of this chapter to demonstrate how these explanations may be applied in actual cases. The life of Bill Bonanno, described at the beginning of this chapter, offers another useful case study to apply these explanations. His father was a well-known target of police and was under surveillance for many years, increasing the odds that Bill Bonanno would be caught if he followed in his father's "family business." At the same time, Bonanno was educated and had opportunities for legitimate success that he

Table 4.1 Four Approaches to Criminal Behavior

Approach to Crime Causation	Primary Cause of Crime	Prescribed Remedy
Positive	External factors (usually social and economic)	Rehabilitation or reform by changing social and economic conditions or by changing a person's reaction to them
Classical	Free-will decision guided by hedonistic tendency to maximize pleasure and minimize pain	Deterrence through threat of apprehension and punishment
Structural	Political and economic conditions promote a culture of competitive individualism where personal gain becomes more important than the social good	More equitable distribution of power and wealth in society, and fewer arbitrary laws, so that all individuals have a greater stake in a better society
Ethical	Free-will decision guided by ethical principles—illegal conduct occurs because it brings pleasure instead of shame due to its wrongfulness and harm to the victim and community	Education and reinforcement in ethical decision-making from an early age; reduction to the extent possible of the external factors that promote unethical decisions

chose not to pursue. Bonanno's life illustrates how positivist and classical explanations of crime have difficulty accounting for his criminal choices and how an ethical perspective adds a needed dimension to understanding how criminal decisions are made and how they might be prevented.

ORGANIZED CRIME BIOGRAPHY

Biographies tell the life story of interesting people. In the world of criminal justice, biographies of organized crime figures offer insight into the background and motivations of the individuals who choose that lifestyle, the reasons for their choices, and their consequences. The following is a brief summary of an organized crime biography, followed by questions that ask you to reflect on the connections between that person's life and the content of this book.

Wiseguy
Nicholas Pileggi (Pocket Books, 1990)

The story of Henry Hill is told from childhood through adulthood and his initiation into the Mafia lifestyle. Hill began running errands for Mafia associates in Brooklyn and later participated in major thefts and organized crimes of all kinds. The book details the characters, mobsters, and others, who formed an underworld of scam artists, thieves, and drug dealers who committed crimes for a living and loved to spend other people's money.

Although clever, these "wiseguys" were not smart, and they often said and did things that were unwise or eventually got them caught by police or killed. Because of their criminal records and current associates, they were targeted by police, making them suspicious of everyone. This constant level of paranoia mixed badly with associates who were thieves and who would turn on one another with little provocation (despite their supposed loyalty to the group). Their chaotic lives as criminals were matched only by their equally chaotic personal lives. Once caught, Henry Hill became a government informant and entered the witness protection program. This book was the basis for the movie *Goodfellas*.

Questions
1. *Wiseguy* is one of the most popular of all nonfiction books about the Mafia lifestyle. What do you think made it so popular?
2. Most people tend to feel guilty or very nervous about living on stolen credit cards, trafficked property, and drug money. Why didn't Henry Hill feel this way?

ORGANIZED CRIME AT THE MOVIES

Movies seek to entertain and inform the audience about a story, incident, or person. Many good movies also hit upon important substantive themes relevant to understanding organized crime. Read the following movie summary (and watch the movie if you haven't already) and answer the questions that follow to make the organized crime subject matter connections.

Goodfellas

Martin Scorsese, Director (1990)

Based on the book *Wiseguy* by Nicholas Pileggi, *Goodfellas* tells the true story of Henry Hill (played by Ray Liotta), who grew up in Brooklyn and admired the Lucchese crime family members in his primarily Italian neighborhood. "As far back as I could remember I've always wanted to be a gangster," said Hill, and he quit school and went to work for the local mob leaders Paul Cicero (played by Paul Sorvino and based on the actual mobster Paul Vario) and Jimmy Conway (played by Robert De Niro and based on the actual Jimmy Burke).

The movie recounts Henry Hill's introduction to, and work for, this New York Mafia group and his ultimate capture and turn to informant. Because Henry Hill is half Irish, he cannot become a "made man" (full member) of the Italian-American crime family. The film portrays actual events in conspiring with Tommy DeVito (Joe Pesci) and Jimmy Conway to steal cargo from the airport, truck hijacking, and the brutal violence of this group.

Henry falls in love and marries Karen (Lorraine Bracco), a Jewish woman, and accompanies her to the Copacabana nightclub several times a week. Karen is not entirely happy with Henry's work, but she enjoys the lifestyle. The marriage suffers when Henry takes a mistress and, in a famous scene, Karen confronts Henry with a gun while he is sleeping. Henry beats her, yelling that he has enough to worry about on the street without waking up to a gun in his face.

Henry and Jimmy Conway are sent to prison for 4 years after dangling a gambler over a lion's cage at the zoo in order to convince him to pay his debts. Henry then turns to drugs to support his family, although Cicero warns him about long prison sentences for drugs and the risk it poses to the crime bosses.

Henry ignores Cicero and involves Karen, Tommy, Jimmy, and a new mistress in a large drug smuggling operation. Simultaneously, Jimmy Conway plans a major heist from the Lufthansa cargo terminal at the airport. The heist works, but Jimmy becomes agitated when some of his associates foolishly flaunt their success, potentially alerting the police, and he begins having them killed off. After receiving a promise that he would be inducted as a "made member" of the crime family, Tommy is killed in retaliation for an earlier murder he committed with Henry and Jimmy.

The many threads of Henry Hill's life come together in a disastrous way as he attempts to balance cocaine shipments, satisfy his mistress, avoid the police, and keep his drug customers happy, while snorting cocaine himself. Henry is arrested as he drives to the airport. Karen bails him out of jail and destroys all the cocaine in the house, leaving him without money.

After his arrest, Henry feels abandoned by his associates and is marked for death for dealing in cocaine (despite Paul's warning not to do so) so he decides to become an informant for the FBI. He enters the witness protection program after he testifies against his former associates, observing, "I get to live the rest of my life like a schnook." His marriage to Karen ends, and she gets custody of their children.

Goodfellas was an extremely popular film, and after seeing it, Henry Hill told others about his true identity, resulting in the government kicking him out of the witness protection program. Joe Pesci received an Academy Award for Best Supporting Actor, and the film was nominated for Best Picture, Best Director, and Best Supporting Actress (Lorraine Bracco).

Questions

1. Why do you think Henry Hill idolized and ultimately joined the mobsters who hung out in his neighborhood?
2. How do you explain Henry's continuing with his criminal lifestyle and associates after being incarcerated and often in fear of his life?

References and Notes

1. Bonanno, B. (2000). *Bound by Honor: A Mafioso's Story*. New York: St. Martin's Press.

2. Durkheim, E. (1964). *The Rules of Sociological Method (1895)*. New York: Free Press, p. 65.

3. Albanese, J. S. (1993). *Dealing with Delinquency: The Future of Juvenile Justice* (2nd ed.). Chicago, IL: Nelson-Hall, ch. 2.

4. Akers, R. L. (2000). *Criminological Theories* (3rd ed.). Los Angeles, CA: Roxbury Press; Williams, F. P., & McShane, M. D. (1999). *Criminological Theory* (3rd ed.). Upper Saddle River, NJ: Prentice Hall.

5. Cloward, R. A., & Ohlin, L. E. (1960). *Delinquency and Opportunity: A Theory of Delinquent Gangs*. New York: Free Press.

6. Merton, R. K. (1938). Social Structure and Anomie. *American Sociological Review, 3*, 672–682.

7. Cloward and Ohlin (1960). *Delinquency and Opportunity*, pp. 22–27.

8. *Delinquency and Opportunity*, pp. 165–166.

9. *Delinquency and Opportunity*, p. 166.

10. O'Kane, M. J. (1992). *Crooked Ladder: Gangsters, Ethnicity, and the American Dream*. New Brunswick, NJ: Transaction Publishers, pp. 27–28.

11. Wyrick, P. A. (2000). *Vietnamese Youth Gang Involvement*. Washington, DC: Office of Juvenile Justice and Delinquency Prevention; see also Ritter, N. M., Simon, T. R., & Mahendra, R. R. (2013). *Changing Course: Preventing Gang Membership*. Washington, DC: National Institute of Justice and Centers for Disease Control.

12. Shaw, C. R., & McKay, H. D. (1969). *Juvenile Delinquency and Urban Areas (1932)*. Chicago, IL: University of Chicago Press.

13. Sutherland, E. H. (1939). *Principles of Criminology*. Philadelphia, PA: Lippincott.

14. Matza, D. (1964). *Delinquency and Drift*. New York: Wiley.

15. Pileggi, N. (1985). *Wiseguy: Life in a Mafia Family*. New York: Simon and Schuster.

16. *Wiseguy*, p. 19.

17. Eckblom, P. (2003). Organised Crime and the Conjunction of Criminal Opportunity Framework. In A. Edwards, & P. Gill (Eds.), *Transnational Organised Crime: Perspectives on Global Security*. Abingdon, UK: Routledge, pp. 242–263; Bullock, K., Calrke, R. V., & Tilley, N. (2010). Introduction. In K. Bullock, R. V. Clarke, & N. Tilley (Eds.), *Situational Prevention of Organised Crimes*. Devon, UK: Willan Publishing.

18. Bouloukos, A. C., Farrell, G., & Laycock, G. (2003). Transnational Organised Crime in Europe and North America: The Need for Situational Crime Prevention. In K. Aromaa, S. Leppa, S. Nevala, & N. Ollus (Eds.), *Report of the Sixth United Nations Survey on Crime Trends and Criminal Justice Systems. Crime and Criminal Justice in Europe and North America 1995–97*. Helinski: European Institute of Crime Prevention and Control; Felson, M. (2006). *The Ecosystem for Organized Crime*. Helsinki: European Institute for Crime Prevention and Control; Aromaa, K., & Viljanen, T. (2006). *International Key Issues in Crime Prevention and Criminal Justice*. Helsinki: European Institute for Crime Prevention and Control [HEUNI]; Van der Schoot, C. R. A. (2006). *Organized Crime Prevention in the Netherlands*. Den Haag: BJU Legal Publishers.

19. Shukla, R. K., & Bartgis, E. E. (2010). Responding to Clandestine Methamphetamine Manufacturing: A Case Study in Situational Crime Prevention. *Criminal Justice Policy Review, 21*, 338–362; Bowers, K. J., & Guerette, R. T. (2009). Assessing the Extent of Crime Displacement and Diffusion of Benefits: A Review of Situational Crime Prevention Evaluations. *Criminology, 47*(November), 1331–1368; Holt, T. J., Blevins, K. R., & Kuhns, J. B. (2008). Examining the Displacement Practices of Johns with On-line Data. *Journal of Criminal Justice, 36*(November), 522–528; Levy, M. P., & Tartaro, C. (2010). Repeat Victimization: A Study of Auto Theft in

Atlantic City Using the WALLS Variables to Measure Environmental Indicators. *Criminal Justice Policy Review, 21*(September), 296–318; Sousa, W. H., & Kelling, G. L. (2010). Police and the Reclamation of Public Places: A Study of MacArthur Park in Los Angeles. *International Journal of Police Science & Management, 12*(Spring), 41–54.

20. Clarke, R. V. (2005). Seven Misconceptions of Situational Crime Prevention. In N. Tilley (Ed.), *Handbook of Crime Prevention and Community Safety*. Portland, OR: Willan Publishing, pp. 46–47; von Lampe, K. (2011). *Criminology & Criminal Justice, 11*, 145–163.

21. Finckenauer, J. O., & Chin, K. L. (2010). Sex Trafficking: A Target for Situational Crime Prevention? In K. Bullock, R. V. Clarke, & N. Tilley (Eds.), *Situational Prevention of Organised Crimes*. Devon, UK: Willan Publishing, pp. 58–80; Kleemans, E. R., Soudijn, M. R. J., & Weenink, A. W. (2010). Situational Crime Prevention and Cross-Border Crime. In K. Bullock, R. V. Clarke, & N. Tilley (Eds.), *Situational Prevention of Organised Crimes*. Devon, UK: Willan Publishing, pp. 17–34; von Lampe, K. (2010). Preventing Organised Crime: The Case of Contraband Cigarettes. In K. Bullock, R. V. Clarke, & N. Tilley (Eds.), *Situational Prevention of Organised Crimes*. Devon, UK: Willan Publishing, pp. 35–57.

22. Gottfredson, M., & Hirschi, T. (1990). *A General Theory of Crime*. Stanford, CA: Stanford University Press, p. 117.

23. Hirschi, T., & Gottfredson, M. (1989). Causes of White-Collar Crime. *Criminology, 25*(November), 959.

24. van Koppen, M. V. (2013). Involvement Mechanisms for Organized Crime. *Crime, Law and Social Change, 59*, 19.

25. *Wiseguy*, pp. 13–14.

26. *Wiseguy*, p. 21.

27. Albanese, J. S. (2005). *Criminal Justice* (3rd ed.). Boston, MA: Allyn & Bacon, pp. 275–276.

28. *Wiseguy*, pp. 141–142.

29. Ruggiero, V. (1993). The Camorra: 'Clean' Capital and Organised Crime. In F. Pearce, & M. Woodiwiss (Eds.), *Global Crime Connections: Dynamics and Control*. Buffalo: University of Toronto Press, p. 142.

30. Woodiwiss, M. (2001). *Organized Crime and American Power*. Buffalo, NY: University of Toronto Press; see also Hobbs, D. L. (2013). *Lush Life: Constructing Organized Crime in the UK*. Oxford, UK: Oxford University Press.

31. Block, A. A., & Chambliss, W. J. (1981). *Organizing Crime*. New York: Elsevier, pp. 9–10.

32. Albanese, J. S., Das, D. K., & Verma, A. (2003). *Organized Crime: World Perspectives*. Upper Saddle River, NJ: Prentice Hall; Einstein, S., & Amir, M. (1999). *Organized Crime: Uncertainties and Dilemmas*. Chicago, IL: Office of International Criminal Justice.

33. Ruggerio, 1993. p. 157.

34. Ruggerio, 1993. p. 145.

35. *Wiseguy*, p. 39.

36. Federal Bureau of Investigation, *Crime in the United States—Uniform Crime Report*. Washington, DC: U.S. Government Printing Office, published annually.

37. *Wiseguy*, pp. 38–39.

38. *Wiseguy*, pp. 24–25.

39. Albanese, J. S. (2012). *Professional Ethics in Criminal Justice: Being Ethical When No One is Looking*. Upper Saddle River, NJ: Prentice Hall.

CHAPTER 5

How Organized Crime Is Organized
Types of Organizations

Empirical studies of organized crime suggest that it is less hierarchical and more entrepreneurial than originally thought.

Everyone knows the story of the blind men asked to identify an elephant. One grabbed the tail and guessed the animal was a snake. Another touched its tusks and thought it was a smooth stone. A third held its ear and surmised it was a large piece of leather. In each case, the perception was based on logical deductions, but the conclusion was wrong.

Models, or paradigms, of organized crime have developed in much the same way. Government investigators, researchers, and scholars have examined various manifestations of organized crime using informants, electronic surveillance, court records, participant observation, interviews with convicted offenders, economic analyses, and historical accounts. By and large, these investigations have been conducted with integrity and true interest in discovering the actual nature of organized crime. Often the perceptions of these individuals have been correct, but the conclusions drawn are misleading. Why?

WHAT IS A MODEL OF ORGANIZED CRIME?

A model, or paradigm, is an effort to draw a picture of a piece of reality in order to understand it better. We make physical models of the structure of the solar system in order to see how it is organized at a level difficult to observe otherwise due to its immense size. We have modeled distinct stages of child development to illustrate the maturation process that is difficult to observe otherwise due to its slow, gradual process. In each case, we use models to "freeze" an object or process in time and space, even though the objects we are modeling are constantly moving and changing. As a result, models are limited but still useful. They make visible physical objects that are too large (or too small) to observe, and make understandable objects that are too fast or too slow to capture. This ability to capture the essence of an object, system, or process without actually witnessing it makes models the most useful of all educational tools.

As noted in Chapter 1, what U.S. Supreme Court Justice Potter Stewart said about obscene material holds equally true for organized crime: I might not know precisely what it is, but "I know it when I see it."[1] Everyone has perceptions of what organized crime is, even when it is difficult to explain in a comprehensive or systematic way. There have been many efforts to model organized crime, most occurring during the past four decades. In every case the goal has been to capture the essence of organized crime in the form of a model because it is so difficult to observe otherwise.

As with the blind men who attempted to identify the elephant, the outcome of efforts to model organized crime invariably reflects the perspective of the investigator. Economists model it in terms of economic factors. Government investigators model organized crime as a hierarchical government-like enterprise. Social scientists view it as a social phenomenon. In too many cases the perceptions are based in reality, but the conclusions drawn are either inaccurate or overgeneralized. Just as in the case of the blind men who disagreed in their conclusions, the elephant still existed in a distinct form. It simply was not identified correctly. The failure of a model to capture the true nature of organized crime should not be construed as proof, one way or the other, about the existence of organized crime. Too often in the past a model shown to have shortcomings in its depiction of organized crime is rejected in its entirety, which overlooks the fact that the investigator's perceptions may have been correct, but the conclusions wrong. As a result, it is important to distinguish between the facts and the perceptions on which models are based and the conclusions drawn from those perceptions and facts. The deduction of wrong conclusions does not mean necessarily that the facts and perceptions on which they are based are also inaccurate.[2]

Models of organized crime can be grouped into three general types: those that focus on hierarchical structure, those that emphasize local ethnic or cultural connections, and those that emphasize the economic nature of organized crime. As this chapter shows, none of these models excludes consideration of the others, as some overlap clearly exists. Nevertheless, the development and the structure of these models are distinct and will be treated separately, in order to make sense of the differing depictions of organized crime from different sources.

HIERARCHICAL MODEL OF ORGANIZED CRIME

"Hierarchical" is defined in the dictionary as "a group of persons or things arranged in order of rank or grade." Various authors over the years have termed this the "bureaucratic," "national conspiracy," or "corporate" model of organized crime. Stated most simply, this model of organized crime characterizes it as a government-like structure, in which organized illegal activities are conducted with the approval of superiors, "policy" is set by higher-ups, and illicit activities are "protected" through the influence of the hierarchy.

This model of organized crime was put forth first in these terms by Estes Kefauver, a U.S. senator who conducted hearings on the subject of organized crime in 1950. His committee concluded that "there is a sinister criminal organization known as the Mafia operating throughout the country with ties in other nations in the opinion of this committee."[3] Unfortunately, Kefauver had little more than the opinions of law enforcement officials to support his contention at that time. The fact that he drew such sweeping conclusions without independent corroboration has been pointed out in several serious critiques of the Kefauver Committee.[4]

It was not until 1963 that evidence was produced that supported the notion that organized crime operated as a hierarchical structure. U.S. Senator John McClellan held public hearings during this period at which the government introduced the first "insider" in organized crime. His name was Joseph Valachi, then serving a prison sentence and agreeing to testify as part of a deal to avoid a possible death sentence for a murder he committed while in prison. Valachi's testimony became the basis for the hierarchical model of organized crime.

Valachi testified that a nationwide criminal organization did exist, as Estes Kefauver had argued in 1950. Unlike Kefauver, Valachi said the organization's name was "Cosa Nostra" rather than "Mafia." (Valachi claimed he had never heard of the term "Mafia," while no law enforcement official who testified had heard of "Cosa Nostra.") The senate committee treated the two names for this apparently identical organization interchangeably.[5] Valachi claimed this organization arose out of a gangland war in New York City during the early 1930s. The main stake in this so-called "Castellammarese War," which was said to have lasted 14 months, was "absolute control of the large segment of the underworld then in the hands of gang leaders of Italian nativity or lineage."[6] See Figure 5.1.

Valachi described the organizational structure, established after this gangland war, as consisting of "the individual bosses of the individual families, and then we had an underboss, and then we had what we call a caporegima which is a lieutenant, and then we have what we call soldiers."[7] In this way, territory and criminal enterprises were divided among "families" of men of Italian descent. According to Valachi, membership was restricted by Lucky Luciano after the Castellammarese War to "Sicilians from the turn of the century through the 1920s," and then it was confined to "full Italians," requiring Italian parentage on both sides of a man's family. This restriction lasted until 1954, when membership was opened to others not meeting these requirements.[8]

Based primarily on Valachi's testimony and the statements of law enforcement officials from some large cities, the McClellan Committee concluded "there exists ... today a criminal organization that is directly descended from and is patterned upon the centuries-old Sicilian terrorist society, the Mafia. This organization, also known as Cosa Nostra, operates vast illegal enterprises that produce an annual income of many billions of dollars. This combine has

FIGURE 5.1 Joseph Valachi, convicted murderer and former Cosa Nostra mobster, testifies before the Senate Permanent Investigation Committee in 1963. *AP Photo*

so much power and influence that it may be described as a private government of organized crime."[9] This characterization of organized crime as a large, centrally controlled, highly organized entity forms the basis for the hierarchical model of organized crime. The major attributes of organized crime according to this model are highlighted in Table 5.1.

As Table 5.1 indicates, the hierarchical model posits a "family" structure with several military-style ranks from the boss down to soldiers. Bosses control the activities of the family. Valachi also testified that a "commission" of bosses exists from approximately 12 families in large cities around the country.[10] This commission handles interfamily relations and disputes, according to the McClellan Committee's conclusions. The source of this information was primarily Joseph Valachi and other criminal informants used by police agencies who also provided testimony at the McClellan hearings.

Over the past 50 years, the hierarchical model has been criticized for its imprecision. Problems with the hierarchical model included (1) the inability to confirm historically that any type of gangland war occurred during the early 1930s;[11] (2) information provided by Valachi himself, and others after him,

Table 5.1 Hierarchical Model of Organized Crime

Structure (That Forms the Basis for Criminal Activity)
1. There is a "family" structure with graded ranks of authority from boss down to soldiers.
2. Bosses oversee the activities of family members.
3. A "commission" of bosses handles interfamily relations and disputes.

show that the "family" actually plays very little role in directing the lives and activities of its members;[12] and (3) subsequent informants, such as Jimmy Fratianno, differed widely in their testimony about the size and structure of Cosa Nostra.[13] Most of the investigations producing findings that contradicted parts of the hierarchical model were historical in nature, relying on court records, testimony, interviews, and archival data. The number, method, and similarity in the conclusions of these investigations are remarkable. What they fail to establish, and perhaps were not intended to prove, is that the hierarchical model is invalid as a description of at least some parts of organized crime.[14] It is true that Valachi's history was faulty, and it is unfortunate that the Senate and subsequent investigators for the President's Crime Commission in 1967 did not assess Valachi's statements more carefully. The President's Commission Task Force on Organized Crime essentially repeated Valachi's testimony and added little new insight.[15] Nevertheless, the most important question remains unanswered: are the errors arising from the McClellan hearings incidental or do they warrant an abandonment of the hierarchical model altogether?

The decade of the 1970s witnessed a growing body of scholarly research into the nature of organized crime. It began with sociologist Joseph Albini in 1971, continued with anthropologists Francis Ianni and Elizabeth Reuss-Ianni in 1972, and was followed by others. In every case, researchers were unable to find any connection between the individuals and groups they studied and a larger, controlling hierarchy. This led to growing doubts about the existence of a national crime syndicate and led to the emergence of a second model of organized crime, discussed in the next section.

Not until the decade of the 1980s was information available that showed conclusively that the hierarchical model accurately portrayed at least some manifestations of organized crime. The "mob trials" of the 1980s and 1990s were the most significant organized crime prosecution efforts in the history of the United States. Several hundred high-level organized crime figures were convicted based on electronic surveillance and protected witnesses that provided documentary evidence of how organized crime operates in some areas. The "Commission" trial of 1986 was perhaps the most notable of the mob trials because it involved the alleged "bosses" of the five New York City "families" of the Cosa Nostra as defendants. The defense conceded that the "Mafia exists and has members" and "there is a commission," which was mentioned in the wiretapped conversations of the defendants. The defendants tried to argue that their membership was not synonymous with criminal activity, but they were each convicted and sentenced to 100 years in prison for various crimes. Interestingly, the defendants argued that the purpose of the "commission" was to resolve disputes rather than to plan crimes, an argument not unlike that made in the 1960s by Joseph Valachi, who characterized the commission as a mechanism for dispute resolution between families. Defense stipulations, wiretap evidence, and jury findings in the commission trial and in the successful prosecution of John Gotti in 1992 make it clear that the hierarchical model clearly characterizes at least some part of organized crime in the United States.[16] Consider the testimony of Salvatore (Sammy the Bull) Gravano in the trial of John Gotti:

> **Assistant U.S. Attorney Gleeson:** Have you ever heard the term "administration?"
>
> **Gravano:** Yes.
>
> **Gleeson:** To you what does that mean?
>
> **Gravano:** There is the boss, the underboss, and the consigliere, it's the higher up in the family. The administration.
>
> **Gleeson:** Were you part of the administration?
>
> **Gravano:** Yes.
>
> **Gleeson:** Who was the rest of the administration?
>
> **Gravano:** John (Gotti) was the boss, I was the underboss, and Frank—and Joe Piney was the consigliere, Frankie was acting consigliere...
>
> **Gleeson:** What's below the administration?
>
> **Gravano:** Captains.

This testimony from Gravano, a criminal informant of higher "rank" than Valachi, is remarkably similar to Valachi's testimony nearly 30 years earlier.[17] Gravano's description of his "induction" ceremony into the Cosa Nostra, and the "commission" made up of leaders of various "families," is quite similar to Valachi's version in 1963.[18] There is no apparent cause or reason for Gravano, or the other criminal informants from the decade of the 1980s, to model their testimony after that of Valachi, so it reasonably can be said that the structure of Cosa Nostra (at least within New York City) is based on the same hierarchical model described by Valachi in the early 1960s.

Given available evidence to date, it is clear that the hierarchical model characterizes organized crime among Italian-Americans in the New York City area who are connected to the Cosa Nostra. There is also evidence from other cities in New England, Philadelphia, and elsewhere that at least within those cities a significant part of organized crime has been controlled by organized criminals with Italian-American roots. The hierarchical model fits best in its description of how the group functions in accord with respect for position and in partnerships and deference to other "connected" individuals in organized crime.

The hierarchical model is weakest, given the evidence to date, in describing whether a true connection exists among organized crime groups in different cities and in specifying the role of Cosa Nostra in the lives of its members. The commission trial in New York City established how the various "families" operate and divide their criminal activities there. The trial sheds little light, however, on (1) the existence and nature of connections among organized crime groups in different cities, (2) the extent of the connections between Italian and non-Italian groups in the same cities, or (3) whether organized crime not connected with Cosa Nostra is structured in a similar fashion. Contemporary investigations suggest that organized crime activities, both within and outside the Cosa Nostra, might be becoming less hierarchical and more entrepreneurial in nature.[19]

Nevertheless, there is evidence that some contemporary gangs are organized hierarchically. According to successful federal prosecutions, the Aryan Brotherhood of Texas (ABT) gang is organized in this way. Some gang members and their associates have committed acts of murder, robbery, kidnapping, and drug trafficking on behalf of the ABT gang, plus assaults against fellow gang members and rival gang members. The ABT was formed in the 1980s inside the Texas prison system and was modeled after the Aryan Brotherhood, a California-based prison gang formed in the California prison system in the 1960s. Originally, the ABT was concerned with the protection of white inmates and promoting white supremacy/separatism, but since then it has expanded its criminal operations to include illegal activities for profit. Members have been required to follow the orders of higher-ranking members, often referred to as "direct orders," indicating a hierarchical structure to the gang.[20]

In an analogous way, a different gang, the Black Guerrilla Family (BGF), is the largest prison gang in Maryland with approximately 1,000 identified members. BGF has its origins in the revolutionary prison writings of a former Black Panther in California. Becoming a "comrade" in BGF requires learning a code of conduct and passing tests on the gang's history and its rules. Law enforcement officials have recovered "graded tests" from jail cells. Membership in the gang becomes a criminal obligation, and the gang has a paramilitary organization including low-level comrades, high-ranking lieutenants, and field generals responsible for specific territories.[21]

LOCAL ETHNIC MODEL OF ORGANIZED CRIME

It was said by some people during the 1980s that once free-market competition was introduced into the U.S. telephone system, the price of making a telephone call would drop considerably. The government was ultimately successful in adding competition to the long-distance telephone marketplace but the results were far from dramatic. A similar logical, but incorrect, prediction often arises from the hierarchical model of organized crime.

Perhaps the biggest problem with the hierarchical model of organized crime is that it leads to the conclusion that prosecution of the "bosses" and others in control will make organized crime less prevalent and less threatening. The successful mob prosecutions of the 1980s and 1990s illustrate that this is not necessarily the case, because the demand for drugs, gambling, stolen property, and a weak regulatory system provoke the emergence of illicit entrepreneurs to cater to the illegal markets or to exploit the legal marketplace. Once these entrepreneurs are removed by arrest or incarceration, others emerge because the demand remains, as do the opportunities for criminal exploitation of the legitimate marketplace.[22]

Social scientists became involved in the study of organized crime in a significant way in the 1970s. For the first time, a series of independent studies appeared that relied on information from sources outside the government. The first was conducted by sociologist Joseph Albini, who found that individuals involved in organized crime "do not belong to an organization." Instead of a "criminal secret society, a criminal syndicate consists of a system of loosely structured relationships" that develops so that each person can maximize profits.[23] The following year anthropologists Francis Ianni and Elizabeth Reuss-Ianni conducted a 2-year study of one specific organized crime "family" in Brooklyn. Francis Ianni became a participant-observer, and based on his observations and those made of two other criminal groups he studied, he found these groups not to be "bureaucratic." In fact, he found them to have "no structure . . . independent of their current 'personnel.'"[24]

Unlike the prevailing view at the time that organized crime operated as "a private government," Albini, as well as Ianni and Reuss-Ianni, found little organization and that friendships based on cultural (i.e., Italian) and economic ties formed the basis for organized crime activities. These authors' findings are limited, of course, by the areas and groups they studied, much in the same way that Valachi was limited in his knowledge about organized crime outside the New York area. The primary difference between Valachi's model of organized crime and the newer local ethnic model developed by social scientists centers on the degree of organization within and between organized criminal groups.

The body of social science evidence continued to grow from the 1970s to the present. Numerous studies now exist of organized crime groups in various locales around the United States and the world that have found (1) cultural and ethnic ties link organized criminals together, rather than a hierarchy; and (2) the groups studied appear to be local in nature without apparent connections to a national crime syndicate.[25]

This model, outlined in Table 5.2, has obvious differences to the hierarchical model first detailed by Joseph Valachi, but there are a few similarities as well. All these studies highlight the importance of heritage (i.e., racial, ethnic, or other cultural ties) in forming the basis for working relationships, and from Valachi forward it has been clear that even those organized crime members who are part of Cosa Nostra obtain relatively little direction in their day-to-day activities. Consider Valachi's statement at the McClellan hearings in 1963:

Senator Javits: That is the function of the family . . . that is mutual protection?

Mr. Valachi: Right.

Senator Javits: Otherwise, everybody operates by himself. They may take partners but that is their option.

> **Table 5.2** Local, Ethnic Model of Organized Crime
>
> **Structure (That Forms the Context for Criminal Activity)**
>
> 1. Cultural and ethnic ties rather than a hierarchical structure bind the group together.
> 2. Individuals control their own activities and take partners as they wish.
> 3. No evidence exists of a connection between these groups with a national crime syndicate in most cases.

> *Gravano:* There is the boss, the underboss, and the consigliere, it's the higher up in the family. The administration.
>
> *Mr. Valachi:* Right.

This exchange shows that the organization of the crime entity, even for a member of the Genovese crime family, as Valachi claimed to be, is rather loose.[26] Therefore, differences between hierarchical and local ethnic models appear to lie entirely in how illicit relationships are structured rather than in the nature or extent of the criminal activity itself.

A contemporary study of tobacco smuggling found that these activities were "born out of and relied upon trust and kinship/acquaintanceship ties as well as the social knowledge developed through locally-based relationships. Transactions were imbued with mutual trust and reliance between actors familiar to one another thanks to their shared local heritage and social frames of reference."[27] So it can be seen that local groups and connections remain an important dimension to some manifestations of organized crime.

A third model of organized crime developed in the late 1970s, when the economics of organized crime drew interest among researchers and policy makers. Instead of focusing on the personal relationships that form the basis for organized crime, this group of investigations focused on the economic relationships that drive the business of organized crime.

ENTERPRISE MODEL OF ORGANIZED CRIME

The enterprise model of organized crime grew out of dissatisfaction with both hierarchical and local ethnic models. A growing number of investigations found that relationships between individuals (hierarchical, ethnic, racial, or friendship) were the genesis of organized crime activity (as opposed to individual, less-organized forms of criminal behavior). The view was that, if factors causing these illicit relationships to form (i.e., conspiracies) could be isolated, a determination might be made about the true causes of organized crime. It is the conspiratorial nature of organized crime that makes it serious. It is not the individual drug dealer and illegal casino operator that cause public concern as much as how these individuals organize their customers, suppliers, and functionaries to provide illicit goods and services for a profit.

The realization that organized crime operates as a business spurred a series of studies in an effort to isolate those factors that contribute most significantly to the formation of criminal enterprises. Dwight Smith was among the first to attempt to explain the economic origins of organized crime in a systematic manner. In his book *The Mafia Mystique* and in subsequent publications, he developed a "spectrum-based theory of enterprise."[28] Applying general organization theory to criminal activity, Smith found that organized crime stems from "the same fundamental assumptions that govern entrepreneurship in the legitimate marketplace: a necessity to maintain and extend one's share of the market." According to this view, organized crime groups form and thrive in the same way that legitimate businesses do: they respond to the needs and demands of suppliers, customers, regulators, and competitors. The only difference between organized crime and legitimate business, according to Smith, is that organized criminals deal in illegal products, whereas legitimate businesses generally do not.

The business enterprise model of organized crime focuses on how economic considerations, rather than hierarchical or ethnic considerations, lie at the base of the formation and success of organized crime groups. Regardless of ethnicity or hierarchy, the enterprise model labels economic concerns as the primary cause of organized criminal behavior. A number of empirical studies of specific organized crime operations support this perspective. Patricia Adler's study of illicit drug sales in the southwest as a participant-observer found that "dealers and smugglers I studied operated within an illicit market that was largely competitive, or disorganized, rather than visibly structured." Disputes were settled in "a spontaneous and unrestricted manner."[29] She concluded that the drug markets she observed consisted of "individual entrepreneurs and small organizations rather than massive, centralized bureaucracies," which were "competitive" rather than "monopolistic" in nature.[30] In a study of bookmaking, loansharking, and numbers gambling in New York City, Peter Reuter found them "not monopolies in the classic sense or subject to control by some external organization." Instead, he observed that "economic forces arising from the illegality of the product tend to fragment the market," making it difficult to control or centralize these illegal activities on a large scale.[31] Letzia Paoli found that the supply of illegal goods is not marked by a tendency toward the development of large-scale criminal enterprises due to the illegal nature of the product.[32] Instead, smaller, more flexible and efficient enterprises characterize this type of organized crime.

A case study of a British organized crime network centered around three legitimate security companies which interacted with professional criminals in small groups. The activities "spanned the spectrum of legitimacy," using illegitimate means to enhance profits of legitimate businesses they owned or worked for.

Some of their activities, especially the collection of debts, clustered "at the margin of legitimacy."[33] The New Jersey State Commission of Investigation found a network of corrupt doctors created a proliferation of painkillers and heroin operating in open-air drug markets in both cities and at malls in affluent communities. A physician told investigators he was expected to write pill prescriptions for anyone who asked and that patients were recruited by word-of-mouth at shelters for the homeless. The practice received $1.6 million in Medicare and Medicaid payments, money turned over to organized crime. In a similar way, open drug markets operating in Chicago's West Side, most specializing in heroin, adopted tactics that allow managers to meet demand and make profits.

"It's not just a bunch of idiots out there," said Aaron Clayton, a former street manager for the drug operation now in prison. "It is like any other business. The only thing is that our business was illegal." Both court records and interviews with former dealers indicate that the drug trade is based on the basic principles of all profitable businesses. In addition, it has capitalized on a plentiful supply of cheap labor of poor young men who find they have few other legitimate options.[34]

Cases like these typify the enterprise model of organized crime. Rather than the product of illicit relationships based on hierarchical or ethnic relationships, this model sees organized crime as the product of market forces, similar to those that cause legitimate businesses to flourish or die in the legal sector of the economy. The major characteristics of the enterprise model are summarized in Table 5.3.

Table 5.3 shows that it is economic relationships, rather than personal relationships (based either in hierarchy or in ethnicity), that form the basis for organized crime activity. Organized crime activity is seen as a deviant variation of legitimate business activity, which is often interethnic and nonviolent, because these latter two factors enhance profit maximization.

Several studies have found that organized crime can be interethnic in nature and also less violent than is commonly believed. Although Jews dominated the cocaine trade in New York City during the early 1900s, historian Alan Block saw that there was also notable "evidence of interethnic cooperation" involving Italians, Greeks, Irish, and Black participants.[35] A contemporary account of the Irish mob the "Westies" on Manhattan's West Side saw that they cooperate

Table 5.3 Enterprise Model of Organized Crime

Structure (Incidental to the Criminal Opportunities)

1. Organized crime and legitimate business involve similar activities on different ends of the "spectrum of legitimacy" of business enterprise.
2. Operations are not ethnically exclusive or very violent in order to enhance profit.
3. It is rarely centrally organized because of the nature of the markets and activities involved.

occasionally with Cosa Nostra groups to further mutual interests.[36] Annelise Anderson's analysis of a single organized crime "family" indicated that there was "no strong evidence" of violence in its legitimate businesses and that the use of force to encourage payments from loanshark customers was "almost non-existent."[37] An investigation of organized crime infiltration of the New York City construction industry showed that "actual violence is only rarely necessary."[38] Reuter, Rubinstein, and Wynn noted that vending machine and waste collection industries in the New York City area had "outgrown the racketeers," inasmuch as "there is no point in a racketeer using force to control machine placement in a bar or restaurant unless he is also able to provide the patrons with the games they desire. If he cannot, the patrons will just move to another bar."[39] Each study demonstrates that organized crime activity operates according to economic factors faced by any business enterprise (i.e., the pressures of suppliers, customers, regulators, and competitors). The enterprise model clearly places these business-related concerns as more significant than hierarchical obligations or ethnic links in the genesis and continuation of organized crime.

CRITICAL THINKING EXERCISE 5.1

The following scenario reports on an actual investigation of organized crime activity. Using the information provided in the chapter, answer the questions that follow.

The Case of Morrisburg

"Morrisburg" (a pseudonym) is an industrial "rust-belt" city that once had booming coal, steel, and railroad industries. Vice and organized crime activity are prevalent and have been throughout most of the city's history. Illicit activities include gambling, loansharking, stolen property, drug trafficking, and prostitution. These activities do not appear to be controlled by a single group, but rather by a number of independent groups and individuals. A single ethnic group characterizes most of those involved, but no one group is dominant.

New groups enter the mix of illegal activities periodically, but older groups do not withdraw. The new groups are merely added to the existing mixture.

Money is generated and laundered through a confusing combination of illegal operations and legitimate businesses that make illegal funds difficult to trace. Activities are protected through political contributions and corruption of individuals in both criminal justice and government agencies.

Critical Thinking Questions

1. Which model of organized crime appears to account for the organized crime in Morrisburg most comprehensively?
2. What strategies do you believe would have the most long-term impact in Morrisburg?

Source: Gary W. Potter (1994). Criminal Organizations: Vice, Racketeering, and Politics in an American City. Prospect Heights, IL: Waveland Press.

FITTING THE MODELS TOGETHER: GROUPS VERSUS ACTIVITIES

Evidence supports each of the three models of organized crime in certain respects. Clear evidence from criminal informants, electronic surveillance, and jury findings indicates that the hierarchical model characterizes relationships among the New York City Cosa Nostra families and some groups in other cities. The mob trials of the 1980s and 1990s removed any doubt that existed after the Valachi testimony in the 1960s. Yet there is clear evidence that much organized crime remains unconnected to Cosa Nostra activity. This evidence has been derived largely from independent case studies (cited earlier) of organized crime groups in many different locations. These groups are usually locally based and bound by ethnic or cultural ties—groups that are often non-Italian. Finally, there is clear evidence that economic considerations are a significant factor in the development and maintenance of criminal enterprises. These findings stem largely from economic analyses of organized crime markets (cited earlier) in different regions of the country.

To what extent do these three models overlap? There are three distinct ways in which these models merge. Cosa Nostra groups are hierarchical (if loosely so), ethnically bound, and perhaps also maintained by market forces. Ethnically bound organized crime groups exist that are not hierarchical in structure, but rather are driven by economic concerns. There are also organized crime groups not hierarchical or ethnically bound that engage in criminal activities corresponding to the nature of the available market. These three possibilities point out the major similarities and differences in the three models of organized crime and suggest how organized crime might be addressed more effectively in the future. Figure 5.2 illustrates the three types of criminal organization discussed in this chapter.

Both hierarchical and local ethnic models focus on how organized crime *groups* are organized; the enterprise model focuses on how organized crime *activities* are organized. This is why the three models do not conflict in any significant

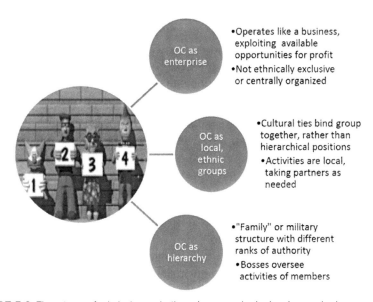

OC as enterprise
- Operates like a business, exploiting available opportunities for profit
- Not ethnically exclusive or centrally organized

OC as local, ethnic groups
- Cultural ties bind group together, rather than hierarchical positions
- Activities are local, taking partners as needed

OC as hierarchy
- "Family" or military structure with different ranks of authority
- Bosses oversee activities of members

FIGURE 5.2 Three types of criminal organization—how organized crime is organized.

way. While it is important to understand how a criminal group is organized if one is to develop a criminal conspiracy case, it is not always necessary to understand the group structure to understand how and why it engages in the activities it does. Perhaps historian Mark Haller said it best, "it makes little sense, for instance, to compare an Italian-American crime family to a Jamaican cocaine distribution group. One is largely a social group that serves its members' business interests; the other is a business group distributing illegal drugs."[40] The Jamaican group, in Haller's view, exists simply as a mechanism to engage in the drug business with little in the way of structure or cultural ties beyond the drug business itself. However, the Cosa Nostra group has both preexisting hierarchical and cultural ties that form the basis for launching illicit enterprises. As Haller puts it, it's like "comparing a Rotary Club and a department store. It is more appropriate to compare stores with stores, and Rotary Clubs with other social organizations."[41]

The perceived inconsistencies among hierarchical, ethnic, and enterprise models of organized crime are incidental for the purposes of both study and crime control. Differences among the models become less significant once one recognizes, as the organized crime literature clearly indicates, that (1) some organized crime is hierarchical in nature, and much is not; (2) some is locally based and ethnically bound in nature, and much is not; and (3) that all organized crime activity is entrepreneurial in nature.

Organized crime is studied most fruitfully as an economic activity and is prosecuted on the basis of the relationship among its participants. For the scholar, the economic activity is paramount inasmuch as it provides more leads to understanding the genesis and maintenance of the illegal acts. For the law enforcement official, the structure of the group is paramount inasmuch as it provides more leads for prosecution purposes. It is hoped that an appreciation of each of these models will enable both scholars and the law enforcement community to understand that the apparent tension among the various models of organized crime is inconsequential rather than contentious.

The enterprise model characterizes all organized crime activity, whereas the precise structure of particular organized crime groups becomes more or less important depending on the group in question (especially whether it predated the current illicit activity or whether it merely arose in response to the criminal opportunity). Future investigations should take greater care to appreciate this dynamic and better distinguish between organized crime activities and organized crime group characteristics as recognized in the three models of organized crime. Just as the three blind men who examined various parts of the elephant had good instincts and made logical judgments, their conclusions were still wrong. When it comes to understanding the true nature of organized crime, it is equally important not to lose sight of the "elephant" as one studies its various structures and activities.

FUTURE FORMS OF ORGANIZED CRIME?

Newer forms of organized crime can occur in the virtual world rather than in the physical world. The virtual world is cyberspace, the electronic arena in which the provision of illicit goods and services is provided without the need for a great deal of physical contact between provider and consumer. Internet pornography, hackers who threaten and extort victims, online gambling, and Internet loan frauds are examples of how the Internet provides a virtual forum to connect criminals to victims without face-to-face contact. Are organized criminal groups and associations important to these offenders?

Criminals associate only when it fulfills a necessary purpose in carrying out a crime. As criminals become more disconnected from victims, it also is likely they will become more disconnected from each other. Continuing criminal associations will become less important, replaced by changing "networks of convenience" in which criminals associate only temporarily when it is necessary to do so. For example, an online pornography Web site that sells access to photos and videos needs a continuing supply of this product to remain attractive to customers. Instead of incurring the risk of constantly recruiting new men and women to perform and video production people to film and manufacture a final product—all risking apprehension—a simple call on the Internet seeking volunteers or other entrepreneurs to sell their own sex videos that are made independently greatly reduces the risk while serving the criminal need. In this way, members of the organized crime "enterprise" (including those who make the pornography, who make it accessible via the Web, and those who sell access) may never even meet in person. Because of the lack of physical contact between provider and consumer, this activity falls short of prostitution, but some jurisdictions have explored revisions to prostitution laws and regulating the marketing of sexually objectionable materials more strict in an effort to curb the spread of sexually oriented Web sites.[42] The legal issues combine with the lack of a traditional continuing group to make prosecutions difficult. Susan Brenner has observed that "the migration of the gang structure to cyberspace is to some extent problematic because a gang's structural advantage in the real world, the concentration of effort, may be of little importance in the cyberworld."[43]

Evidence indicates that even organized crimes in the physical world, such as extortion and the sale of stolen property, are becoming less "organized" and more "networked." Separate empirical studies of extortion and frauds by Russians, human smuggling by Chinese, and other disparate groups have found a trend toward "networking," where *ad hoc* associations are formed in which individuals come together for a specific "job" and, once completed, disperse.[44] An analysis for the Congressional Research Service summarized it this way:

Modern organized criminals often prefer cellular or networked structural models for their flexibility and avoid the hierarchies that previously governed more traditional organized crime groups such as the Cosa Nostra. Fluid network structures make it harder for law enforcement to infiltrate, disrupt, and dismantle conspiracies. Many 21st century organized crime groups opportunistically form around specific, short-term schemes and may outsource portions of their operations rather than keeping it all 'in-house.'[45]

Contemporary organized crime, therefore, may be moving away from longer-term traditional relationships and structures to more fluid, less formal, and temporary associations. This may reflect a wider characteristic in society in general, where long-term relationships in families and the workplace are increasingly rare, reducing personal loyalty and commitment among individuals and institutions. In the world of organized crime, this is a further argument to distinguish the acts of organized crime from the offenders who engage in it. The acts have remained quite stable, reflecting only changes in opportunity (e.g., the Internet, globalization of commerce), whereas the structure of organized crime (e.g., groups and networks) mirror parallel changes in the social structure.

CRITICAL THINKING EXERCISE 5.2

The following scenarios report on actual events. Using the information provided in this chapter and thus far in the book, answer the questions that follow.

The Case of the Hackers

A hacker claimed that he had the stolen credit card numbers of 300,000 customers of the Web site "CD Universe." The hacker said he was a 19-year-old from Russia. The company refused to pay his ransom demand of $100,000, so he released thousands of credit card numbers over the Internet. In another case, a hacker traced to Russia stole 55,000 credit card numbers from Creditcards.com, a company that processes credit card transactions for online merchants. This hacker's demand for $100,000 was ignored, so he posted 25,000 stolen credit card numbers on the Internet.

A senior at the University of Missouri was arrested on suspicion of using his girlfriend's e-mail account to send out thousands of spam e-mails in an effort to crash the computer network. In another case, a 20-year-old student at the University of Texas was arrested for breaking into the university's computer system and taking the social security numbers and personal information of 55,000 students, faculty, and staff.

These are some of the many cases of systematic efforts to steal credit card numbers and other personal information from nonsecure Web sites. Examining the organization of these crimes is helpful in trying to assess the characteristics of the criminal enterprise that underlie the criminal activity.

Critical Thinking Questions

1. Explain the crimes with which these hackers could be charged.
2. Would you consider these hackers part of organized crime?
3. Given the nature of their criminal conduct, what model of organized crime would best describe these hackers?

Sources: "Companies Warned about Organized Hacker Attacks," USA Today (March 8, 2001); "Texas Student Charged," Information Week (March 14, 2003); "University of Missouri System Hackers Nailed," Intelligence Wire (March 13, 2003).

SUMMARY

Three paradigms, or models, of organized crime include hierarchical, local ethnic, and enterprise models. These models differ in their focus on the nature of organized crime groups versus the nature of organized crime activity. Empirical studies of organized crime suggest that organized crime is less hierarchical and more entrepreneurial than originally thought. Likewise, ethnicity is a means by which groups connect and form trusted bonds rather than the only way in which organized crime forms. Studies find a great deal of interethnic organized crime activity. In all cases, however, organized crime functions as entrepreneurial activity in which economic criminal opportunities are exploited based on their availability, competition from other crime groups, the size of the market for that illegal product, and concerns similar to those of legitimate businesses in the legal marketplace. In the future, it is likely that even less formal, more fluid connections among organized crime interests will exist in order to keep the risk of apprehension low. In addition, the changing nature of communication and illegal products available via the Internet will enable offenders to avoid face-to-face contact with each other and with their victims in many cases. These criminal networks will be more difficult to detect and track, and they are a significant departure from traditional forms of organized crime in the past.

ORGANIZED CRIME BIOGRAPHY

Biographies tell the life story of interesting people. In the world of criminal justice, biographies of organized crime figures offer insight into the background and motivations of the individuals who choose that lifestyle, the reasons for their choices, and their consequences. The following is a brief summary of an organized crime biography, followed by questions that ask you to reflect on the connections between that person's life and the content of this book.

The First Family: Terror, Extortion, Revenge, Murder, and the Birth of the American Mafia
Mike Dash (Ballantine Books, 2010)

The author, a historian, documents the early beginnings of the so-called "Mafia" in America, concentrating on the period from the 1890s through the 1920s. He documents the life of Giuseppe Morello, called the "Clutch Hand" due to his deformed arm, who came to New York with his family from Corleone, Sicily, in 1892.

Morello's criminal operations are fully described, including counterfeiting American and Canadian bills, extorting local businesses, and kidnapping. The author claims that the term "Mafia" was never used by members, but only by outsiders, and was in its early stages during the early 1900s. Morello was killed in 1930, but by that time, several other Mafia groups had emerged in New York and a few other cities.

Although Morello is not widely known today, the author argues that he was the true father of the Mafia in America.

Continued

ORGANIZED CRIME BIOGRAPHY—CONT'D

Rather than Prohibition creating the Mafia, as some accounts have it, the author makes the case that groups of organized gangsters had already formed by then, making them able to exploit the criminal opportunity provided by the prohibition of alcohol in the early 20th century. The author characterizes his subject in this way: "Morello and his henchmen were parasites who terrorized their fellow countrymen, exploited the weak, and dealt in fear." They came to the United States as private citizens, not as part of any existing criminal enterprise, but in order to make a better living they gradually organized into various, and often competing, groups in which

murder was common as a means of enforcement and intimidation was needed to maintain control.

Questions
1. Why do you believe that the U.S. government did not foresee how Prohibition would strengthen organized crime groups?
2. Some historical crime figures, such as Morello, are less well known than others who lived during the same time (e.g., Luciano, Capone). Why do you believe this happens?

ORGANIZED CRIME AT THE MOVIES

Movies seek to entertain and inform the audience about a story, incident, or person. Many good movies also hit upon important substantive themes relevant to understanding organized crime. Read the following movie summary (and watch the movie if you haven't already) and answer the questions that follow to make the organized crime subject matter connections.

Carlito's Way
Brian DePalma, Director (1993)

Carlito's Way is based on two novels by Judge Edwin Torres. Carlito Brigante (Al Pacino) is a Puerto Rican ex-convict who wants to change from his former life as a drug dealer, but he finds it difficult to do so. After serving 5 years in prison, Carlito's attorney, Dave Kleinfeld (Sean Penn), has secured his release due to illegal evidence gathering in the case against him.

Carlito has been a gangster and drug dealer for many years and announces his plans to go straight and open a car dealership in the Bahamas. Carlito is shocked by how his old neighborhood has changed while he was in prison; many of his friends are either dead or in jail. A young cousin is now involved as a low-level drug courier and asks Carlito to back him up on a pending deal. The deal goes bad, the cousin is killed, and Carlito has to shoot his way out of the situation,

taking the money from the deal with him.

Carlito uses the money to buy into a nightclub owned by a struggling pathological gambler. Carlito manages the club well, turning a profit and saving the money for his planned new life. His lawyer, Kleinfeld, is not doing as well, he's snorting cocaine and drinking heavily. One of his clients is a mobster, Tony Taggalucci, who believes that Kleinfeld has stolen a million dollars from him and intends to use it as a bribe to avoid his current prison sentence. Tony tells Kleinfeld to help him break out of jail or else become the target of a mob hit.

Kleinfeld asks Carlito for help in the escape plan for Tony. During the escape, Kleinfeld decides to kill both Tony and his son and dump them into the river. Carlito knows the mob will come after them so he plans to leave town earlier than expected with his girlfriend Gail (Penelope Ann Miller). His preparations are interrupted by a call into the prosecutor's office, where he learns that Kleinfeld has offered to testify against Carlito. The prosecutor realizes, however, that Kleinfeld is a more serious criminal than Carlito, but Carlito refuses to cut a deal.

Instead, he goes to the hospital where Kleinfeld is recovering from an assault, and Kleinfeld admits to betraying Carlito. Carlito secretly unloads Kleinfeld's gun in the

ORGANIZED CRIME AT THE MOVIES—CONT'D

hospital room, and Tony's surviving son later kills Kleinfeld in the hospital.

Carlito goes to his nightclub to get money to leave town, but is confronted by a group of mobsters who want to know if he was involved in the killing of Tony, and he is caught in a lie. Carlito manages to escape from the club, and a major chase ensues through New York City's subway system, where Carlito almost makes the train out of town where Gail is waiting. It becomes clear that Carlito's failure to heed warnings about danger from others was a fatal flaw. Carlito manages to hand Gail the money to start a new life before he dies.

Questions
1. Why do you think Carlito actively sought to leave the criminal life, whereas many others, such as Henry Hill, never make that decision? Explain the reasons why it is difficult for Carlito to escape his prior life as a career criminal.
2. What paradigm of organized crime is portrayed in this movie?

References and Notes

1. *Jacobellis v. Ohio*, 84 S. Ct. 1676 (1964).

2. Rogovin, C. H., & Martens, F. T. (1992). The Evil That Men Do. *Journal of Contemporary Criminal Justice*, *8*(February), 62–79.

3. U.S. Senate Special Committee to Investigate Organized Crime in Interstate Commerce (1951). *Third Interim Report*. Washington, DC: U.S. Government Printing Office, p. 2.

4. Bell, D. (1953). Crime as an American Way of Life. *The Antioch Review*, *13*(June), 131–154; Moore, W. H. (1974). *The Kefauver Committee and the Politics of Crime, 1950–1952*. Columbia, MO: University of Missouri Press.

5. U.S. Senate Committee on Government Operations Permanent Subcommittee on Investigations (1965). *Report on Organized Crime and Illicit Traffic in Narcotics*. Washington, DC: U.S. Government Printing Office, p. 117.

6. U.S. Senate Committee on Government Operations Permanent Subcommittee on Investigations. *Report on Organized Crime and Illicit Traffic in Narcotics*, p. 12.

7. U.S. Senate Committee on Government Operations Permanent Subcommittee on Investigations. *Organized Crime and Illicit Traffic in Narcotics: Hearings Part I*. Washington, DC: U.S. Government Printing Office, pp. 80, 215.

8. U.S. Senate Committee on Government Operations Permanent Subcommittee on Investigations. *Organized Crime and Illicit Traffic in Narcotics: Hearings Part I*, p. 13.

9. U.S. Senate. *Report on Organized Crime and Illicit Traffic in Narcotics*, p. 117.

10. U.S. Senate. *Report on Organized Crime and Illicit Traffic in Narcotics*, p. 117.

11. Block, A. A. (1978). History and the Study of Organized Crime. *Urban Life*, *6*, 455–474; Nelli, H. S. (1981). *The Business of Crime: Italians and Syndicate Crime in the United States*. Chicago, IL: University of Chicago Press.

12. Anderson, A. G. (1979). *The Business of Organized Crime*. Stanford, CA: Hoover Institution Press, p. 44; Haller, M. H. (1991). *Life under Bruno: The Economics of an Organized Crime Family*. Conshohocken, PA: Pennsylvania Crime Commission.

13. Demaris, O. (1981). *The Last Mafioso*. New York: Bantam, pp. 20–22; U.S. Senate Committee on Governmental Affairs Permanent Subcommittee on Investigations (1981). *Organized Crime and Violence: Hearings Part I*. Washington, DC: U.S. Government Printing Office, p. 88.

14. Kelly, R. J. (1992). Trapped in the Folds of Discourse: Theorizing About the Underworld. *Journal of Contemporary Criminal Justice, 8*(February), 11–35.

15. President's Commission on Law Enforcement and Administration of Justice (1967). *Task Force Report: Organized Crime.* Washington, DC: U.S. Government Printing Office; Cressey, D. R. (1969). *Theft of the Nation.* New York: Harper & Row.

16. Gotti, J. (1992). *The Gotti Tapes.* New York: Times Books.

17. *The Gotti Tapes,* pp. 134–135.

18. *The Gotti Tapes,* pp. 146–149.

19. Reuter, P. (1983). *Disorganized Crime: The Economics of the Visible Hand.* Cambridge, MA: MIT Press; Adler, P. A. (1985). *Wheeling and Dealing: An Ethnography of an Upper-Level Drug Dealing and Smuggling Community.* New York: Columbia University Press; Arlacchi, P. (1986). *Mafia Business: The Mafia Ethic and the Spirit of Capitalism.* London, UK: Verso; Finckenauer, J., & Waring, E.(2001). *Russian Mafia in America.* Boston, MA: Northeastern University Press.

20. U.S. Department of Justice (2013). *Aryan Brotherhood of Texas Gang Member Pleads Guilty to Federal Racketeering Charges.* Washington, DC: Office of Public Affairs, September 9.

21. Marimow, A. E., & Hermann, P. "How the Black Guerrilla Family Gang Took Root in Maryland's Prisons," *The Washington Post* (July 15, 2013), 3; Mikutis, M. J. (2013). Prison Gangs. In J. Albanese (Ed.), *Encyclopedia of Criminology and Criminal Justice.* Malden, MA: Wiley-Blackwell.

22. Abadinsky, H. (1981). *The Mafia in America: An Oral History.* New York: Praeger; Albini, J. L. (1971). *The American Mafia: Genesis of a Legend.* New York: Irvington, p. 289; Reuter, P., Rubinstein, J., & Wynn, S. (1983). *Racketeering in Legitimate Industries: Two Case Studies.* Washington, DC: National Institute of Justice; Smith, D. C. (1978). Organized Crime and Entrepreneurship. *International Journal of Criminology and Penology, 6,* 161–177.

23. Albini, *The American Mafia: Genesis of a Legend,* p. 288.

24. Ianni, F. A. J., & Ianni, E. R. (1972). *A Family Business: Kinship and Social Control in Organized Crime.* New York: New American Library, p. 20.

25. Abadinsky, *The Mafia in America;* Albini, *The American Mafia;* Anderson, *The Business of Organized Crime;* Ianni and Reuss-Ianni, *A Family Business;* Adler, *Wheeling and Dealing;* Chin, K.-l. and Zhang, S. (November 2002). Enter the Dragon: Inside Chinese Human Smuggling Organization. *Criminology, 40,* 737.

26. U.S. Senate. *Organized Crime and Illicit Traffic in Narcotics: Hearings Part I,* pp. 116, 194.

27. L'Hoiry, X. D. (2013). "Shifting the Stuff Wasn't Any Bother": Illicit Enterprise, Tobacco Bootlegging and Deconstructing the British Government's Cigarette Smuggling Discourse. *Trends in Organized Crime, 16,* 413–434.

28. Smith, *"Organized Crime and Entrepreneurship,"* pp. 161–177; Smith, D. C. (1980). Paragons, Pariahs, and Pirates: A Spectrum-Based Theory of Enterprise. *Crime & Delinquency, 26*(July), 358–386; Smith, D. C. (1990). *The Mafia Mystique* (revised ed.). Lanham, MD: University Press of America; Gottschalk, P. (2009). *Entrepreneurship and Organized Crime: Entrepreneurs in Illegal Business.* Northampton, MA: Edward Elgar.

29. *Wheeling and Dealing,* p. 80.

30. *Wheeling and Dealing,* p. 82.

31. *Disorganized Crime,* p. 176.

32. Paoli, L. (2002). The Paradoxes of Organized Crime. *Crime, Law and Social Change, 37,* 51–97.

33. Windle, J. (2013). Tuckers Firm: A Case Study of British Organised Crime. *Trends in Organized Crime, 16,* 382–396; also quoting Smith, D. C. (1980). Paragons, Pariahs, and Pirates: A Spectrum-Based Theory of Enterprise. *Crime & Delinquency, 26,* 358.

34. Dumke, M. "Heroin, LLC," *Chicago Reader* (December 4, 2013); New Jersey State Commission of Investigation. *Scenes from an Epidemic: A Report on the SCI's Investigation of Prescription Pill and Heroin Abuse*. www.state.nj.us/sci/pdf/PillsReport.pdf, July.

35. Block, A. A. (1979). The Snowman Cometh: Coke in Progressive New York. *Criminology, 17* (May), 75–99.

36. English, T. J. (1991). *The Westies*. New York: St. Martin's Press, pp. 136–178.

37. Anderson. *The Business of Organized Crime*, pp. 66, 117.

38. Goldstock, R., Marcus, M., Thacher, T. D., & Jacobs, J. B. (1990). *Corruption and Racketeering in the New York City Construction Industry*. New York: New York University Press, p. 31.

39. *Racketeering in Legitimate Industries*, p. 33.

40. Haller. "*Bureaucracy and the Mafia*," p. 7.

41. Haller. "*Bureaucracy and the Mafia*," p. 8; Haller. "*Life Under Bruno*," p. 227.

42. Green, M. (2002). Sex on the Internet: A Legal Click or an Illicit Trick? *California Western Law Review* (Spring), 527; Wolak, J., Mitchell, K., & Finkelhor, D. (2007). Unwanted and Wanted Exposure to Online Pornography in a National Sample of Youth Internet Users. *Journal of the American Academy of Child and Adolescent Psychiatry, 46*(May), 652.

43. Brenner, S. W. (2002). Organized Cybercrime?: How Cyberspace May Affect the Structure of Criminal Relationships. *North Carolina Journal of Law & Technology, 4*(Fall), 29.

44. Chin, K. -l., & Zhang, S. (2002). Enter the Dragon: Inside Chinese Human Smuggling Organization. *Criminology, 40*(November), 737; Finckenauer, J. O., & Waring, E. (2001). *Russian Mafia in America: Immigration, Culture, and Crime*. Boston, MA: Northeastern University Press; Llewellyn, H. (2005). Spain Steps Up Piracy Fight. *Billboard, 117*(May), 14; Levi, M. (2008). Organized Fraud and Organizing Frauds: Unpacking Research on Networks and Organization. *Criminology & Criminal Justice: An International Journal, 8*, 389–419.

45. Bjelopera, J. P., & Finklea, K. M. (2012). *Organized Crime: An Evolving Challenge for U.S. Law Enforcement*. Washington, DC: Congressional Research Service.

CHAPTER 6

The Mafia
100 Years of Historical Facts and Myths

How many things which served us yesterday as articles of faith, are fables for us today.

—Michel de Montaigne (1580)

Martin Bosshart, age 31, was found dead, shot in the back of the head, on a street corner in Queens, New York. No motive or suspects were found, although Bosshart had been arrested more than a dozen times in the past for crimes relating to a stolen car ring. He was on parole after serving 5 years in prison. Police say he once ran one of the largest Mafia-owned chop shops in Queens, where cars were stolen, dismantled, and parts were sold illicitly.[1]

Bosshart's case is typical of how we hear about the Mafia. It appears to be the result of a feud among gangsters. But how are they organized? How do individual events like this fit into the larger picture of the Mafia and organized crime? Finding the answers to these questions is imperative if an accurate understanding of organized crime is to be established. This chapter examines the origins of the "Mafia" link to organized crime in America and separates myth from reality on the basis of firsthand investigations of the historical record.

The term "Mafia" is synonymous with LCN (La Cosa Nostra), referring primarily to groups of organized crime "families" in the United States and Italy. The members of these groups are of Italian descent and often are unrelated to each other; hence, the term "family" is not descriptive. Nevertheless, the group exists for noncriminal socializing as well as for carrying out criminal acts; they are connected by both their ethnicity and their sworn allegiance to each other (which in recent years has eroded with numerous cases of Mafia members testifying against each other).

THE HENNESSEY MURDER IN NEW ORLEANS, 1890

Interest in a Mafia in the United States can be traced to the murder of David Hennessey in 1890. Hennessey was the superintendent of police in New

Orleans when he was shot and seriously wounded on his front doorstep by a group of unknown assassins. His deathbed statement was said to be either "Sicilians have done for me" or "Dagoes," which was interpreted as indicating an Italian connection with his death.

Seventeen Italian immigrants were arrested as a result of this alleged statement, and they were called part of a "Sicilian Assassination League." The prime count of murder against nine of the defendants was the first to come to trial. Before the trial, however, the prosecution dropped its case against one of the defendants, and the judge directed a verdict of acquittal against another due to lack of evidence. Nevertheless, it was widely assumed that the other seven suspects would be convicted, but they were not.[2]

On March 13, 1891, the jury acquitted four of them, and a mistrial was declared in the case of the other three. The citizens of New Orleans were outraged by this apparent miscarriage of justice. Soon after the trial, a mass town meeting was called, which turned into an angry mob. The crowd marched on the jail, broke into it, shot 9 of the 11 defendants, and publicly hanged two others. In response, the Italian government recalled its foreign minister to the United States in protest. Diplomatic relations were resumed, however, when the United States made an indemnity payment to the Italian government.

Most contemporary explanations now indicate that Hennessey's death was actually the result of a business rivalry between two Italian families: the Matrangas and the Provenzanos.[3] The Provenzanos controlled the dock areas of New Orleans, but the Matrangas had begun to take business away from them. In early 1890, several of Matranga's workers were killed or wounded, and the Provenzanos were accused. In July 1890, several of the Provenzanos were convicted, but a new trial was subsequently ordered due to inconclusive identification of the suspects. The Matrangas objected to this and were especially unhappy with Police Chief Hennessey, who supported the Provenzanos during the trial and who was thought to have influenced the judge in setting aside the verdict.

At the retrial of the Provenzanos, Hennessey was scheduled to testify against the Matrangas, claiming that they were part of a Mafia in New Orleans. Hennessey was, of course, shot before he testified, and many concluded that his death proved that a Mafia existed. In the eventual retrial of the Provenzanos, however, the Mafia issue was never raised, and there has never been any hint that Hennessey ever had any evidence of a New Orleans Mafia. If such evidence existed, it never came out, either before or after his death.

During this period, many people in North America generally assumed that some sort of Mafia existed in Italy (or Sicily). As a corollary to this belief, it was commonly held that if there was a Mafia there, some of its members were probably included in the mass of immigrants from southern Italy during the 1880s.[4] As a result, a common explanation given for these murders was lax immigration controls that permitted entry to North America of numerous ex-convicts and criminals escaping from Italian justice.[5]

THE ITALIAN CONNECTION

In the late 1800s, it was claimed that there were many unsolved murders of Italians in New Orleans—fueling belief in a Mafia. However, less than four Italian deaths per year have been documented. As Dwight Smith has observed, "In retrospect, it appears that a desire to believe in a local Mafia society outstripped any objective investigation of fact. Shreds of evidence—even hearsay assertions—that would support the theory were accepted without reservation, and contrary evidence was ignored."[6]

In addition, because local feelings were very much anti-immigrant during this period, it would not be surprising that Hennessey's death caused an anti-Italian campaign. It was said during this period that more than 1,000 Italian immigrants with criminal records in Italy had come to the United States during the previous few years. However, a grand jury investigation of the lynching of the Italians charged with Hennessey's murder found that only about 300 Italian immigrants had been offenders in Italy; most were petty offenders. In any case, this total of 300 was less than 1% of the Italian population of New Orleans. In some ways, assertions of an imported Italian Mafia were similar to allegations made against more recent immigrant groups, such as Cubans, Mexicans, and Asians, that they are somehow part of a criminal conspiracy.

Despite these facts, many people continue to believe, even today, that a Mafia was somehow imported to North America from Italy. Now, it is only possible to examine this claim through historical investigations. Fortunately, a number of these have been conducted to determine the existence of a Mafia in Italy and/or its importation to North America.

Sociologist Joseph Albini conducted an investigation based on archival data and information provided by confidential informants gathered in both Italy and the United States. In a book entitled *The American Mafia: Genesis of a Legend*, he attempted to examine the historical basis for the popular belief that a Mafia exists in Sicily, which somehow formed the basis for a similar organization in the United States. Albini found no formal organization that could be called a Mafia. Instead he found there was a less organized arrangement.

> It is not a centralized, highly complex national and international organization with a supreme head in Palermo. It does not have a rigidly defined hierarchy of positions. It does not have specific rules and rituals. In other words it has none of the characteristics generally attributed to it in popular and clandestine descriptions. In noting the absence of these characteristics the author is not alone, as evidenced by the agreement found in the works of Pitre [1904],

Barzini [1954], Bruno [1900], Sladen [1907], Hood [1916], King and Okey [1901], Neville [1964], Candida [1964], Maxwell [1960], Paton [1900], Monroe [1909], Pantaleone [1966] to mention only a few.[7]

As Albini notes, numerous authors before him found a similar result: rather than a formal organization called "Mafia" in Italy, there is much evidence to indicate that persons considered "mafioso" came about during the 1800s in Sicily, when feudalism was legally abolished. The end of feudalism resulted in a large class of landowners (who had land to be cultivated) and a large class of peasants (who could now cultivate the land if they paid rent to the landowner). This situation led to the demand for a person who could (1) make sure that the landowner received an adequate yearly rent for his land and (2) provide protection for the landowner because the government could not guarantee it. As a result, a middleman called a "gambellotto" or "mafioso" emerged who provided protection for landowners, while ensuring that the peasants paid for their use of the land. As Albini discovered,

> By using violence, by subjugating the tenant into accepting impossible leases, by extorting the small farmer with threats of attacks upon person and property, the "gambellotto" entrenched himself in a patronage system which continues today. As a client to his landowner in return for certain favors he promised continued suppression of the peasant. As a patron to the peasant he promised work and the continuation of contracts.[8]

This system of protection and patronage provided by the "gambellotto" or "mafioso" was not a centralized or organized system. In fact, Albini did not find evidence of an organization called "Mafia," but rather, the term "Mafia" refers to the role of the mafioso in Sicilian society.

> "Mafia" then is not an organization. It is a system of patron-client relationships that interweaves legitimate and illegitimate segments of Sicilian society. "Mafioso" is not a rank or position within a secret organization. Rather it represents a type of position within the patron-client relationship of Sicilian society itself.[9]

It is useful to examine the work of subsequent investigators who conducted independent historical investigations using different methods in their research.

Henner Hess published the results of his historical investigation into Italian organized crime in a book entitled *Mafia and Mafiosi: The Structure of Power*, where he examined Sicilian archives of police reports and trial transcripts from the period 1880-1890. Hess found "there is no organisation, no secret society called mafia."[10] Instead, there was the mafioso type, which existed in Sicily due to Italy's weak central government, located far from Sicily. "The moral, social, economic and geographical conditions of Western Sicily, combined with the decisive political factor of a weak central power situated outside Sicily, thus led to the emergence and continued existence of a mafioso self-help which stepped into a power vacuum" to enforce contracts and other relationships that the state could not carry out effectively. Hess concluded that "Mafia is neither an organisation nor a secret society, but a method."[11] Like Albini, Hess saw the idea of a Mafia as a general term applied to these individuals who provided "protection" and other services to citizens that the government was unable to provide.

In other research, Hess found that it is "easy to misinterpret [the actions of mafiosi] as actions planned and supervised by a single command group." This is because these individuals have similar interests. He uncovered no evidence of a central organization that controlled mafiosi; rather, he found evidence of individual mafiosi who shared "the same profession and the same problems" and who occasionally "turn to each other as to colleagues for help."[12]

Anton Blok published an anthropological study of a Sicilian village entitled *The Mafia of a Sicilian Village, 1860-1960*. Blok's study followed the emergence of the concept and role of a Mafia through an examination of archival data.

Similar to the findings of Albini and Hess, Blok found the emergence of a Mafia in Italy to be the result of tensions among the central government of Italy, landowners, and peasants.

> Mafia emerged in the early 19th century when the Bourbon State tried to curb the power of the traditional landowning aristocracy and encouraged the emancipation of the peasantry. . . . Feudal rights and privileges were abolished by law, and the peasants were offered a prospect of land which had become marketable. This so-called anti-feudal policy touched off tensions between the central government and the landowners, who sought to maintain their control over both the land and the peasants . . . "mafiosi" were recruited from the ranks of the peasantry to provide the large estate owners with armed staffs to confront both the impact of the State and the restive peasants, especially in the inland areas of the island where the Bourbon State failed to monopolize the use of physical power.[13]

According to Blok, therefore, mafiosi came about due to the need for power brokers to mediate between the landowners and the weak central government, which was attempting to alter the long-standing privileges of the landowners, and between the landowners and the peasants, whom the government was attempting to liberate.

> Even after the unification of Italy, the State failed to monopolize the use of physical force in large areas of western Sicily and, therefore, could not hope to enforce legislation. . . . "Mafia" was born of the tensions between the central government and local landowners on the one hand, and between the latter and peasants on the other.[14]

Blok did not find evidence of an organization called the "Mafia," but uncovered evidence of private citizens who found themselves in a position to gain by using violence to control a political situation. So Albini, Hess, and Blok each found the "Mafia" to be a term applied to individuals who were employed by private citizens for protection. They did not find evidence that these "mafiosi" were coordinated or organized in any systematic way.

Still another investigation was summarized in a book entitled *Mafioso*, published by journalist Gaia Servadio. The book attempted to assess the historical accuracy of a belief in an Italian Mafia. Interestingly, Servadio's findings concur with those of previous investigators:

> When Sicily became part of the new-born state of Italy in 1860 it had been under continual foreign occupation for more than two thousand years. ... To the outsider, Sicilian society appeared brutal, corrupt and secretive. It was not difficult to lump these qualities together, and in fact it was during the decade of 1860-70 that the myth of a "secret society" was born and baptized. Italy, and soon Europe, discovered "the Mafia."[15]

Like Albini, Hess, and Blok, Servadio saw "the Mafia" as the result of the inability of a central government to deal effectively with the people of Sicily who, historically, had resisted foreign occupation by an outside government. She goes on to note how the idea of a secret society may have come about.

> For an administrator or policeman confronted with the complex criminal machinery of Sicilian society the conspiratorial notion of a mysterious secret entity made a kind of sense, and glossed over any more far-reaching speculations. They saw the symptoms, but diagnosed the wrong disease. If the Mafia were in fact a secret society, it would be long defunct. Even a weak police force would have uncovered names and details of its organization, and the Mafia whose rise we have traced is not secret: on the contrary, it thrives on publicity.[16]

Servadio points out it is improbable that a secret society could have survived, especially when the acts of mafiosi thrive on publicity (i.e., violence or murders are rarely kept secret; under most circumstances, it is desired that the evidence be discovered to serve as an example of influence or power).[17]

A fifth historical investigation of the roots of the Mafia was published by Italian sociologist Pino Arlacchi. Using archival data that included official inquiries and court records, he found the "mafia was a form of behaviour and a kind of power, not a formal organization."[18] Arlacchi found, like the investigators before him, that individuals, called mafioso, emerged as power brokers due to a weak central government. Given the conditions "typical of the local community, there was very little security of property, wealth or person, anyone who owned anything had to entrust its protection to the leading mafioso of the area."[19] Those refusing to pay protection money suffered from fires, robberies, vandalism, and, occasionally, murder. Therefore, Arlacchi's investigation of the origins of the Mafia drew conclusions similar to those of Albini, Hess, Blok, and Servadio: the term "Mafia" describes an individual criminal lifestyle, rather than an organization.

A sixth historical investigation was conducted of the origins of organized crime in northern Italy rather than in Sicily. Sociologist James Walston examined court records, police archives, and newspaper sources and conducted interviews to examine the nature of organized crime in Naples, Italy, during the nineteenth and twentieth centuries. Walston examined the origins of the "Camorra," a term used to describe Neapolitan organized crime. He found that "there has been organized crime in Naples since the beginning of the [nineteenth] century." He discovered that the "rise to a position of power and prestige of Neapolitan gangsters has not changed" over the years and, in fact, "it is a similar path taken by mafiosi and gangsters everywhere."[20]

Nevertheless, "Neapolitan society is too fragmented, as indeed one would expect a city of two million people to be, to allow a single figure [or group] to control the whole or even a fractional part of the whole" of political power necessary for the protection of organized crime activities. In the villages around Naples, Walston found "gangsters might control the local council. . . . But in the city and region as a whole there is too great a heterogeneity for one social group to gain control."[21]

Although there is much evidence of continuing organized crime activity by "Camorra" groups, Walston expressed doubts about the existence of a "strictly ordered secret society" that has continued for several hundred years. First, the education level of organized criminals and the very high illiteracy rate cast doubt that they are "sufficiently literate" to write or read rules. Second, an ordered society governed by "codes" or internal "laws" would be quite vulnerable to police discovery once the "secret is out." Third, the "supposed submissiveness of members" to a "code" ignores the fact that "internal conflict within 'the society'" did occur, and continues to occur.[22] Indeed, a continuing "gang war" resulted in the trials in Italy of several hundred defendants originally recruited as members while in prison. Conflicts among these Neapolitan groups have arisen due to resistance to an attempted organization along geographical lines, the profitability of the narcotics trade, and disagreements over control of various illicit markets, such as cigarette smuggling.[23] Similarly, Robert Lombardo found that extortion rackets ("Black Hand" activity) in the Italian-American community in Chicago in the early 1900s was not imported from Sicily as is commonly believed, but instead has its roots in America.[24]

Testimony from Tommaso Buscetta, a Sicilian organized crime figure who became a government informant in 1985, put all this historical research into perspective when he testified that there was no central organization of criminal groups in Sicily until the 1950s. Interestingly, the suggestion for such an organization, according to Buscetta, was made by Joseph Bonanno, a well-known American organized crime figure. The purpose for the organization of criminal groups (via a "commission") was "to resolve disputes" among the various criminal groups.[25] The "commission" in Sicily did not last very long, however, and continuing disputes among criminal groups over territory, control, and markets resulted in mass trials of defendants there during the 1980s.

Each of the separate historical investigations discussed here, as well as others, has ended with similar conclusions.[26] First, none found evidence of a single organization called "Mafia" in Italy. Rather, it is a "collection of groups."[27] Second, the violence attributed to a Mafia in Italy appears to have resulted from individuals filling the need for power brokers among the conflicting interests of the government, landowners, and peasants. Therefore, it is more accurate to think of the Mafia as a loose collection of individual criminals and criminal groups than as a single entity.

In recent years, organization of the Mafia in Sicily has taken on new importance. The so-called "Pizza Connection" case in New York established that Sicilian Mafia figures had conspired with American Mafia figures to import heroin through pizza parlors in the United States. Tons of morphine were smuggled from Turkey to Sicily, processed there into heroin, and then smuggled through U.S. airports.[28] This case prompted a realization on the part of U.S. investigators that, regardless of the form, organized criminals did engage in mutually beneficial arrangements, sometimes on an international scale.[29] The Mafia "maxi-trial" in Sicily during the 1980s charged 464 defendants with multiple murders and with operation of a worldwide heroin ring covering the years 1975-1985. In Italy, this was momentous for two reasons: Mafia members and names were made public and never before had such a huge trial occurred. Tomasso Buscetta testified, as he did in the Pizza Connection trial in New York. A total of 1,337 witnesses testified, and 342 of the defendants were convicted. From the Italian point of view, "this was the first serious assault ever made on the entire, infinitely complex Mafia phenomenon."[30] It also prompted recognition that, regardless of its structure, some Sicilian organized crime figures were now operating worldwide. Mafia groups struck back at the government in 1992 when they killed two Italian judges with bombs, but this had the effect of strengthening the resolve in Italy to continue its prosecution efforts against organized crime.[31]

This prosecution effort continued with the conviction of 97 members of the Ndrangheta crime "family," after a 4-year trial. This Mafia group operated out of Calabria in southern Italy. They were found guilty of 20 murders, extortion, drug smuggling, and other crimes. Thirteen of the members received life terms, with other sentences totaling 460 years.[32]

Most Italian organized crime, like its American counterpart, remains primarily local in nature. The confession of Antonio Calderone, an alleged "boss" of a Mafia group in Sicily, illustrates this. The city of Palermo has long been known to be the most active Mafia city in Sicily, and Calderone claims "there are more than 50 of them [Mafia families], at least one for each neighborhood" in Palermo.[33] But he claims, "a family is autonomous in its own territory."[34] Therefore, the organization of organized crime can be characterized as locally based, but its activities, especially in recent years, can span the globe. According to the U.S. Drug Enforcement Administration, alliances have been struck between several Sicilian Mafia "families" and drug cartels in Colombia.[35]

FROM CITY GANGS TO A NATIONAL CONSPIRACY

After the Hennessey murder in 1890, and subsequent lynchings of the Italian suspects, public interest in a Mafia faded quickly. In fact, during the 25-year period from 1918 to 1943, the word "Mafia" appeared in *The New York Times* only four times.

During the early 1900s, there existed concern about organized crime, but not about the Mafia. John Landesco's work for the Illinois Crime Survey in 1929 is illustrative of this. His examination of "Organized Crime in Chicago" found crime "organized on a scale and with resources unprecedented in the history of Chicago." He found that the "leading gangsters were practically immune from punishment" and that organized crime had corrupted local politicians.[36] This report identified gangsters by name, including Giacomo "Big Jim" Colosimo, who ran the rackets up until his murder in 1920, followed by John Torrio, who organized a bootlegging syndicate from 1920 to 1924, followed by Al Capone, who consolidated all forms of commercialized vice and gambling in Chicago during the late 1920s.[37]

Ironically, concern about these "gangsters" was seen as a local phenomenon rather than a problem of any national significance. A similar situation existed in New York during the early 1900s. Keep in mind that this was the era of Prohibition (the period between 1920 and 1933 in the United States when the laws, passed pursuant to the 18th Amendment to the U.S. Constitution [1920], prohibited the making or selling of alcoholic liquors). Prohibition is probably more responsible than any single event for the emergence of strong organized crime groups. Organized crime developed around the underground market created by the void left between the public demand for alcoholic beverages (and the other vices of gambling and prostitution) and the prohibition of them.

Illegal alcohol manufacturing, smuggling, and operation of speakeasies were predominant forms of organized crime during this period as Prohibition took effect in January 1920. Brewers of alcoholic beverages had a choice in 1920: shut down, convert their equipment to make legal one-half percent liquor, or do business as usual by becoming partners with questionable people who would market their product. Organized crime groups slowly evolved into more sophisticated criminal enterprises, as was made necessary by competition from other criminal entrepreneurs, to evade law enforcement and to bribe public officials when necessary. This evolution was slow, as evidenced by the fact that most local crime leaders of this period did not die natural deaths. Gang warfare was common, as mostly uneducated, first- or second-generation immigrants attempted to make their fortune. In Chicago, Giacomo "Big Jim" Colosimo was murdered by Johnny Torrio's people before Prohibition was 6 months old. Torrio was later to be shot five times, but lived because his assassin ran out of bullets. He left for New York to become a mentor to the up-and-coming Lucky Luciano. Hymie Weis controlled part of Chicago's vices, with Al Capone as his primary competitor. Weis was killed by Al Capone's gang in 1926.[38] Given the profits from the Prohibition era, the Chicago "Outfit" was a powerful force in Chicago crime and politics for the next 50 years.[39]

CRITICAL THINKING EXERCISE 6.1

The Case of Al Capone Versus John Gotti

The criminal careers of Al Capone and John Gotti had many interesting parallels. Al Capone's career as a leader of a criminal group in Chicago lasted for a few years during the 1920s and 1930s, while Gotti's leadership career in New York City also was brief at the end of the 1980s into the 1990s. Both men ran "gangs" of adult men, specialized in hijacking, and competed with rival crime groups in their cities. In Capone's case, hijacking focused on alcoholic beverages, whereas Gotti hijacked trucks carrying clothing and other types of goods that could be resold illegally as stolen property. Both were uneducated men and were big gamblers, losing a lot of money. Both men were popular in their neighborhoods, often more popular than the politicians of their day because their neighborhoods were "safe" from other criminals (most of the violence occurred between members of rival groups that did not involve the general public). Capone fed the poor during the depression in a soup kitchen, and Gotti put on free fireworks shows on the fourth of July, adding to their popularity as local "heroes" who earned respect out of fear.

Both Capone and Gotti were violent. Instead of dividing up territory or negotiating agreements with rival criminal groups, they murdered rivals and anyone perceived to be a threat to them. Their propensity toward violence ultimately served to focus the government's attention on them, resulting in their conviction and imprisonment. Both Capone and Gotti took pride in their appearance, dressed well, and liked to have their pictures taken, which added to their celebrity status, but also focused police attention on them. They are the only two crime figures to appear on the cover of *Time* magazine. Finally, both were convicted and sentenced to long jail terms in the most secure prisons of their time (Alcatraz and Marion) based on the testimony of former criminal comrades. Ironically, both died before their sentences were completed, Capone from complications from syphilis and Gotti from throat cancer.

Critical Thinking Questions

1. Given the similarities between Al Capone and John Gotti, why was Capone considered to be a Chicago "gangster" or "hoodlum," while Gotti was considered a leader of the Mafia?
2. Why do you believe other organized crime figures have not tried to become as high profile as Al Capone or John Gotti?

In New York, the story was similar. Arnold Rothstein organized the vices there and mentored such infamous figures as Frank Costello and Jack "Legs" Diamond.[40] An attempt on the life of Frank Costello failed. Legs Diamond was shot and recovered, only to be challenged by Dutch Schultz. Rothstein himself was ultimately murdered in 1928, a crime blamed on Legs Diamond.[41] Dutch Schultz was later murdered by Charles "Lucky" Luciano in 1935.[42]

It may be difficult to remember who murdered whom during this period, but the general point is clear.[43] Organized crime in the early 1900s was centered around the vices (especially alcohol), involved a great deal of corruption to maintain a degree of immunity from law enforcement, and the competition to control these vices was violent, at least in selected large cities. In describing Luciano's mob in the 1920s, whose crimes included bootlegging, drugs, and brothels, there may have been as many as 200 men, but as one historian concluded, "it should be emphasized that the structure was very loose. Anybody searching for an organizational chart with lines of authority would be disappointed."[44] This violence, and the reign of these gangs, declined somewhat as the Great Depression took hold in 1930 and law enforcement slowly became professionalized and more effective, followed by the end of Prohibition in December 1933.[45] The Depression took much of their customers' income, and the repeal of Prohibition dried up the huge illegal alcohol market. Despite these setbacks, however, many organized crime groups maintained themselves largely on the illicit profits made by gambling. As a historical account concluded, these gangsters "never managed to create an all-powerful, national syndicate that was imagined by their opponents," yet Prohibition forced gangsters to become more organized in handling their supply, demand, the threat of enforcement, and dealing with competitors.[46]

THE KEFAUVER HEARINGS, 1950

It was not until 1950 that the term "Mafia" made a dramatic return to the headlines. U.S. Senator Estes Kefauver chaired the Special Senate Committee to Investigate Organized Crime in the United States (Kefauver Committee). The committee spent 12 months holding public hearings in major cities across the country. Kefauver's investigation received much attention because there was live television coverage of the hearings (at a time when television was new and there were very few channels to choose from). A number of law enforcement officials testified, as did a number of individuals with criminal records. Interestingly, all the criminal offenders denied membership in, or knowledge of, a Mafia, while the law enforcement officials claimed such an organization existed, although they offered no objective evidence to substantiate their belief. Despite these conflicting views and lack of evidence, the Kefauver Committee concluded,

> There is a sinister criminal organization known as the Mafia operating throughout the country with ties in other nations in the opinion of the committee. The Mafia is a direct descendant of a criminal organization of the same name originating in the island of Sicily. ... The Mafia is a loose-knit organization ... the binder which ties together the two major criminal syndicates as well as numerous other criminal groups throughout the country.[47]

William Moore, a historian, conducted an extensive investigation of the Kefauver Committee, and he found that the political environment at the time worked against the possibility of conducting any significant investigation into the true nature of organized crime. Because the committee was created at a time when there were "rampant fears and rumors about politico-criminal conspiracies," Moore found that the Kefauver Committee did not investigate the problem so much as it dramatized it.

> Particularly in the case of the Mafia, the senators lacked adequate evidence for their conclusions. Because such groups as the press and the academic community failed to point out the weaknesses in the Committee's overblown and unfounded statements, the public accepted them, and the popular myths and misunderstandings grew stronger, buttressed by the "proofs" of the Kefauver Committee. Sensational journalists and publishers enjoyed a field day ... gangster movies and television programs dramatized variations of the same theme. ... Even after the initial shock and novelty of the Kefauver findings had lifted and critics began to question the more sweeping Committee statements, the public at large continued to hold to the older conspiracy view, thus making more difficult an intelligent appraisal of organized crime.[48]

The Kefauver Committee adopted the conspiratorial view that most organized crime was controlled by a single Mafia. It "implied that [the Mafia] essentially originated outside of American society and was imposed upon the public by a group of immoral men, bound together by a mysterious ethnic conspiracy." As William Moore discovered, the Kefauver Committee "unquestionably exaggerated the degree of centralization in the underworld." Treating organized crime as a conspiracy rather than as a social and economic problem allowed the committee to focus on legal remedies and to dismiss underlying factors that give rise to organized crime. In discussing gambling, the Kefauver Committee even suggested that "those who supported legalization might themselves be part of an underworld plot."[49]

Even more disconcerting, in the view of historian William Moore, was the fact that the Kefauver Committee misled the public into believing that a thorough investigation of organized crime had taken place when, in fact, it had not.

> If it is unfair to criticize the Committee for an investigation it did not make, it is hardly unjust to point out that they did not make it and that the scope of their authoritative judgment should have been lessened by that failure. The real tragedy, of course, is that the public thought such a study had been made, and popular opinion being set, later investigations enjoyed less flexibility for reeducating the public.[50]

As a result, the Kefauver Committee, largely through its televised hearings in various parts of the country, brought the concept of Mafia to the forefront of public concern, but added nothing to what little was known about the nature and causes of organized crime in America. As Joseph Albini remarked, Kefauver did not prove the existence of the Mafia. Rather, he "merely assumed its existence."[51]

Other investigations have subsequently examined the evidence that exists to support the claims of the Kefauver Committee. The Kefauver Committee claim that Lucky Luciano was "the czar of a vast and secret underworld government" is characterized by historian Marc Mappen as "simply wrong. By the early 1950s Luciano was an aging man with little power, authority, or wealth."[52]

One of the early critics of the Kefauver Committee was sociologist Daniel Bell.

> Neither the Senate Crime Committee in its testimony, nor Kefauver in his book, presented any real evidence that the Mafia exists as a functioning organization. One finds police officials asserting before the Kefauver Committee their "belief" in the Mafia; the Narcotics Bureau "thinks" that a worldwide dope ring allegedly run by Luciano is part of the Mafia; but the only other real evidence presented . . . is that certain crimes bear "the earmarks of the Mafia."[53]

Bell's conclusion was corroborated by Burton Turkus, a New York prosecutor who broke up the "Murder, Inc." ring, who denied the existence of a unified Mafia.[54]

In place of this conspiratorial view, Daniel Bell offered an alternative explanation for the existence of organized crime based on ethnic succession into positions of political power. Bell argued that it was necessary to look at the waves of immigrant groups that have entered the United States. During the middle 1800s, for example, the Irish comprised the largest group of immigrants, the late 1800s were characterized by German-Jews, and the early 1900s saw a large number of Italian immigrants. Bell claims that as these ethnic groups attempted to enter the mainstream of American life, some of them did so through illegal means. He provides examples of well-known Irish criminals in politics and in the trucking industry, as well as Jewish gangsters in the garment industry in years past. According to Bell, as each ethnic group became established in American life, the next wave of immigrants received the bulk of attention when crimes were perpetrated.

> There is little question that men of Italian origin appeared in most of the leading roles in the high drama of gambling and mobs, just as twenty years ago the children of East European Jews were the most prominent figures in organized crime, and before that individuals of Irish decent were similarly prominent. To some extent statistical accident and the tendency of newspapers to emphasize the few sensational figures gives a greater illusion about the domination of illicit activities by a single ethnic group than all the facts warrant.[55]

The Outfit, the traditional Italian-American organized crime group in Chicago, has also been explained by ethnic succession. A study found that Sicilian mafiosi were not responsible for organized crime in Chicago, and that most of Al Capone's gangsters weren't even Italian. Chicago gangsters did not come from Italy, but from the slum neighborhoods of Chicago, and grew correspondingly to the corrupt politics in Chicago.[56]

Ultimately, following the year-long hearings of the Kefauver Committee, rediscovered interest in the Mafia was not lasting in terms of either public interest or legislative response. But the idea of a Mafia was to return to the public spotlight for good in 1957.

THE APALACHIN INCIDENT, 1957

On November 19, 1957, *The New York Times* had a page-one story headlined, "65 Hoodlums Seized in a Raid and Run Out of Upstate Village." As it turned out, 65 Italians, some with criminal records, were gathered at the home of Joseph Barbara in Apalachin, New York. The incident itself was unremarkable. Speculation about the event was fueled primarily by a lack of information. New York State Police Sergeant Edgar Croswell had set up a roadblock on the only route away from the Barbara home because a large number of unknown guests were visiting a man about whom he had long been suspicious. Sergeant Croswell had no evidence to bring against the men he detained as they left or against those who were found later, inexplicably, in the woods adjoining the Barbara property. He learned the names, addresses, and stated occupations of 58 men (including the Barbaras, father and son) and was able to determine whether any were wanted by police in New York State or in their home jurisdiction. He checked those who drove for valid driver's licenses and those armed for pistol permits, and he searched each vehicle and its occupants, finding nothing incriminating. Beyond that, there was little Croswell could do except let them go. "It was a baffling event, and we can appreciate why, amid all the tantalizing news stories in the first few days after the incident, there were few government leaders willing to be quoted."[57]

There was great interest in finding out what this supposed meeting was all about, which was sparked by election year publicity-seeking in New York State. None of the 65 men at Barbara's house would talk to government officials or say that it was anything more than a friendly visit, but John Cusack, New York district director of the Federal Narcotics Bureau, testified in early 1958 before a committee of the New York State legislature. Rather than discuss the fact that eight of the men at Joseph Barbara's house had previous drug convictions, he attempted to link the meeting with a Mafia. No other witness mentioned the Mafia, but it raised the specter of Mafia in a government forum for the first time since the Kefauver hearings.[58]

The New York State committee incorporated Cusack's allegations in its interim report, claiming that "the Apalachin meeting ... is strong evidence that there exists in this country an active association or organization of criminals whose operations are nationwide and international."[59] When the report was submitted to the New York State legislature in April 1958, the media reported that the Apalachin incident was considered to be a "gathering of the Grand Council of the Mafia." In this way, Cusack's unsupported allegations were eventually interpreted as the conclusions of an official government investigation.

Despite these assertions, the most striking feature of the entire Apalachin incident was the unwillingness of those gathered to testify before a grand jury or investigative committee about their purpose. Most of Barbara's guests employed the Fifth Amendment protection against self-incrimination and refused to testify.

In the autobiography of reputed organized crime figure Joseph Bonanno, published much later, he claimed that the Apalachin incident was a meeting of leaders of organized crime groups in the New York area to discuss implications of the recent murder of Albert Anastasia. This account may, or may not, be accurate as Joseph Bonanno did not attend the meeting, and it is not clear whether any meeting ever took place at Apalachin.[60]

In May 1958, New York State established the Temporary State Commission of Investigation to uncover the purpose of the alleged meeting at Apalachin.

The commission had subpoena power to force the appearance of reluctant witnesses, and it had the power to grant immunity to prevent witnesses from invoking the Fifth Amendment when testifying about incriminating activities. Of those men that appeared, most refused to testify and were jailed for contempt. Those that did testify gave unsatisfactory answers to the commission, explaining their presence as a "wrong turn" or as a visit to a sick friend. The commission hoped that by jailing the reluctant witnesses for refusing to testify under a grant of immunity, they would eventually hear what they were looking for. Unfortunately, the commission's efforts were unsuccessful.

By 1959, 14 men had been subpoenaed, 8 were jailed, 2 were fugitives, 1 was contesting the subpoena, and only 3 had chosen to answer the commission's questions. In March 1959, New York State's highest court upheld the jailing of the first seven men. As a result, the men began to answer the questions posed by the commission. Their responses, however, were considered to be "inherently incredible," and the commission continued to hold the men in contempt and held them in jail. In October 1959, New York State's Court of Appeals held that the commission could not continue to hold the men in jail just because it did not like the answers given. The court found "it has not been established that the answers to questions are so preposterous as to offer not the slightest possibility of truthfulness." To hold these men in jail indefinitely, it was thought, could result "in life imprisonment without trial by jury."[61]

Following this decision, the remaining five witnesses also won their release, the last being released after nearly 2 years of confinement. In February 1963, the Temporary State Commission of Investigation released its final report, which reflected the lack of success of its tactics.

> Apalachin attendees subpoenaed to testify at the Commission's public hearings, who refused to answer Commission questions, were confined to jail for various periods ranging up to sixteen months—the only prison term ever served by these major racketeers. Although the full story as to the purpose of the meeting has not been divulged by any participant, much was accomplished by this investigation to shake up the members of this criminal syndicate; many have departed from the State, others have gone into full or semi-retirement and their overall strength and influence in this State has been diminished substantially.[62]

It is clear that the commission attempted, in vain, to justify its actions by referring to the witnesses as "major racketeers," even though none had prison records and no conviction resulting from the commission investigation withstood court review. The Apalachin incident did not die easily, however.

In May 1959, 27 of the men at Barbara's house were indicted for conspiracy to obstruct justice through their failure to explain the meeting at Apalachin. Thirty-six other attendees were named as coconspirators. The trial lasted 8 weeks and consisted of testimony from 69 prosecution witnesses. None of the defendants took the stand. The case went to the jury in December 1959, and all the defendants were found guilty. In June 1960, however, the U.S. Court of Appeals unanimously reversed the convictions. An excerpt from the opinion of Chief Judge Lumbard provides the court's rationale:

> The fact that none of those present admitted that he was asked to attend a meeting for other than social purposes and that at least some of those present must have lied, does not warrant a jury's conclusion that any or all lies were told pursuant to an agreement made [among the attendees]. There is nothing in the record or in common experience to suggest that it is not just as likely that each one present decided for himself that it would be wiser not to discuss all that he knew.
>
> Indeed, the pervasive innuendo throughout this case that this was a gathering of bad people for an evil purpose would seem to us to rebut any possible argument that only as a result of group action would any individual lie. Even an otherwise law abiding citizen who is stopped and interrogated by police, and who is given no reason for his detention and questioning, may feel it his right to give as little information as possible and even perhaps to respond evasively if he believed he might thereby be earlier rid of police inquiry.

The other judges also expressed concern about the apparently indiscriminate roundup of citizens without cause and the supposed link to organized crime that "was given unusual and disturbing publicity." As the court concluded,

> This is vastly unfortunate; not only does it go beyond the judicial record necessary for its support, but it suggests that the administration of the criminal law is in such dire straits that crash methods have become a necessity. But it seems we should have known better, and a prosecution framed on such a doubtful basis should never have been allowed to proceed so far. For in America we still respect the dignity of the individual, and even an unsavory character is not to be imprisoned except on definite proof of specific crime. And nothing in present criminal law administration suggests or justifies sharp relaxation of traditional standards.[63]

The result of the Apalachin episode was much more far-reaching than the substance of the event. Like the Kefauver hearings, a great deal of publicity surrounded the Apalachin incident, and it went a long way toward cementing public attitudes about the nature of organized crime, despite the absence of hard information gathered by either of these events. A subsequent event in 1963 held the spotlight on organized crime.

THE VALACHI HEARINGS AND THE COSA NOSTRA, 1963

In September 1963, Joseph Valachi appeared before the U.S. Senate Sub-committee on Investigations and testified to the existence of a nationwide organization involved in widespread criminal activity. Valachi was an admit-ted lower-level criminal associated with the Genovese crime "family" in New York City. This testimony, together with more detailed information obtained by federal investigators during months of interviews with Valachi, constituted the record of the first time someone had ever admitted "belonging to or openly talking about a huge criminal conspiracy in this country, indeed an entire subculture of evil ... the Cosa Nostra."[64] In addition to providing his view of the structure of organized crime in the United States, Valachi also discussed the processes by which this structure engaged in crime in a systematic manner.

Valachi's testimony was significant because, unlike the Kefauver hearings and the Apalachin incident, it resulted in far-reaching new laws designed to combat organized crime more effectively. His accounts became part of the rationale for legislation permitting widespread use of wiretaps, special grand juries, witness immunity, and other prosecution tools.

When Valachi testified, he told of the existence of activities and organization not previously known to exist by the U.S. government. His willingness to testify resulted, not because of his involvement in these activities, but due to circum-stances beyond his control. Valachi felt he was marked to be killed in prison by his "boss," Vito Genovese. In order to prevent that from happening, he killed a fellow inmate who turned out to be an innocent bystander. To escape the death penalty for his crime, and feeling betrayed by his organization, Valachi agreed to cooperate with federal investigators.

Valachi's testimony before the Permanent Subcommittee on Investigations of the Senate Committee on Government Operations described a number of activ-ities and an organization, providing new information about the nature and extent of organized crime in the United States. The two major subjects covered by Valachi were:

1. A power struggle among Italian-American gangs that took place during the early 1930s, called the Castellammarese War.
2. The existence of a structured organization, called the Cosa Nostra, whose principal activity is to pursue crime.

In addition, Valachi gave the details of a number of murders in New York City, which were confirmed as previously "open" cases by the New York City Police Department.

The veracity of Valachi's testimony became an important issue because of his unsavory past and also because he was facing a murder charge. The primary method used to establish his truthfulness was confirmation by police that the murders he described did indeed occur. During the so-called "Castellammarese War," for example, Valachi stated that up to 60 killings may have taken place. He was able to name only a few, however. Valachi also claimed the Castellammarese War was national in scope but provided no evidence that this was actually the case.

> **Mr. Alderman (counsel to the committee):** Did Masseria declare or condemn
> anybody who came from that area (the Castellammarese area of Sicily),
> no matter where they came from in the United States, to death?
>
> **Mr. Valachi:** All Castellammarese. That is the way I was told. I never found out
> the reason. I never asked for the reason. All I understand is that all the
> Castellammarese were sentenced to death.
>
> **Senator McClellan:** That is when all-out war was declared by the other side?
>
> **Mr. Valachi:** That is, I would put it, national.
>
> **Senator McClellan:** It was made national.
>
> **Mr. Valachi:** It was made in all cities, wherever the members were—in
> Chicago, Cleveland, and California.[65]

The question that arises is how a national war occurred when only a handful of sites were mentioned, and actual events can only be described in one location (New York City). This was not pursued further by the subcommittee. Neither was an alternative account of the same killings given a decade earlier.[66] Inexplicably, there was not even a check as to whether 60 people were killed during this period in the manner Valachi described. Two historical investigations have subsequently confirmed only four or five deaths and no evidence of a national "gangland war."[68] A separate study of homicides in Chicago during the Prohibition era (1919-1933) found similar results. Forty-three percent of the killings were unrelated to organized crime, and only 40% were tied to bootlegging, and the victim was found to belong to one of the major bootlegging gangs in only 40% of those cases. So although violence occurred during this era, the casualties were much smaller than expected.[67]

Valachi's version of events was accepted by senate investigators (and the Justice Department) even though law enforcement officials admitted they had not even heard of a Cosa Nostra prior to his testimony, and despite available conflicting evidence. This is a serious concern, as Valachi's testimony to the existence and structure of the Cosa Nostra, and the Castellammarese War as its immediate precursor, became the basis for conclusions drawn about organized crime by the President's Crime Commission and by others in subsequent years.[69]

Valachi described the organizational structure of the Cosa Nostra as consisting of "the individual bosses of the individual families, and then we had an underboss, and then we had what we call a caporegima which is a lieutenant, and then we have what we call soldiers."[70] When it came to specifying the role of the organization in the lives of its members, however, the Cosa Nostra appeared less organized.[71]

> **Senator Javits:** Now, what he (Vito Genovese) got out of it then, your actions and these of other members of the family, was to kill off or otherwise deal with people who were bothering him; is that right?
>
> **Mr. Valachi:** Anybody bothering him, naturally he has the soldiers.
>
> **Senator Javits:** That is the function of the family?
>
> **Mr. Valachi:** Right.
>
> **Senator Javits:** That is mutual protection?
>
> **Mr. Valachi:** Right.
>
> **Senator Javits:** Otherwise, everybody operates by himself. They may take partners but that is their option.
>
> **Mr. Valachi:** Right.

Given this scenario, it appears that the Cosa Nostra was a very loose association of criminals.

Valachi also provided information about the members of Cosa Nostra "families" in the New York area. While all the law enforcement personnel who testified, including Attorney General Robert Kennedy, claimed that a nationwide criminal organization existed, no one could provide supporting information independent of Valachi.

> **Senator Muskie:** Would it have been possible for you to reconstruct these charts (of Cosa Nostra families) without his testimony?
>
> **Mr. Shanley** (of the Intelligence Unit of the New York City Police Department): No, sir.

Another important question about Valachi's testimony is why it did not result in convictions of organized crime figures.[72] The willingness to accept Valachi's often uncorroborated testimony might be explained by the senate committee wanting to hear Valachi's version because it corresponded with the preconceptions established by the Kefauver hearings and the Apalachin incident. As Dwight Smith explains, "It was a case of the story being true because it sounded like what ought to be heard."[73]

FRATIANNO, THE FBI, AND THE *TIERI* TRIAL, 1980

Gordon Hawkins has argued that, like the existence of God, the history of organized crime has been based largely on unprovable assumptions. He claimed that to the believer in a Mafia or Cosa Nostra, no evidence is enough to prove its nonexistence.

> Thus, denials of membership in, or knowledge of, the syndicate can not only be dismissed as self-evidently false, but also adduced as evidence of what they deny. If there is gang warfare, this indicates that "an internal struggle for dominance over the entire organization" is going on; and also provides "a somber illustration of how cruel and calculating the underworld continues to be." If peace prevails this may be taken either as evidence of the power of the syndicate leadership and the fear in which it is held; or alternatively as reflecting the development of "the sophisticated and polished control of rackets that now characterize that organization." In the end, it is difficult to resist the conclusion that one is not dealing with an empirical phenomenon at all, but with an article of faith.[74]

Hawkins, of course, believed that organized crime exists. The point he attempted to make was that, although belief in God relies essentially on faith, believers in a North American Mafia or Cosa Nostra expect others also to believe it based on a similar leap of faith.

At the time of Hawkins's writing in 1969, the only "independent" evidence that had been produced in support of a North American criminal conspiracy was the testimony of Joseph Valachi in 1963. As discussed in the previous section, Valachi was a criminal who became a government informant and testified about the existence of a nationwide criminal conspiracy that he said controlled the bulk of the illegal gambling, prostitution, and narcotics trade in North America. Although the 1967 President's Crime Commission and many subsequent writers have accepted Valachi's description of organized crime as fact, Hawkins and many others have pointed to a number of inconsistencies that cast doubt on the veracity of Valachi's testimony.

In 1980, this debate over the true nature of organized crime was rekindled with the introduction of another criminal turned government informant, Jimmy Fratianno. The testimony of Fratianno was seen by many as being more important than Valachi's because, unlike Valachi, Fratianno was said to be (1) a high-ranking member of an organized criminal group, and (2) his testimony resulted in the conviction of a number of suspected organized criminals.

It is appropriate to reevaluate Hawkins's thesis to determine whether the uncorroborated assertions of Valachi were supported or refuted by Fratianno. Fratianno testified at several trials that ended in convictions, one of which is selected for discussion here because of its focus on proving the existence of a national conspiracy of organized criminals. The case of *United States v. Frank Tieri* took place in federal district court in Manhattan in 1980. After a month-long trial, Frank Tieri was convicted of racketeering and conspiracy and was, according to court records, the first person ever proven to be a "boss" of a Cosa Nostra "family."

Frank Tieri was originally indicted on charges of racketeering, conspiracy, bankruptcy fraud, and income tax evasion under the Racketeer Influenced and Corrupt Organization (RICO) provisions of the Organized Crime Control Act. This statute is particularly important to the *Tieri* case because the "enterprise" he was alleged to have illegally operated or received income from was the Cosa Nostra. According to the indictment, the grand jury alleged that

> a criminal organization known by various names including La Cosa Nostra was a criminal group which operated throughout the United States through entities known as "Families" with each "Family" having as its leader a person known as a "Boss." At all times relevant to this Indictment, the defendant Frank Tieri, a.k.a. "Funzi Tieri," a.k.a. "Funzuola," a.k.a. "The Old Man," was the "boss" of one of five New York City "Families" of La Cosa Nostra and which "Family" constituted and continues to constitute an "enterprise," as defined by [the Organized Crime Control Act of 1970].

The significance of this case, therefore, lies in its attempt to prove in court the existence of the Cosa Nostra as a continuing illegal enterprise, that Tieri was the "boss" of one of its families, and that he committed various organized crimes in that capacity.

Fratianno's role in this case was not only to testify to the existence of the Cosa Nostra, but also to implicate Tieri in at least two indictable offenses during the past 10 years in order to establish the "pattern" of racketeering activity necessary for conviction under RICO. One of the illegal acts about which Fratianno testified was Tieri's alleged involvement in a bankruptcy fraud of the Westchester Premier Theatre in New York State. During a conversation with prosecution and defense counsel (while the jury was excused), the presiding federal trial judge acknowledged how important Fratianno's testimony was to the prosecution's case and how much the jury had to rely on his "fragmentary" testimony.[75]

> ***Court:*** So, this may be absolutely far out, but I wonder if there is somebody who really is an expert on the relationship crime families who could—you see, I don't really know. I know nothing about the subject virtually, and I don't know whether it is part of the protocol or part of the custom and usage to have two families involved in one operation. Now, there was that very fragmentary testimony of Fratianno. You know, it's two questions or one question or whatever, and it doesn't solve very much. He said what he said. But it's almost a subject you'd like a Yale professor to come in and . . .

Mr. Goldberg: Harvard.

Court: Harvard. You know, I will take any one of those modern schools, and come in and explain to me—I would like to know.

Mr. Goldberg: Maybe I can do it. I was on both sides.

Court: But what is it, because it may be that people who know about this know that it is impossible to have a situation where you've got the kind of relationship the government is talking about. Maybe that's just an impossibility. On the other hand, maybe there is enough of a fraternity between the different families, if they are families, there is enough of a fraternity that they go to each other's wakes, they will go to each other's theatres, they will lend each other money, and if Frank Sinatra comes to the Westchester Premier Theatre it wouldn't be unusual to have Mr. Tieri, who is not a high profile type, he is in the background controlling it, maybe the Gambino people are a little more, you know, social, and they go to the theatre and they get photographed with Sinatra and all this goes on. Maybe this is perfectly standard. I haven't the faintest idea, and what do I have? That's a one-liner. It's a one-liner by Mr. Fratianno. I don't know.

Later that same day the trial was nearing completion, but the prosecutor's request to charge (i.e., recommendations to the judge for his legal instructions to the jury for their deliberations) claimed that Fratianno's testimony about the Westchester case was not essential for a conviction.

Mr. Goldberg: Judge, before he offers an expert, will he have an offer of proof?

Court: You mean expert testimony by Cantalupo?

Mr. Goldberg: No. He's going to have expert testimony by an FBI agent about the interrelationship of families, no doubt plugging up the holes created by Mr. Fratianno.

Court: He didn't say that.

Mr. Ackerman: No.

Court: No.[76]

It can be seen from these two excerpts from the trial record that Fratianno's testimony was significant, yet uncertain.[77] It is clear from these exchanges that the credibility of Fratianno's testimony had not been well established at this point.

The most important aspect of the *Tieri* case was the government's effort to prove the existence of Cosa Nostra. This effort was based entirely on the testimony of Fratianno.

Mr. Ackerman: Now, directing your attention to late 1947, early 1948, did you become a member of any organization?

Mr. Fratianno: Yes, sir.

Mr. Ackerman: What is the name of that organization?

Mr. Fratianno: La Cosa Nostra.

Mr. Ackerman: How long have you been a member of La Cosa Nostra?

Mr. Fratianno: Thirty-two years, sir.

Mr. Ackerman: Would you tell the jury what La Cosa Nostra is?

Mr. Fratianno: Well, I would say it is a secret organization, sir.

Mr. Ackerman: What does it do, primarily?

Mr. Fratianno: Well, it engages in different businesses, illegal activities.

Mr. Ackerman: What kinds of illegal activities?

Mr. Fratianno: I'd say shylocking, bookmaking, taking bets on horses, football games, baseball games, labor racketeering, all sorts of illegal activity . . .

Mr. Ackerman: Mr. Fratianno, would you please tell the jury what requirements there are for one to become a member of La Cosa Nostra?

Mr. Fratianno: Well, you are more or less proposed by somebody. Sometimes you do something significant. Then there is times when you have a brother or a father in it, and you get in that way. There's different ways, sir.

Mr. Ackerman: Is there any kind of background requirement that's necessary?

Mr. Fratianno: You have to be Italian, sir.

Mr. Ackerman: Would you please tell the jury where La Cosa Nostra is located?

Mr. Fratianno: Well, it is located in different parts of the United States, sir, most of the big cities.

Mr. Ackerman: How is this national organization broken down with respect to the big cities?

Mr. Fratianno: It is broken down into families, sir.

Mr. Ackerman: Now, I am going to put up a map of the United States which has been marked as Government's Exhibit 4 for identification. Mr. Fratianno, starting from the West Coast, could you tell the jury where there are families, and which cities have families of La Cosa Nostra?[78]

Fratianno went on to claim that "families" of LCN exist in 25 cities, including San Francisco, San Jose, Los Angeles, Denver, Dallas, Kansas City (Missouri), Chicago, Detroit, Cleveland, Buffalo, St. Louis, Pittsburgh, Steubenville (Ohio), Milwaukee, Philadelphia, Pittston (Pennsylvania), New Orleans, Tampa, an unknown city in Connecticut, Providence, and five families in New York City. He also testified that he met Frank Tieri in 1976 when Tieri was boss of one of the New York City "families."

Unfortunately, there are problems with Fratianno's account of the Cosa Nostra. The head of the FBI's organized crime operations testified before the Senate Permanent Subcommittee on Investigations in April 1980 and said 26 "active" families of LCN exist in the United States. Interestingly, he claimed there were LCN families in Tucson (Arizona), Rockford (Illinois), Madison (Wisconsin), and Elizabeth-Newark (New Jersey) that Fratianno did not acknowledge. Further, he did not acknowledge that any families existed in Steubenville, Ohio, or in Connecticut or that there was an active group in Dallas, as Fratianno had testified.[79]

A comparison of the Fratianno and FBI testimony both in 1980, and Valachi's 1963 testimony, about the cities where LCN "families" are alleged to exist, reveals some further unaccountable differences.

> **Mr. Alderman (counsel to the senate subcommittee):** Mr. Valachi, we have covered New York rather extensively. Now are there any other members, any other families outside of the area of New York?
>
> **Mr. Valachi:** You mean like Chicago, Boston?
>
> **Mr. Alderman:** Yes. Could you mention the cities where other families exist of the Cosa Nostra, and if you know, the numbers of the members as you know them, could you mention them?
>
> **Mr. Valachi:** I will start with Philadelphia. In Philadelphia I would say about a hundred. Boston, when I left the streets, was about 20, 18 or 20. Chicago, about 150. Cleveland, about 40 or 50. Los Angeles, about 40. Tampa, about 10. Newark, about a hundred. Detroit, I am not familiar at all with Detroit ...
>
> **Mr. Alderman:** How about Buffalo?
>
> **Mr. Valachi:** Buffalo, about 100 to 125.
>
> **Mr. Alderman:** Utica, NY?
>
> **Mr. Valachi:** Utica, 80 to 100.
>
> **Mr. Alderman:** I think you covered New Orleans, did you?
>
> **Mr. Valachi:** No, I didn't cover New Orleans. Very few in New Orleans.
>
> **Mr. Alderman:** Now you mentioned you don't know any in Detroit. Do you know if any families exist there?
>
> **Mr. Valachi:** Yes, they exist.
>
> **Mr. Alderman:** But do you know the number they have there?
>
> **Mr. Valachi:** I have no idea of Detroit.
>
> **Mr. Alderman:** Did you mention Tampa?
>
> **Mr. Valachi:** Tampa, I did, yes, about 10. When I left the streets.
>
> **Mr. Alderman:** In other words, the 10 cities [sic] are Boston, Chicago, Los Angeles, San Francisco, New Orleans, Tampa, Buffalo, Utica, Philadelphia, Cleveland, and Detroit?
>
> **Mr. Valachi:** Right.[80]

Counting the 5 New York City families, Valachi identified a total of 16 LCN groups in the United States. Fratianno dropped 2 cities from Valachi's list, but added 9 others for a total of 25 LCN cities. The FBI testified to the existence of 26 LCN groups, disagreeing with two of the cities Fratianno included, while adding four others. The disparate claims of Valachi, Fratianno, and the FBI are summarized in Table 6.1.

Whether one believes Fratianno or the FBI, the number of LCN groups apparently increased from between 40% and 60% after 1963, which is inconsistent with testimony about changes in the number of members. At the beginning of the same 1980 senate hearings, the FBI director and his unit chief responsible

Table 6.1 Cities Where Families of La Cosa Nostra Are Alleged to Exist

Valachi (1963)	Fratianno (1980)	FBI (1980)
Boston	_[a]	Boston-Providence
Buffalo	Buffalo	Buffalo
Chicago	Chicago	Chicago
Cleveland	Cleveland	Cleveland
Detroit	Detroit	Detroit
Los Angeles	Los Angeles	Los Angeles
New York (5)	New York (5)	New York (5)
New Orleans	New Orleans	New Orleans
Philadelphia	Philadelphia	Philadelphia
San Francisco	San Francisco	San Francisco
Tampa	Tampa	Tampa
Utica, NY	-	-
-	San Jose	San Jose
-	Denver	Denver-Pueblo
-	Dallas	(inactive)
-	Kansas City, MO	Kansas City, MO
-	Pittsburgh	Pittsburgh
Milwaukee	Milwaukee	
-	Providence	(see Boston)
-	St. Louis	St. Louis
-	Pittston, PA	Pittston-Scranton-Wilkes-Barre, PA
-	Steubenville, OH	-
-	Connecticut (one city)	-
-	-	Tucson
-	-	Rockford, IL
-	-	Madison, WI
-	-	Elizabeth-Newark, NJ
-	-	Springfield, IL (inactive)

[a]No family reported.

for organized crime investigations gave testimony as to the "family" structure and size of the Cosa Nostra.

Senator Cohen: May I also ask for a clarification for the record that, when you say "families" that does not necessarily intimate they are blood relations, although there may be blood relations within the "family."

Mr. Nelson (FBI unit chief): That is correct, there may be blood relationships, but "family" comes from the Italian "famiglia" and it does not necessarily mean that they are blood related. In most cases, of course, they are not.

Mr. Steinberg (counsel to the senate committee): Mr. Nelson, how many members of La Cosa Nostra exist today?

Mr. Nelson: There are approximately 2,000 members. However, I must say that is probably the most misleading figure I could throw out because these are the initiated members, the people who are considered by other people as part of the organization. Our most conservative estimate is that for every initiated member, there are approximately at least 10 people aligned with them and associated with them on a daily basis whose day-to-day activities are criminal and associated with La Cosa Nostra. So the conservative figure of the number of people in this country who are doing La Cosa Nostra's work is 20,000, and that is conservative.[81]

Compare this 1980 description of the size of LCN with Valachi's original description in 1963.

Mr. Alderman: Mr. Valachi, along those lines, how many active members do you feel there are in the New York area that belong to the various families? ... All of the five families.

Mr. Valachi: About 2,000.

Mr. Alderman: Those whom you have been able to identify in the five families, you have marked with stars on these charts?

Mr. Valachi: Yes.

Mr. Alderman: But they do not represent all of the members of families? I mean in any family you don't know all of the members of the family?

Mr. Valachi: Well, I tell you, I am off the street for about 4 years. I am sure I know more than what I have got up there.

Mr. Alderman: These charts portray something over 400 names.

Mr. Valachi: Something like that.

Mr. Alderman: You say there are 2,000 members. So there are quite a number of members whom you do not know.

Mr. Valachi: Yes, there is quite a number, yes.

Mr. Alderman: How many inactive members are there?

Mr. Valachi: I would say about 2,500 or 3,000.

Mr. Alderman: You are just talking about New York City alone?

Mr. Valachi: I am talking about New York, including Newark.[82]

Valachi estimated LCN membership in the New York City area alone to be 2,000 in 1963, while the FBI claimed that the nationwide membership was only 2,000 in 1980, so it is difficult to see how the Cosa Nostra has grown. If we accept both Valachi's and the FBI's upper estimates of LCN participants, a New York City-only membership of 5,000 in 1963, compared to a nationwide estimate of 20,000 in 1980, there does not appear to be growth in the size of the Cosa Nostra (considering that the FBI counts only 5 New York City families out of a nationwide total of 26) in 1980. Furthermore, if LCN membership has not increased in size between 1963 and 1980, how could it have established "families" in 7-10 additional cities during that period? As a result, there not only appears to be contradictions between Fratianno and the FBI's testimony in 1980, but the Justice Department claims about the Cosa Nostra in 1980 cannot be reconciled with the claims of their 1963 witness, Joseph Valachi.

A final note of concern relates to how the Cosa Nostra is organized. At the *Tieri* trial, Fratianno testified about the organization of LCN "families."

Mr. Ackerman: Now, is there any structure in La Cosa Nostra above the families which are located in the cities as we have in Government's Exhibit 4?

Mr. Fratianno: Yes, sir.

Mr. Ackerman: What is the name of that structure?

Mr. Fratianno: Well, they have a commission, sir.

Mr. Ackerman: Now, who comprises the commission?

Mr. Fratianno: The five bosses of the New York family plus the boss of the Chicago family, sir.

Mr. Ackerman: Now, what is the purpose of the commission?

Mr. Fratianno: Well, they more or less handle disputes with other families. If you have a problem with another family, they more or less handle it, sir.

Mr. Ackerman: Now, when a new boss is selected by a family, who is notified?

Mr. Fratianno: The commission is notified, sir.

Mr. Ackerman: Would you describe to the jury how a family of La Cosa Nostra is actually run?

Mr. Fratianno: Well, it's run by the boss. He's the main one. And then they have an underboss. They have a consigliere, and then they have capos ...

Mr. Ackerman: What is the consigliere's job in the family?

Mr. Fratianno: Well, he is more or less the counselor of the family, you know.

Mr. Ackerman: You mentioned the capos. What are they?

Mr. Fratianno: Well, they are like captains. They more or less—they break the soldiers into units and they belong to the capos, certain capos.

Mr. Ackerman: You referred to soldiers. Is everybody who is not a capo, a boss, underboss, and consigliere, a soldier in La Cosa Nostra?

Mr. Fratianno: That's correct.[83]

Therefore, each "family" has ranks from "soldier" up to "boss," and the families are, according to Fratianno, regulated by a six-member commission of six "family" bosses (of the five New York City families and Chicago). When the FBI unit chief testified before the senate the same year, however, he arrived at a different formulation.

At that time [when the commission was allegedly formed in 1931], there were seven members on the Mafia Commission, the La Cosa Nostra Commission. ... Currently, there are nine. It is made up of the five bosses of the New York families, the boss in Philadelphia, the boss in Buffalo, the boss in Detroit, and the boss in Chicago.[84]

This confusion over the existence and size of the "commission" is further amplified when Fratianno's 1981 biography offers still a third version of the commission structure. In it, the commission is said to be composed of 10 Cosa Nostra bosses. Fratianno's credibility suffers, not only due to his self-contradiction, but also because he admits in his biography that he was told of the family and commission structure by someone else in 1947.[85] This inconsistency is especially disturbing because Fratianno claims he was the one-time "boss" of the Los Angeles "family," so presumably he would have firsthand knowledge of such a crucial fact. Therefore, Fratianno's testimony on this subject is not only inconsistent, but it also appears to be hearsay.

Fratianno's testimony is suspect on other grounds as well. At other points during the *Tieri* trial, Fratianno was found to have contradicted his prior grand jury testimony, admitted violating the "family" code in setting up a fellow member to be murdered, admitted lying under oath in the past, and admitted defrauding the FBI while receiving money as a paid informant. These facts, in addition to his unsavory background, did not enhance his credibility at trial.

Nevertheless, Frank Tieri was ultimately convicted of racketeering and conspiracy, undoubtedly due to the testimony of other witnesses at trial and the failure of the defense to call a single witness in Tieri's behalf. Tieri was in poor health throughout his trial, and he died only 3 months after his conviction in March 1981 at age 77. A conviction cannot stand when death has deprived an offender the opportunity to appeal his conviction; Tieri's indictment was formally dismissed and the conviction vacated in May 1981.

But the *Tieri* case was the beginning of a massive prosecution effort against organized crime. Many other informants came forward, and electronic eavesdropping of conversations saw some alleged organized crime figures literally convict themselves.

MOB TRIALS OF THE 1980S TO THE PRESENT

The period from the 1980s to the present will be remembered for the U.S. Justice Department taking new initiative to prosecute large numbers of reputed organized crime figures around the country. It has been the largest organized crime prosecution effort in U.S. history. The alleged leaders of 16 of the 24 Mafia groups identified by the government were indicted by 1986. Nearly 5,000 federal organized crime indictments were issued by grand juries in 1985 alone.[86] By 1988, the FBI reported that 19 bosses, 13 underbosses, and 43 "captains" had been convicted.[87] The year 2003 marked the first time in history that all five leaders of the New York City families of Cosa Nostra were in jail at the same time.[88]

This dramatic increase in prosecutions was not due to new laws, but simply was the result of devoting more existing resources to the problem and changing strategy. Many of these prosecutions took place in New York City and relied on the investigative efforts of a reorganized New York State Organized Crime Task Force. On the national level, there were changes as well. In President Reagan's first 4 years in office, his attorney general authorized more than 700 federal wiretaps, more than twice the number allowed during Carter's

CRITICAL THINKING EXERCISE 6.2

The Case of Whitey Bulger

James "Whitey" Bulger was born in 1929 to Irish immigrant parents living in Boston's Dorchester neighborhood. His platinum blonde hair earned him his nickname. As the leader of the Winter Hill Gang, he ran a criminal network from South Boston and controlled much of the surrounding area during the 1970s and 1980s. Bulger and his associates engaged in numerous illegal activities such as loansharking, extortion of local business owners and bookmakers, trafficking of narcotics and firearms, and murder.

In 1975, Bulger cut a deal with FBI agent John Connolly to provide information on the Italian Mafia in New England (a higher investigative priority at the time) in exchange for protection from the FBI. This served to deflect police attention from Bulger's ongoing criminal activities.

Four years later, a former business associate implicated Whitey Bulger and Steve "The Rifleman" Flemmi in a horse race-fixing scheme, but FBI agent Connolly persuaded federal prosecutors to leave the two out of the indictment. Twenty-one people were charged, leaving Bulger and Flemmi to assume control of the Winter Hill Gang. In 1982, Bulger and Flemmi allegedly gunned down a former henchman in broad daylight to prevent him from telling about a murder, but Connolly filed a report with the FBI saying that rival gangsters made the hit.

FBI agent Connolly was subsequently convicted and sentenced to prison for warning Bulger and Flemmi that they were about to be indicted. So in late 1994, upon learning of his pending indictment, Bulger fled. He evaded capture for years until 2011, when he was caught with his girlfriend in his apartment in California, living under a false name. In 2012, his girlfriend, Catherine Greig was sentenced to 8 years in prison for helping Bulger evade authorities.

Bulger was convicted of racketeering and other crimes, including extortion, conspiracy, money-laundering, drug dealing, and roles in 11 killings during his years as leader of the Winter Hill gang in the 1970s and 1980s. He was sentenced to two life prison terms in 2013 at age 84.

Critical Thinking Questions

1. Interest was high in the case of Whitey Bulger because he was able to evade capture for 17 years. How do you think a known crime figure from South Boston was able to stay on the run for so long?
2. Bulger's corrupt relationship with FBI agent Connolly was also an important part of this case. Should Connolly be held liable for Bulger's crimes if Connolly protected him from arrest?

Sources: Mark Memmott, "Bulger Trial's Most Memorable Moments," NPR.org, August 13, 2013; "Key Events in the Life of James 'Whitey' Bulger," Associated Press, August 12, 2013; Katharine Q. Seelye, "Crime Boss Bulger Gets 2 Life Terms and Is Assailed by Judge for His 'Depravity'", The New York Times, November 14, 2013; Dick Lehr and Gerard O'Neill, Whitey: The Life of America's Most Notorious Mob Boss (Broadway Books, 2013).

presidency.[89] In a similar way, prosecutors began to make use of the racketeering law (RICO), enacted in 1970 but not used much until the 1980s, which provides for extended sentences and large fines and forfeitures for convicted offenders. In addition, undercover agents and government informants were being employed more often in organized crime investigations.

The significance of this investigation and prosecution effort is difficult to capture without illustration. The leaders of many Cosa Nostra (a.k.a. Mafia) groups were convicted and sentenced to long terms, including John Gotti in New York, Nicky Scarfo in Philadelphia, and Gennaro Anguilo in Boston, and many others.[90] Table 6.2 lists the outcome of many of the significant mob trials since the *Tieri* trial, including a growing number of non-Mafia prosecutions of ongoing criminal enterprises, showing their emerging importance in organized crime in the United States.

Table 6.2 Major Organized Crime Trials and Outcomes, 1985-2013

Year	Name	Age	Alleged Role	Offense	Outcome
1985	Gennaro Langella	47	Underboss of Colombo group in New York City	Perjury, obstruction of justice	10 years in prison, $15,000 fine
1986	Matthew Ianniello Benjamin Cohen (and six others)	65 66	No mention of organized crime in indictment	Skimming from NYC bars, restaurants	6 years, 5 years
1986	Michael Franzese (and four others)	35	Son of "captain" in Colombo group	Racketeering and tax conspiracy	10 years, plus $15 million fine, forfeit
1986	Gennaro Anguilo (and four others)	67	Underboss of New England (Patriarca) group	Racketeering, gambling, loansharking, murder	45 years prison, $120,000 fine
1986	Anthony Spilotro (and eight others)	47	Overseer of Las Vegas operations for Chicago group	Conspiracy, racketeering in Las Vegas burglary ring	Mistrial (found murdered 2 days before retrial)
1986	Paul Castellano Anthony Gaggi Ronald Ustica Henry Borelli	72 60 41 37	Leader and members of Gambino crime group in New York	Car theft conspiracy and murder (Ustica and Borelli)	Castellano killed during trial; Gaggi, 5 years; others, life in prison
1986	Matthew Ianniello Benjamin Cohen (and four others)	65 66	"Captain" and associates in Genovese group	Racketeering, fraud, extortion in garbage collection	Acquitted
1986	Anthony, Joseph, and Vincent Colombo	41 39 35	Members of Colombo group in New York City	Racketeering, conspiracy, narcotics	14 years prison, 5 years prison, 5 years prison
1986	Santo Trafficante	71	Leader of Florida group	Racketeering, gambling	Mistrial
1986	Joseph Bonanno	81	Retired boss of Bonanno group	Contempt for refusal to testify	14 months jail
1986	Carmine and Alphonse Persico, Gennaro Langella (and seven others)	53 33 47	Head of Colombo crime group and associates in NYC	Labor and construction racketeering, extortion	39 years prison, 12 years prison, 65 years prison
1986	Paul Vario	73	Counselor in NYC Lucchese group	Extortion at JFK Airport	6 years prison, $25,000 fine
1986	Chang An-lo (and seven others)	30s	Leader and members of the United Bamboo Chinese gang in New York	Narcotics distribution, murder	25 years prison
1987	Paul Castellano Anthony Salerno Anthony Corralo Gennaro Langella Philip Rastelli (and four others)	72 75 73 48 69	"Commission" trial of leaders of Gambino, Genovese, Lucchese, Colombo, and Bonanno groups in NYC	Racketeering, conspiracy, loansharking, labor bribery, extortion in construction	Castellano murdered during trial, other leaders each received 100 years in prison

Continued

Table 6.2 Major Organized Crime Trials and Outcomes, 1985-2013—cont'd

Year	Name	Age	Alleged Role	Offense	Outcome
1987	Philip Rastelli (and seven others)	69	Leader of Bonanno group in New York	Labor racketeering in moving industry	12 years prison
1987	Ilario Zannino	67	Underboss in New England group	Gambling, loansharking	30 years prison
1987	John Gotti Armand and Aniello Dellacroce (and six others)	46 38 71	Leader of Gambino crime group and associates	Gambling, loansharking, hijacking, murder	Gotti acquitted, Armand Dellacroce disappeared, Aniello Dellacroce died before trial
1987	Gaetano Badalementi Salvatore Catalano (and 14 others)	64 46	"Pizza Connection" Turkey-Sicily-Brazil-New York drug importation via pizzerias	Narcotics distribution, conspiracy	Each received 45 years prison and $1.1 million fine
1987	Nicodemo Scarfo	58	Boss of Philadelphia group	Extortion from developers	14 years prison
1987	Nicodemo Scarfo	58	Boss of Philadelphia group	Narcotics distribution	Acquitted
1988	Carlos Lehder	38	A Medellin Cartel leader	Drug smuggling, conspiracy	Two consecutive life terms, plus 135 years prison
1989	Loren Piccarreto	38	Head of Rochester, NY, crime group	Gambling and extortion	7 years prison
1989	Albert Tocco	60	Alleged boss southside of Chicago	Racketeering, extortion, obstruction of justice	200 years prison (died in prison in 2005)
1989	Nicodemo Scarfo (and seven others)	59	Boss of Philadelphia group	Murder	Life in prison (overturned on appeal due to prosecutorial misconduct)
1989	Nicodemo Scarfo Philip Leonetti (and 13 others)	59 36	Boss of Philadelphia group	Racketeering, murder, extortion, narcotics, gambling	55 years prison, 45 years prison
1990	John Gotti	49	Boss of Gambino crime family in New York	Assault	Acquitted
1990	Rayful Edmond III	25	Head of Washington, DC, cocaine ring	Drug trafficking	Three life terms
1990	Matthew Ianniello	70	Captain in Genovese group	Racketeering, extortion	5 years prison
1990	Charles Porter Louis Raucci	58 61	Underboss and member of Pittsburgh group	Racketeering, narcotics, tax violations	28 years prison
1991	Raymond Patriarca Jr.	47	Leader of New England group	Racketeering	8 years prison

Table 6.2 Major Organized Crime Trials and Outcomes, 1985-2013—cont'd

Year	Name	Age	Alleged Role	Offense	Outcome
1991	Nicholas Bianco	59	Boss of Patriarca (New England) group	Racketeering	11 years prison
1992	Joseph Russo (and four others)	58	Counselor in New England group	Kidnapping, extortion, murder	16 years prison
1992	Victor Orena	58	Acting boss of Colombo family	Racketeering, murder, loan-sharking, conspiracy	Life in prison
1992	Thomas Pitera	37	Soldier in Bonanno group	Six drug-related murders	Life in prison
1992	John Gotti	51	Boss of Gambino group in New York	Five murders, including that of Paul Castellano	Life in prison (died in prison of throat cancer in 2002)
1993	Michael Tacetta Michael Perna	46 50	Head of Lucchese group in New Jersey	Racketeering and murder conspiracy	30 years prison
1993	Thomas Gambino	64	Captain in Gambino group	Racketeering gambling, loansharking	5 years prison
1993	Johnny Eng	36	Head of Flying Dragons in New York's Chinatown	Racketeering, heroin trafficking	24 years prison, $3.5 million fine
1993	Salvatore Lombardi (and six others)	54	Captain in Genovese group in New Jersey	Racketeering, extortion, gambling	22 years prison, $175,000 fine
1993	John Riggi	69	Boss of New Jersey crime group	Murder conspiracy	7 years prison
1993	Gregory Scarpa Sr.	65	Captain in Colombo crime group in New York	Murder conspiracy	10 years prison (Scarpa was terminally ill)
1993	Joseph "Joey Bang Bang" Massaro	50	Soldier in Lucchese crime group	Racketeering, murder, extortion, arson, loansharking	Life in prison
1994	John Gambino Joseph Gambino	53 47	Members of Gambino crime group	Racketeering, narcotics trafficking	15 years prison
1994	Joseph Lovett	44	Former chapter leader of Pagans motorcycle gang	Trafficking in methamphetamines	27 years prison
1994	Salvatore Avellino Jr.	58	Associate of Lucchese group on Long Island	Racketeering and murder conspiracy	10 years prison plus 21 years probation
1994	Leonard Falzone	59	Enforcer in Buffalo crime group	Racketeering and loansharking	5 years prison
1995	Nicholas Gio	28	Enforcer in Chicago crime group	Murder	Life in prison
1995	Marco D'Amico	59	Chicago organized crime group	Racketeering, bookmaking, extortion	12 years prison
1996	Anthony Carollo (with 11 others)	72	Head of New Orleans crime group	Video poker fraud enterprise	4 years prison

Continued

Table 6.2 Major Organized Crime Trials and Outcomes, 1985-2013—cont'd

Year	Name	Age	Alleged Role	Offense	Outcome
1996	Sam Carlisi	74	Head of street crew for Chicago organized crime	Racketeering, extortion, gambling, loansharking	13 years prison
1996	John Stanfa	54	Head of Philadelphia crime group	Murder, conspiracy, racketeering	Life in prison
1996	Vincent Pagano	60	Philadelphia crime group	Murder, conspiracy, racketeering	80 years prison
1996	Anthony Volpe	63	Genovese crime group in Hartford, CT	Racketeering, gambling, loansharking	4 years prison
1997	Vincent Gigante	69	Head of Genovese crime group in NYC	Racketeering	12 years prison (died in prison in 2005)
1999	John A. Gotti (son of John Gotti)	35	Leader in Gambino crime group in NYC; capo in Gambino family	Racketeering and extortion at NYC topless club	6 years prison, 1 year prison
	Salvatore Locascio (son of Frank)	39			
2000	Frank Salemme	66	Head of Patriarca organized crime group in New England	Racketeering, loansharking, extortion	11 years prison
2001	Alphonse Persico (son of Carmine)	47	Acting boss of Colombo crime group in NYC	Racketeering, loansharking, extortion	13 years prison
2001	Robert Santana	31	Mexico-U.S. drug smuggling ring	Narcotics distribution	15 years prison
2001	Carmine Agnello (son-in-law of John Gotti)	41	Gambino crime group in NYC	Racketeering and tax evasion—taking over rival scrap yard	9 years prison
2001	Salvatore Avellino	65	Lucchese organized crime group	Extortion conspiracy in garbage hauling business	5 years (already serving 10 years for murder conspiracy)
2001	Robert Cechini	53	Linked to Chicago organized crime	Video gambling enterprise, money laundering	16 years prison
2001	Robert Lino	34	Alleged capo in Bonanno crime group; Colombo associate	Securities fraud—Wall Street stock scam	6 years prison
	Frank Persico (with eight others)	38			
2001	Joseph Merlino	39	Philadelphia-South Jersey crime group leader; group associate	Racketeering, extortion, illegal gambling, loansharking	14 years prison, 9 years prison
	Angelo Lutz	38			
2002	Sammy "The Bull" Gravano	57	Former underboss in Gambino crime group, now in Arizona	Drug dealing (ecstasy), money laundering	20 years prison

Table 6.2 Major Organized Crime Trials and Outcomes, 1985-2013—cont'd

Year	Name	Age	Alleged Role	Offense	Outcome
2002	Stephen "The Whale" Cino	65	Reputed Chicago mob soldier involved in business takeover in Las Vegas	Extortion conspiracy	Sentence reduced to 13 years prison
2002	Charles Pipkins	57	Called "granddaddy" of Atlanta's pimps	Racketeering and child prostitution	30 years prison
2002	John Connolly	60	Former FBI agent leaked information to protect informants Whitey Bulger and Stephen Flemmi in Boston	Racketeering and obstruction of justice	10 years prison
2003	Anthony Calabrese	42	Mob enforcer for hired beating in Florida	Aggravated assault	7 years prison
2003	Michael "Hollywood" Davis	42	Forced 14-year-old girls into prostitution as pimp in Atlanta	Forced prostitution and child molestation	15 years prison
2003	John Riggi	78	Former leader of DeCavalcante family in New Jersey	Murder conspiracy	10 years prison (already serving 12 years for extortion)
2003	Carmine Manzi Anthony DeLevo	54 63	Springfield, Massachusetts, associates of Genovese crime group in NYC	Racketeering (involving gambling and loansharking), money laundering	3.5 years prison
2003	Peter Gotti Anthony "Sonny" Ciccone	64 69	Gambino crime group in NYC	Racketeering involving extortion	20 years prison
2004	Louis "Bagels" Daidone	56	Acting boss of Lucchese crime group in NYC	Racketeering and loansharking (involving murder)	Life in prison
2004	Louis "Lump Lump" Barone	67	Associate of Lucchese crime group	Murder	15 years prison
2005	Dominick "Quiet Dom" Cirillo (with three others)	76	Acting boss of Genovese crime group in NYC	Rackteering, murder conspiracy, extortion, loansharking	4 years prison
2005	Joseph "Big Joey" Massino	62	Boss of Bonanno crime group in NYC	Murder conspiracy, racketeering, extortion	Life in prison
2006	Anthony "The Genius" Megale	52	Acting underboss of Gambino crime group in NYC	Racketeering, extortion, gambling enterprise	7 years prison
2006	Peter "Rabbit" Calabrese Louis "HaHa" Attanasio	58 62	Captains in Bonanno crime group	Murder conspiracy	15 years prison
2006	Alex Dudaj (and five others)	38	Albanian organized crime group leader in NYC	Racketeering, extortion, gambling	27 years prison

Continued

Table 6.2 Major Organized Crime Trials and Outcomes, 1985-2013—cont'd

Year	Name	Age	Alleged Role	Offense	Outcome
2006	Arnold "Sylvester" Squiteri	70	Underboss of Gambino crime group in NYC	Racketeering, assault, extortion, loansharking	7.5 years prison
2006	Peter Ojeda (with 25 others)	64	Mexican mafia smuggling into California	Racketeering, narcotics conspiracy	14 years prison
2006	Baldassare "Baldo" Amato	54	Soldier in Bonanno crime group in NYC	Racketeering conspiracy and murder	Life in prison
2006	Gregory DePalma	74	Captain in Gambino crime group in NYC	Racketeering	12 years prison
2007	Ronald Trucchio Steven Catalano	55 45	Gambino crime group in NYC and Florida	Racketeering, murder, extortion, robbery	Life in prison; 16 years prison
2007	Jose Miguel Battle	77	Leader of Cuban mafia in Florida	Racketeering	20 years prison
2007	Renaldi "Ray" Ruggiero	73	Head of Genovese crime group in south Florida	Racketeering, extortion, robbery, money laundering	14 years prison
2008	Domenico Cefalu	61	Acting underboss of Gambino group	Extortion	2 years prison
2008	John Caggiano	59	Genovese group associate in NYC	Illegal gambling enterprise	4 years prison
2008	Michael Mancuso Anthony Aiello Anthony Indelicato Anthony Donato	54 32 62 51	Acting boss and members of Bonanno crime group	Murder conspiracy	15 years prison, 30 years prison, 20 years prison, 25 years prison
2009	Ivaylo Vasilev Pletnyov Nikolay Georgiev Minchev	39 45	Eastern Europe organized crime (Bulgaria) fraudulent eBay sales scheme	Conspiracy to commit money laundering and wire fraud	4 years prison 2.5 years prison
2009	Louis Eppolito Stephen Caracappa	60 66	Former NYPD detectives	Eight murders for Lucchese crime group	Life in prison
2009	Nicholas (Little Nick) Corozzo	69	Gambino crime group capo	Murder conspiracy	13.5 years prison
2009	Charles Carneglia	62	Soldier in Gambino crime group	Four murders	Life in prison
2009	Willie Valdez, Rene Gonzales Jr, Johnny Perez Jr, Francisco Nuncio Jr, Roberto Ybarra, and five others	"ages not confirmed"	Texas Syndicate members and associates of prison/street gang	Murder, robbery, drug trafficking	27 years prison 22 years prison 22 years prison 20 years prison 20 years prison
2009	Angelo Prisco	69	Captain in Genovese crime group	Racketeering, extortion, murder, conspiracy	Life in prison

Table 6.2 Major Organized Crime Trials and Outcomes, 1985-2013—cont'd

Year	Name	Age	Alleged Role	Offense	Outcome
2009	Joseph "Joey the Clown" Lombardo Frank Calabrese Sr. James Marcello	80 71 66	Leaders of Chicago outfit-family secrets trial	Murder conspiracy	Life in prison
2009	Alphonse (Allie Boy) Persico	55	Boss of Colombo crime NYC group (son of Carmine)	Murder in 1999	Life in prison
2009	John A. "Junior" Gotti	45	Alleged one-time boss of Gambino crime group	Four hung juries 2005-2009 for racketeering	Government ends Gotti prosecution effort in 2010
2010	Hieu Phan	36	Benjamin Ton drug trafficking organization	Drug smuggling from Canada into U.S. via Asian OC groups	10 years prison
2010	Francisco "King Pone" Ortiz	26	Latin Kings street gang leader (Maryland)	Attempted murders, robbery, witness tampering	21 years prison
2010	Jerome Rico Evans	25	Narcotics importation and trafficking enterprise (Operation Don Quixote)	Drug offenses involving heroin, cocaine, and ecstasy	14 years prison
2011	Terrance "Doo Wop" Clark Lamon "M-Dot" Street	22 20	Members of Pittsburgh Crips street gang	Racketeering, attempted murders, drug trafficking, witness intimidation	13 years prison 10 years prison
2011	Jack "Milwaukee Jack" Rosga	53	President of Outlaws motorcycle gang	Racketeering and assault	20 years prison
2011	Juan Gloria-Perales Orlando Guerrero Arturo Villarrel Ernesto Ramon Abel Melendrez	33 32 33 21 38	Texas Mexican Mafia gang members	Racketeering involving drug trafficking and extortion at Mexican border	25 years prison 15 years prison 14 years prison 10 years prison 10 years prison
2011	Vincent "Vinnie Gorgeous" Basciano	51	Former acting boss of Bonanno crime group	Murder conspiracy	Life in prison
2011	Anthony "Tony D" Palumbo	62	Former capo of Genovese crime group in New York	Murder conspiracy, extortion	10 years prison
2011	John "Sonny" Franzese	93	Former underboss of Colombo crime group	Extortion of New York strip clubs and a pizzeria	8 years prison
2011	Arthur Nigro Fotios Geas Ty Geas	66 44 39	Former acting boss and two associates of Genovese group in New York and Massachusetts	Multiple murders, racketeering, extortion	Life in prison Life in prison Life in prison

Continued

Table 6.2 Major Organized Crime Trials and Outcomes, 1985–2013—cont'd

Year	Name	Age	Alleged Role	Offense	Outcome
2011	Joseph Watts	69	Associate of Gambino crime group	Murder and assault conspiracy	13 years prison
2012	Anthony L. Dinunzio Alfred "Chippy" Scivola Jr Richard Bonafiglia Thomas Iafrate	53 71 58 70	Acting leader of New England Cosa Nostra group, member, associates	Racketeering, extortion from adult entertainment businesses	6.5 years prison 4 years prison 7 years prison 2.5 years prison
2012	Gaeton Lucibello	59	Member of Philadelphia Cosa Nostra group	Racketeering, extortion, loansharking, illegal gambling	4 years prison
2013	John Burke	51	Associate of Gambino crime group	Two murders and racketeering	Life in prison
2013	Kaboni Savage Steven Northington	38 41	Leaders of drug trafficking enterprise in Philadelphia	12 counts of murder (including a witness)	Death sentence Life in prison
2013	Christian Fernando "Tony" Borda	49	Leader of Colombian drug trafficking organization	Conspiracy to import cocaine	25 years prison
2013	James "Dirty" Meldrum (one of 36 charged)	40	Member of Aryan Brotherhood of Texas	Racketeering involving multiple murders, robbery, arson, kidnapping, drug trafficking	12 years prison
2013	Antonio C. Martinez Jr. Hiluterio "Tails" Chavez Jermaine "J-Dub" Ellis	40 37 21	Latin Kings street gang (w/Chicago Police Officer)	Racketeering conspiracy involving drugs and robberies	12 years prison 20 years prison 17 years prison
2013	Joseph Massimino Anthony Staino	63 57	Underboss and capo of Philadelphia Cosa Nostra group	Racketeering, extortion, loansharking, illegal gambling	15 years prison 8 years prison
2013	Louis Fazzini	46	Member of Philadelphia Cosa Nostra group	Racketeering involving illegal gambling and theft from employee benefit plan	4.5 years prison
2013	Damion Canalichio Gary Battaglini	43 52	Member and associate of Philadelphia Cosa Nostra group	Racketeering involving loansharking and illegal gambling	11 years prison 8 years prison
2013	James "Whitey" Bulger	84	One-time boss of Winter Hill gang in Boston	11 murders, extortion, money laundering	Two life sentences
2013	Armen Kazarian	47	Mirzoyan-Terdjanian Organization, an Armenian-American OC enterprise	Racketeering conspiracy in Medicare fraud scheme	3 years prison

Table 6.2 Major Organized Crime Trials and Outcomes, 1985-2013—cont'd

Year	Name	Age	Alleged Role	Offense	Outcome
2014	Bajram Lajqi	38	International drug trafficking syndicate (led by ethnic Albanians)	Drug trafficking into U.S. from multiple other countries	10 years prison
2014	Ricky Timothy "Knuckles" Wyatt Jr.	27	Member of the Nine Trey Gangster (NTG) organization, part of the United Blood Nation (UBN)—started in Riker's Island prison	Illegal firearms, manufacturing counterfeit currency, and drug trafficking	9.5 years prison

Outcomes of the Organized Crime Prosecution Effort

Five outcomes become apparent as one reviews the positions, offenses, and sentences of the principals in these cases. First, it is clear that many of these organized crime cases were significant. Many involved racketeering convictions that entailed the infiltration of legitimate or illegitimate businesses through bribery and extortion. The sentences imposed on the principals in these cases were severe. The average sentence was more than 20 years per offender. It is apparent from the ages of the principals involved in these cases that many are senior citizens. The average age of these offenders was nearly 60. Given an average sentence of 20 years, even accounting for parole eligibility, an entirely new leadership will emerge among many Italian-American organized crime groups. Perhaps the continued existence of some of these established groups is now in jeopardy, as new groups attempt to take over given the weakened position of some of these Italian-American groups. Note the patterns of age differences in Table 6.2 of those convicted in Italian-American groups versus those convicted in other kinds of "emerging" organized crime groups. The age difference (also reflected in Figure 6.1) reflects the shift in the relative dominance of different groups in organized crime in general, and what the future might hold.

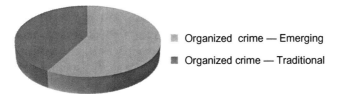

    Organized crime — Emerging

    Organized crime — Traditional

FIGURE 6.1 Federal organized crime convictions by type of crime group. Organized crime—Emerging = 58% of convictions. Organized crime—Traditional = 42% of convictions. Source: Transactional Records Clearinghouse at trac.syr.edu (September 2013).

Second, it can be seen that although many of these cases took place in New York City, a number occurred in other parts of the country. Convictions affecting organized crime operations in New England, New Jersey, Chicago, Las Vegas, Pittsburgh, Philadelphia, and Washington, DC, attest to the national scope of the prosecution effort. It is important to realize that outside of the New York City, Chicago, Boston, and Philadelphia areas, Italian-American organized crime groups are nowhere near the size and influence of years past. This has been due to the success of prosecution efforts, and also to the encroachment of other, non-Mafia organized crime groups who have taken control over criminal opportunities in narcotics, the smuggling of immigrants, and fraud in many areas (see Chapters 7 and 8). Some estimates place the number of sworn members of Cosa Nostra or Mafia members at less than 1,000, and many observers see Mafia-linked crime as a declining presence in the overall picture of organized crime.[91] According to Ronald Goldstock, former director of the New York State Organized Crime Task Force, "The shrinking of Italian-American neighborhoods results in a lack of gangs, which means that there are no minor leagues to supply the majors anymore. And it used to be that only some children of mobsters would go legitimate, but now most of them are going legitimate."[92] It is also likely that the sustained and successful prosecution effort over the past three decades has played a role in these decisions. Nevertheless, the New York District Attorney comments after another arrest of a group of Italian-American mobsters, "Whatever name it's called—the Mafia, La Cosa Nostra, the mob—this indictment demonstrates that organized crime is still operating in New York City and still has its hooks in the labor movement."[93]

Third, the prosecution focus has remained on the organized crime of Italian-Americans. The overwhelming majority of cases were of alleged Mafia groups, although convictions of members of the "United Bamboo" Chinese gang, the leader of the "Flying Dragons," leaders of motorcycle gangs, Mexican drug smugglers, Cuban organized crime, an Albanian group in New York, Washington, DC, cocaine ring leader, and other groups (listed in Table 6.2) are a sign of the recognition of serious, continuing organized crime enterprises among non-Italians. For example, 36 members of the Aryan Brotherhood of Texas (ABT) were shown to commit multiple acts of murder, robbery, arson, kidnapping and narcotics trafficking on behalf of the ABT gang. ABT gang members met on a regular basis at various locations throughout Texas to report on gang-related business, collect dues, commit disciplinary assaults against fellow gang members and discuss acts of violence against rival gang members, among other things. The ABT was established in the early 1980s within the Texas prison system and was modeled after the writings of the Aryan Brotherhood, a California-based prison gang that was formed in the California prison system during the 1960s.

Earlier, the ABT was primarily concerned with the protection of white inmates and white supremacy/separatism but over time, the ABT expanded its criminal enterprise to include illegal activities for profit.[94] In an unrelated case, a group was convicted of involvement in an ongoing enterprise to engage in prostitution and distribution of synthetic drug. The group enticed predominantly Asian women to travel to Massachusetts from other locations to engage in prostitution in brothels located there. The women were also transported from one brothel to another.[95] So it can be seen how many organized crime enterprises are carried out by groups and networks unconnected to Italian-American organized crime (as Table 6.2 summarizes). The number of cases involving relatives and even sons of known organized crime figures demonstrates the persistence of organized crime activity as a lifestyle in some local areas.

The shift in organized crime activity among groups is reflected in current prosecution initiatives. Figure 6.1 illustrates the focus of contemporary federal organized crime prosecutions, indicating that the largest number of convictions as of September 2013 were for "organized crime-emerging organizations," followed by "organized crime-traditional organizations" (e.g., Mafia-related groups), accounting for 42% of organized crime convictions. These figures demonstrate the growing importance of organized crime committed by non-Mafia groups, which is a consequence of the successful mob trials of the last 30 years.

Fourth, the debate over the existence of a Mafia was finally rendered moot in a 1986 trial, when the defendants in the "commission" trial (i.e., the alleged "bosses" of the New York City crime "families") conceded that the "Mafia exists and has members." Furthermore, the defense claimed, "there is a commission," which is mentioned in wiretapped conversations of the defendants. Testimony from Sicilian informer Tommaso Buscetta corroborated this claim. He stated that he was told by Joseph Bonanno in 1957 that "it was very advisable" to set up a commission in Sicily "to resolve disputes" among criminal groups.[96] If this testimony is true, it appears that any organization of criminal groups in Sicily was modeled after that in America rather than the common belief (discussed earlier in this chapter) that a Mafia organization was imported to America from Sicily. In his autobiography, Joseph Bonanno claims to have set up such a commission in America, but he refused to testify in the "commission" trial and was jailed for contempt.

Similar to both Valachi's and Fratianno's earlier testimony, the role of the commission, according to the defendants in the "commission" trial, is only to approve new members and to avoid conflicts between the groups. The prosecution argued, however, that four of the defendants participated in "the ruling council of La Cosa Nostra, or the 'Mafia,' which directed criminal activity."[97] The defendants maintained that "just because someone is a Mafia member, it doesn't mean that he has committed the crimes in this case." The distinction the defense attempted to make was that the Mafia was a loose social and business association of individuals with similar backgrounds, but without a criminal purpose, that could be likened to a plumber's or businessman's professional association that has as a purpose the avoidance of conflict.[98] The purpose of the defense's admissions in the "commission" trial was to challenge the government "to prove that it has actually engaged in the crimes of which it has been accused."[99] The charges included bid rigging of concrete prices, extortion, and (in the case of one defendant) murder. The charges were ultimately proven, and the defendants were each sentenced to 100 years in prison.

Fifth, several of the mob trials resulted in acquittals and mistrials. It has been argued by some that the government's heavy reliance on former criminals as paid government witnesses is a questionable practice. Juries may not be willing to convict a defendant when the case is based largely on the testimony of a criminal-turned-informant.[100] The issues posed by the use of paid government informers are assessed in Chapter 8.

Impacts

Although it is difficult to assess the long-term result of these successful organized crime prosecutions, several immediate impacts have already been felt: increased violence, more sophisticated criminal operations, and a possible shift in the primary activities of organized crime groups.

First, the shooting of Paul Castellano by members of his own Gambino family demonstrates how the threatened incapacitation of a crime leader through imprisonment can lead to murder, as other members either fear they will be implicated in crimes or are seeking to replace the leader. It has been argued that successful prosecution of organized crime leaders will bring to power younger, more aggressive leaders who will use violence more freely to protect their interests and avoid prosecution.[101] The car-bombing murder of Frank DeCiccio in New York City soon after Castellano's death was seen as a retaliatory act. More violence followed in the struggle for leadership of organized crime groups and the effort to avoid prosecution by "protecting" illicit enterprises and "eliminating" suspected informants.[102]

Second, there will be a shift in organized crime activities. Interviews with law enforcement officials reveal that organized criminals may be shifting to "safer" activities that are better protected from street-level investigations. Increasing organized crime involvement in credit card fraud, counterfeiting, stock frauds, and illicit waste disposal have been cited as examples of this trend.[103] As a result, the infiltration of legitimate business may prove to be an area of greater interest to organized crime rather than the more visible activities necessary in catering to the vices of narcotics and gambling, which have greater apprehension risks (see Figure 6.2).

Third, organized crime will have to become more sophisticated in its operation to maintain acceptable levels of success. As sociologist Mary McIntosh has suggested, the "technology" or sophistication of organized criminal activity responds to law enforcement effectiveness. Once law enforcement strategy becomes more effective, as mob trials indicate, "we can expect the criminal technology to reach rapidly the same level of efficiency in order to maintain

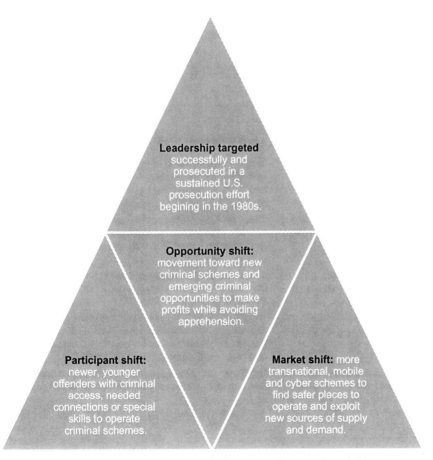

Leadership targeted successfully and prosecuted in a sustained U.S. prosecution effort begining in the 1980s.

Opportunity shift: movement toward new criminal schemes and emerging criminal opportunities to make profits while avoiding apprehension.

Participant shift: newer, younger offenders with criminal access, needed connections or special skills to operate criminal schemes.

Market shift: more transnational, mobile and cyber schemes to find safer places to operate and exploit new sources of supply and demand.

FIGURE 6.2 The impacts of successful organized crime prosecutions over the last 30 years.

acceptable levels of success."[104] This sophistication may take the form of greater dealings in the financing of criminal activities than in the operation of criminal enterprises. Gambling and narcotics sales have been claimed to be the two largest sources of organized crime revenue. It is possible that traditional racketeers who wish to remain in the gambling and narcotics business will back off from operating these higher risk enterprises and be content to finance other illicit entrepreneurs for a percentage of the profits. Illegal profits can then be laundered through legally owned businesses, such as restaurants and nightclubs. In order to accomplish this, there may be greater effort among organized criminals in the future to infiltrate legitimate businesses to obtain access to money for financing and to have the means to launder illicitly obtained cash.[105] Labor union funds and the construction industry have been favorite targets in the past, and obtaining a "mob tax" percentage of the motor fuel tax frauds run by Russian groups provides recent examples of this phenomenon.[106] A summary of the outcomes and implications of the mob trials is presented in Table 6.3.

Table 6.3 Summary of Mob Trial Outcomes and Implications

Results of 30 Years of Mob Prosecutions	Implications for the Future
Many significant cases involving leaders of crime groups who received lengthy sentences. Many of these leaders are older, effectively ending their criminal careers	Lengthy incarceration of group leaders has resulted in (and will continue to cause) violence within and among crime groups for leadership and control of criminal markets (e.g., narcotics, gambling)
Most cases occurred in New York City area, but many prosecutions are occurring in large cities in many parts of the United States	In some cities, Mafia groups have been prosecuted almost out of existence, leaving the door open for other groups to take over illicit markets and criminal opportunities
Italian-Americans have been the focus of these prosecutions, although there are a growing number of large-scale prosecutions of non-Italian groups	It is likely that the majority of trials in the future will involve non-Mafia groups, as other groups become dominant in the illegal economy
The "commission" trial caused the defense to stipulate the existence of the Mafia and communication among crime groups in different locations	The extent to which Mafia and non-Mafia groups are organized and work together will vary widely, although more sophisticated and international schemes will require participation of multiple criminal partners
Successful prosecutions in traditional areas of organized crime (e.g., narcotics, gambling, extortion) have caused some groups to shift to more sophisticated activities that engender less street-level exposure to law enforcement efforts	Organized crimes will use more sophisticated schemes to hide criminal activities from law enforcement efforts, such as money laundering, stock market and investment scams, use of the Internet, and frauds

Prosecution is a necessary tool in addressing organized crime, but it is important to understand and anticipate its impacts. Figure 6.2 illustrates how the effective targeting of organized crime (especially mob) leadership over the last 30 years has impacted organized crime in the United States significantly. It can also be seen that there is a ripple effect caused by this success: shifts occur in organized crime participants, opportunities, and markets, often in response to this prosecution success. Participants shift in that newer, younger offenders with criminal access, needed connections, or special skills move up to operate criminal schemes. Opportunities shift as organized criminals move toward new criminal schemes and emerging criminal opportunities to make profits while avoiding apprehension. Markets shift in response to prosecution as more transnational, mobile, and cyber schemes are developed to find safer places to operate and exploit new sources of supply and demand. See Figure 6.3.

FIGURE 6.3 Reggio Calabria head of Police Guido Longo, left, gives the thumbs up next to FBI special agent Leo Taddeo following a joint Italian-U.S. authorities' press conference on an anti-Mafia blitz with numerous arrests reported on both sides of the Atlantic on February 11, 2014. *AP Photo/Alessandra Tarantino*

CRITICAL THINKING EXERCISE 6.3

A Case of Murder Among Gangsters

Much has been made of "honor among thieves" and the "oath of loyalty" taken by traditional Mafia members. From Valachi to Gravano there have been accounts of secret induction ceremonies in which males of Italian decent are asked to hold their hand over a flame and have their finger pricked to take a "blood oath" of loyalty to "this thing of ours" (which has come to be roughly translated into Mafia or Cosa Nostra). Loyalty to fellow Mafia members is said to be stronger than one's allegiance to their own family.

Despite this professed loyalty, there have been thousands of instances in which members have doubled-crossed, betrayed, and murdered each other for little or no reason. Consider the case of Herbert Blitzstein, a gangster with ties to the Cosa Nostra group in Chicago. He gave $25,000 to Joseph DeLuca to set up "Any Auto Repair" in Las Vegas, a shop to repair, buy, and sell cars. According to DeLuca, he would give the money he made from the business to Blitzstein, who would lend it to others at usurious rates. Both the loan-shark money and auto repair money were split evenly between DeLuca and Blitzstein.

A few years into this scheme, Peter Caruso, a person with links to crime groups in Buffalo, Chicago, and Los Angeles, told DeLuca that he was being cheated by Blitzstein. Caruso said he planned to steal Blitzstein's share of both the auto shop and the loanshark business and wanted DeLuca's help. DeLuca said he needed the advice and consent of Robert Panaro, with whom he had dealt in the past and trusted, and who was a "made" (i.e., inducted) member of the Mafia. After several meetings involving other criminals, there was disagreement over whether Blitzstein should be forced out of the business by threats or whether he should be killed. It was clear, however, that Panaro and the others would profit from Blitzstein's removal from the enterprises.

DeLuca expressed fear that Blitzstein would retaliate against him, but Panaro said, "you wanted him shut up, so we're here to shut him up ... we're here to protect you." Besides, if Blitzstein refused to forfeit his interest in the businesses, Panaro indicated that Branco (a Panaro associate) would "pick him up bodily" and throw him out of the building. Panaro told DeLuca that Blitzstein would be robbed and "if something was going to happen to him, oh well." Blitzstein's body was discovered by police 2 days later.

After Blitzstein's death, Panaro asked DeLuca to compile a list of all the outstanding loanshark debts (which totaled $250,000), and Panaro and his associates split these proceeds. They also agreed to let DeLuca make regular payments to them for the privilege of operating the auto shop.

Critical Thinking Questions

1. Why do you believe DeLuca went to Panaro for help when he could have handled the problem himself?
2. How do you explain the fact that DeLuca came to Panaro for help, but Panaro ultimately exploited him, despite their previous relationship?

Source: United States v. Panaro, *241 F.3d 1104 (2001).*

SUMMARY

The history of Mafia-linked crime in the United States is a long one, but it resulted in very few important prosecutions until the 1980s. Since then, we have witnessed the most significant organized crime prosecution effort in U.S. history. The successful prosecution of organized crime leaders in recent years may be a mixed blessing, in that prosecutions disrupt operations for a short period, but also have been shown to bring to power younger and more violent leaders. Successful prosecutions also shift organized crime activities to "safer" but more complex scams; and possibly encourage further organized crime infiltration into legitimate business to finance illicit business and launder illegally obtained profits. Therefore, successful prosecutions of organized crime figures is only one step in reducing its incidence. Changes in the nature of organized crime, and the law enforcement response to it, are considered in the next chapters.

ORGANIZED CRIME BIOGRAPHY

Biographies tell the life story of interesting people. In the world of criminal justice, biographies of organized crime figures offer insight into the background and motivations of the individuals who choose that lifestyle, the reasons for their choices, and their consequences. The following is a brief summary of an organized crime biography, followed by questions that ask you to reflect on the connections between that person's life and the content of this book.

A Man of Honor: The Autobiography of Joseph Bonanno
Joseph Bonanno (St. Martin's Press, 2000)

Bound by Honor: A Mafioso's Story
Bill Bonanno (St. Martin's Press, 2003)

Books by father and son, written more than 15 years apart, reveal the lives of career members of organized crime. Joe Bonanno was the first (and only) Mafia leader ever to write an autobiography. An immigrant from Italy, he provides the history of Italian-American organized crime in New York and his role in it, arguing that he retired years ago as boss of the New York crime family (which still bears his name) and moved to Arizona. His son, Bill Bonanno, is college educated and served in the military, but still ended up as an organized crime figure (by choice) and ultimately doing time in prison. His book explains how that happened.

Together, these books offer a unique perspective on the development of a powerful Italian-American group in New York. Joe was uneducated, but had good leadership skills until he was kidnapped by his own mobster cousin; he was eventually released unharmed. Bill ended up following in the footsteps of his father, marrying the niece of another Mafia family leader, and concluding that he has "no apologies" for his life and that the "best values of my world" are "loyalty within a group, honor, devotion to one another, [and] responsibility for one's actions."

Questions
1. How would you explain Bill Bonanno's decision to follow in his father's footsteps (and become a target of law enforcement) rather than pursuing a legitimate career?
2. Do you agree with Bill Bonanno's statement about the "best values" of his world? Why or why not?

ORGANIZED CRIME AT THE MOVIES

Movies seek to entertain and inform the audience about a story, incident, or person. Many good movies also hit upon important substantive themes relevant to understanding organized crime. Read the following movie summary (and watch the movie if you haven't already) and answer the questions that follow to make the organized crime subject matter connections.

A Bronx Tale
Robert De Niro, Director (1993)

A Bronx Tale is a coming-of-age story of a young man raised in New York City's Bronx during the 1960s. The film is based on a one-man play written by Chazz Palminteri about his own difficult childhood. Palminteri agreed to sell the movie rights to first-time director Robert De Niro on the condition that he was able to play the role of the local Mafia boss, Sonny.

The movie focuses on the life of Calogero Anello, a 9-year-old child living in a violent neighborhood filled with mobsters and racists. Calogero witnesses a murder by a local Mafia boss, Sonny, but he says nothing when questioned by the police. Sonny is impressed by Calogero who starts to visit Sonny and his gang almost every day, something that meets the

Continued

ORGANIZED CRIME AT THE MOVIES—CONT'D

strong disapproval of his father, Lorenzo (Robert De Niro), who is a bus driver struggling to make ends meet. He tells Calogero, "You want to see a real hero? Look at a guy who gets up in the morning and goes off to work and supports his family. That's heroism."

The film moves forward 8 years and Calogero is now 17 years old. He continues to see Sonny, who gives him a "street" education, but tells him that being a gangster is too dangerous. Calogero doesn't hear the message, however, and becomes involved with racist friends who attack without reason blacks who have moved into the neighborhood. His life gets complicated when he falls in love with a black girlfriend, and the movie is filled with interesting neighborhood characters.

Ultimately, Calogero must choose between his education in school and the influence of his father versus the life of the street as a gangster. The advice of Sonny and Lorenzo is sometimes similar, but it leads to entirely different lives and Calogero must make a choice.

Questions

1. This movie asks fundamental questions about how a person raised in a tough neighborhood with conflicting influences can avoid becoming a criminal. Can you explain how this occurs?

2. How do you explain the lure of the Mafia lifestyle and why it is rejected by many but is attractive to some?

References and Notes

1. McPhee, M. "Mobster Shot Dead in Queens," *New York Daily News* (January 4, 2002).

2. Smith, D. C., Jr. (1990). *The Mafia Mystique*. Lanham, MD: University Press of America, p. 28.

3. Albini, J. L. (1971). *The American Mafia: Genesis of a Legend*. New York: Irvington, pp. 159–167. Nelli, H. S. (1981). *The Business of Crime: Italians and Syndicate Crime in the United States*. Chicago, IL: University of Chicago Press, ch. 2; Smith. *The Mafia Mystique*, pp. 27–44.

4. Albini. *The American Mafia*, ch. 5; Nelli. *The Business of Crime*, ch. 3; Smith. *The Mafia Mystique*, p. 32.

5. Pitkin, T. M., & Cordasco, F. (1977). *The Black Hand: A Chapter in Ethnic Crime*. Totowa, NJ: Littlefield Adams, pp. 22–30.

6. *The Mafia Mystique*, p. 32.

7. *The American Mafia*, p. 125. Some of the sources he cites are in Italian, except Barzini, L., Jr. "The Real Mafia," *Harper's Magazine* (June 1954); Sladen, D. (1907). *Sicily*. New York: E.P. Dutton; Hood, A. N. (1916). *Sicilian Studies*. New York: Dodd, Mead and Co.; King, B., & Okey, T. (1901). *Italy Today*. London: James Nisber and Co.; Neville, R. "The Mafia Is Deadlier," *The New York Times Magazine* (January 12, 1964). Maxwell, G. (1960). *Ten Pains of Death*. New York: E.P. Dutton; Paton, W. A. (1900). *Picturesque Sicily*. New York: Harper and Brothers; Pantaleone, M. (1966). *The Mafia and Politics*. New York: Coward-McCann.

8. *The American Mafia*, p. 133.

9. *The American Mafia*, p. 135.

10. Hess, H. (1998). *Mafia & Mafiosi: Origin, Power and Myth*. New York University Press, p. 155.

11. Hess, H. (1998). *Mafia & Mafiosi: Origin, Power and Myth*. New York University Press, p. 127.

12. Hess, H. (1986). The Traditional Sicilian Mafia: Organized Crime and Repressive Crime. In R. Kelly (Ed.), *Organized Crime: A Global Perspective*. Totowa, NJ: Rowan and Littlefield, p. 123.

13. Blok, A. (1996). *The Mafia of a Sicilian Village, 1860–1960*. Prospect Heights, IL: Waveland Press, pp. 10–11.

14. Blok, A. (1996). *The Mafia of a Sicilian Village, 1860–1960*. Prospect Heights, IL: Waveland Press, p. 92.

15. Servadio, G. (1978). *Mafioso: A History of the Mafia from Its Origins to the Present Day*. New York: Dell, p. 3.

16. *Mafioso*, pp. 19–20.

17. See also Barzini. *"The Real Mafia."*

18. Arlacchi, P. (1986). *Mafia Business: The Mafia Ethic and the Spirit of Capitalism*. London: Verso, p. 4.

19. Arlacchi, P. (1986). *Mafia Business: The Mafia Ethic and the Spirit of Capitalism*. London: Verso, p. 26.

20. Walston, J. (1986). See Naples and Die: Organized Crime in Campania. In R. Kelly (Ed.), *Organized Crime: A Global Perspective*. Totowa, NJ: Rowan and Littlefield, p. 139.

21. Walston, J. (1986). See Naples and Die: Organized Crime in Campania. In R. Kelly (Ed.), *Organized Crime: A Global Perspective*. Totowa, NJ: Rowan and Littlefield, pp. 143, 153.

22. Walston, J. (1986). See Naples and Die: Organized Crime in Campania. In R. Kelly (Ed.), *Organized Crime: A Global Perspective*. Totowa, NJ: Rowan and Littlefield, p. 137.

23. Dionne, E. J. "Naples Gang War: And Now the Courtroom Scene," *The New York Times* (April 16, 1985), 2.

24. Lombardo, R. M. (2002). The Black Hand: Terror by Letter in Chicago. *Journal of Contemporary Criminal Justice*, 18, 394–409.

25. Lubasch, A. H. "Mafia Member Testifies on Sicily 'Commission,'" *The New York Times* (November 1, 1985), B3.

26. Ferrarotti, F. (1989). The Sicilian Mafia: 1860–1977. *Italian Journal*, 5, 17–28.

27. Catanzaro, R. (1992). *Men of Respect: A Social History of the Sicilian Mafia*. New York: The Free Press, p. 18.

28. Blumenthal, R. (1988). *Last Days of the Sicilians: The FBI Assault on the Pizza Connection*. New York: Times Books; Alexander, S. (1988). *The Pizza Connection: Lawyers, Money, Drugs, Mafia*. New York: Weidenfeld and Nicolson; Stoler, P. "The Sicilian Connection," *Time* (October 15, 1984), 42–51.

29. Sterling, C. (1990). *Octopus: The Long Reach of the International Sicilian Mafia*. New York: W. W. Norton.

30. *Octopus: The Long Reach of the International Sicilian Mafia*, p. 289.

31. Jamieson, A. (2000). *The Anti-Mafia: Italty's Fight against Organized Crime*. New York: St. Martin's Press; Dickie, J. "Mob Rule and Dirty Money," *The Observer (London)* (February 10, 2002), 17.

32. "Italian Court Sentences 97 After Four-Year Trial," *Organized Crime Digest* (March 9, 1994), 8.

33. Arlacchi, P. (1993). *Men of Dishonor: Inside the Sicilian Mafia*. New York: William Morrow, p. 21.

34. *Men of Dishonor: Inside the Sicilian Mafia*, p. 35.

35. Attanasio, A. Sr. "The Sicilian Mafia Enters the 21st Century," *Organized Crime Digest* (August 11, 1993), 1.

36. Landesco, J. (1968). *Organized Crime in Chicago, Part III of the Illinois Crime Survey, 1929*. Chicago, IL: University of Chicago Press, p. 277.

37. Bergeen, L. (1994). *Capone: The Man and the Era. Organized Crime in Chicago*. New York: Simon and Schuster, p. 278.

38. Browning, F., & Gerassi, J. (1980). *The American Way of Crime*. New York: G.P. Putnam & Sons; Morgan, J. (1985). *Prince of Crime*. New York: Stein and Day.

39. Russo, G. (2003). *The Outfit: The Role of Chicago's Underworld in the Shaping of Modern America*. New York: Bloombury.

40. Peterson, V. (1983). *The Mob: 200 Years of Organized Crime in New York*. Ottawa, IL: Green Hill; Joselit, J. (1983). *Our Gang: Jewish Crime and the New York Jewish Community, 1900–1940*. Bloomington, IN: Indiana University Press; Wolf, G., & DiMona, J. (1975). *Frank Costello*. New York: Bantam.

41. *The Mob*.

42. Jacobs, T. (1990). *The Gangsters*. New York: Mallard Press; Feder, S., & Joesten, J. (1972). *The Luciano Story*. New York: Award Books.

43. Monaco, R., & Bascom, L. (1991). *Rubouts: Mob Murders in America*. New York: Avon Books.

44. Mappen, M. (2013). *Prohibition Gangsters: The Rise and Fall of a Bad Generation*. New Brunswick, NJ: Rutgers University Press, p. 49.

45. Ness, E., & Fraley, O. (1957). *The Untouchables*. New York: Pocket Books.

46. Mappen, M. (2013). *Prohibition Gangsters: The Rise and Fall of a Bad Generation*. New Brunswick, NJ: Rutgers University Press, pp. 6, 159.

47. U.S. Senate Special Committee to Investigate Organized Crime in Interstate Commerce (1951). *Third Interim Report*. Washington, DC: U.S. Government Printing Office, p. 2.

48. Moore, W. H. (1974). *The Kefauver Committee and the Politics of Crime, 1950–1952*. Columbia, MO: University of Missouri Press, p. 134.

49. *The Kefauver Committee*, pp. 237–238.

50. *The Kefauver Committee*, p. 241.

51. Albini, J. L. (1971). *The American Mafia: Genesis of a Legend*. New York: Irvington, p. 210.

52. Mappen, M. (2013). *Prohibition Gangsters: The Rise and Fall of a Bad Generation*. New Brunswick, NJ: Rutgers University Press, p. 170.

53. Bell, D. (1953). Crime as an American Way of Life. *The Antioch Review*, 13(June), 131.

54. Turkus, B. B., & Feder, S. (1951). *Murder, Inc*. New York: Manor Books.

55. Bell, "*Crime as an American Way of Life*"; Ianni, F. A. J. (1974). *Black Mafia: Ethnic Succession in Organized Crime*. New York: Simon and Schuster, p. 144

56. Lombardo, R. M. (2013). The Chicago Outfit: Alien Conspiracy or Machine Politics? *Journal of Contemporary Criminal Justice, 29*, 233–255.

57. *The Mafia Mystique*, pp. 162–163.

58. *The Mafia Mystique*, p. 171.

59. New York State Joint Legislative Committee on Government Operations (1958). *Interim Report on the Gangland Meeting at Apalachin Part III*. Legislative Document No. 25, p. 101.

60. Bonanno, J. (2001). *A Man of Honor*. New York: St. Martin's Press; Bonanno, B. (2000). *Bound by Honor: A Mafioso's Story*. New York: St. Martin's Press.

61. *The Mafia Mystique*, p. 194.

62. New York State Temporary Commission of Investigation (1963). *The Apalachin Meeting*. New York: State Investigations Commission, p. 20.

63. *United States v. Buffalino et al.*, 285 F.2d 408 (2d Cir. 1960).

64. Maas, P. (1969). *The Valachi Papers*. New York: Bantam, p. 1.

65. U.S. Senate Committee on Government Operations Permanent Subcommittee on Investigations (1963). *Organized Crime and Illicit Traffic in Narcotics: Hearings Part I 88th Congress, 1st Session.* Washington, DC: U.S. Government Printing Office, p. 180.

66. *Murder, Inc.*, p. 201.

67. Binder, J. J., & Eghigian, M., Jr. (2013). Gangland Killings in Chicago, 1919–1933. *Journal of Contemporary Criminal Justice, 29,* 219–232.

68. Block, A. A. (1978). History and the Study of Organized Crime. *Urban Life, 6,* 455–474; Humbert S. Nelli, *The Business of Crime*, pp. 179–218; Mappen, M. (2013). *Prohibition Gangsters: The Rise and Fall of a Bad Generation.* New Brunswick, NJ: Rutgers University Press.

69. President's Commission on Law Enforcement and Administration of Justice (1967). *Task Force Report: Organized Crime.* Washington, DC: U.S. Government Printing Office; Cressey, D. R. (1969). *Theft of the Nation.* New York: Harper & Row.

70. U.S. Senate. *Organized Crime and Illicit Traffic in Narcotics*, p. 80.

71. U.S. Senate. *Organized Crime and Illicit Traffic in Narcotics*, pp. 116, 194.

72. *The Mafia Mystique*, pp. 217–242.

73. *The Mafia Mystique*, p. 234.

74. Hawkins, G. (1969). God and the Mafia. *The Public Interest, 14,* 50–51.

75. *United States v. Tieri*, trial transcript, 80 S.D.N.Y. Cr. 381, pp. 2181–2183.

76. *United States v. Tieri*, trial transcript, 80 S.D.N.Y. Cr. 381, pp. 2304–2305.

77. It should be noted that, prior to trial, defense counsel Jay Goldberg sought to have the prosecutor disqualified from this case. A letter Ackerman submitted to the U.S. Parole Commission asking for Fratianno's early release from prison claimed that Fratianno's testimony led to the conviction of four persons in an earlier case involving fraud at the Westchester Premier Theatre. Goldberg pointed out that no one was convicted at the trial in which Fratianno testified. The presiding judge, Thomas Griesa, denied this motion to disqualify the prosecutor, however.

78. *United States v. Tieri*, trial transcript, pp. 863, 870.

79. U.S. Senate Committee on Governmental Affairs Permanent Subcommittee on Investigations (1980). *Organized Crime and the Use of Violence: Hearings Part I 86th Congress, 2nd Session.* Washington, DC: U.S. Government Printing Office, pp. 114–116.

80. U.S. Senate. *Organized Crime and Illicit Traffic in Narcotics*, pp. 386–387.

81. U.S. Senate. *Organized Crime and the Use of Violence*, pp. 90, 91.

82. U.S. Senate. *Organized Crime and Illicit Traffic in Narcotics*, pp. 270–271.

83. *United States v. Tieri*, trial transcript, pp. 875–878.

84. U.S. Senate. *Organized Crime and the Use of Violence*, p. 88.

85. Demaris, O. (1981). *The Last Mafioso.* New York: Bantam, pp. 20–22.

86. Powell, S., Emerson, S., Orr, K., Collins, D., & Quick, B. "Busting the Mob," *U.S. News & World Report* (February 3, 1986), 24–31.

87. James, B. (1994). *Jacobs, Busting the Mob: United States v. Cosa Nostra.* New York: New York University Press, p. 4.

88. McShane, L. "All Five NYC Family Heads Simultaneously Behind Bars for First Time," *Associated Press* (January 25, 2003).

89. McShane, L. "All Five NYC Family Heads Simultaneously Behind Bars for First Time," *Associated Press* (January 25, 2003), 25.

90. Davis, J. H. (1993). *Mafia Dynasty: The Rise and Fall of the Gambino Crime Family.* New York: Harper–Collins; Cox, D. (1992). *Mafia Wipeout: How the Feds Put Away an Entire Mob Family.* New York: SPI Books; Friel, F., & Gunther, J. (1992). *Breaking the Mob.* New York: Warner Books; O'Neill, G., & Lehr, D. (1989). *The Underboss: The Rise and Fall of a Mafia Family.* New York: St. Martin's Press; Cummings, J., & Volkman, E. (1990). *Goombata: The Improbable Rise and Fall of John Gotti and His Gang.* Boston, MA: Little, Brown; McShane, L. "All Five NYC Family Heads Simultaneously Behind Bars for First Time," *Associated Press* (January 25, 2003); Rashbaum, W. K. "FBI and Police Arrest More Than 100 in Mob Sweep," *The New York Times* (January 20, 2011).

91. Finckenauer, J. O. (2001). *La Cosa Nostra in the United States.* Washington, DC: National Institute of Justice International Center; Lindberg, R. C. (2001). *The Mafia in America: Traditional Organized Crime in Transition.* www.search-international.com/Articles/crime/mafiaamerican. htm. organizedcrime.about.com/blnyfamilies.htm; El-Ghobashy, T., & Gardiner, S. "Is the Mob Done or Bouncing Back?," *The Wall Street Journal* (January 21, 2011); U.S. Department of Justice (2013). *Philadelphia La Cosa Nostra Underboss Sentenced to 188 Months in Prison.* Washington, DC: Office of Public Affairs, July 11.

92. Goldberg, J. "The Don Is Done," *The New York Times* (January 31, 1999), 25.

93. Shapiro, R. "Well-armed Bonanno Crime Crew Busted on Charges including Viagra Trafficking, Extortion: DA," *New York Daily News* (July 9, 2013).

94. U.S. Department of Justice (2013). *Aryan Brotherhood of Texas Gang Member Sentenced in Houston to 150 Months in Prison for Role in Racketeering Conspiracy.* Washington, DC: Office of Public Affairs, June 27.

95. U.S. Department of Justice (2013). *Associate of Asian Organized Crime Organization Sentenced.* Boston, MA: U.S. Attorney District of Massachusetts, July 22.

96. Lubash, A. H. "Mafia Member Testifies on Sicily 'Commission,'" *The New York Times* (November 1, 1985), B3.

97. Lubash, A. H. "Persico Asks Jury Not to Be Duped by Mafia Label," *The New York Times* (September 19, 1986), 1, 24; Smothers, R. "Tapes Played at Mob Trial Focus on Money and Power," *The New York Times* (January 26, 1986), 20.

98. Magnuson, E. "Hitting the Mafia," *Time* (September 29, 1986), 14–22.

99. Oreskes, M. "Commission Trial Illustrates Changes in Attitude on Mafia," *The New York Times* (September 20, 1986), B29–B30.

100. Dershowitz, A. M. "Gotti Case Shows Flaws and Buying Witnesses," *The Buffalo News* (March 20, 1987), C3; Murphy, S., & Cambanis, T. "Connolly Convicted but Jury Acquits Ex-Agent of Most Serious Charges," *The Boston Globe* (May 29, 2002), A1; Riley, J., & DeStefano, A. "Prosecutors Give Up on Gotti after 4 Hung Juries," *Newsday (New York)* (January 14, 2010), 8.

101. Anderson, A. G. (1979). *The Business of Organized Crime.* Stanford, CA: Hoover Institution Press, p. 144.

102. McPhee, M. "Fuhgeddaboud the Old Mob: After Gotti, Mafia Ordered to Clean House," *New York Daily News* (July 7, 2002), 4.

103. Powell et al. *"Busting the Mob,"* p. 26.

104. McIntosh, M. (1975). *The Organisation of Crime.* London: Macmillan.

105. Glaberson, W. "Old Mobs Never Die, and Cliched but Brutal Methods Refuse to Fade Away," *The New York Times* (January 26, 2003), 27; Marzulli, J., Zambito, T., & Smith, G. B. "Kill the Mafia? Forget About It—How Families Adapt to the 21st Century," *Daily News (New York)* (June 7, 2009), 12; Gardiner, S., & Shallwani, P. "Mafia Is Down—but Not Out: Crime

Families Adapt to Survive, Lowering Profile and Using Need-to-Know Tactics," *The Wall Street Journal* (February 18, 2014).

106. Rush, R. J., & Scarpitti, F. R. (2001). Russian Organized Crime: The Continuation of a Tradition. *Deviant Behavior, 22*, 517–540; Jacobs, J. (2007). *Mobsters, Unions, and Feds: The Mafia and the American Labor Movement.* New York: New York University Press; Jacobs, J. R., & Cooperman, K. T. (2011). *Breaking the Devil's Pact: The Battle to Free the Teamsters from the Mob.* New York: New York University Press.

CHAPTER 7

Changes in Organized Crime
From Local to Transnational

*The true history of the President's Commission on
Organized Crime is a saga of missed opportunity.*
**—Ten members of the 18-member
President's Commission (1987)**

The founder of the witness protection program, Gerald Shur, said "a presidential commission had recommended that we begin protecting witnesses, and this gave the idea credibility and tremendous political clout. I jumped on that report. It was exactly what I needed to get the ball rolling."[1] Presidential commissions are appointed to investigate a problem when it is not immediately clear what to do about it. Their conclusions are important because they present official views of a subject, and they often set the agenda for future law and policy decisions in the area. Gerald Shur's elation about the commission's recommendation to support his idea shows the power of their conclusions. (The witness protection program is discussed in Chapter 10.)

Two U.S. presidential commissions have focused specifically on organized crime in the past 50 years. The Task Force on Organized Crime of the President's Commission on Law Enforcement and Administration of Justice reported to President Johnson in 1967, and the President's Commission on Organized Crime reported to President Reagan in 1986 (although the final report was not released until 1987). Each of these investigations took approximately 2 years to complete, relying on hearings, testimony, and research staff to conduct their analyses. Since the latter report was completed, there have been dramatic changes in the world political landscape and significant changes in the global economy, in communications, and in ease of travel that have had direct impacts on organized crime.

This chapter compares the observations and conclusions of the two presidential commissions in their assessment of (1) the proper definition of organized crime, (2) the primary activities of organized crime groups, (3) their role in public and private corruption, (4) national efforts to prevent organized crime, and (5) recommendations for the future. The chapter then presents major organized crime issues that have arisen during the past 30 years since the last commission, corresponding to political and economic changes around the world, so the reader can see the changes from the 1960s to the 1980s to the present day.

PRESIDENTIAL INVESTIGATIONS OF ORGANIZED CRIME

The Task Force Report (TFR) on Organized Crime concluded in 1967 that organized crime was a "society." In particular, the "core of organized crime in the United States consists of 24 groups" exclusively of Italian origin and totaling 5,000 members. The term "Mafia" was not mentioned in the text of the report, although it was mentioned in a footnote as the name of this "nationwide crime syndicate."[2] It was claimed that the 24 groups of this syndicate worked with and controlled other racket groups of other ethnic derivations.

This information was credited to the Kefauver and McClellan Senate Committee investigations of the 1950s and 1960s, which brought national attention to organized crime. Based on the testimony of criminal-turned-informant Joseph Valachi in 1963, who said he had never heard of a Mafia but, rather, the Cosa Nostra, the TFR concluded that this Italian-based syndicate had changed its name from the Mafia to La Cosa Nostra.[3]

The report went on to detail the structure of each organized crime group, or "family," relying heavily on the testimony of Joseph Valachi 4 years earlier. The now-familiar vernacular of "commission," "boss," "underboss," and "soldier" were all detailed in this report. Although it was admitted that knowledge of organized crime at that time was comparable to "the knowledge of Standard Oil which could be gleaned from gasoline station attendants," the task force was not deterred from publishing elaborate charts and schematic diagrams of how these groups of the Cosa Nostra were supposedly organized in the United States.[4]

President Reagan's Commission on Organized Crime published seven volumes of hearings and four reports during its more than 2 years of existence. Although the commission disbanded and submitted its final report to the president on April 1, 1986, the final report was not published and made available to the public until April 1987. The Reagan Commission held public hearings in a number of large cities at which primarily law enforcement officials testified about organized crime. The commission's four ultimate reports included the subjects of money laundering, labor racketeering, drug use and trafficking, and a final report.

It is clear that the definition of organized crime offered by the Reagan Commission was broader than that given 20 years earlier. In its hearings on organized crime of Asian origin, the commission concluded

> Since the early 1960s, when Joseph Valachi provided dramatic testimony concerning activities of La Cosa Nostra (LCN), many people (including representatives from leading law enforcement agencies) have gained the

impression that organized crime in the United States is dominated by, or consists almost totally of, the LCN "families" whose members are of Italian origin.[5]

The commission observed, "it is misleading to describe the more prominent Asian groups as 'emerging groups' inasmuch as they engage in much illicit activity, corruption, and violence to protect their activities."[6]

This view of organized crime involving much more than Italian-Americans is a significant departure from the focus of the 1967 report. This emphasis was further evidenced in other parts of the 1986 commission investigation. At the conclusion of the hearings on cocaine distribution, for example, the commission declared,

> The testimony in this record portrays a state of war . . . a situation in which large, sophisticated organizations, based abroad but with agents and collaborators within our borders, have launched a massive, well-armed and well-financed invasion of our country by sea and air, resulting in thousands of our citizens being killed or disabled.[7]

Similarly, the hearings on heroin distribution had a multiethnic perspective. The commission concluded "more and more groups of different ethnic origins are becoming substantially involved in heroin importation and distribution networks."[8] The commission's report on drugs concluded, "America's cocaine supply at present originates exclusively from South America."[9] It also claimed that in the mid-1980s, "Mexican traffickers provided a 32% share of the heroin consumed in the United States."[10] Finally, the commission noted in the hearings on gambling that "not only the traditional organized crime groups, but also numerous emerging groups, participate in the lucrative gambling market."[11] In its final report, the commission outlined the operations of organized crime among Italian-American groups, outlaw motorcycle gangs, prison gangs, and Chinese, Vietnamese, Japanese, Cuban, Colombian, Irish, Russian, and Canadian criminal groups.[12]

It can be seen that a great deal of emphasis was placed on organized criminal activity apart from the traditional focus on Italian-American organized crime. This emphasis distinguishes the 1986 commission investigation from the 1967 TFR.

Activities of Organized Crime Groups

The 1967 TFR was emphatic in its claim that "law enforcement officers agree almost unanimously that gambling is the largest source of revenue" for organized crime.[13] The report provided estimated figures of this revenue, but admitted the figures may not be accurate.

The TFR claimed that loansharking "is the second largest source of revenue for organized crime" and is funded by gambling profits.[14] No reliable estimates of its magnitude were available. Interestingly, only two paragraphs in the entire TFR were devoted to narcotics. It was found that narcotics are "imported by organized crime" and sold by independent pushers. Heroin was the only drug mentioned by name in the report. It was also concluded that prostitution and bootlegging "play a small and declining role in organized crime operations," and little attention was given these in the report.[15]

The TFR discussed the infiltration of legitimate business and how organized criminals invest illegal profits to establish a "legal source of funds." It was mentioned twice that organized criminals pay no taxes on these funds, but the "cumulative effect" of this problem "cannot be measured."[16]

One additional form of organized criminal behavior addressed by the task force was labor racketeering, a discussion that consisted of only three paragraphs. The infiltration of labor unions was seen as a way to "enhance other illegal activities," such as "stealing from union funds and extorting money by threats of possible labor strife."[17]

It is apparent that the 1967 presidential investigation of organized crime focused heavily on gambling and loansharking, especially as conducted by groups of Italian-Americans. Much less attention was given to narcotics trafficking or labor racketeering.

The conclusions of the 1986 President's Commission ranked the prevalence of the activities of organized crime quite differently from that offered in 1967. In addition, the types of activities addressed were somewhat different.

The report on narcotics, for example, concluded, "This Commission has found drug trafficking to be the most widespread and lucrative organized crime activity in the United States."[18] Furthermore, it accounts "for nearly 40% of this country's organized crime activity," and it generates an "annual income estimated to be as high as $110 billion."[19] This is a marked departure from the conclusions of the 1967 TFR, which found gambling to be the largest and most lucrative organized crime activity.

The report on labor-management racketeering brought much more attention to the problem of labor racketeering than was given in the 1967 report. The commission noted that although "the majority of unions and businesses have not been tainted by organized crime," there are severe problems in those organizations where organized crime exists.[20]

Money laundering also received much more attention in the 1986 report than in the report 20 years earlier. Although no estimates were given of the amount of money laundered, it was concluded that police agencies recognize that "narcotics traffickers, who must conceal billions of dollars in cash from detection by the government, create by far the greatest demand for money laundering schemes."[21]

Finally, the commission's hearings on gambling involved testimony regarding casino skimming, basketball betting, and boxing, but no separate report on gambling was issued.

Political and Commercial Corruption

The 1967 TFR found that "all available data indicate that organized crime flourishes only where it has corrupted local officials."[22] This was because "neutralizing local law enforcement is central to organized crime's operations." A degree of immunity from prosecution is required to ensure continuance of the criminal enterprise. Although the TFR found "no large city is completely controlled by organized crime," it observed, nonetheless, "in many there is a considerable degree of corruption."[23]

The major problem faced by the task force was that it was "impossible to determine" the extent of the corruption of public officials in the United States. This lack of information may have been aggravated by the fact that most of those providing information to the task force were, themselves, public officials (i.e., police or politicians).

The 1986 President's Commission on Organized Crime found there had been a failure of banks to cooperate adequately with the intent of the Bank Secrecy Act in reporting large cash transactions, suggesting the possibility of commercial corruption in not questioning the source of large cash deposits. Such cooperation was seen as necessary to fight the laundering of illegally obtained cash. The clear connection between labor racketeering and corruption was addressed by the commission: "By manipulating the supply and costs of labor, organized crime can raise its competitor's costs, force legitimate businesses to deal with mob-run companies, and enforce price-fixing, bid-rigging, and other anticompetitive practices throughout an industry."[24]

The commission went on to recommend increased penalties and law enforcement efforts against narcotics, claiming such a policy "will not undermine organized crime policy."[25] It noted, however, that there is evidence to the contrary, suggesting that by making narcotics a higher-risk market through more severe penalties, there will be fewer, more sophisticated organizations that increase the price of the product and the violence associated with that increase.

The commission's hearings found that gambling continues to be most conducive to corruption due to the wide perception that it is a nonserious activity.

> Unlike illegal drugs, for example, which are in large part controlled by some form of organized crime and which are universally condemned, gambling is not an activity which is thought to be a harmful practice in and of itself, notwithstanding organized crime's persistent involvement. Much of what we saw and heard in the three days of hearings lends credence to the view that gambling, legal or illegal, is considered to be a relatively harmless pursuit, with no serious negative effects on society or the individual.[26]

Corruption was seen by the 1986 commission as a more concrete issue with more definable limits than in the 1967 report, which had found it was "impossible to determine its extent." The 1986 commission was also more specific as to the causes of corruption. Nevertheless, the 1986 commission, like the 1967 investigation, was dominated by information provided by public officials themselves.

National Efforts to Control Organized Crime

The TFR blamed the pervasiveness of organized crime on "belated recognition" of the problem. It was not until the publicity generated by the Kefauver Committee in 1950, the Apalachin incident in 1957, and the McClellan Committee hearings in the early 1960s that organized crime received much public or official attention (see Chapter 6 for a discussion of these events).

In 1954, the Department of Justice formed the Organized Crime and Racketeering Section to focus specifically on organized crime prosecutions, although by the early 1960s IRS tax investigations still netted the bulk of convictions related to organized crime. The TFR noted that the discovery of illicit federal wiretaps and electronic surveillance in 1965 "slowed the momentum" of the prosecution effort against organized crime.[27]

Of the 71 cities surveyed by the task force, it was found that 17 of the 19 cities with admitted organized crime problems had specialized organized crime units within their police departments. It was discovered that few special prosecutors were assigned to organized crime cases and that few programs to gather intelligence existed.

The TFR concluded that public and private crime commissions are among "the most effective vehicles for providing public information" about organized crime. They were found to be particularly helpful in "exposing organized crime and corruption and arousing public interest."[28]

Unlike the 1967 report, which proposed many new tools to combat organized crime, the 1986 commission generally found existing tools to be adequate, but they were simply not seen as the answer in preventing organized crime over the long term. With regard to narcotics, for example, the commission found that interdiction "is at best a random and occasional threat" as long as cocaine continues "in its current flood, unabated at its source." Furthermore, it was found that source country eradication will not succeed "unless it is comprehensive, long-term, and visibly supported by a national commitment" in the United States to stamp out demand.[29]

Prosecution was not seen as an effective solution for labor racketeering either. It was concluded that these rackets are "not easily deterred by prosecutive efforts that merely 'count bodies' as a measure of success."[30]

> The data compiled by the Commission confirm that the government's emphasis on the "big four" international labor unions has been both justifiable and fruitful, but has not ended the control racketeers exercise over the unions.[31]

The existing prosecution effort was found to be "fragmented, and lacks adequate coordination" among government agencies. A greater emphasis on civil remedies was encouraged "to bankrupt individual mobsters and to discourage union officers, employees, and public officials from accommodating organized crime."[32] Unfortunately, the commission undertook no evaluation of federal prosecution efforts due to a lack of cooperation by the Justice Department. This failure to carry out one of its primary objectives led to dissension among many of the commissioners and to criticism of the commission's work.[33]

Government Recommendations

The TFR cited in 1967 many existing shortfalls of efforts to combat organized crime, which were used as the basis for recommendations for change. The most significant recommendations can be grouped into five categories: proof, resources, coordination, sanctions, and commitment.

First (as to proof), the task force found that there were "difficulties in obtaining proof" in organized crime investigations. There were instances of noncooperation in victimless crimes and the reluctance of informants "to testify publicly."[34] The TFR recommended, among other suggestions, a witness protection program, a federal wiretapping law, and a provision for special grand juries to be enacted by Congress. These recommendations were later to become law within the next 3 years.

Second (as to resources), the task force found a "lack of resources" in the fight against organized crime. Staffing problems, arrests for minor offenses, and poor pay for prosecutors were all cited as examples. As the TFR concluded, an effective investigation and prosecution effort may not be fruitful "without years of intelligence gathering." The push for agencies to pile up numbers of arrests and convictions "may divert investigative energy to meaningless low-level gambling arrests that have little effect on the criminal organizations."[35] It was recommended that state attorney generals and police departments in large cities establish specialized organized crime units.

Third (as to coordination), the task force found that there was an apparent "lack of coordination" among investigators of organized crime. It was found that agencies "do not cooperate with each other in preparing cases, and they do not exchange information with each other." The threat of police corruption in organized crime cases results in officers and agencies that "do not trust each other." In addition, jurisdictional problems and the failure to develop strategic intelligence were cited as continuing problems. Once strategic intelligence information was developed, it "would enable agencies to predict what directions organized crime might take, which industries it might try to penetrate, and how it might infiltrate." The need for special prosecutors, federal technical assistance, and a federal computerized information system for organized crime were suggested. It was noted, however, that "comprehensive strategic planning" will not be possible "even with an expanded intelligence effort" until "relevant disciplines, such as economics, political science, sociology, and operations research, begin to study organized crime intensively."[36]

Fourth (as to sanctions), the task force criticized the "failure to use available sanctions" in organized crime cases. Gambling was cited as a specific example. It was recommended that extended prisons terms for felonies committed as part of a continuing enterprise be established. This subsequently became law through the Racketeer Influenced and Corrupt Organizations (RICO) section of the Organized Crime Control Act in 1970.

Fifth (as to commitment), the task force cited the "lack of public and political commitment" in the fight against organized crime. Without public pressure, politicians "have little incentive" to be serious in efforts against organized crime. Permanent investigating commissions with subpoena power were recommended for the states, as were citizen crime commissions, and better investigative reporting on organized crime that emphasizes its costs to the public.

The 1967 TFR concluded with four consultants' papers. Donald Cressey described the structure of Italian-American organized crime in the United States, as first outlined by Joseph Valachi in 1963. John Gardiner conducted a case study of political corruption in a small city. G. Robert Blakey wrote a paper that set forth the elements of the eventual federal wiretapping law and parts of the Organized Crime Control Act of 1970. Finally, Thomas Schelling attempted to explain the existence of organized crime as a study in economics.

The 1986 President's Commission made recommendations for each of its identified problem areas: drugs, labor racketeering, money laundering, and gambling. The report on drugs made 13 recommendations arguing that drug policy "must emphasize more strongly efforts to reduce the demand for drugs."[37] It was recommended that the cost of drug enforcement be subsidized by seizure and forfeiture of traffickers' assets and that the United Nations should sponsor a model "International Controlled Substances Act" to assist in eradicating narcotics distribution at its source.

With regard to labor-management racketeering it was found that the 1970 RICO provisions "and union decertification laws have been underutilized."[38] Prosecution efforts to remove racketeer influence over unions and legitimate businesses were seen as "largely ineffective."

> This situation does not stem simply from too few laws or unavailable remedies. It arises from a lack of political will, a lack of fixed responsibility, and a lack of a national plan of attack.[39]

The need for a national strategy to combat labor racketeering was recognized, as was better organization of prosecution efforts. It was suggested that antitrust offenses become eligible for electronic surveillance under Title III. Similarly, Title III wiretap authority was recommended for money laundering offenses, as was improved cooperation of financial institutions in enforcing the Bank Secrecy Act.

There was less consensus about strategies to fight gambling. There appeared to be disagreement over the priority that gambling enforcement should have in a strategy to reduce organized crime.

> The extent to which illegal gambling should be targeted, either as unacceptable per se or as a revenue source for other ... organized criminal activities, and the priority to be given to any such targeting, is one of the more challenging subjects facing policy makers and law enforcement officials in the near future.[40]

Similar to the 1967 investigation, the 1986 commission recommended several new laws, but many of these were suggestions that states adopt laws that already exist on the federal level, such as those regarding wiretapping, witness immunity, special grand juries, and broad racketeering.[41] As noted earlier, however, the impact of these existing laws on the federal level was not examined.

The 1986 commission report concluded with several appendices. First was a summary of five case studies of "mob-connected lawyers." This was followed by an economic model proposed by Wharton Econometric Forecasting Associates for estimating the income of organized crime. Third, there was a survey of prosecutors regarding their access and use of various tools to combat organized crime. Finally, there was a paper by G. Robert Blakey that summarized how organized crime is defined in statutes and case law.

Table 7.1 outlines the major differences between the 1967 and the 1987 presidential investigations of organized crime. As discussed previously, the 1987 commission investigation is more expansive in its perception of the scope of organized crime and, if the commissions were both correct in their conclusions, there was a significant shift in organized crime activities over two decades.

Summary of Similarities

Three interesting similarities can be noted in the two presidential investigations of organized crime. First, both commissions recognized the pivotal role of money in funding organized criminal activity. In 1967, it was argued "It is the accumulation of money, not the individual transactions themselves ... that has a great and threatening impact on America."[42] Twenty years later, it was concluded that "without means to launder money, thereby making cash generated by a criminal enterprise appear to come from a legitimate source, organized crime could not flourish as it now does."[43] Therefore, it is the generation

Table 7.1 Comparison of Findings and Recommendations of the Two Presidential Investigations of Organized Crime

Subject	Task Force Report, 1967	President's Commission, 1987
Crime groups	Nearly exclusive focus on Italian-Sicilian groups	Specific recognition of organized crime among at least 10 other ethnic, national, and geographic groups
Narcotics	Only two paragraphs on narcotics in the report; heroin the only drug mentioned by name	Five days of hearings on cocaine and heroin, and a 500-page interim report on the drug-organized crime link, recognizing the problems of interdiction and source country eradication, and the need to reduce demand
Labor racketeering	Only three paragraphs devoted to labor racketeering in report	Two days of hearings and a 400-page interim report and appendix on labor racketeering, encouraging civil remedies and a less fragmented prosecution approach
Money laundering	No specific mention of money laundering in the report	One day of hearings and a 90-page report on money laundering, focusing on the collusion of some banks with organized crime
Gambling	Gambling seen as largest source of organized crime revenue	Uncertain of the attention that should be devoted to gambling; narcotics found to be largest source of revenue
Penalties	Emphasis on criminal penalties to reduce organized crime involvement in drugs and other crimes	Recognized that civil remedies and reduced demand may be more effective in reducing organized crime activities
New laws	Many proposals for new laws, including wiretapping, witness immunity and protection, and RICO, which have since become law	Recognized that existing laws have been underutilized; fewer proposals for new laws, except for state versions of federal laws and better interagency law enforcement cooperation

and accumulation of income that lie at the heart of organized crime. This would argue strongly for greater reliance on civil remedies in organized crime prosecutions.

Both presidential investigations suggested more severe drug penalties on the grounds that they would affect drug trafficking. The basis for this belief is debatable, as noted earlier, and the experience of the past 50 years does not make it clear that long sentences for drug traffickers reduced their incidence. Still more attention must be given to civil penalties and to efforts to reduce demand. Without reduced demand, the market for illicit drugs will never disappear, as the 1987 commission noted.

Third, both investigations cited similar problems on more than one occasion. Both mentioned a lack of investigative resources, a lack of coordination among agencies, a failure to share information, a failure to make use of existing sanctions, and a lack of political or public conviction to fight organized crime. There is a continuing problem among law enforcement agencies in their unwillingness to cooperate in criminal investigations. Organized crime activity often takes place across several jurisdictions, and yet local, county, state, and federal enforcement agencies appear unable to cooperate in most instances in the fight against organized crime. In many ways, the inefficiency of the law enforcement response assists the maintenance of criminal enterprises in keeping the risk of detection low.

This inefficiency of law enforcement efforts was a major component of the political controversy that surrounded the release of the 1987 commission report. The commission consisted of 18 members, yet 10 of them filed a joint supplemental report claiming that the commission did not do "an adequate job in assessing the effectiveness of the [law enforcement] response to organized crime."[44] Likewise, these commissioners believed that the commission's efforts were also not adequate in assessing the criminality of "other ethnic groups," and the commission itself was poorly organized in that final drafts of commission reports "were not even shown to commission members before publication."[45] As a consultant to the commission concluded, "The commission will not be remembered for what it did. It will be remembered for the job that it didn't do."[46]

Nevertheless, similarities in the findings and recommendations of the two commissions provide a framework for the criminal justice response to organized crime. Subsequent chapters on investigation, prosecution, defense, and sentencing will assess the extent to which these recommendations have been adopted in practice.

CRITICAL THINKING EXERCISE 7.1

The Case of the Unmaking of a Mobster

The conclusions of the two president's commissions on organized crime suggest that organized crime has changed a great deal in both its activities and the groups involved. Joseph DeFede was a traditional organized crime figure, once the acting boss of the Luchese crime family in New York City. He was a native New Yorker with a raspy Brooklyn accent.

He pleaded guilty to extortion in 1998, serving most of his 5-year prison sentence when another member of the Luchese group visited him in prison saying the "money didn't jive" and accusing DeFede of stealing money from the crime family's funds. DeFede was also told he was being demoted from acting boss to soldier (from the highest rank in the group to the lowest).

Several of his relatives were subsequently threatened, so DeFede began cooperating with prosecutors. According to DeFede, the Mafia no longer honors an unwritten code that protects family members from violence: "I was hoping they would kill me and leave my family alone. I'm protecting my wife. I'm protecting my family."

DeFede's cooperation brought him and his relatives into the witness protection program and they were relocated to another part of the country. "If they want, they can kill me. (But) I was afraid of my family getting hurt," said DeFede.

Testifying at a trial of another crime figure, DeFede's truthfulness was questioned by the defense attorney, "You would shoot anybody, but you wouldn't lie?" DeFede said, "I wouldn't lie to protect my family. I'd kill to protect my family."

Critical Thinking Questions

1. If DeFede's account is true, why would a former colleague (in crime) falsely accuse him?
2. Why do you believe DeFede drew such a distinction between threats against him versus threats against his family?
3. What are some reasons why threats against a person's family are now acceptable in some criminal circles when they were unacceptable years ago?

Source: Larry Neumeister, "Ex-Mafia Boss Says He Became Turncoat after Family Was Threatened," The Associated Press (October 28, 2002).

CHANGING ORGANIZED CRIME PATTERNS: FROM LOCAL TO TRANSNATIONAL

Since the publication of the presidential commission reports, organized crime has continued to evolve to new levels as new criminal opportunities emerge. This evolution of organized crime is shaping national and international responses to the problem. The 1990s began a time of dramatic political and technological change. This section examines several types of organized crime that reflect its increasingly globalized nature.

The fall of the former Soviet Union and other remarkable political changes in eastern Europe and Asia made international travel easier, while weak developing nations have trouble controlling smuggling goods such as vehicles, drugs, and humans. In a similar way the dramatic expansion of computer usage and the Internet and access to it created new opportunities for crime. The nature of hijacking has also changed. These political and technological changes could not have been anticipated by the earlier presidential commissions, and they illustrate how organized crime adapts to exploit emerging opportunities to obtain a criminal advantage. A result of these changes was the *Strategy To Combat Transnational Organized Crime: Addressing Converging Threats to National Security* issued by President Obama in 2011, which announced new enforcement measures including a sanctions program to block property and cash transactions involving major transnational criminal networks that threaten national security interests.[47] In addition, transnational criminal aliens who have been targeted for financial sanctions will be denied entry into the county, and a new rewards program was established for information leading to the conviction of leaders of transnational crime groups. This report linked the power of transnational organized crime groups to their ability to raise significant amounts of money and thereby threaten U.S. security. The crimes discussed below provide examples of how transnational organized crime engages in multinational schemes to profit illegally.

International Stolen Vehicle Smuggling

The international trade in stolen vehicles expanded greatly with the globalization of trade and ease of travel brought about by the growing worldwide economy. Of the 1.5 million vehicles stolen each year in the United States, approximately 200,000 are shipped overseas for resale, a market that barely existed during the 1980s. At the busiest seaport in the United States, Los Angeles-Long Beach, 225 vehicles valued at $10 million were seized in a single year. The most popular vehicles to be stolen and smuggled out of the country are newer luxury cars, sport utility vehicles, and motorcycles because they are difficult to obtain overseas. In the United Kingdom, for example, more than

85,000 cars stolen in Japan are believed to be on the road in England. In Hong Kong, police have made arrests in an organized scheme to steal cars and ship them to the mainland. In Bulgaria, car theft rings often steal the cars in Spain and either ship them from there (or Portugal) or drive them through France and Italy and ship them from there into Greece and Turkey. The ultimate buyers are often citizens of Arab countries. The Bolivian government started an amnesty process to legalize undocumented vehicles in the country, and thousands of stolen vehicles originating from Bolivia's bordering countries were discovered.[48]

Given the need to steal, transport, evade customs, and deliver stolen vehicles to their destination, these schemes must be organized, sometimes by different networks of individuals at the supply stage, transport stage, and delivery stage of the enterprise. An analysis by Interpol found that 90% of countries acknowledged that transnational organized crime operates international stolen vehicle smuggling.[49] A large operation uncovered in New Jersey found it operated in multiple layers. Often gang members or associates stole the cars, which were sold to "fences," who would buy the stolen vehicles for a few thousand dollars (even though the market value of the car was much higher). The fences employed "runners" to drive the stolen vehicles from one location to another and collect purchase payments. A third layer of criminals "retagged" the stolen vehicles by altering the Vehicle Identification Numbers (VINs) in each car, and creating a counterfeit Certificate of Title to match the new fictitious VIN. Finally, the cars were sold to customers for use in the United States or shipped overseas using falsified shipping documents.[50]

To hide stolen cars from investigators, thieves often conceal them behind false container walls or in large steel containers bound for overseas shipping (see Figure 7.1). VINs are often altered as well, making it difficult to trace the movement of a specific vehicle. A single ship holds as many as 4,000 steel containers, each as large as a semitrailer. The United States has 130 seaports, and 10 million containers leave the Los Angeles-Long Beach seaport alone each year. Criminals pay thieves to steal desired cars off the street or the cars are bought or rented using false identification, making a cash deposit, and then driving away never to return. On the foreign end, ownership and registry of stolen vehicles are not very difficult. Some countries have no central registry of vehicles. In others, registration requirements can be overcome with cash payoffs from aspiring car owners. In some countries, crimes of violence and political unrest are the focus of police attention so police are not overly concerned with imports of stolen cars.

A major reason why people in other countries do not simply buy the cars legally is lack of availability in many places and huge import duties. A $50,000 Lexus, for example, was found selling in a Thailand showroom for $180,000. The total cost of international vehicle smuggling is estimated at $1-4 billion annually.

FIGURE 7.1 A U.S. customs agent looks over stolen auto parts displayed in a shipping container that is used to export stolen vehicles. *AP Photo/Nick Ut*

A representative of the National Insurance Crime Bureau remarked, "It's getting to be of epidemic proportion." A total of 200,000 stolen vehicles are exported each year according to the National Crime Insurance Bureau, and the vast majority of illegal exports are undetected.[51] Interpol developed a Stolen Motor Vehicle database to support police in its 190 member countries to better respond to international vehicle theft and trafficking. The database has 7.2 million records of reported stolen motor vehicles, and nearly 116 million searches of the database were conducted by police agencies worldwide during 2013, resulting in more than 116,000 motor vehicles being identified (see Figure 7.2).[52]

International Drug Smuggling

International drug smuggling mirrors many of the problems faced in international vehicle smuggling, and the globalization of organized crime activity. Drug smuggling begins at a source country where coca or opium is grown, usually in Central or South America or Asia. Next, the raw plant must be processed, which can be done in the source country or in a nation where smuggling is relatively easy. Once the substance has been transformed into a consumable product, it must be smuggled to the consumer drug market (North America and Europe are the largest consumers). After the drug has been sold, money must be "laundered" through a legitimate business and transferred by wire overseas or else large amounts of cash must be physically smuggled by couriers back to

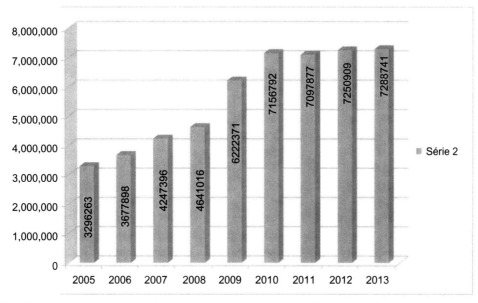

FIGURE 7.2 More than 7.2 million records of reported stolen motor vehicles from 130 countries in 2013. Source: *Vehicle Crime, www. interpol.int (January 27, 2014). www.interpol.int/Crime-areas/Vehicle-crime/Database-statistics*

the manufacturing and source countries. Laundering consists of reporting drug money as part of the income from a legitimate business, such as a restaurant or other business that has a large number of cash transactions, making it look as if it were earned lawfully as part of the legitimate business.

Here is an example of how this works in practice. Nigerian heroin smugglers recruited non-Nigerian residents of Dallas to serve as couriers, smuggling heroin into the United States. The recruiters provided airline tickets and expense money for the couriers, in addition to a salary of $5,000-10,000 per trip. The first courier was sent to Thailand, the heroin source, and took the heroin from there to an intermediate nonsource nation (such as the Philippines, Kenya, Poland, or western Europe), where it was delivered to a second courier. The second courier concealed the heroin in a suitcase or strapped it to his or her body and smuggled it into the United States. The strategy was designed to deceive U.S. authorities, who would not suspect a courier who had not been to a source country. This scheme capitalized on multiethnic cooperation among criminals and points to the need for international cooperation and surveillance by law enforcement agencies. Some schemes are more desperate, such as launching large cans containing marijuana over the U.S. border via a gas-powered cannon in Mexico, filling lollipops with heroin, hollowing replicas of famous works of art in order to stuff them with contraband, or molding cocaine paste into plaster casts in fake designer shoes.[53] All of these cases have taken place, reflecting higher levels of organization required to evade authorities, and making surveillance and apprehension more difficult by crossing national borders.

The two primary opportunities for intervening in drug smuggling occur at the courier stage, when the finished product is being smuggled to the market, or when the illicit cash is being returned from the consuming country to the supply country. In the United States, profiles have been established for drug couriers and for "high-risk" and "source" nations and airports that lack effective controls on drug manufacturing or contraband. The profiles are descriptions of travelers who appear likely to be carrying drugs, such as those making short international trips, carry little luggage, appear in a hurry, and pay for their tickets in cash.[54] "Top-down" approaches targeting leaders often are ineffective because of the nature of drug smuggling operations. A study involving interviews with 34 federal prisoners convicted of smuggling large volumes of cocaine into the United States found a general lack of formal organization structure. Instead, drug smuggling operations were composed of isolated groups lacking any formal connections. These drug smugglers did not take orders or commands came from a centralized authority but the smugglers worked in loosely connected nodes.[55] As a result, drug trafficking occurs across both jurisdictions and groups, making international cases difficult to build.

International Human Trafficking

Illegal immigration is a third example of organized crime that has increased globally since the 1990s. There are many people throughout the world who wish to come to the United States and other developed countries, but have little chance of lawful immigration because they lack the skills or wealth desired by the developed country. Sometimes people are tricked into coming to Europe or America for promised work as nannies, dancers, or housekeepers. Smuggling rings have transported illegal immigrants to New York City by boat for a charge of $30,000 or more per person. Sometimes the "cargo" is smuggled by boat to Canada or Mexico and is then transported by land to the United States. Sometimes this human cargo is shipped in containers, resulting in injury and death. The huge smuggling fee often turns the new arrivals into virtual slaves to their transporters.[56] Because they are illegal aliens, it is difficult for them to obtain legitimate employment so they are often exploited in sweatshops by unscrupulous employers, become prostitutes or drug couriers, or become involved in criminal activity to raise the money to pay their smuggling fee.[57] In this way, the illegal immigrants become victims of their human traffickers.

Human trafficking involves three elements: (1) exploitive labor (sex, manual labor, domestic servitude), (2) harboring of victims (through recruitment, transport, or exploitation), and (3) coercion (through deception, threats, or force).[58] Trafficking for sexual exploitation is more common in Europe, Central

Asia, and the Americas, whereas trafficking for forced labor is more common in Africa, the Middle East, and Southeast Asia. According to an analysis by the United Nations, almost half of the human trafficking victims detected worldwide were trafficked across borders within their region of origin, but 24% were trafficked to a different region and the remainder were trafficked within their borders.[59] In virtually all cases, victims can be exploited because there are few opportunities for work in their local region or country, and they are desperate to support themselves or their families. This desperation is exploited by traffickers who recruit them and make connections with those who can move them across borders, and others who arrange for exploitive work on the destination end. Of course, victims do not know in advance that they will be exploited, but they take a calculated risk for promised work as a dancer, restaurant worker, or laborer, and are often exploited after their journey has begun.

Based on information provided to the United Nations by more than 50 countries, males comprise two-thirds of traffickers. But the fact that one-third of traffickers are women is twice the rate of females offending for most other crimes, suggesting significant involvement of women as both traffickers and victims, especially in sexual exploitation cases.[60] This data has been found in other smaller studies as well, although it appears that female involvement in trafficking is most often at lower levels of the enterprise.[61] Information from nearly 40 countries reveals that most convicted human traffickers are of the same nationality as their victims, but 25% are not. However, this varies dramatically by country. For example, while foreign nationals comprised 3% of convicted traffickers in El Salvador, in Oman the proportion was 58%, reflecting differences in local conditions in supply, demand, enforcement, and competition in this illegal market. Most importantly, three-fourths of all human trafficking victims are foreign nationals in the country where they are discovered, illustrating the transnational nature of most human trafficking enterprises.[62]

Immigrants suffer victimization by their traffickers in many ways. In Los Angeles, for example, 8 Thai nationals were arrested for enslaving 56 illegal immigrants. Money was extorted from the immigrants in exchange for safe passage to the United States, where they were required to work 17-hour days.[63] As William McDonald has remarked, "the problems of organized crime involved in the fraud, corruption, smuggling, and victimization associated with illegal immigration represent a growing area of need for transnational police cooperation which threatens to eclipse international drug trafficking as a social problem in the global village."[64]

U.S. authorities are able to identify only 5% of the vessels carrying illegal immigrants.[65] Given the vast extent of the nation's borders and the inability of any nation to search every person, car, boat, and plane that crosses its borders, there is a clear need for international cooperation and coordination of law enforcement efforts and intelligence gathering.

The issue of human trafficking is serious in terms of the harm caused to the victim, the loss of human potential to the home country, the impact of illegal labor on the destination country's economy, and the fact that victims can be trafficked repeatedly (re-sold) to a new "owner." This makes human trafficking perhaps the most heinous form of organized crime.

Computer and Internet Crime

The United States and the world have become completely dependent on computers and electronic telecommunications, a technological revolution that began during the 1980s and exploded during the 1990s into the present. Most American households now have computers, as do the vast majority of governments, businesses, and schools. Computers have now become central to our lives at home and at work. The opportunities for misuse of information systems and communications technologies grow daily.

In the same way that the invention of the automobile early in the twentieth century nearly doubled the number of offenses in the criminal codes of the United States, the invention of the computer will have the same impact in the twenty-first century. Automobiles provided opportunities for illegal activity ranging from substandard manufacturing and repair frauds to auto theft. Computers have a similar impact, as computer viruses and cyber theft threaten property, privacy, and the public order. Legal codes have been modified to eliminate opportunities for crime or misuse, similar to changes needed as automobiles became commonplace. Organized crime elements have often been involved in taking advantage of the criminal opportunities provided by computers.

Computers are used most often to steal, but they can be used to commit other crimes as well. Computer crimes can be grouped into two basic categories: crimes in which computers are used as the *instrument* of the offense and crimes in which computers are the *object* of the offense. Computers are used as an instrument in crimes such as embezzlement, fraud, extortion, or harassment where computer access is compromised to steal money in various ways. The spread of computer "viruses" (hidden programs that annoy a user or threaten to alter a user's computer files) is an example. In one case, thousands of Internet users received unsolicited e-mails stating that their orders had been processed and their credit card would be charged $300, but these people had not ordered anything. They were advised to call a phone number with a 767 area code if they had questions. That phone number turned out to be a phone-sex line that incurred an automatic charge when connected. The number was located in the West Indies. The conspirators received their money from the phone companies who charged the customers for their connection to the phone-sex line.

Individuals behind the conspiracy had still not been located, but the Federal Trade Commission obtained a court order to freeze the funds collected by phone companies for calls to the phone-sex number.[66]

These kinds of theft-by-computer operations usually involve multiple offenders with sophisticated computer skills, plus those who provide illicit access from the inside companies. In one scheme, a 28-year-old Moldovan man learned of a vulnerability in the computer network of a major credit card processing company in Atlanta. He passed that information to a hacker living in Estonia, who evaluated the network's vulnerabilities and shared his information with another hacker in Russia. Enlisting three other hackers, the Russian was able to obtain illegal entry into the electronic network, reproduce the PIN codes from the encrypted system, and raised the limits on the amount of money that could be withdrawn from the prepaid payroll debit cards. (These cards are used by many employers to enable employees to withdraw their salaries from an ATM.) One of the hackers managed a global network of criminals who used 44 counterfeit cards to withdraw $9 million from multiple ATMs at different locations. Those who withdrew funds from the ATMs were able to keep a percentage of the funds with the rest going to the original hackers.[67] In another large operation, five men from Russia and Ukraine were charged in a scheme in which they stole and sold 160 million credit card numbers from Visa, J.C. Penney, JetBlue Airways, and other companies that cost the companies more than $300 million. Each member of the scheme had specialized tasks: two hacked into networks, another mined them for data (account numbers and identifying information), another provided anonymous web-hosting services to hide the group's activities, and another sold the stolen data and distributed the profits.[68] The multinational, networked nature of these organized computer breaches is apparent.

A frightening type of computer crime is the use of a computer to harass or extort a victim. A notorious case of this type is that of Donald Burleson, who inserted a "virus" program that duplicated itself continuously into the computer system at a brokerage firm from which he had been fired. The virus erased 168,000 sales commission records.[69] In another kind of extortion-by-computer case, a computer science student pleaded guilty to hacking the computers of Miss Teen USA and other young women, secretly photographing them and threatening to post the pictures online if they didn't send him more naked photos (see Figure 7.3).[70]

The second category of computer crime involves damage to the computer itself (hardware or software) as the object of the offense. The damage can be physical or financial in terms of costs and competitive value. One example of this kind of cybercrime is use of bots. A bot (web robot) is an automated malware program that scans network addresses and infects vulnerable computers. A network of these infected computers is called a botnet (robot network), and each computer is

FIGURE 7.3 Nineteen-year-old Jared James Abrahams was arrested in September 2013 in an investigation into the hacking of webcams at the homes of Cassidy Wolf, shown here being crowned Miss Teen USA 2013, and other young women in an attempt to extort nude photographs and videos, the FBI said. *AP Photo/Miss Universe L.P., LLLP, File*

connected to a command-and-control server operated by the criminal. Once the botnet is in place, it can be used in distributed denial of service attacks, proxy and spam services, malware distribution, and other organized criminal activity. Botnets can also be used for covert information collection, or to instigate fear, intimidation, or public embarrassment. The head of an international securities fraud ring was convicted for manipulating stock prices by using botnets to distribute spam/false information that promoted those stocks. In another case, 10 members of an international cybercrime ring were arrested for using botnets to steal more than $850 million by obtaining personal financial information from compromised computers.[71] In another case, a computer systems manager at Lawrence Berkeley Laboratory in California realized that an unauthorized user was looking at his computer files, so he set up a phony Star Wars computer file that the hacker could not resist. The suspect was eventually tracked to Hanover, West Germany, where three people were charged with selling secrets to the Soviet Union.[72]

Two individuals from Latvia were indicted and more than 65 computers, servers, and bank accounts in 8 countries seized as part of a scheme that victimized more than one million computer users through the sale of fraudulent computer security software known as "scareware." Scareware is malicious software that poses as legitimate computer security software to detect threats on the affected computer that do not actually exist. Users are informed with aggressive and disruptive on-screen notifications that they must purchase specific antivirus software in order to repair their computers. The users are barraged with messages until they supply their credit card number and pay for the "antivirus" product, which is fake. Consumers lost more than $70 million in this scheme.[73]

It appears that computers are being used to commit organized crimes both by and against computers, and that improved law enforcement sophistication, cooperation, and expertise will be needed to combat them successfully to avoid a predicted wave of cybercrime.[74]

Hijacking

A man told a flight attendant on a Southwest Airlines flight from San Diego to San Jose, California, to "tell the captain that he should take the plane to Hollywood or else he was going to start killing people."[75] The flight attendant convinced the man to allow the plane to land in Burbank because there is no airport in Hollywood, and the man was taken into custody there, after a brief struggle. None of the 74 passengers or flight crew was injured, although not all incidents of this kind end so well. The suspect in this case was indicted for hijacking, which is the unauthorized seizure of a land vehicle, aircraft, or other conveyance while it is in transit. The term *"hijacking"* originated during the 1920s referring to thefts of truckloads or boatloads of liquor manufactured illegally in the Prohibition era. Organized crime groups continue to hijack trucks carrying clothes, furs, electronic equipment, cigarettes, or any other product that can be sold illicitly to unscrupulous buyers.

The hijacking of an airplane is sometimes called skyjacking, and the first incident of this kind occurred in the United States in 1961 when a man forced a plane bound for Florida to go to Cuba. This began a rash of hijacking attempts in the United States, usually carried out for political asylum or to obtain ransom for releasing passengers. The United States responded by beginning mandatory point-of-departure screening and searches of all airline passengers in the early 1970s and by placing federal agents on certain flights. During the past 30 years skyjacking dropped in the United States but increased in the Middle East and Europe, where political dissidents used hijacking as a means for releasing political prisoners in foreign countries or obtaining ransom money to support their political cause. Skyjacking made a dramatic return in 2001 when terrorists commandeered jets in the United States and used them as missiles to target the World Trade Center in New York and the Pentagon in Washington, DC.

Piracy on the seas is another modern form of hijacking; holding ships and crews for ransom, especially off the coast of Somali where the government is not functioning effectively and there are limited economic opportunities for those living there, either legitimate or illegitimate.[76] Hijacking continues today in developed countries such as the United States, but for most organized crime groups it has shifted back to truck and boat hijacking of legal products for sale as stolen merchandise, and hijacking of illegal goods such as drugs and guns.[77]

Well known New York City crime figure John Gotti and his group, including Sammy Gravano, worked as hijackers for years, commandeering trucks full

CRITICAL THINKING EXERCISE 7.2

The Case of Tracking Immigrants Within Our Own Borders

Concern began when it was discovered that at least 13 of the 19 terrorists suspected in the terrorist attacks of September 11, 2001, originally entered the United States legally on visas. How did these terrorists obtain visas? Why weren't they under surveillance? A closer look at America's monitoring system of immigrants on visas revealed serious problems of security and law enforcement. (A visa is a document attached to a passport that a government issues when permission is given for a noncitizen to enter and travel within its borders for a specified period of time.)

It is estimated that there are more than eight million illegal immigrants in the United States. As many as 40% of them originally entered on a legal visa and simply never left when their visas expired. Each year, millions of foreign tourists, workers, and students enter the United States on visas, but they are not tracked by the U.S. Immigration Service or by any other agency. Hani Hanjour, one of the suspected hijackers of the jet that hit the Pentagon, obtained a student visa to enroll at an English-language program in Oakland. He never showed up at the school, and there was no law that required the school to notify the government of his absence.

A little more than 1 month after the September 11 terrorist attacks, Congress held hearings to discuss better ways of monitoring noncitizens within the United States. Senator Dianne Feinstein (D-California) recommended suspending any new foreign-student visas for 6 months while immigration officials improve a system to monitor them, but she encountered immediate opposition. The opposition occurred on economic grounds and on grounds of government capabilities.

Foreign tourists spend billions of dollars in the United States every year. This income has become an important part of the United States' hotel, restaurant, entertainment, airline, and tourism industries. More than 500,000 foreign students are enrolled at U.S. universities, providing a significant source of income and diversity for higher education (even though they account for only 2% of annual foreign entries into the United States). In addition, technically skilled foreign workers are highly desired by the computer industry and by other high-tech employers.

Of the 30 million foreigners entering the United States each year, about one-half come from Japan, Germany, France, the United Kingdom, and 25 other countries from which visas are not required ("friendly" nations). Therefore, many legal immigrants do not possess visas to be monitored. Another quarter of those entering are tourists, workers, and students entering on time-specific visas issued by the U.S. State Department.

The State Department has been criticized because visa applications are not screened adequately to check the background of the applicant. Criminal background checks are rare, as are checks with their stated U.S. destination to reduce the likelihood of fraud in visa applications.

Once foreigners are granted a visa, no effort occurs to track their movements or even determine whether they leave the country when their visa expires. The Immigration and Naturalization Service was ordered in 1996 to develop a tracking system and was given until December 2003 to complete it, a deadline it did not meet. Funding such a huge effort is very expensive, and some argue the effort should be placed on prevention of the *entry* of suspicious foreigners rather than on surveillance of their activities *after* they arrive. Nevertheless, a program now tracks foreign students through an electronic database and covers the costs by charging students a fee. Schools report whether foreign students are enrolled or have changed their status, including dropping out, changing majors, or moving to a new address.

Critical Thinking Questions

1. Why do you believe the United States historically has not monitored the status of those entering the country on visas?
2. As President, how would you weigh the economic benefits of the many foreign visitors to the United States against the expense required to check their backgrounds more thoroughly and monitor their movements more closely?
3. To what extent do you believe border screening and immigrant monitoring will impact organized crime in the United States?

of merchandise coming from Kennedy Airport and then selling it to stores and individuals who were unscrupulous about the source.[78] Joe Pistone worked as an undercover agent for 6 years, infiltrating the Bonanno crime family in New York City. According to Pistone,

> They would hijack any kind of truck from 18-wheelers down to little straight jobs. They would seize the truck, unload the stuff into smaller trucks or vans, and take it to the "drop," which might be a vacant warehouse or factory ... to show prospective buyers (or fences). When they hijacked a truck, they would usually just tie the driver up. But most of the hijacked loads were giveaways—setups. The drivers of the heisted trucks would be in on the heist for a percentage.[79]

In these cases, the truck driver would tip off the organized crime group that he had a load of desirable merchandise, describe his route, and allow himself to be "hijacked" for a percentage of the load's value. Hijacking has a long history in organized crime, but the hijacking of airplanes has a much shorter history— becoming more common as both flying and knowledge of technology (the ability to pilot) become more common. It illustrates how organized crime activity exploits the available opportunities in pursuing a criminal advantage. See Figure 7.4.

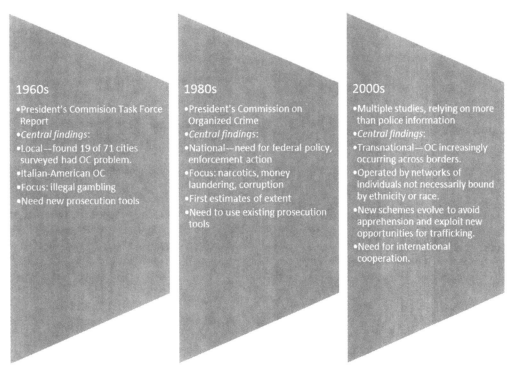

1960s
- President's Commission Task Force Report
- *Central findings*:
- Local—found 19 of 71 cities surveyed had OC problem.
- Italian-American OC
- Focus: illegal gambling
- Need new prosecution tools

1980s
- President's Commission on Organized Crime
- *Central findings*:
- National—need for federal policy, enforcement action
- Focus: narcotics, money laundering, corruption
- First estimates of extent
- Need to use existing prosecution tools

2000s
- Multiple studies, relying on more than police information
- *Central findings*:
- Transnational—OC increasingly occurring across borders.
- Operated by networks of individuals not necessarily bound by ethnicity or race.
- New schemes evolve to avoid apprehension and exploit new opportunities for trafficking.
- Need for international cooperation.

FIGURE 7.4 Mapping our understanding of organized crime from the 1960s to the present.

SUMMARY

This chapter has shown how changes in the nature of organized crime have occurred since the 1967 President's Crime Commission Report, which focused on illegal gambling and Italian-American organized crime and the need for new legislation to combat it effectively. The 1987 President's Commission reflected the emergence of non-Italian organized crime and focused attention on the overlapping problems of drug trafficking, money laundering, and corruption. Since then, dramatic political and technological changes around the world have expanded opportunities for criminal conduct in ways that attempt to evade local and national jurisdictional boundaries. Organized crime groups are increasingly operated by networks of individuals not necessarily bound by ethnicity or race, and new schemes continue to evolve to avoid apprehension and exploit new opportunities for trafficking people and goods illegally around the world. The response to these new forms of organized crime will require significant cooperation both within and among nations to deal effectively with stolen vehicle smuggling, drug smuggling, human trafficking, computer and Internet crimes, hijacking, and other crimes.

ORGANIZED CRIME BIOGRAPHY

Biographies tell the life story of interesting people. In the world of criminal justice, biographies of organized crime figures offer insight into the background and motivations of the individuals who choose that lifestyle, the reasons for their choices, and their consequences. The following is a brief summary of an organized crime biography, followed by questions that ask you to reflect on the connections between that person's life and the content of this book.

Underboss: Sammy the Bull Gravano's Story of Life in the Mafia
Peter Maas (Harper, 2000)

The life story of Sammy Gravano is recounted. Gravano is best known for being John Gotti's underboss in the New York City Mafia. The book recounts Gravano's childhood and offers insights into his criminal life choices. It follows his lack of success in school, the effects of his diminutive stature, to becoming a neighborhood tough guy, a reputation he enjoyed. These experiences were followed by an unsuccessful military experience and very brief efforts to work a legitimate job. However, that lifestyle lacked the excitement and potential rewards of a life of scams, stolen property, and drug trafficking while associating with a series of people who were also predisposed to violence and generally less well adjusted than he was.

Gravano's many crimes and multiple murders over the years set the stage for his ultimately becoming a government informant and entering the witness protection program. His testimony against his former boss, John Gotti, resulted in Gotti's sentence to life in prison. Many of Gravano's friends, and also his family, were unhappy with his decision to testify against Gotti, believing it somehow violated the criminal friendships he had established. Gravano was seeking a short prison sentence (which he received), and then he entered the witness protection program and was relocated. Within a few years, however, he was caught trafficking drugs and was returned to prison.

Questions
1. What do you see as the important causes of Gravano's involvement in organized crime as a criminal career?
2. How do you explain Gravano's choice not to go straight (and lead a law-abiding life) after his "second chance" in the witness protection program?

ORGANIZED CRIME AT THE MOVIES

Movies seek to entertain and inform the audience about a story, incident, or person. Many good movies also hit upon important substantive themes relevant to understanding organized crime. Read the following movie summary (and watch the movie if you haven't already) and answer the questions that follow to make the organized crime subject matter connections.

The Departed
Martin Scorcese, Director (2006)

The Departed is a fictional portrayal of an Irish mob boss, Frank Costello (Jack Nicholson), who manages to place Colin Sullivan (Matt Damon) as an informant inside the Massachusetts State Police. At the same time, the police have assigned Officer Billy Costigan (Leonardo DiCaprio) as an undercover operative to infiltrate Costello's gang. The tension in the movie occurs when both the mobsters and the police realize that the other side has moles inside their organizations, and they desperately try to determine the identities of the infiltrators.

An all-star cast captures the two-pronged story of the police, Captain Queenan (Martin Sheen) and the foul-mouthed Sergeant Dignam (Mark Wahlberg), who supervise the undercover Costigan (selected because of Costigan's family's past ties to the underworld). In parallel fashion, Costello's plant inside the police, Sullivan, is soon promoted to the detective unit by the very funny Captain Ellerby (Alec Baldwin).

Costigan gains favor with Costello's crew, given his fights with Italian mobsters from Providence and engaging in crimes with Costello's second-in-command. But a major complication emerges when Sullivan begins a relationship with the police department psychiatrist (Vera Farmiga), who also has Costigan as a client, because he is on probation for assaulting the Providence mobsters.

Costello learns from Sullivan that there is a mole inside his organization, and a crescendo is reached when Captain Queenan meets with Costigan in an old building. Sullivan tells Costello's men that the mole they are seeking is inside the building. Costigan manages to flee unnoticed, but Queenan is thrown from the building to his death. Sergeant Dignam and Sullivan have a fight back at the police department over the circumstances of Queenan's death, and

Dignam refuses to identify the department's undercover person inside the Costello crew. But Sullivan unexpectedly finds information in Queenan's files that mob boss Costello is actually an informant for the FBI.

A few days later, Costello and his gang are tailed to a warehouse pickup of a drug shipment. Costigan fears that the police know about this operation and he slips away. A shoot-out ensues and Costello's entire crew is killed. At the end of the shooting, Sullivan confronts Costello, who admits being an informant, and Sullivan kills him.

Most movies end at this point, but *The Departed* goes further to see how it ends for the two undercover principals. Sullivan is praised at the police station for defeating Costello and his crew. He meets Costigan, who again slips away when he finally comprehends the connection between Sullivan and Costello.

The next morning, the psychiatrist is at Sullivan's apartment and finds an envelope from Costigan in the mail containing recordings of conversations between Costello and Sullivan as well as a telephone number. The psychiatrist confronts Sullivan and ends their relationship. Sullivan calls the phone number and Costigan tells him that Costello kept the recordings as "insurance" if he was ever arrested.

Sullivan and Costigan agree to meet on the same roof where Captain Queenan was killed. Costigan handcuffs Sullivan while former police academy classmates who arrive at the scene try to convince Costigan that they have evidence that Sullivan is the mole. Costigan is shot by Agent Barrigan (James Badge Dale) and tells Sullivan that he is the second mole on the police force and that they must look out for each other. Shockingly, Sullivan shoots Barrigan in the head, blames everything on him, and recommends Costigan posthumously for the Medal of Merit.

At Costigan's funeral, the psychiatrist continues to shun Sullivan. When he returns to his apartment, Sergeant Dignam is waiting with a gun, and he kills Sullivan.

The Departed was a very successful film, earning nearly $300 million worldwide and receiving four Academy Awards for Best Picture, Best Director, Best Screenplay, and Best Editing, and a nomination for Best Supporting Actor (Mark Wahlberg). The film is an American adaptation of the 2002 Hong Kong film

Continued

ORGANIZED CRIME AT THE MOVIES—CONT'D

Mou gaan dou (*Infernal Affairs*), although the film takes elements from Boston's organized crime and police history as described in the book *Black Mass*.

Questions

1. The movie makes several references to Costello's leadership and the changing nature of organized crime. Why do you think Costello was cooperating with the FBI, even though he was the mob boss?

2. Undercover police and inside informants have resulted in many important organized crime prosecutions. Why are these techniques particularly effective (and also extremely dangerous)?

References and Notes

1. Earley, P., & Shur, G. (2002). *Witsec: Inside the Federal Witness Protection Program.* New York: Bantam Books, p. 71.

2. President's Commission on Law Enforcement and Administration of Justice (1967). *Task Force Report: Organized Crime.* Washington, DC: U.S. Government Printing Office, pp. 1, 6.

3. There is no evidence whatsoever that any name change occurred from Mafia to Cosa Nostra.

4. President's Commission on Law Enforcement and Administration of Justice (1967). *Task Force Report: Organized Crime.* Washington, DC: U.S. Government Printing Office, p. 33.

5. President's Commission on Organized Crime (1984). *Organized Crime of Asian Origin Record of Hearing III.* October, 1984, Washington, DC: U.S. Government Printing Office, p. v.

6. President's Commission on Organized Crime (1984). *Organized Crime of Asian Origin Record of Hearing III.* October, p. 407.

7. President's Commission on Organized Crime (1984). *Organized Crime and Cocaine Trafficking Record of Hearing IV.* Washington, DC: U.S. Government Printing Office, p. 477, November.

8. President's Commission on Organized Crime (1985). *Organized Crime and Heroin Trafficking Record of Hearing V.* Washington, DC: U.S. Government Printing Office, p. 389, February.

9. President's Commission on Organized Crime (1986). *America's Habit: Drug Abuse, Drug Trafficking and Organized Crime Interim Report.* Washington, DC: U.S. Government Printing Office, p. 73, March.

10. President's Commission on Organized Crime (1986). *America's Habit: Drug Abuse, Drug Trafficking and Organized Crime Interim Report.* March, p. 109.

11. President's Commission on Organized Crime (1985). *Organized Crime and Gambling Record of Hearing VII.* Washington, DC: U.S. Government Printing Office, p. vi, June.

12. President's Commission on Organized Crime (1987). *The Impact: Organized Crime Today.* April, 1986, Washington, DC: U.S. Government Printing Office, pp. 58–128.

13. *Task Force Report*, p. 2.

14. *Task Force Report*, p. 3.

15. *Task Force Report*, p. 4.

16. *Task Force Report*, p. 5.

17. *Task Force Report.*

18. *America's Habit*, pp. 2–3.

19. *America's Habit*, p. 71.

20. President's Commission on Organized Crime (1986). *The Edge: Organized Crime, Business, Labor Unions Interim Report.* Washington, DC: U.S. Government Printing Office, p. 2, March; President's Commission on Organized Crime (1985). *Organized Crime and Labor-Management Racketeering in the United States Record of Hearing VI.* Washington, DC: U.S. Government Printing Office, p. vi, April.

21. President's Commission on Organized Crime (1984). *The Cash Connection: Organized Crime, Financial Institutions, and Money Laundering Interim Report.* Washington, DC: U.S. Government Printing Office p. 7.

22. *Task Force Report*, p. 6.

23. *Task Force Report*.

24. *The Edge*, p. 1.

25. *America's Habit*, p. 464.

26. *Organized Crime and Gambling*, p. 637.

27. *Task Force Report*, pp. 11–12.

28. *Task Force Report*, p. 14.

29. *Organized Crime and Cocaine Trafficking*, p. 477.

30. *The Edge*, p. 6.

31. *The Edge*, p. 245.

32. *The Edge*, pp. 5–6.

33. Shenon, P. "Crime Panel Issues Its Final Report," *The New York Times* (April 2, 1986), 1, B8; "Writing the Book on the Mob," *The New York Times* (April 5, 1986), 26.

34. *Task Force Report*, p. 14.

35. *Task Force Report*, p. 15.

36. *Task Force Report*, p. 15.

37. *America's Habit*, p. 463.

38. *The Edge*, p. 5.

39. *The Edge*, p. 307.

40. *Organized Crime and Gambling*, p. 637.

41. *The Impact: Organized Crime Today*, pp. 129–170.

42. *Task Force Report*, p. 2.

43. *The Cash Connection*, p. 3.

44. *The Impact: Organized Crime Today*, p. 176.

45. *The Impact: Organized Crime Today*, p. 173.

46. Blakey, G. R. cited in Philip Shenon, "U.S. Crime Panel: Discord to the End," *The New York Times* (April 4, 1986), 16.

47. President of the United States (July 2011). *Strategy to Combat Transnational Organized Crime: Addressing Converging Threats to National Security.* www.whitehouse.gov/sites/default/files/Strategy_to_Combat_Transnational_Organized_Crime_July_2011.pdf.

48. "Car Smuggling Ring Uncovered," *BBC News* (July 24, 2001); "Vehicle-Stealing and Smuggling Syndicates Neutralised," Press Release, Hong Kong Special Administrative Region Government, www.info.gov.hk/gia/200102/11/0211128.htm (2001); Gounev, P., & Bezlov, T. (2008). From the Economy of Deficit to the Black-Market: Car Theft and Trafficking in Bulgaria. *Trends in Organized Crime, 11*, 410–429; "Bolivian Government Promises Neighbouring Countries

to Return Thousands of Stolen Cars," *MercoPress* (February 3, 2012); Aldaba, R. M. "Can the Philippine Auto Industry Survive Smuggling?" *Policy Notes*, dirp4.pids.gov.ph/ris/pn/pidspn1305.pdf (March, 2013).

49. Interpol, *Analytical Report: Motor Vehicle Crime in Global Perspective*, www.interpol.int/Crime-areas/Vehicle-crime/Vehicle-crime (January 2014).

50. Grant, J. "Ring that Stole Cars Worth $6 Million and Shipped Them to Africa is Busted in Newark," *The Star-Ledger (Newark)* (May 23, 2012); see also Petrossian, G., & Clarke, R. V. (2012). *Export of Stolen Vehicles Across Land Borders.* Washington, DC: Community Oriented Policing Services. www.popcenter.org/problems/pdfs/export_stolen_vehicles.pdf.

51. U.S. Comptroller General. (1999). *Efforts to Curtail the Exportation of Stolen Vehicles.* Washington, DC: U.S. General Accounting Office; Federal Bureau of Investigation. *Uniform Crime Reports.* www.fbigov (published annually).

52. "Vehicle Crime," www.interpol.int/Crime-areas/Vehicle-crime/Database-statistics (January 27, 2014).

53. "Worldwide Nigerian Heroin Smuggling Ring Smashed," *Organized Crime Digest* (May 27, 1992), 3; "New Breed of Smugglers," *USA Today* (September 23, 1991), 3; "From Heroin Lollipops To Cocaine Implants, Smuggling Methods Increasingly Endanger Mules," *Organized Crime and Corruption Project* (December 13, 2012).

54. U.S. Comptroller General (1994). *Drug Control: Interdiction Efforts in Central America Have Had Little Impact on the Flow of Drugs.* Washington, DC: U.S. General Accounting Office; Unlu, A., & Ekici, B. (2012). The Extent to Which Demographic Characteristics Determine International Drug Couriers' Profiles: A Cross-Sectional Study in Istanbul. *Trends in Organized Crime, 15*, 296–312.

55. Benson, J. S., & Decker, S. H. (2010). The Organizational Structure of International Drug Smuggling. *Journal of Criminal Justice, 38*(March–April), 130–138.

56. Verhovek, S. H. "Wretched Masses, Smuggled," *The New York Times* (January 16, 2000), 2; Bales, K. (1999). *Disposable People.* Berkeley: University of California Press.

57. Hughes, D. M. (2001). The 'Natasha' Trade: Transnational Sex Trafficking. *National Institute of Justice Journal*, (March), 1–5; Richard, A. O. N. (2000). *International Trafficking in Women to the United States: A Contemporary Manifestation of Slavery and Organized Crime.* Washington, DC: Center for the Study of Intelligence; McDonald, W. F. (1997). Illegal Immigration: Crime, Ramifications, and Control (The American Experience). In W. F. McDonald (Ed.), *Crime and Law Enforcement in the Global Village.* Cincinnati: Anderson, pp. 65–88.

58. Albanese, J. (2011). *Transnational Crime and the 21st Century.* New York: Oxford University Press.

59. United Nations Office on Drugs and Crime (2012). *Global Report on Trafficking in Persons 2012.* Vienna: UNODC. www.unodc.org/documents/data-and-analysis/glotip/Trafficking_in_Persons_2012_web.pdf.

60. Ibid.

61. Ciccone, E. (2005). *The Trafficking Flows and Routes of Eastern Europe. WEST Project*; Surtees, R. (2008). Traffickers and Trafficking in Southern and Eastern Europe. *European Journal of Criminology, 5*, 39–68.

62. United Nations Office on Drugs and Crime (2012). *Global Report on Trafficking in Persons 2012.* Vienna: UNODC.

63. Swaboda, F., Webb, J., & Pressler, M. "U.S. Targets 'Slave Labor' Sweatshop," *Washington Post* (August 16, 1995), 1; Marosi, R. (2006). "An Immigrant Underground," *Los Angeles Times* (May 25, 2006), 1.

64. McDonald, W.F. "*Illegal Immigration*," p. 83.

65. U.S. Comptroller General (1993). *Immigration Enforcement: Problems in Controlling the Flow of Illegal Aliens.* Washington, DC: U.S. General Accounting Office; U.S. Comptroller General (2007). *Department of Homeland Security Progress Report on Implementation and Mission and Management Functions.* Washington, DC: U.S. General Accountability Office.

66. Mannix, M. "Spammed and Scammed," *U.S. News & World Report* (May 31, 1999), 79.

67. Federal Bureau of Investigation. *High-Tech Heist: 2,100 ATMs Worldwide Hit at Once,* www.fbi.gov (November 16, 2009).

68. Jones, D., & Finkle, J. "U.S. Indicts Hackers in Biggest Cyber Fraud Case in History," *Reuters* (July 25, 2013).

69. Lewyn, M. "Computer Verdict Sets Precedent," *USA Today* (September 21, 1998), 1.

70. Risling, G. "Computer Science Student Pleads Guilty in Teen USA Extortion Case," *The Washington Times* (November 13, 2013).

71. Federal Bureau of Investigation. *Botnets 101: What They Are and How to Avoid Them,* www.fbi.gov (June 5, 2013).

72. Stoll, C. (1989). *The Cuckoo's Egg: Inside the World of Computer Espionage.* New York: Doubleday.

73. U.S. Department of Justice (2011). *Department of Justice Disrupts International Cybercrime Rings Distributing Scareware.* Washington, DC: Office of Public Affairs, June 22.

74. Douglas, D., & Timberg, C. "Experts Warn of Coming Wave of Serious Cybercrime," *The Washington Post* (February 9, 2014).

75. "Man Who Threatened Airline Crew Indicted," *USA Today* (October 6, 2000), 3.

76. Dua, J., & Menkhaus, K. (2012). The Context of Contemporary Piracy: The Case of Somalia. *Journal of International Criminal Justice, 10,* 749–766.

77. Gottschalk, J. A., Flanagan, B. P., & Kahn, L. J. (2000). *Jolly Roger with an Uzi: The Rise and Threat of Modern Piracy.* Naval Institute Press; Haywood, R. (2012). *Maritime Piracy.* New York: Routledge.

78. Maas, P. (1997). *Underboss.* New York: Harper Collins.

79. Pistone, J. D., & Woodley, R. (2002). Donnie Brasco. In C. Willis (Ed.), *Mob: Stories of Death and Betrayal from Organized Crime.* New York: Thunder's Mouth Press, p. 38; Hijacking, T. Million Dollar Business. *New Zealand Herald* (October 6, 2008); Smith, B. C. "Highway Hijackers Target Truckers' Loot," *USA Today* (February 25, 2010).

CHAPTER 8

Transnational Organized Crime

Although the size and organization of these groups and networks vary,
their methods of creating and exploiting criminal opportunities
are remarkably consistent.

More than 100 celebrities were subpoenaed by the U.S. government in an investigation of shahtoosh wool shawls and scarves, which cost $2,000 to $3,000 and are popular among the wealthy as status symbols.[1] The wool comes from Tibetan antelopes, an endangered species. Dealers claimed that the wool came from wild goats, but it later was found that illegal killing of Tibetan antelopes occurred, clothing was fashioned illegally from the animals' hides in other Asian countries, and they were then illegally imported and sold in the United States. In this case crimes were committed in at least three countries, but the overarching offense is transnational in nature. Transnational crime occurs where the planning and execution of a crime involve more than one country. This chapter addresses specific examples of transnational crime and how the changing nature of criminal opportunities is the driving force behind the surge in organized crime across borders.

THE SCOPE OF TRANSNATIONAL CRIME

Concern about transnational crime began during the 1990s, when criminal activity began to cross national borders to a significant extent. The United Nations (UN) identified 18 categories of transnational offenses, which were found to have direct or indirect effects in two or more countries. This UN list was quite broad and included money laundering, terrorist activities, theft of art and cultural objects, theft of intellectual property, illicit arms trafficking, aircraft hijacking, sea piracy, insurance fraud, computer crime, environmental crime, trafficking in persons, trade in human body parts, illicit drug trafficking, fraudulent bankruptcy, infiltration of legal business, and corruption and bribery of public officials. These wide-ranging offenses can be grouped according to the general definition of organized crime presented in Chapter 1. They are all

Table 8.1 United Nations List of Transnational Crimes (by Category)

Provision of Illicit Goods	Provision of Illicit Services	Infiltration of Business
• Theft of arts and cultural objects	• Money laundering	• Insurance fraud
• Theft of intellectual property	• Trafficking in persons	• Bankruptcy fraud
• Illicit arms trafficking	• Computer crime	• Computer crime
• Sea piracy	• Environmental crime	• Corruption and bribery
• Trade in human body parts		of public officials
• Illicit drug trafficking		

manifestations of the provision of illicit goods, the provision of illicit services, or the infiltration of business. Viewed in this way the offenses identified by the UN can be categorized as shown in Table 8.1.

It can be seen from Table 8.1 that most of the transnational crimes identified by the United Nations are forms of organized crime. Other transnational crimes, such as terrorist activities and aircraft hijacking, are not necessarily organized crimes (although they can be when they meet the general definition of organized crime provided in Chapter 1). Of course, depending on the circumstances, some of the crimes listed in Table 8.1 can be categorized differently. For example, corruption of a public official may be provision of an illicit service in order to make it possible for an organized crime group to operate with impunity rather than be part of the infiltration of legitimate business. The UN listing is illustrative because it shows that most concern about transnational crime is centered on organized crime activity rather than on traditional or political crimes.

In recognition of the central role of organized crime in the concern about transnational crime in general, the United Nations drafted the international Convention against Transnational Organized Crime in December 2000. The convention provides model law, policies, enforcement techniques, and prevention strategies against transnational criminal groups, money laundering, witness protection, and shielding organized crime figures. The convention had to be signed by at least 40 countries in order to become binding, and this occurred in 2003. Now, 179 of the world's 193 UN Member States (nations) have ratified this convention (93%). Countries that are party to the convention must adopt laws that prohibit participation in organized criminal groups, money laundering, corruption, and obstruction of justice. The convention directs participating countries to engage in mutual legal assistance, training, extradition agreements, joint investigations, and witness protection. Three separate protocols were added for countries to ratify on the related issues of trafficking in persons, smuggling of migrants, and illicit manufacture and trafficking in firearms. Similar to the Convention against Organized Crime, these three protocols direct countries to criminalize these behaviors and take affirmative steps to investigate and prosecute suspects, as well as devote resources to training and prevention efforts.[2]

A separate United Nations Convention against Corruption entered into force in 2005 and is now ratified by 170 countries (88% of UN Member States). The UN Corruption Convention holds promise internationally because it places binding requirements on parties to criminalize corruption-related acts, aid in the recovery and return of stolen assets, cooperate with other countries in prosecution, establish anticorruption bodies, and enhance transparency in election financing. It also takes specific measures to prevent corruption in the judiciary and in public procurement. These UN efforts are important because they demonstrate that a multinational response is required to address the problem of transnational crime effectively. Efforts in a single country cannot succeed due to the nature of the criminal market, as producers, transporters, sellers, and buyers now often cross national boundaries.

USING ETHNICITY TO EXPLAIN ORGANIZED CRIME?

There is a tendency to describe organized crime around the world in ethnic terms, but the use of ethnicity as a descriptor of criminal activity is extremely limited; it fails to explain the existence of the activity itself, and it often comes perilously close to racial and ethnic stereotyping. "Italian" is no more a descriptor of organized crime in New York, for example, than is "African-American" in describing armed robbery or "Caucasian" in describing embezzlement. In each case, overbroad generalizations are made, and a variety of criminal activity committed by others is overlooked. In a similar way, the term "Russian organized crime" does not help us explain crime in Russia or the crimes committed by Russians in general, so something more than national or ethnic identity is needed in our search to explain the nature and extent of organized crime in its various manifestations.

Consider this case example: more than 500 residents were evacuated from their homes for the second time in a year when a gas vapor escaped after thieves had stolen raw ammonia from a fertilizer plant in town. Large quantities of ammonia were stolen from plants in many different places. The ammonia was traced to secret laboratories that manufactured methamphetamine.[3] Where did this occur? What types of organized crime groups are involved? In the case of methamphetamine, old stereotypes about organized crime no longer hold. Major locations for these ammonia thefts and drug manufacturing have been places such as Arkansas, Missouri, and Iowa and were committed by entrepreneurial groups that came together to exploit the criminal opportunities. Traditional boundaries and stereotypes about organized crime appear to have changed as the available opportunities have expanded.

Instead of describing organized crime in terms of the nature of the groups that engage in it, it is more useful to describe the nature of the organized crime activity itself and how and why various groups specialize in certain activities (or fail to). In this way, we can see organized crime as the result of exploitation of criminal opportunities rather than as a problem of particular ethnic groups.

The Ethnicity Trap

When the President's Commission on Organized Crime attempted to characterize "Organized Crime Today" in its final report, it fell into the "ethnicity trap." Instead of focusing on the causes and prevention of criminal opportunities and the crimes themselves, it identified 11 different groups: 9 by ethnicity, 1 by location (prison gangs), and 1 by means of transportation (motorcycle gangs). This typology lacks both clarity and logic.

You will recall the ethnic groups included in the President's Commission report (described in Chapter 7) included Italian, Mexican, Chinese, Vietnamese, Japanese, Cuban, Colombian, Irish, Russian, and Canadian. This is xenophobic in several important respects. First, the United States' two bordering neighbors, Mexico and Canada, are identified, and the other ethnic groups represent most of the recent immigration waves of the twentieth century. Only the Irish and Italian groups are nineteenth century immigrants. It is interesting that no British, French, German, or other western European groups were identified. Are we to assume no people are involved in organized crime from western Europe? The point here is that a list of ethnic groups, focusing primarily on our nearest neighbors and newest immigrants, is an extremely constricted and paranoid view of organized crime. Empirical studies offer significant evidence that ethnicity is not a good predictor of organized crime. Instead, special skills, patron–client relationships, and bonds of friendship are more important to the development of organized crime activity. Studies of organized crime in other countries, such as the Netherlands and Greece, have also found that considerations of ethnicity are secondary to the roles of opportunity, networks, and situational context.[4]

In its discussion of prison gangs, the President's Commission identified four specific gangs: Mexican, Aryan Brotherhood, Black Guerillas, and the Texas Syndicate. Once again, we are faced with a querulous mix of ethnicity, racism, race, and geographic location as descriptors of organized crime groups. This offers little guidance to the investigator, policy maker, scholar, or student who attempts to understand the problem of organized crime. A more logical and systematic approach is needed.

Criminal Networks versus Organizations

Traditional organized crime groups such as the Mafia are often characterized as "formal" groups because of the hierarchical structure from "soldiers" to "bosses." The actual operations of Mafia groups are much less formal, however, with individual members engaging in their own businesses and scams with little oversight from associates and higher-ups. The testimony of Joseph Valachi (see Chapter 6) and many others since that time has illustrated the loosely knit nature of Mafia groups. Historian Mark Haller studied traditional organized crime in Philadelphia extensively. He summarized the nature of the organization in an interview:

> There was in Philadelphia somebody called the boss, Angelo Bruno. But it was largely a fraternal organization. If you're a member of the Catholic Church that doesn't mean the Pope runs your business, you see? If you're a member of the Bruno family that certainly doesn't mean he runs anybody's businesses. Because I've seen transcript after transcript of his conversations. They never suggest "I've got to run this past Bruno." They run their own businesses and Bruno doesn't have anything to do with their businesses, except of course they feel a kind of fraternity among themselves, but they are independent. [5]

Studies of other kinds of organized crime groups show even less organization. Take the case of oxycodone (brand name, OxyContin), a prescription painkiller, a drug that has been trafficked illegally throughout the United States in recent years. Some of it has been trafficked illegally by physicians and a great deal by drug dealers who often operate in rural parts of the country. For example, a small county in Mississippi had 14 drug-related homicides in two years, giving it a higher homicide rate per capita than the most dangerous cities.[6] Clearly, this was a case of a new product being exploited in illegal ways by both criminal groups (drug dealers) and professionals (physicians) in a loosely organized fashion, more closely resembling networks than criminal organizations.

Organized crime activity committed by Russian émigrés in the Brighton Beach area of Brooklyn in New York City has been found to operate as "networks" in which there is little loyalty based on shared ethnicity or friendship. These networks are not centralized nor are they dominated by a few leaders. Organization of the networks is fluid because individuals have many indirect connections to others and take on partners as needed for a criminal activity, but no hierarchy exists independent of the crime, as is the case in many Mafia groups. Therefore, Russian organized crime in the United States is not the separate acts of individuals nor is it ethnically based organized crime on the Italian model. Finckenauer and Waring distinguish "organized crime and crime that is organized," meaning that Russian organized crime in the United States thus far has been organized, but it is not organized crime that is operated out of one or more organizations.[7] Instead, Russian émigrés have been found to be criminal entrepreneurs and extortionists who do not have the honor and respect of their community (most of whom, of course, are law-abiding). These criminals sometimes take on partners as needed to exploit a particular criminal opportunity (such as forgery specialists or enforcers), but these partnerships do not endure and form an ongoing criminal group. A study of professional criminal organizations in Finland also found loosely structured ad hoc groups to dominate organized crime activity there. As Jeffrey McIllwain observed, social networks become their own social system, which are not bound by culture or local practices, so these human network connections form the basis for organized crime activity rather than any hierarchal structure.[8]

Findings within Russia and Ukraine are similar; comparatively few significant, continuing organized crime groups are found and fewer still have international connections. For example, one study found only about 5% of organized criminal groups could be classified as major cartels. In Ukraine, only 3% of organized crime groups were found to have international ties.[9] A study by Federico Varese concluded, "the picture that emerges from post-Soviet Russia is one of many gangs with a grip on a specific bit of turf such as a neighborhood or a number of 'clients.'"[10]

A look at studies of organized crime in other countries suggests a similarity in structure and operation to the Russian and Ukrainian "network" model. In South Africa, for example, it was found that "organized crime remains comparatively fragmented" with little penetration or influence in higher levels of government.[11] Other examples would be heroin trafficking by Turks and Kurds occurring in the Netherlands and Germany, human smuggling of Chinese to the United States, and similar situations in other countries, where the structure of the enterprise is more horizontal/networked, rather than vertical/hierarchical.[12] These findings around the world suggest that organized crime has "degrees" of organization and that most groups are smaller, local networks while a much smaller number are larger ongoing and more powerful criminal enterprises.

The way in which organized crime groups and networks intertwine across borders is illustrated in Figure 8.1. Using Europe as a case example (the European Union is composed of 27 countries), and the information gathered by Europol (the European Union's law enforcement agency), the data presented in Figure 8.1 are based on their analysis across multiple countries.[13] The figure illustrates how opportunity factors combine to shape the nature of operations by organized crime. First, there are opportunities presented by the broader economic, social, and technological environment, including uncertain economic stability, the presences of many weak and corrupt governments, growth of multinational trade and travel, growth in the use of Internet and e-commerce, and the need for documentation for travel and trade. Second, these larger opportunities create criminal opportunities, including new synthetic drugs, opportunities to corrupt weak government to protect criminal enterprises, a growing market for counterfeited documents and products, opportunities for cybercrime to commit fraud across borders, environmental crime given the large waste disposal market, the large

Aligning Opportunity Factors with the Operations of Organized Crime Groups

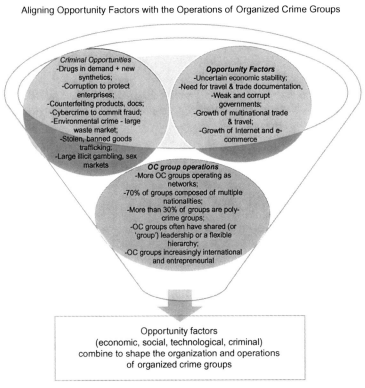

FIGURE 8.1 Linking opportunity factors with the operations of organized crime groups.

market for trafficking in stolen and banned goods, and the large markets for illicit gambling and sex. Third, organized crimes adapt to exploit these opportunities; there are more organized crime groups operating as networks, 70% of the groups in the EU are composed of multiple nationalities, more than 30% of the groups are poly-crime groups specializing in more than one kind of criminal activity, organized crime groups often have shared (or 'group') leadership or a flexible hierarchy, and organized crime groups are increasingly international and entrepreneurial. Figure 8.1 illustrates how opportunities and the nature of organized crime are closely linked.

Like all organized crime groups, European groups are impacted based on their proximity to major destination markets, geographic location, history of organized crime, and migration flows. Many non-European groups operate in Europe because it is a highly developed continent and therefore has both high demand and money to patronize illegal goods and services. Here again, the situation is similar to that in the United States where non-U.S. organized crime largely caters to indigenous U.S. demand.

TRANSNATIONAL ORGANIZED CRIME GROUPS

The United Nations Office on Drugs and Crime developed a detailed questionnaire about transnational organized crime groups, which was completed by 16 countries and one region (the Caribbean). Each country was asked to provide an analysis about what was known about three prominent organized crime groups in their country. The result was information collected on a total of 40 specific criminal groups.

The 40 organized crime groups identified were found to be of five different types.

- Rigid hierarchy—single boss with strong internal discipline within several divisions.
- Devolved hierarchy—regional structures, each with its own hierarchy and degree of autonomy.
- Hierarchical conglomerate—a loose or umbrella association of otherwise separate organized crime groups.
- Core criminal group—a horizontal structure of core individuals who describe themselves as working for the same organization.
- Organized criminal network—individuals engage in criminal activity in shifting alliances, not necessarily affiliated with any crime group, but according to skills they possess to carry out illicit activity.

This typology of groups ranged from the most to least organized, and the countries reported more rigidly hierarchical groups than any other type (about one-third of the total).[14] This finding might be due to the fact that these groups are often larger, and better documented, than other groups.

The UN study found only about one-third of the 40 groups identified to be ethnically based. The other groups either had no strong social or ethnic identity, or members were simply drawn from the same social background. Significantly, two-thirds of the groups identified had activities in three or more countries, which demonstrates the pervasiveness of transnational organized crime.

Transnational organized crime and the groups that commit this type of crime can be understood in a manner consistent with the typology presented in Chapter 1: the provision of illicit services, the provision of illicit goods, and the infiltration of legitimate business. Using these three categories of organized crime activity, the different types of organized crime groups can be examined to discover their degree of organization, whether they specialize in certain activities, and the extent to which they work across regional and national boundaries in conjunction with other groups. This presentation should enable the reader to see the interrelationships among different types of organized crimes and the types of criminals who engage in them.

PROVIDING ILLICIT SERVICES

The provision of illicit services involves primarily gambling, loansharking, and sex, as detailed in Chapter 2. These are among the oldest vices, and organized crime groups have engaged in these activities for many years and continue to do so. Like most organized crimes, illicit services are entirely demand-driven, as the public appetite for illegal gambling, borrowing, and sex knows few bounds.

Gambling and Loansharking

The roots of the gambling–organized crime link in the United States lie primarily on the prohibition of most forms of gambling on the one hand and the prohibition of alcoholic beverages on the other. These legal changes spurred the organization of illicit entrepreneurs to provide liquor and gambling opportunities to a customer base that remained after these prohibitions were passed. During the 1920s and 1930s, bootleggers of illegal alcohol became intertwined with providers of illegal gaming. As historian Mark Haller explains, bootleggers and gambling entrepreneurs originally "co-existed," but bootleggers ultimately infiltrated the illegal gambling industry for three reasons: they were younger, more violent, and sought "coordination of the nightlife and commercialized entertainment of a city."[15] Therefore, bootleggers, who existed because of Prohibition, eventually became involved in illegal gambling as another profitable way to serve their customers. It was this predictable expansion of the illegal bootlegging market that began the notorious associations of Al Capone, Sam Giancana, Lucky Luciano, Bugsy Siegel, and others with illegal gambling.[16]

In contemporary America and around the world, illegal gambling continues everywhere, given the persistent demand to play games of chance. Cosa Nostra groups have been identified in only 25 cities or so in the United States and Italy, there is a great deal of room for other groups to cater to the existing demand. A study by Potter and Gaines of rural organized crime in eastern Kentucky found interesting similarities with the urban "Cosa Nostra" version. First, vices in highest demand formed the basis for the illicit services provided. In Kentucky, this was primarily marijuana, alcohol (there are some dry counties there), sex, and gambling. Most of the syndicates were run by people related to each other, and corruption of government officials was extensive.[17] In fact, the familial nature of the groups is reminiscent of the Cosa Nostra, although their structure is more fluid.

Criminal groups have operated illegal lotteries for many years. Even with the passage of state-sponsored lotteries in most states, illegal lotteries continue to flourish because they have no minimum bet, credit is available, and the odds are better. For example, several African-American groups throughout New Jersey have been found to receive financing, lay-off bets, or split proceeds with

New York City and Philadelphia families of the Cosa Nostra.[18] In Francis Ian-ni's pioneering study titled *Black Mafia*, he found no "Mafia" or other structure that linked together black organized crime operations.[19] Nevertheless, large African-American organized crime groups have endured, such as Nicky Barnes in New York and El Rukns in Chicago, gangs that have matched the power and influence of any existing group.[20] Most of these large, independent groups have dealt primarily in drugs, while gambling in urban settings has often been conducted in conjunction with Cosa Nostra groups.

The Yakuza in Japan have been known to be involved in the vices, especially in gambling and loansharking. The Yakuza include at least seven distinct groups with a long history in Japan. Their presence in the United States was limited to Hawaii and California, but they have spread to Canada and eastern U.S. cities.[21] Interestingly, the membership is openly flaunted, and the Yakuza consider themselves legitimate businessmen. A primary activity of Yakuza is extortion, and their structure and other activities are explained more fully later.

The rise of gambling via the Internet was a predictable expansion given widespread access to Internet sites globally and the ability to use credit cards to place bets. Therefore, gambling from one's home became convenient and safe. The United States criminalized the use of credit cards to place online bets in 2006 when it passed the Unlawful Internet Gambling Enforcement Act, which makes it illegal for non-U.S. firms to collect gambling debts and prohibits U.S. banks (i.e., credit card issuers) from making payments for illegal gambling. This law is not fully implemented because of confusion in determining which types of gambling are legal in different states and the difficultly in knowing whether a vendor has submitted a claim for payment of a gambling debt versus another kind of service. It also does not require that checks or wire transactions related to Internet gambling be monitored or blocked. The U.S. House of Representatives proposed a law that would create a licensing system for online gambling, but it has not been passed into law.

The result is that criminal prosecutions continue, and they are transnational cases. Several Internet gambling operators were charged criminally (e.g., BetOnSports and Partygaming) (see Figure 8.2) for providing gambling services to U.S. customers in violation of the law.[22] Thirty-four individuals and 23 businesses were indicted and accused of operating illegal sports bookmaking businesses that solicited more than $1 billion in illegal bets. They operated Internet and telephone gambling from San Jose, Costa Rica, and Panama City, which took wagers almost exclusively from gamblers in the United States. In another case, 11 defendants pleaded guilty to running a gambling enterprise with more than 1,000 bettors and generating millions of dollars annually. The organization used websites (www.betroma.com and www.betrose.com) and telephone numbers that allowed bettors to place sports bets on football, baseball,

FIGURE 8.2 Former online gambling executive David Carruthers, left, exits the federal courthouse with his attorney. Carruthers, the former chief executive of online gambling company BetOnSports, was freed on $1 million bond after spending nearly a month behind bars following his arrest on racketeering and fraud charges. *AP Photo/Tom Gannam*

basketball, golf, horse racing, and other sporting events, and laundered the gambling proceeds by using a check cashing agency, two private bank accounts, and numerous international bank accounts.[23] It is not difficult to see that criminal entrepreneurs will work to find a way to cater to the demand for online gaming, despite legal prohibitions. Gambling proceeds historically have been used for loansharking—lending money at illegal, high-interest rates (often used to cover gambling debts).[24]

Human Trafficking and Prostitution

Chicago was identified by the President's Commission on Organized Crime as "one of the few cities" where prostitution is "controlled" by the Cosa Nostra. In most cities, however, prostitution is a mixed bag: a combination of voluntary prostitution and increasingly human trafficking involving force, fraud, or threat. In one international scheme, a Chinese tong flew young Asian women from Taiwan to Guatemala and then drove them to Mexico. Mexican smugglers then sneaked them into the United States. Madame Shih ran brothels in seven American cities, charging $20 at the door and $50 to $80 more for the prostitutes' services. The Madame and a Chinese film director ultimately were found to be behind the scheme.[25] Such a complex, international, and multiethnic scheme illustrates how organized crime groups adapt to changes in criminal opportunities, the law, and enforcement strategies.

In 2000, the United Nations adopted the Protocol to Prevent, Suppress and Punish Trafficking in Persons, Especially Women and Children, which supplemented the United Nations Convention against Transnational Organized Crime. This protocol has been ratified by three-fourths of the world's nations, illustrating the global attention to and seriousness of this issue. The basic elements of human trafficking are three:

- Exploitive labor (sex, manual labor, servitude)
- The harboring of victims (through recruitment, transport, or receipt)
- Coercion (accomplished through deception, force, or threats)

Human trafficking is different from alien smuggling because of the added elements of coercion and/or fraud. A case can begin as migrant smuggling, but the rules are changed en route and the victims are deceived or threatened, turning it into a case of human trafficking. One investigation found that "It was a common scenario in all countries (i.e., the Bahamas, Barbados, Guyana, Jamaica, The Netherlands, Antilles, St. Lucia, Suriname) that women and girls were deceived, being offered work as waitresses, cashiers, bartenders, dancers, salesclerks, or masseuses, only to be told soon after arrival that they would have to engage in prostitution."[26]

The National Human Trafficking Resource Center (NHTRC) is a 24-hour national hotline and resource center in the United States. It is funded primarily by the U.S. Department of Health and Human Services. Over five years, 1,488 individual trafficking victims contacted the hotline directly, and more than 9,298 unique cases of human trafficking were reported: 64% involved sex trafficking, 22% involved labor trafficking, 3% involved both sex and labor trafficking, and 11% were unspecified. The NHTRC provided victims of human trafficking with referrals to services, including legal services, emergency shelter, and mental health services.[27]

In England, Albanians took over more than 70% of the brothels in Soho (a district in London), smuggling women from eastern Europe to work illegally as prostitutes, undercutting the prices of the local brothels. Some of these women were kidnapped, and some were simply tricked into leaving their home countries, arriving on false passports or having their legal papers taken from them, and then forced to act as sex slaves to pay off their captors. The Albanian groups are organized into clans rather than around leaders or bosses, and although their influence in local prostitution is significant, they have had little influence elsewhere in Britain. Likewise, Albanians have been found to dominate prostitution in northern and central Italy, but not elsewhere.[28] In another British case, a group of five members (Hungarian and British) were convicted of human trafficking after they flew more than 50 young women into the UK from Hungary and set them up as prostitutes in various locations.[29] In Bosnia-Herzegovina, the United Nations mission closed, for labor and tax law violations, 15 bars where women were being forced into prostitution. Most of the women came from Romania, Moldova, Ukraine, and Belarus.[30]

Prostitution also has been the result of Chinese gangs smuggling illegal immigrants into the United States. Large fees are charged, and the only way many women can hope to repay the debt is through prostitution. This method of racketeering and extortion by Chinese gangs is discussed in the next section.

In Australia and the Asia Pacific region, a combination of political instability, armed conflict, rapid population growth, and widening economic disparities have contributed to "migration pressures," causing women from developing countries or countries in conflict to seek employment in developed nations or those without the conflict and with greater opportunities for jobs.[31] The result is risk-taking and a susceptibility to become victims of fraud and manipulation, contributing to a growing problem of illegal migration and forced prostitution.

Russian mafia groups run prostitution enterprises in Russia, but it is not clear that prostitution is an enterprise they are pursuing actively in the United States. Nevertheless, there is evidence of young women being recruited from Russia, a number of whom are trafficked abroad.[32] Stolen property and extortion appear to be the primary focus of Russian crime groups, as explained later.

In a related way, there have been reports of trafficking in body organs to feed the need for transplants in developed countries. A worldwide shortage of donors has combined with a high-profit potential to create a market. In India, five men took out an ad in an Indian magazine to offer their kidneys for sale, and there have been cases in which victims of human smuggling have had body organs missing. In another case, kidney donors from Israel sold their kidneys through middle-men who earned a high price from buyers needing transplants in the United States.[33] The need for skilled surgeons to participate in such a criminal enterprise probably limits the size of this market, but the dynamics of a high demand for organs, combined with the high prices and potential profits that can result, can attract criminal entrepreneurs from all walks of life.

PROVIDING ILLICIT GOODS

The provision of illicit goods primarily involves drug trafficking and dealing in stolen and banned property of various kinds. Drug trafficking was the international organized crime of choice during the 1990s. Stolen property has become an illicit industry in many countries, especially those where a weak economy and weak government structure combine to provide an underground market for goods. Of course, stolen property remains pervasive in developed countries as well because of the high demand for "bargains" by many who do not consider the source of the goods. The cases that follow describe the multiethnic and multinational nature of many of these criminal operations.

Drugs

Drug trafficking is often a transnational crime because common drugs of choice can only be grown effectively in certain regions of the world, and these regions are far from the high demand and affluent drug users. Drug trafficking occurs when psychoactive substances are moved across international borders in violation of international law. International drug laws consist of three major drug control conventions enacted in 1961, 1971, and 1988. These three drug control conventions have been ratified by more than 95% of United Nations members. The Convention on Narcotic Drugs (1961) merged all existing multilateral treaties that existed up until that time, created an International Narcotics Control Board, and extended drug control to cultivation of plants grown as raw material to manufacture narcotic drugs. The Convention controls more than 116 narcotic drugs (including the production, distribution, and use of opium, heroin, cocaine, cannabis, and related substances), and divides them into four groups, or schedules, organizing a greater or lesser degree of control for the various drugs. Opium smoking and eating, coca leaf chewing, cannabis-resin smoking, and the nonmedical use of cannabis are prohibited under this convention. The Convention on Psychotropic Substances (1971) extended international drug control to include hallucinogens, stimulants, and sedatives, such as LSD, amphetamines, and barbiturates. The UN Convention against Illicit Traffic in Narcotic Drugs and Psychotropic Substances (1988) focused on control of precursor chemicals in the manufacture of illicit drugs, as well as the growing problem of international trafficking. The convention includes money laundering and illicit traffic in precursor chemicals as drug trafficking activities. International cooperation between law enforcement and judicial bodies was promoted through mechanisms for the extradition of major drug traffickers and mutual legal assistance between countries in drug-related investigations and prosecutions. It also introduces provisions for the tracing, freezing, and confiscation of proceeds and property derived from drug trafficking.

These three conventions are important because they are binding on the ratifying nations, which now include nearly all of the world. Therefore, they reflect international consensus and cooperation against illicit drug trafficking. Of course, because the three conventions have no police force of their own, enforcement requires action by individual nations. A multinational Commission on Narcotic Drugs meets annually at the UN to assess the world drug situation, and it monitors the implementation of the three international drug control conventions across borders.[34]

Three major groups of illicit drugs are of major concern in terms of their global implications: cocaine, opiates, and amphetamines. Cannabis (marijuana) trafficking is not discussed here because cannabis cultivation and production occurs in nearly every country in the world (because it can be effectively grown indoors), and its cultivation and consumption are most often local. As a result, transnational trafficking of marijuana affects fewer cross-border regions, and increasing possibilities of decriminalizing it in many locations contributes to making marijuana trafficking a local problem rather than a transnational one.

The world's cocaine supply comes from the coca bush (its leaves are made into paste), and it thrives only in tropical climates. Virtually all the supply comes from three countries: Colombia (41%), Peru (41%), and Bolivia (17%).[35] Global demand for cocaine has been dominated by two major consumer markets: North America and Western and Central Europe.

These two markets together are estimated to account for half of cocaine users globally, although increases have been seen in other world regions in recent years. This shift in cocaine demand (produced by prevention efforts, treatment, and law enforcement and seizures) has caused South American cocaine traffickers to use areas of West Africa as transit zones, where law enforcement presence and risk is low. In some cases, maritime and private air shipments are owned and managed by South Americans, who exchange logistical assistance for payment in cocaine. This creates another trafficking route in which West Africans transport these drugs to Europe using commercial air flights. The introduction of cocaine into this region of Africa also fuels local violence and drug use in a place without the resources to control it effectively and with high levels of corruption. Cocaine seizures reveal some patterns. More than 80% of the seized cocaine destined for Spain was taken from nationals of Nigeria, Guinea-Bissau, Mali, and Cape Verde. In the United Kingdom, 75% of the couriers discovered were Nigerian or British nationals.[36]

Drug trafficking north through Mexico continues to be a problem in the Americas. More than 15,000 were killed in 2010 alone, although the vast majority of those killed are believed to be persons connected in some fashion to criminal organizations. When tourists or police officers are occasional victims of this violence, public attention is drawn back to this ongoing situation involving competition among drug cartels as well as challenges to the authority of the Mexican government. The criminal groups are called "cartels" or "drug trafficking organizations" (DTOs), and their activities are not limited to drug trafficking, but include trafficking in persons, kidnapping, extortion, and trafficking in stolen and pirated goods. These groups are primarily trafficking businesses that are motivated by profits, rather than ideology. The DTOs are horizontally organized and often subcontract with local criminal organizations or youth gangs to move product through a particular port of entry.[37] This array of criminal enterprises is aggravated by persistent corruption as illustrated by a case in which a former Colombian prosecutor was found to be providing information to drug traffickers. In this case, the DTO was responsible for transporting cocaine by speedy vessels from Colombia to Central America and ultimately to the United States. Wire intercepts recorded the prosecutor speaking to representatives of the DTO about his receiving regular monthly payments from the Colombian drug trafficking organization in exchange for information about criminal investigations the governments of Colombia or the United States were conducting against the drug traffickers.[38]

Opiates are a second major category of controlled drug. Afghanistan dominates opium production (65%), followed by Myanmar (21%). It is estimated that 60% of the opium in Afghanistan is converted into heroin and morphine within the country, and about 40% is exported as opium. Opium is usually converted into heroin inside or close by the country where opium poppy is cultivated. Opiates are transported via several different routes from Afghanistan to Iran to Turkey and into Europe. Another route is through Central Asia and Russia into Europe. There has also been an increase in heroin seizures in East Africa at seaports or on the open sea, indicating growing opiate trafficking via Africa to other parts of the world.[35] In one case, the alleged leader of a Ghana-based heroin trafficking organization was charged with recruiting couriers to hide heroin in their specially-designed carry-on bags for smuggling into the United States through Dulles International Airport in Washington, DC. The organization paid couriers up to $15,000 to transport the heroin, along with providing airfare, passports, and hotel accommodations until the drugs were transferred to distributors within the United States.[39]

A third category of controlled drugs are amphetamines (including ecstasy), which are stimulants that can be produced anywhere in the world using certain chemical combinations. Monitoring and control of the precursor chemicals used to make amphetamine-type stimulants has caused substitution of these chemicals with alternate precursors that are not yet controlled. The market for amphetamine-type drugs is expanding as indicated by the number of labs seized, trafficking seizures, and demand. The emergence of new psychoactive substances (such as bath salts, synthetic cannabinoids [Spice], and phenethylamines) has introduced an added layer of concern in which chemicals are mixed with a variety of substances to produce stimulant or hallucinogenic effects. As of 2012, there were 251 new psychoactive substances identified by UN member nations that are not covered under the existing drug conventions.[40]

Project Synergy, an operation of the Drug Enforcement Administration (DEA) in Houston, Texas, discovered a wholesale distributor who was selling synthetic cannabinoid products. The manager of this illegal operation told undercover

DEA agents that he initially invested $80,000 and turned it into $6 million, stating "you can't rob banks and make this kind of money." More than $53 million was seized in currency and assets in this case.[41]

An important example of a multinational drug case was *United States v. Vasquez-Velaso*. The defendant, Javier Vasquez-Velaso, was convicted of racketeering and murder. Along with three codefendants, Vasquez-Velaso was part of the "Guadalajara Narcotics Cartel," which distributed large amounts of drugs from Mexico to the United States.[42] The U.S. DEA was having some success against the drug cartel that resulted in millions of dollars in drug losses and cash seizures. As a result, the cartel engaged in retaliatory actions against DEA agents in Mexico. This included the killing of DEA agent Enrique Camarena, informants, and others mistakenly believed to be associated with the DEA.

These murders took place in Mexico and raised an important issue about the ability of the U.S. government to enforce its laws against those who violate them outside its borders. Vasquez-Velaso was not charged with the killing of Camarena, although his associates were. Instead, he was charged with murder and racketeering for participating in the beating deaths of two persons in Mexico mistakenly believed to be DEA agents.

Vasquez-Velaso argued that he could not be charged with crimes not committed in the United States. The U.S. Court of Appeals looked to "congressional intent" in deciding on extraterritorial application of the law and considered two important principles of international law:

1. *Objective Territorial Principle*—jurisdiction is asserted over acts performed outside the United States that produce detrimental effects within the United States.
2. *Protective Principle*—jurisdiction is asserted over foreigners for an act committed outside the United States that may impinge on the territorial integrity, security, or political independence of the United States.

The court held that extraterritorial application of the law in this case was not unreasonable because it corresponded with the principles of international law. Because "drug smuggling is a serious and universally condemned offense, no conflict is likely to be created by extraterritorial regulation of drug traffickers."[43] Similarly, the court relied on its holding in an earlier case involving an accessory to the murder of DEA Agent Camarena:

> We held that because drug trafficking by its nature involves foreign countries and because DEA agents often work overseas, the murder of a DEA agent in retaliation for drug enforcement activities is a crime against the United States regardless of where it occurs. [44]

Therefore, the U.S. Court of Appeals found that Congress would have intended extraterritoriality in cases like this. Even though Vasquez-Velaso did not murder a DEA agent, the court declared "the record clearly supports the government contention that [the two victims] were murdered in retaliation for the DEA's activities in Mexico."[45]

The issue of extraterritoriality is likely to arise again as organized crime's global reach grows.[46] Consider the case of the indictments brought against 18 people in Dallas for international drug smuggling. Nigerian heroin smugglers recruited non-Nigerian Dallas residents to smuggle heroin into the United States. According to the indictment, the Nigerian recruiters provided airline tickets and expense money for the couriers, in addition to a salary of $5,000 to $10,000 per trip. The first courier would be sent to Thailand, the heroin source, and would take the heroin from there to an intermediate nonsource nation (such as the Philippines, Kenya, Poland, or western Europe) and deliver it to a second courier there. The second courier would conceal the heroin in a suitcase or strap it to his or her body and then smuggle it into the United States. The strategy was designed to deceive U.S. authorities who would not suspect the courier who had not been to the source country, and the suspicious courier who had been there would possess no drugs.[47] Such a scheme capitalizes on multiethnic cooperation among criminals, as well as points to the need for international cooperation and surveillance by law enforcement agencies.

The "internationalization" of organized crime activities is typified by narcotics trafficking. The immense problems posed by manufacture, transportation, smuggling, and distribution have resulted in "marriages of convenience" in which criminal groups work together, albeit suspiciously, to make a mutual profit, and sometimes the money ends up being used to fund terrorist activities. An example of this phenomenon is the alliance between some Sicilian mafia groups and the Medellin cartel in Colombia. The shooting death of Pablo Escobar during a police raid on his home in 1993 did not slow the flow of cocaine from Colombia. In his absence, the Cali cartel gained control of the bulk of cocaine manufacturing and distribution in Colombia.[48] The Cali cartel may have learned from the murderous ways of Escobar in that they are less prone to violence and more skilled at bribery and corruption. Therefore, organized crime groups come to live off one another in carrying out international criminal schemes, and also learn from each other's mistakes.

Stolen Property

In times past, trafficked stolen property consisted primarily of clothing, electronics, currency, and precious stones. As the economy has become globalized, international trafficking cases have been made involving caviar from Russia, pirated CDs from Ukraine, video games from Asia, nuclear materials from the former Soviet Union and eastern European nations, and rare bird eggs from

Brazil.[49] As travel, technology, and communication have all been made easier, the ability of criminals to reach eager consumers of illicit products around the world has been strengthened.

Political changes throughout central and eastern Europe, Asia, Africa, and Central and South America have produced new opportunities for organized crime, most associated with the precipitous drop in the standard of living. Growing unemployment, high inflation, and scarcity of goods have led "more and more people turning to the black market and to crime as a means of supplementing their income."[50] The subterranean economy has formed the wellspring of many organized crime groups over the years, including the Bahamas once it became politically independent of Great Britain.[51]

Although the true extent of Russian organized crime around the world is not well documented, it is known that many Soviet Jews emigrated to the United States and elsewhere when the Soviet Union liberalized its Jewish emigration policy in the mid-1970s. It is estimated that as many as 100,000 former Soviets came to the United States with more than 40,000 settling in Brighton Beach, Brooklyn. It is also alleged that criminals from Soviet jails were included in this wave of immigration.[52] Significant cases involving Russian organized crime entailed motor fuel tax fraud in New Jersey. Scams involved a number of Russian immigrants who bought fuel oil, sold it as diesel, charged the customer taxes, but never paid those taxes to the government. Schemes involved dummy corporations, which hoped to "lose" the taxes in a paper trail of buyers, sellers, oil refineries, and distributors.[53] An important aspect of these cases was that the Russians knew they had to pay "tribute" to Cosa Nostra families in the area where they were operating and did so. Loosely knit groups of Russian immigrants also have been found to be engaged in money laundering, fraud, and murder.[54]

It has been discovered that nuclear materials are "missing" from the former Soviet Union and eastern European nations. That material is being offered for sale illegally in western Europe, primarily in Germany. The Stanford Database on Nuclear Smuggling identified more than 700 illicit trafficking incidents in 10 years.[55] Most of these cases involved theft by employees in nuclear facilities around the world who sell to criminal groups or individuals, although cases involving weapons-grade materials are rare. See Figure 8.3.

In Toronto, luxury car thefts have been blamed on Russian organized crime connected to Brighton Beach in Brooklyn. Sought-after automobiles, especially large Buicks and Cadillacs, can be shipped legally from Canada to Russia for less than $1,000. They can be sold in Russia for $40,000.[56] An investigation in the United Kingdom occurred when a random car check in Southampton found that 50% of the cars were identified as stolen, even though the owners had no idea they were driving stolen property. It was discovered that up to 85,000 cars were stolen in Japan, shipped to Dubai where they are given false papers and new identification numbers and then transported to the

FIGURE 8.3 Part of a seizure of radioactive substances including iridium-192 and europium-152 being smuggled in 2011. Police in Kutaisi, Georgia, arrested three people involved in the smuggling, one who was arrested trying to sell radioactive material to two Turkish men. *AP Photo/Georgia Interior Ministry*

United Kingdom.[57] In Hong Kong, similar investigations have recovered more than 2,000 stolen vehicles per year. They are often found inside containers on cargo ships, where the cargo reference numbers are altered, making it difficult to trace their origins.[58] Police often find a combination of left-hand-drive and right-hand-drive vehicles, indicating that the thefts are occurring in different parts of the world.

The President's Commission on Organized Crime found "firearms trafficking" to be common in Cosa Nostra groups in the north central United States, although Jamaican posses (gangs) appeared to be most active in gunrunning. Guns were either bought illegally or stolen and then smuggled back to Kingston, Jamaica, where they were sold to local gangs at inflated prices.[59] The demand for guns by organized crime groups sometimes leads them to suppliers not affiliated with their own group. One "independent" illegal trafficker was said to have sold weapons to members of the Genovese crime family in New York, as well as to Chinese gangs in Manhattan.[60]

Outlaw motorcycle clubs vary widely in the extent to which they engage in criminal activity. Members of Hells Angels, Outlaws, Pagans, Bandidos, and Satan's Choice have been documented committing a wide array of crimes.[61] Drug trafficking is the most common, along with robbery and extortion. Like the Chinese Tongs, motorcycle gangs are composed of many noncriminals, making it difficult to distinguish criminal members from the others. For example, the Toronto chapter of Satan's Choice was found to operate a drug laboratory that manufactured methamphetamines, "Canadian Blue," that was exported to the U.S.-based Outlaws motorcycle club. It was found that "mixed in with the narcotics dealers ... were labourers and tradesmen, such as an electrician, a plumber, and a truck driver, along with a stock-market executive."[62] A sociologist who rode with the Rebels motorcycle club reported that they "are outlaws, but they are not professional criminals." They broke laws, but "rarely for profit." He found them to be criminal opportunists who committed misdemeanors, assaults, weapons offenses, drug possession, and other crimes, but did not organize their criminal activity.[62] This variation both among and within motorcycle gangs makes it difficult to generalize about them beyond specific cases, although Canada sees a continuing rivalry among chapters of Hells Angels, Bandidos, and Outlaws, and their associations with drug trafficking networks and street gangs in cities around the country.[63]

In different world regions, the nature of the stolen and banned property market varies by the available opportunities. The largest source of financing for these crime groups in Central Africa is the minerals trade. The illicit trade in Congolese gold is estimated at 10 times the value of the country's legal gold exports and is twice the value of coffee, its largest agricultural export. In the developing world, such large scale theft and profit provide incentives for armed groups to perpetuate the instability to make it difficult for the rule of law to take hold (in terms of improving the capacity of police, prosecution, courts, and corrections systems to respond effectively).[64] In West African countries the situation is similar. Contraband most often includes drugs, weapons, counterfeit medicine, and smuggled migrants, requiring public education, and a more effective and less corrupt response from government agencies.[65]

In China, there is a centuries-old tradition of intricately carving rhinoceros horn cups. Drinking from such a cup is believed to bring good health, and antique carvings are sought by collectors in Asian countries and also in the United States. The value of such items has resulted in a demand for rhinoceros horn that fuels a black market (including fake antiques). In one case, a conspiracy was found to smuggle objects carved from rhinoceros horn and elephant ivory out of the United States illegally. Due to their dwindling populations, all rhinoceros and elephant species are protected under international trade agreements. In one case, packages were falsely labeled in order to conceal their true contents and helped to "create and sustain a marketplace for goods made from endangered wildlife."[66]

A new variation of stolen property crimes is the theft of intellectual property. Online piracy involves placing illegally copied movies, music, games, and software on the Internet, generating thousands of illicit digital copies. This market is dominated by "a handful of highly structured, security conscious groups which exist solely to engage in piracy [online]." They are called "warez" groups, which compete with each other to obtain the fastest, highest quality, and free access to pirated digital materials. The groups use high-end technology to shield their activity from law enforcement. These groups have hierarchies and divisions of labor, but unlike more traditional forms of organized crime, "they do not engage in piracy for monetary gain."[67]

However, there are organized crime groups that endeavor to profit from the theft of intellectual property. These groups manufacture optical disks that contain pirated music, movies, software, and video games that are distributed around the world. This form of digital piracy occurs primarily in Asia and parts of the former Soviet Union, with distribution networks through Central and South America into North America, Europe, and Australia. For example, the Business Software Alliance (BSA) reports that nearly two-thirds of the software used in eastern Europe and Greece is illegal (pirated digitally), followed by Latin America (57%) and the Asia-Pacific region (57%). Nearly one-half of the software in France and Spain is similarly illegal. In the United States, it is estimated that 25% of software used is pirated. This results in a combined global loss of $11 billion. If the world piracy rate was lowered to the U.S. level, the BSA estimates 44,000 jobs would be created to meet the demand for software. The BSA investigated 15,000 reports of pirated software in 2012.[68] The Motion Picture Association estimates that illegal videos account for 5% of the video business in Australia, but the rate is significantly higher in Asia. In China, Hong Kong, and Malaysia, pirated DVDs comprise more than 80% of the video business. During a conference in Australia, for example, an exhibitor was able to purchase a copy of *Spiderman* for less than $10, a week before the movie was released in theaters. In a typical case, a DVD fraud and counterfeiting case is made by undercover investigators from the Motion Picture Association of America who, along with police, make purchases of suspect DVDs (usually movies are still in theaters and illicit copies are leaked by insiders). Subsequent search warrants find evidence of packaging of pirated DVDs, equipment used to make the illegal recordings, blank disks, as well as computers used to sell counterfeit DVDs over the web.[69] Clearly, the theft of intellectual property has been facilitated by dramatic advances in technology and by the ability to transmit stolen materials electronically.

INFILTRATING LEGITIMATE BUSINESS

The President's Commission on Organized Crime found that "labor racketeering and infiltration of the construction trades" are "primary" activities of Cosa Nostra groups in the northeast United States. Forgery and arson for profit were found to be "prominent" among Cosa Nostra groups in the southern and western regions of the United States. In addition, the New Orleans Cosa Nostra group was found to generate "most of its income" through the infiltration of legitimate business.[70] The extent to which other criminal groups are involved in these, and related, kinds of criminal infiltration is described next.

CRITICAL THINKING EXERCISE 8.1

The Case of the Nigerian Advance Fee Fraud

You receive a "desperate" letter from the widow of a well-known government official or businessperson in Africa. Your bank account number is needed to process an inheritance, buy real estate, convert currency, or obtain funds from a foreign bank account in the sum of millions of dollars. You are impressed with various official-looking forms, stamps, and documents and are requested to travel to Nigeria or a country nearby. Eventually, you must provide up-front or advance fees for taxes, attorneys' fees, transaction fees, or bribes. After you have paid these fees, nothing happens, and sometimes your entire bank account is drained. You have been the victim of an advance fee fraud (AFF).

These AFFs are known internationally as "4-1-9" frauds, named after the section of the Nigerian penal code that addresses fraudulent schemes. Most people around the world have received these e-mails, and some actually believe they have been singled out to share in a multimillion dollar windfall for doing absolutely nothing. The most successful AFF is the fund transfer scam. The victim receives an unsolicited letter or e-mail from a Nigerian claiming to be a senior civil servant. The Nigerian is looking for a reputable foreign company to take receipt of funds of $10 million or more that the Nigerian government overpaid on a contract. Once the victim is persuaded to reveal his or her bank account number or transfer funds to facilitate this transaction, the fraud occurs. More than 10,000 U.S. Internet users reportedly receive AFF letters each year, and more solicitations come from Nigeria than any other country.

Reasons for the escalation in AFFs in recent years are many. Mass unemployment and a culture that tolerates widespread fraud continue in Nigeria, despite efforts to control it. On the victim end, the "get-rich-quick" syndrome and the greed of many in countries around the world make them susceptible to suspicious offers they desperately want to be genuine. The Financial Crimes Division of the U.S. Secret Service receives 100 telephone calls a day from victims and potential victims of AFF. A number of citizens from the United States and other countries have gotten into legal trouble, and some have disappeared when they traveled to Nigeria or bordering countries to complete an AFF transaction.

Critical Thinking Questions

1. Nigerian cyber-cafés charge about $1 per hour for Internet usage, and these have been used to conduct "4-1-9" scams. How might this be controlled?
2. Potential AFF victims are selected in large numbers from e-mail lists of various kinds. How can the misuse of this information be prevented?
3. Why do you believe Nigeria is a center for this kind of activity rather than other countries?

Sources: *David E. Kaplan, "A Land Where Con Is King," U.S. News & World Report (May 7, 2001); Sam Olukoya, "Nigeria Grapples with E-mail Scams" (April 23, 2002); "Fraudsters Dupe Americans N50 Million," Africa News Service (April 17, 2002); Advance Fee Fraud Schemes www.sec.gov/answers/nigeria.htm (April 28, 2010).*

Racketeering

Peter Reuter conducted a study of the garbage collection industry in the New York City area. He found that companies in this area were "dominated by males of Italian origin" and that numerous firms were family enterprises. Interestingly, he found that "ethnic homogeneity" is characteristic in the waste carting industry, although the ethnicity varies. In Chicago, most firms are run by those of Dutch origin. In Los Angeles, the Armenians and Jews dominate, and in San Francisco, the Italians appear to dominate.[71] Reuter found this ethnic homogeneity not to be accidental or conspiratorial. Instead, it is due to the fact that most of these firms are small and cannot afford to have a truck fail or an employee not show up for work in order to conduct that day's business. There-fore, there is a need for carters to cooperate with each other to provide backup if one of their members experiences problems. Reuter also argues that the "low repute of the industry" left it to new immigrant groups with traditions of entre-preneurship.[72] Criminal conspiracies emerged largely in allocating customers among carters in violation of antitrust laws. In this way, carters establish monopolies and large profits from not bidding against each other in open com-petition. Reuter found that the reputation of being a racketeer (i.e., being "con-nected" to a larger criminal organization) was more important than being an actual member of a conspiracy. The label of racketeer involvement "provides a reputational barrier to entry" into the market, where other potential carting competitors do not enter the market due to fear of retaliation by racketeers.[73]

Reuter admits that it is difficult to determine how the industry operates outside the New York City area with regard to monopolies, customer allocation agree-ments, and the involvement of racketeers. In most areas of the country "there are neither Mafia families nor any other comparable racketeering group."[74] An analysis of the customer market and prices charged for carting in different juris-dictions can provide clues, however, regarding overcharging and potential con-spiratorial arrangements.

Racketeering appears to have become a multiethnic enterprise in recent years. Cosa Nostra groups have been found to supply and service illegal video gam-bling machines that Chinese gangs have forced on bars and nightclubs. Russian groups have been found to be no longer exclusively Russian or even Slavic, but rather a network comprised of various ethnicities.[75] The Irish, Russian, Chinese, Japanese, and groups from other ethnic background have engaged in racketeering. Such racketeering usually involves extortion, and the tactics employed mirror those first used in the country where the group originated.

Since the collapse of the Soviet Union, Russian organized crime groups have been engaged in racketeering activities there, in the United States, and in other countries. Businessmen have been found to hire gangsters for protection from other criminals. As the new capitalist economy emerges, businesses have a need to protect their property interests, protection which the government and police are unable to provide. This creates a market for criminal groups to provide "pro-tection" to these businesses. Sociologist Vadim Volkov calls this "violent entre-prenuership."[76] These activities are often part of a wider assortment of criminal activities that involve drug trafficking and frauds of various kinds.[77] Lydia Ros-ner uses the term "buccaneer capitalism" to refer to the expansion of criminal enterprises that previously existed only within countries but now extend across borders, and the transformation of criminal enterprises in new markets into legitimate businesses through money laundering and the investment of illegal profits into legal businesses.[78]

Extortion

Interviews with people from more than 600 businesses owned and operated by Chinese in New York City found that more than 70% were approached by gang members for some type of extortion, most often demands for money. Most of these businesses (55%) made the payments and, although threats were common, violence was rare (less than four times per year). Interestingly, Tongs have emerged as "power brokers" or "middlemen" between the businesses and the gangs. The problem, of course, is that "merchants who resort to tong protection for a fee may find themselves in new partnerships."[79]

From a purely economic calculus, merchants appear to be content to deal with a powerful tong or gang boss rather than face the chaos of shakedowns from every street hoodlum. Thus, in a sense, there are as many "voluntary victims" as "involuntary victims" in a commercial environment where the lines of demarcation between the legal and illegal are blurred.[80]

The intergang murders that have occurred in the Chinese community appear to originate with territorial conflicts in which gangs compete for extortion targets or market share.

The smuggling of aliens has become an enterprise for some Chinese gangs, most notably the Fuk Ching. In one case, this group smuggled hundreds of illegal immigrants from mainland China to New York City, charging $23,000 each. The illegal aliens had the option of working as indentured servants (i.e., mules, enforcers, prostitutes) or becoming part of the Fuk Ching gang to pay off their debts, ensuring the continuity of the illegal enterprise. There are more than 50,000 Chinese aliens smuggled by criminal groups into the United States each year, according to one estimate.[81] Studies of Chinese smuggling organizations found them to be informal groups: most were ordinary citizens from diverse backgrounds who formed temporary alliances to conduct smuggling operations. Chinese "organized crime" groups involved in transnational criminal activities include Hong Kong-based Triads, Taiwan-based crime groups, China-based crime groups, U.S.-based Tongs, U.S.-based gangs, drug traffickers, and human smugglers (called "Snakeheads").[82]

Vietnamese gangs arose in California during the early 1980s, after the arrival of thousands of Vietnamese refugees in the United States. These gangs are highly localized in nature, but they engage in common activities. Several of these gangs seek "donations" from legitimate Vietnamese businesses in the United States with promises of using them to help free Vietnam. These "requests" are sometimes accompanied with threats of being labeled a "procommunist." Such a label is tantamount to being called a traitor to one's homeland. These extortionate methods are used to support further criminal activity. In a Vietnamese gang in New York City it was found that "the gang's weekly extortion rounds were the backbone of their entire operation . . . by continuously reasserting its presence, the gang was making it clear to area merchants who was boss on Canal Street."[83] Collection of a "street tax" by the Vietnamese gang mirrors that of traditional Italian-American and Chinese groups operating in different neighborhoods of the same city.

Extortion on an international scale became a significant problem in the late twentieth century. Strong Western economies promoted both international business expansion and tourism to all parts of the world, especially in developing nations. The kidnapping of business executives and tourists from wealthy nations grew to the highest level ever during the 1990s. It is estimated that nearly two-thirds of the largest companies in the United States buy kidnap insurance to pay for professional negotiators, counselors, and ransoms. Kidnappings like these have been used in some nations as a form of illicit business to earn income in otherwise impoverished areas. Blackmail is used to extort ransom payments from corporations and families in exchange for the return of the victims. Kidnapping for purposes of blackmail was common in the United States early in the twentieth century. In 1933, for example, the *New York Times* covered 27 major kidnappings for ransom.[84] The development and the success of the Federal Bureau of Investigation as an agency designed to deal with interjurisdictional crimes have made it difficult to conduct kidnappings successfully for purposes of blackmail and this has reduced its occurrence greatly in the United States, although it continues transnationally in the form of piracy and ransom of ships off the coast of Africa and kidnapping of business executives is some developing countries,

Variations of the crime of blackmail or extortion continue to occur in response to changes in society, the economy, and technology. For example, the Vatican charged Chinese authorities with employing prostitutes to subject Roman Catholic priests to sexual blackmail, thereby weakening their loyalty to the church. Computer hackers infiltrated the sites of nonsecure companies and then threatened to cripple company computers with a flood of data or messages unless an extortion payment was made. Two collection agency owners were convicted of extortion after they were given a list of nonpaying clients of a sex-chat phone service. Instead of collecting unpaid bills, they threatened to inform the clients' bosses and wives about their use of the phone service if extra payments were not made. Mexican drug gangs use kidnapping and extortion to control their territories.[85] It appears that the variations of extortion are limitless and will grow as the opportunities for it expand.

It is likely that the extent of extortion is associated with rates of other forms of theft. Therefore, it should occur with some frequency in impoverished jurisdictions, but blackmail can also be justified for political or ideological purposes, and changes in technology simply make blackmail easier to carry out. For example, kidnappings for extortion are sometimes justified in developing nations as a way to strike back against perceived injustices caused by developed nations with operations in their countries. In addition, the growing ease of international travel and communication makes it easier than ever to locate suitable blackmail targets and victims. The secretive nature and implicit coercion make it impossible to know the true extent of extortion, but there is no reason to believe it will diminish given recent international trends.

Traditional organized crime groups have been found to turn to nontraditional groups for "subcontracting" purposes. Cecil Kirby, a Canadian biker, was contracted by an alleged Mafia group to commit murder.[86] Similarly, Clarence Smith, a member of the Outlaws motorcycle club, was convicted for the murder of a witness who had testified against a nephew of Carlos Marcello, the alleged boss of the Cosa Nostra group in New Orleans.[87] There is continuing evidence of outlaw motorcycle gangs that both contract and use subcontractors to commit crimes in support of ongoing criminal operations, including extortion.[88]

The generic term for organized crime groups in Japan is "boryokudan," which means "violent ones." The criminals call themselves "Yakuza," which stands for "8,9,3." This is the worst possible hand in a popular Japanese card game (hana-fuda), so the term is taken to mean a "loser."[89] Yakuza commonly have ornate tattoos and dress distinctively. If a member has committed a transgression in the eyes of his "boss," he may atone for it by cutting off the last joint of his little finger. This may be repeated for other transgressions on other fingers. Unlike organized crime groups in the United States, gangs in Japan are usually open about their Yakuza affiliation. They consider themselves part of a "mutual aid society." As a result, membership in Yakuza groups is much larger than that of the American Mafia, which attempts to remain invisible.[90]

There are at least seven major Yakuza gangs. Membership involves an initiation and sworn oath of loyalty, much like that of traditional Italian organized crime. The structure of the gang is also much like that of a Cosa Nostra family, although it is somewhat more structured. Extortion is a primary activity of Yakuza groups. Sometimes they purchase stock in a targeted corporation, disrupting corporate meetings, and extort payment for "peace." Police in Japan are limited in combating the Yakuza because undercover police work and electronic surveillance are not permitted in Japan. In addition, informants are unpopular and are not used in Japan. Therefore, prosecutions usually result only after a witness comes forward voluntarily. This is rare.

The four Mafia-type organizations in Italy are associated with their geographic locations: the Sicilian Mafia, Calabrian Ndrangheta, Neapolitan Camorra, and Apulian Organised Crime. Italian criminal groups are reported as active in only a handful of European countries besides Italy, according to Europol. The racketeering and extortion associated with Italian Mafias are connected to their local control of specific areas in Italy (enabled by government ineffectiveness and Italian

CRITICAL THINKING EXERCISE 8.2

Read the following case study. Using the concepts from this chapter, answer the questions that follow, explaining your rationale.

The Case of Video Slot Machines

The structure of this gang is very fluid. Old gangs dissolve and are replaced quickly by new groups. Several of these groups distribute illegal video gambling machines to selected neighborhoods throughout the city. One individual has distributed more than 20 "Cherry Master" video slot machines to businesses, selected by their ownership, which include bars, nightclubs, and massage parlors. These groups cannot place their machines in other neighborhoods because they are controlled by different gangs who would demand a split of the profits, as well as protection money.

Businesses that refuse these gambling machines are threatened or damage is inflicted. Money is also extorted from these businesses for "protection" from damage or disruption. Business owners in the neighborhoods affected pay the extortion because it protects them from harassment, and they do not believe that the police, if called, can do anything about it.

Critical Thinking Questions

1. Given the facts just provided, can you guess which organized crime group is being described?
2. If gambling and extortion are used by a large number of organized crime groups to produce illegal income, what solutions would you recommend?

culture), which cannot occur effectively when operating overseas. The more organized crime groups act at transnational level, the more they develop networked organizational structures, so control of territory and the centrality of extortion is reduced, because it relies on local reputation, connections, and control.[91]

CRIMES AGAINST GOVERNMENT

Corruption and terrorism are two types of offenses in which governments are targeted for the purposes of bribery, extortion, fear, or overthrow. Corruption is an endemic problem around the world as countries attempt to administer government business and the rule of law in an impartial way in the face of private demands for favorable treatment. Terrorism has grown as a concern because terrorist groups increasingly engage in organized crime activity to fund their larger political objectives.

Corruption

Political and law enforcement corruption around the world is the largest impediment to effective action against transnational crime. Corruption occurs in the form of bribery or extortion, by which an official position is misused for personal gain or threats of harm or legal action are used to force payment. In both cases it is misuse of an elected or appointed government position that lies at the heart of corruption. Interviews with police officers in Mexico City reveal that most officers take or solicit bribes in a system that requires them to make payments in turn to higher government officials.[92] This situation has led to charges that police in some nations operate as outlaws, using their government authority to enrich themselves rather than protect public safety. Police corruption scandals in Nigeria, China, and Japan have been seen as symptomatic of larger political corruption at higher levels. The result is cities and nations where the government victimizes the people instead of working to improve their lives. In China, for example, "Red Mafia" is the collective term for corrupt public officials there (primarily in the criminal justice system) who abuse their power in the extortion/protection business. The Red Mafia has developed into an alternative system of government that can exert control over both communities and organized crime groups. The corrupt nature of this situation is made more troubling because it is not always clear to what extent "protection" by the Red Mafia is demanded by customers versus imposed upon them.[93]

The problem of transnational crime is worsened when corrupt government agencies use their power to exploit their citizens further. For example, a group arranged for aliens from Mexico to be smuggled into the United States through the inspection lanes of a corrupted border control officer in exchange for bribe payments ranging from $500 to $3,000 per alien. The officer admitted that he organized and directed a total of approximately 80 to 150 different smuggling events and that he knowingly permitted approximately 80 to 165 aliens to gain illegal entry into the United States. A study suggests that significant corruption in Mexico continues to be present throughout governmental institutions including local, state, and federal law enforcement agencies, congress, and the military.[94] This defeats the proper role of government in protecting citizens from predatory behavior.

Improvements in levels of corruption will occur when changes are made internationally that were made in the United States starting in the 1930s. When policing is professionalized through better training and higher pay, loyalty to the job is enhanced and corruption is less likely to succeed. This change in law enforcement can only be successful, however, when democracies are established where power is balanced, thus preventing any abuse of that power for personal gain. At this point in history, the world has a large number of new democracies, and the future of transnational crime and corruption will depend to a significant degree on the ability of these nations to develop into stable governments that strive to advance the interests of their citizens. The adoption of the UN Convention against Corruption, which entered into force in 2005, is now ratified by 170 countries (nearly 90% of the world). This Convention is the only legally binding universal anticorruption instrument, and it holds promise internationally because it places binding requirements on ratifying countries to criminalize corruption-related acts, recover and return stolen assets, cooperate with other countries in prosecution, establish anticorruption bodies, and enhance transparency in election financing, and they also must take specific measures to prevent corruption in the judiciary and in public procurement. Therefore, the UN Convention against Corruption promotes anticorruption activities through technical assistance and training (e.g., assistance with legislative implementation and training), combined with the possibility of sanctions for those countries not making serious anti-corruption efforts.[95]

Terrorism Connections

A growing link has been found between transnational organized crime and terrorism. Much of it stems from a decline in state-supported terrorism, causing these groups to rely more on organized crime activities to fund their terrorist activities. Joseph Albini found that terrorists increasingly possess technological skills and are becoming more mercenary (and perhaps less ideological).[96] The result is a joining of forces between terrorists and organized crime in some cases. Actual cases have appeared in which an organized crime investigation becomes a terrorist investigation after the profits made are traced to a terrorist destination.[97]

The term "narcoterrorism" has been sometimes used in connection with drugs and organized crime. The phrase conjures up notions of drug manufacturers who are also terrorists. This does not appear to be the case. Instead, the term more aptly describes the terrorist-type tactics used by drug organizations such as the Medellin cartel in Colombia to intimidate governments. As head of the Medellin cartel, Pablo Escobar had a private army of an estimated 1,000 men. His propensity to kill rivals, friends, politicians, and police earned him the label of "narco-terrorist." He was said to be responsible for some 400 murders. He was killed by police in a raid in 1993, a death possibly encouraged by his many enemies both within and outside the drug world.[98] Narcoterrorism also describes interactions between drug traffickers and revolutionary organizations against an incumbent regime, such as has been found in some South American and Asian nations.[99]

After the terrorist attacks in the United States in September 2001, narcoterrorism received renewed interest concerning the use of drug trafficking proceeds to fund terrorist operations. For example, a drug trafficking group was discovered smuggling pseudoephedrine from Canada to the United States to use in manufacturing methamphetamine. The smugglers were of Middle Eastern descent, and the proceeds were traced back to terrorist groups in Lebanon and Yemen.[100] According to the U.S. State Department, one-third of the groups on its foreign terrorist organization list have drug trafficking links.[101]

To improve their preparedness to respond to terrorist incidents, federal agencies have conducted hundreds of exercises, about one-third of which include state and local participants. The National Commission on Terrorism, created by Congress after the bombings of U.S. embassies in East Africa, recommended in 2000 even more aggressive steps to prevent terrorism. These included making the U.S. military the agency to lead the government's response to terrorist attacks rather than police agencies. It was also recommended that foreign students in the United States be monitored and that sanctions be taken against nations that fail to cooperate fully with terrorism investigations.[102] These actions all pre-dated the terrorist attacks in the United States of September 11, 2001, and show that concern about terrorism has not resulted in a coordinated, unified response. The recommendations made have sparked some controversy, but they point to flaws in the readiness and lack of coordinating mechanism of the United States in preventing or responding to acts of terrorism and the underlying criminal acts that support it. The New Jersey State Commission of Investigation found that traditional organized crime activities are increasingly supplemented by financial frauds, identity theft, and global money laundering operations, pointing to the need for greater vigilance in looking for terrorist links that may be found hidden in organized crime activity.[103] Studies in other countries in conflict areas, such as Iraq, have found organized crime to be a method used by traditional for-profit groups, as well as by insurgents, militia, sectarian groups, and political parties to fund their political (and sometimes terrorist) objectives.[104] In Afghanistan, many of the President's "most senior aides and cabinet ministers have grown wealthy in the past dozen years," as their political power is used to gain influence in profitable businesses serving foreign militaries and development projects, "or simply demanding a cut of business from other Afghans, much as organized crime bosses offer protection in exchange for regular payoffs."[105] This illustrates the close connection that can exist among corruption, terrorism, and organized crime.

SUMMARY

Organized crime committed by traditional, nontraditional, and transnational groups can be characterized by a typology of criminal activity. Although the size and organization of these groups and networks vary, their methods of creating and exploiting criminal opportunities are remarkably consistent. All these groups engage in a definable scope of activity, most groups engage in more than one type of illicit enterprise, interethnic cooperation is common, and the globalization of organized crime is upon us. With all the differences of the various crime groups, "there is one thing that remains the same: all the groups delve into illegal activities to make the 'all-important' dollar," pointing to the need for following the money trail to assess the true scope of organized crime activity.[106] The study of organized crime groups of diverse origins is important, as the former director of the FBI has recognized:

> We cannot allow the same kinds of mistakes to be made today in Russia, Europe and the U.S. that were made in responding to the threat of gangsterism that swept through the United States in the [1920s] and [1930s]. The failure of American law enforcement, including the FBI, to take effective measures against developing organized crime groups then, and subsequently through the [1940s] and [1950s], permitted the development of a powerful, well-entrenched, American organized crime syndicate, which . . . has required over 35 years of concerted law enforcement effort and the expenditure of incredible resources to address . . . It still has not been overcome.[107]

Many nontraditional groups are still in their early stages in the United States. Early efforts to understand their native underpinnings, language, culture, and method of operation will go a long way to preventing their existence as entrenched organized crime groups in the future.

As the President's Commission on Organized Crime concluded after its hearings on organized crime of Asian origin, "these groups have frequently exhibited the same characteristics as La Cosa Nostra families: significant involvement in illegal activities such as narcotics, gambling, and prostitution; efforts to corrupt police authorities . . . and the willingness to use violence" for purposes of intimidation.[108] In order to combat these groups, and the others described in this chapter, effectively, "law enforcement officers will need to explore methods to overcome barriers of language, culture, and tradition even more formidable than those on which La Cosa Nostra has long depended for its success."[109] The overlapping nature of the threat of organized crime, corruption, and sometimes terrorism, led the U.S. government to publish a *Strategy to Combat Transnational Organized Crime* in 2011 (its first such assessment since 1995). It concluded that "today's criminal networks are fluid, striking new balances with other networks around the world and engaging in a wide vary of illicit activities," concluding that transnational organized crime poses a national security threat. It proposed some of the changes that are part of the two UN Conventions against Transnational Organized Crime and against Corruption, as well as re-emphasizing the need to enhance intelligence sharing, protect the financial system, and strengthen investigations and prosecutions.[110] These measures to improve the effort in responding to organized crime are examined in the following chapters.

ORGANIZED CRIME BIOGRAPHY

Biographies tell the life story of interesting people. In the world of criminal justice, biographies of organized crime figures offer insight into the background and motivations of the individuals who choose that lifestyle, the reasons for their choices, and their consequences. The following is a brief summary of an organized crime biography, followed by questions that ask you to reflect on the connections between that person's life and the content of this book.

McMafia: A Journey through the Global Criminal Underworld
Misha Glenny (Vintage, 2009)

McMafia is a broad journalistic account of transnational organized crime, showing how the suppliers and consumers of illicit goods and services are connected. The author describes in detail how opportunistic exploiters develop sources, smuggling methods, and distribution routes around the world. The story concentrates on the Balkans in southeastern Europe, but the book works its way through most world regions.

Contraband (including drugs, untaxed cigarettes, nuclear material, and smuggled people) are traced to the collapse of the Soviet Union with markets located in India, South Africa, Colombia, and the United States. The author attempts to make clear the necessary connection required to make global provision of illicit goods a profitable enterprise. Dominated largely by networks of individuals and other small groups, it is claimed that these illicit markets comprise as much as 20% of global gross national product.

Many different types of operations are described by product and world region. The business of illicit sex in Bulgaria and Internet frauds in Nigeria are examples of organized crime activities with transnational roots and connections. The chaos existing in many developing and postconflict countries has combined with the buying power and demand of developed countries to create the incentives for exploitative criminal markets around the world. These criminal opportunities are seized upon by a host of individuals, small groups, and networks who work cooperatively and corruptly with some governments to take advantage of desperate people, available products, and weak countries for illicit profit.

Questions
1. Why do you believe the author titled the book *McMafia*?
2. Why is transnational organized crime often more profitable than domestic organized crime?

ORGANIZED CRIME AT THE MOVIES

Movies seek to entertain and inform the audience about a story, incident, or person. Many good movies also hit upon important substantive themes relevant to understanding organized crime. Read the following movie summary (and watch the movie if you haven't already) and answer the questions that follow to make the organized crime subject matter connections.

Blood Diamond
Edward Zwick, Director (2006)

Blood Diamond opens with the capture of fisherman Solomon Vandy (Djimon Hounsou) by Revolutionary United Front (RUF) rebels in Africa. Solomon is forced to work in the diamond mines as a slave to fund the RUF war with diamonds being traded for weapons. Solomon's overseer is Captain Poison (David Harewood), who sees Solomon bury a rare 100-karat pink diamond just as they are both captured by government troops.

Danny Archer (Leonardo DiCaprio) is a white mercenary from Zimbabwe who trades guns for diamonds with the RUF. He was earlier imprisoned smuggling diamonds into Liberia and is looking for a way to repay a South African mercenary, Colonel Coetzee (Arnold Vosloo), for the diamonds he lost when captured. Coetzee works, in turn, for a South African diamond company. Archer overhears talk about the discovery of the large pink diamond by Solomon and offers to help him find his family in exchange for the diamond.

Continued

ORGANIZED CRIME AT THE MOVIES—CONT'D

Archer meets an American journalist, Maddy Bowen (Jennifer Connelly), who is covering the war and the illegal diamond trade. He convinces Bowen to help him find Solomon's family, ultimately locating them in a massive UN refugee camp. Solomon's son is found to have been kidnapped and brainwashed by the RUF into becoming a child soldier, and Archer promises to get Solomon's son back if he can get the diamond.

Archer and Solomon pretend to be a part of Bowen's group of journalists and find themselves under attack as they locate both the diamond and Solomon's brainwashed son in the RUF-controlled camp. There is a violent struggle, and Archer kills Colonel Coetzee, and is shot himself. Archer and Solomon escape up a mountain being chased by soldiers, and Archer, suffering from his wound, makes a final call to Bowen for help in getting Solomon out of the country, selling the diamond, and reuniting him with his family.

Bowen secretly photographs the diamond's sale to the diamond company executive and publishes a magazine article exposing the trade in "conflict" or "blood" diamonds from countries experiencing civil unrest and war. The film closes with Solomon speaking to a conference on blood diamonds in Kimberly, South Africa, referring to an actual meeting in 2000 that led to the Kimberly Process Certification Scheme aimed at certifying the origin of diamonds in order to curb the illicit trade in conflict diamonds. *Blood Diamond* was nominated for five Academy Awards, including Best Actor (DiCaprio) and Best Supporting Actor (Hounsou).

Questions

1. *Blood Diamond* shows shifting alliances among the company seeking diamonds, rebels seeking guns, mercenaries seeking money, and innocent civilians caught in the middle. Explain how this can be considered a transnational criminal enterprise and conspiracy.

2. This movie highlights the power of the media in spotlighting injustices and helping to bring about change. Can you provide other examples in which media attention to criminal activity helped provoke positive changes?

References and Notes

1. Whitman, D. "Better Burn That Shawl," *U.S. News & World Report* (October 18, 1999), 74; Gray, R. "Inside the World of Wildlife CSI," *The Daily Telegraph* (London) (February 3, 2009), 23.

2. www.unodc.org (January 2014).

3. Parker, S. "Ammonia's New Cachet," *U.S. News & World Report* (September 27, 1999), 37.

4. Kleemans, E. R., & van de Bunt, H. G. (2002). The Social Embeddedness of Organized Crime. *Transnational Organized Crime, 5,* 19–36; Soudijn, M. R. J., & Kleemans, E. R. (2009). Chinese Organized Crime and Situational Context: Comparing Human Smuggling and Synthetic Drugs Trafficking. *Crime, Law and Social Change, 52,* 457–474; Antonopoulos, G. A. (2009). Are the 'Others' Coming?: Evidence on Alien Conspiracy from Three Illegal Markets in Greece. *Crime, Law and Social Change, 52,* 475–493; Siegel, D. (2014). Transnational Organized Crime. In J. Albanese (Ed.), *Encyclopedia of Criminology and Criminal Justice.* Malden, MA: Wiley-Blackwell.

5. Yeager, M. G. (2012). Fifty Years of Research on Illegal Enterprise: An Interview with Mark Haller. *Trends in Organized Crime, 15,* 1–12.

6. Butterfield, F. "As Drug Use Drops in Big Cities, Small Towns Confront Upsurge," *The New York Times* (February 11, 2002); see also Cumming, C. "Former West Orange Pharmacist Admits to Illegal Oxycontin Distribution," *The Alternative Press* (January 24, 2014).

7. Finckenauer, J. O., & Waring, E. J. (2000). *Russian Mafia in America: Immigration, Culture, and Crime*. Boston, MA: Northeastern University Press.

8. Scott McIllwain, J. (1999). Organized Crime: A Social Network Approach. *Crime, Law and Social Change, 32*, 301–323; Coles, N. (2001, Autumn). It's Not What You Know—It's Who You Know That Counts: Analysing Serious Crime as Social Networks. *British Journal of Criminology, 41*; Junninen, M. (2009). Finnish Professional Criminals and Their Organisations in the 1990s. *Crime, Law and Social Change, 51*, 487–509.

9. Fogelsong, T. S., & Solomon, P. H. Jr. (2001). *Crime, Criminal Justice, and Criminology in Post-Soviet Ukraine*. Washington, DC: National Institute of Justice, p. 36.

10. Varese, F. (2001). *The Russian Mafia: Private Protection in a New Market Economy*. New York: Oxford University Press, p. 188; Serio, J. D. (2008). *Investigating the Russian Mafia*. Durham, NC: Carolina Academic Press.

11. Shaw, M. (1999). The Development and Control of Organized Crime in Post-Apartheid South Africa. In S. Einstein, & M. Amir (Eds.), *Organized Crime: Uncertainties and Dilemmas*. Chicago, IL: Office of International, Criminal Justice, p. 114.

12. Albanese, J. S., Das, D. K., & Verma, A. (Eds.). (2003). *Organized Crime: World Perspectives*. Upper Saddle River, NJ: Prentice Hall; Bovenkerk, F., & Yesilgoz, Y. (2007). *The Turkish Mafia. A History of the Heroin Godfathers*. Preston, UK: Milo Books; Zhang, S. (2008). *Chinese Human Smuggling Organizations. Families, social networks, and cultural imperatives*. Stanford, CA: Stanford University Press; Kegö, W., & Maïga, A. (2013). *The Rise of Transnational Russian-Speaking Organized Crime*. Stockholm: Institute for Security and Development Policy Brief.

13. Europol (2013). *EU Serious and Organised Crime Threat Assessment*. The Hague: Europol.

14. United Nations Centre for International Crime Prevention (2000, Winter). Assessing Transnational Organized Crime: Results of a Pilot Survey of 40 Selected Organized Criminal Groups in 16 Countries. *Trends in Organized Crime, 6*, 44–140.

15. Haller, M. H. (1979). The Changing Structure of American Gambling in the Twentieth Century. *Journal of Social Issues, 35*, 110.

16. Mappen, M., & Gangsters, P. (2013). *The Rise and Fall of a Bad Generation*. New Brunswick, NJ: Rutgers University Press.

17. Potter, G. W., & Gaines, L. K. (1992). Country Comfort: Vice and Corruption in Rural Settings. *Journal of Contemporary Criminal Justice, 8*, 36–61.

18. New Jersey State Commission of Investigation (1991). *Afro-Lineal Organized Crime*. Trenton, NJ: State Commission of Investigation, pp. 6–7.

19. Ianni, F. A. J. (1974). *Black Mafia: Ethnic Succession in Organized Crime*. New York: Simon and Schuster.

20. Schatzberg, R. (1994). African American Organized Crime. In R. J. Kelly, K. Chin, & R. Schatzberg (Eds.), *Handbook of Organized Crime in the United States*. Westport, CT: Greenwood Press, pp. 189–212.

21. Kaplan, D. E., & Dubro, A. (2003). *Yakuza: Japan's Criminal Underworld*. Berkeley, CA: University of California Press; "Seven Large Chinese Triads Active in U.S. and Canada," *Organized Crime Digest* (June 24, 1992), 1.

22. "Betonsports Admits Racketeering," *BBC News* (February 1, 2009); U.S. Department of Justice Federal Bureau of Investigation. New York Office, Partygaming Founder Pleads Guilty in Internet Gambling Case and Agrees to $300 Million Forfeiture (December 16, 2008); "U.S. Defers Bank Rules on Internet Gambling," *Wall Street Journal* (November 28, 2009), 2.

23. U.S. Department of Justice. (2013). *Fifty-Seven Charged with Operating Illegal Online Sports Gaming Business: Indictment Seeks Forfeiture Money Judgment of $1 Billion*. Washington, DC: Office of

Public Affairs, April 10; U.S. Department of Justice (2014). *Leader of Alleged Sports Betting Ring Pleads Guilty to Racketeering Charges.* Washington, DC: Office of Public Affairs, January 31.

24. "Drugs Gang Linked to Chopra Jailed for 33 Years," *The Blackpool Gazette* (UK) (January 26, 2014); Roebuck, J. "Star Mob Witness is Both Disappointed and Satisfied," *Philadelphia Inquirer* (January 31, 2014).

25. President's Commission on Organized Crime (1987). *The Impact: Organized Crime Today.* Washington, DC: U.S. Government Printing Office, p. 46; Kleinknecht, W. (1996). *The New Ethnic Mobs: The Changing Face of Organized Crime in America.* New York: Free Press.

26. International Organization for Migration (2005). *Exploratory Assessment of Trafficking in Persons in the Caribbean Region.* Washington, DC: IOM, p. 151.

27. The National Human Trafficking Resource Center (2013). *Human Trafficking Trends in the United States, 2007-2012.* Washington, DC: Polaris Project.

28. Kennedy, D., Tendler, S., & Phillips, J. (2002). *Albanian Gangs Corner Britain's Sex Trade.* London: The Times.

29. Bowcott, O. (2014). "Gang Guilty of Trafficking 50 Women for Sexual Exploitation in UK: Four Hungarian men and one British woman found guilty of conspiring to traffic women into UK to work as prostitutes," *The Guardian.*

30. Kroeger, A. "UN Cracks Down on Bosnia Prostitution," *BBC News* (November 2, 2001); Aronowitz, A. A. (2009). *Human Trafficking, Human Misery: The Global Trade in Human Beings.* New York: Praeger.

31. Schloenhardt, A. (2001). Trafficking in Migrants: Illegal Migration and Organized Crime in Australia and the Asia Pacific Region. *International Journal of the Sociology of Law, 29,* 331–378; Tailby, R. "Organized Crime and People Smuggling/Trafficking to Australia," *Australian Institute of Criminology Trends & Issues in Crime and Criminal Justice* (May 2001), 1–6; "More Boat People Found Off Australia's Northwest," *Reuters* (December 10, 2001).

32. Duffy, B., & Trimble, J. "The Looting of Russia," *U.S. News & World Report* (March 7, 1994), 36–47; Satchell, M. "Fighting the Child Sex Trade," *U.S. News & World Report* (May 8, 2000), 32; United Nations Centre for International Crime Prevention (Winter 2000). "Assessing Transnational Organized Crime: Results of a Pilot Survey of 40 Selected Organized Criminal Groups in 16 Countries," *Trends in Organized Crime, 6,* 118; Peterson, H. "Racketeering Rap's First against Russians," *New York Daily News* (October 28, 1998); Kegö, W., & Maïga, A. (2013). *The Rise of Transnational Russian-Speaking Organized Crime.* Stockholm: Institute for Security and Development Policy Brief, September 6.

33. Sen, A. "Impoverished Indians Advertise Kidneys," *BBC News* (March 27, 2002); Moors, C. (May 2001). Body Brokers in Organ Trafficking. *Crime & Justice International, 17;* Mayeda, A. "Ottawa Sets Rules for Visiting Organ Donors: Danger of Trafficking," *National Post* (Canada) (November 6, 2006), 8; Sherman, T., & Margolin, J. (2012). *The Jersey Sting.* New York: St. Martin's Griffin.

34. United Nations Office on Drugs and Crime. www.unodc.org/unodc/en/commissions/CND/index.html (February 4, 2014).

35. "United Nations Office on Drugs and Crime," *World Drug Report 2013* (Vienna: UNODC, 2013).

36. United Nations Office on Drugs and Crime (2008). *Drug Trafficking as a Security Threat in West Africa.* Vienna: UNODC.

37. Salazar, M. R., & Olson, E. L. (2011). *A Profile of Mexico's Major Organized Crime Groups.* Washington, DC: Woodrow Wilson International Center for Scholars Mexico Institute.

38. U.S. Department of Justice (2012). *Former Colombian Prosecutor Pleads Guilty to Role in International Drug Trafficking Conspiracy.* Washington, DC: Office of Public Affairs.

39. U.S. Attorney. Eastern District of Virginia (2011). *Members Of Ghana-Based Heroin Smuggling Ring Charged International Traffickers Used Dulles International Airport as Entry Point for East Coast Distribution of Heroin from West Africa*. Washington, DC: Office of Public Affairs, July 14.

40. United Nations Office on Drugs and Crime (2013). *World Drug Report 2013*. Vienna: UNODC; see also Drug Enforcement Administration. *2013 National Drug Threat Assessment: Summary*. www. justice.gov/dea/resource-center/DIR-017-13%20NDTA%20Summary%20final.pdf (November, 2013).

41. Statement of Joseph T. Rannazzisi, Deputy Assistant Administrator, Office of Diversion Control, Drug Enforcement Administration. U.S. Department of Justice. Before the Senate Caucus on International Narcotics Control For a Hearing Entitled "Dangerous Synthetic Drugs" www. justice.gov/iso/opa/ola/witness/09–25–13-dea-rannazzisi-testimony-re-dangerous-synthetic-drugs.201312231.pdf (September 25, 2013), p. 25.

42. *United States v. Vasquez-Velaso*, 15 F.3d 833 (9th Cir. 1994).

43. *United States v. Vasquez-Velaso* at 841.

44. at 840–841; *United States v. Lopez-Alvarez*, 970 F.2d 583 (9th Cir.) cert. denied, 113 S. Ct. 504 (1992).

45. at 842.

46. Thaarp, M. "Battling It Out on the Border: Mexican Traffickers Target U.S. Lawmen," *U.S. News & World Report* (May 29, 2000), 21; Chabat, J. "Mexico's War on Drugs: No Margin for Maneuver," *The Annals of the American Academy of Political and Social Science* (July 2002).

47. "Worldwide Nigerian Heroin Smuggling Ring Smashed," *Organized Crime Digest* (May 27, 1992), 3; "New Breed of Smugglers," *USA Today* (September 23, 1991), 3; see also Statement of Thomas Harrigan, Deputy Administrator, Drug Enforcement Administration. Senate Caucus on International Narcotics Control. U.S. Senate. Countering Narcotics Threats in West Africa. www.justice.gov/ola/testimony/112–2/05–16–12-dea-harrigan.pdf (May 16, 2012).

48. Gately, W., & Fernandez, Y. (1994). *Dead Ringer: An Insider's Account of the Mob's Colombian Connection*. New York: Donald I. Fine; Thoumi, F. E. (2002). *Illegal Drugs in Colombia: From Illegal Economic Boom to Social Crisis. The Annals of the American Academy of Political and Social Science*; Watson, R., et al. (1993). Death on the Spot. *Newsweek*, 16; Decker, S. H., & Townsend, M. (2008). *Drug Smugglers on Drug Smuggling*. Philadelphia, PA: Temple University Press.

49. *United States v. Koczuk*, 252 F.3d 91 (2001); "Ukraine Backs CD Piracy Purge," *BBC News* (January 17, 2002); Jagan, L. "Thailand's Struggle with Goods Piracy," *BBC News* (December 13, 2001); Zaitseva, L., & Hand, K. (February 2002). Nuclear Smuggling Chains: Suppliers, Intermediaries, and End-Users. *American Behavioral Scientist, 46*; "Austrian in Rio Caught with Rare Eggs in Underwear," *CNN.com* (February 14, 2001).

50. Joutsen, M. (1995). The Growth of Organized Crime in Central and Eastern Europe. In J. Albanese (Ed.), *Contemporary Issues in Organized Crime*. Monsey, NY: Willow Tree Press, p. 201.

51. Block, A. A. (1991). *Masters of Paradise: Organized Crime and the Internal Revenue Service in the Bahamas*. New Brunswick, NJ: Transaction Publishers.

52. Attanasio, T. A. How Russian Organized Crime Took Root in the U.S. *Organized Crime Digest, 15*, 71; Adams, N. M. "Menace of the Russian Mafia," *Reader's Digest* (August 1992), 33–40; Friedman, R. I. "Brighton Beach Goodfella," *Vanity Fair* (January 1993), 26–41.

53. Murray, C. "Seven Indicted in Tax Evasion: Organized Crime Figures Ran Gas Scam," *Newsday* (May 30, 2001), A45; Moore, R. H. Jr. (1995). Motor Fuel Tax Fraud and Organized Crime: The Russians and the American-Italian Mafia. In J. Albanese (Ed.), *Contemporary Issues in Organized Crime*. Monsey, NY: Willow Tree Press.

54. Freeh, L. (June 22, 1994). Russian Organized Crime Groups Spread in U.S. *Organized Crime Digest, 15*, 1; Duffy, D. & Trimble, J. "The Looting of Russia," *U.S. News & World Report* (March 7, 1994), 46.

55. Zaitseva, L., & Hand, K. (February 2003). Nuclear Smuggling Chains: Suppliers, Intermediaries, and End-Users. *American Behavioral Scientist, 46*, 822; Hersh, S. "Hijack the State," *Atlantic Monthly* (June 1994).

56. (May 11, 1994). Russian Emigres Are Canada's Newest Organized Crime Threat. *Organized Crime Digest, 15*, 1.

57. "Car Smuggling Ring Uncovered," *BBC News* (July 24, 2001).

58. "Vehicle-Stealing and Smuggling Syndicates Neutralized," www.info.gov.hk/gia (February 11, 2002).

59. Seamonds, J. "The New Face of Organized Crime," *U.S. News & World Report* (January 18, 1988), 29–37; Jones, M. J. "Policy Paradox: Implications of U.S. Drug Control Policy for Jamaica," *Annuals of the American Academy of Political and Social Science* (July 2002): Williams, C., & Roth, M. P. "The Importation and Re-exportation of Organized Crime: Explaining the Rise and Fall of the Jamaican Posses in the United States," *Trends in Organized Crime* (July 2011), 1–16.

60. Seamonds, J. "Ethnic Gangs and Organized Crime," *U.S. News & World Report* (January 18, 1988), 35; Ladd, S. "Armed with Law," *New York Newsday* (March 15, 1994), 15.

61. President's Commission on Organized Crime (1987). *The Impact: Organized Crime Today.* Washington, DC: U.S. Government Printing Office, pp. 58–73.

62. Wolf, D. R. (1991). *The Rebels: A Brotherhood of Outlaw Bikers.* Toronto, ON: University of Toronto Press, p. 268.

63. Criminal Intelligence Service Canada (2002). *Annual Report on Organized Crime in Canada,* www.cisc.gc.ca.

64. United Nations Office on Drugs and Crime (2011). *Organized Crime and Instability in Central Africa: A Threat Assessment.* Vienna: UNODC.

65. United Nations Office on Drugs and Crime (2013). *Transnational Organized Crime in West Africa: A Threat Assessment.* Vienna: UNODC.

66. U.S. Department of Justice (2013). *New York Antiques Dealer Sentenced to 37 Months in Prison for Wildlife Smuggling: Wang Smuggled Artifacts Carved from Rhinoceros Horns from New York to China.* Washington, DC: Office of Public Affairs, December 5.

67. Malcolm, J. U.S. Deputy Assistant Attorney General "Testimony: Organized Online Piracy Groups," *U.S. House of Representatives Subcommittee on the Courts, the Internet, and Intellectual Property of the Committee on the Judiciary* (March 13, 2003).

68. "Software Piracy," *Tech Europe* (June 13, 2002), 207; www.bsa.org/anti-piracy/anti-piracy-agenda (February 6, 2014).

69. Groves, D. "Pirated DVDs," *Reuters* (June 3, 2002); Dymski, G. "DA: Manhasset Man Sold Bootleg Copies of Oscar-nominated Hits," *Newsday* (January 30, 2014).

70. President's Commission on Organized Crime (1987). *The Impact: Organized Crime Today.* Washington, DC: U.S. Government Printing Office, pp. 45–46.

71. Reuter, P. (1933). The Cartage Industry in New York. In Tonry, M., & Reiss, A. J., Jr. (Eds.), *Beyond the Law: Crime in Complex Organizations.* Chicago, IL: University of Chicago Press, p. 154.

72. *Beyond the Law: Crime in Complex Organizations,* p. 155.

73. *Beyond the Law: Crime in Complex Organizations,* p. 179.

74. *Beyond the Law: Crime in Complex Organizations*, p. 198.

75. Kleinknecht, W. "Ethnic Mix Is Crime Recipe," *New York Daily News* (December 14, 1993), 3; Kegö, W., & Maïga, A. (2013). *The Rise of Transnational Russian-Speaking Organized Crime*. Stockholm: Institute for Security and Development Policy Brief, September 6.

76. Volkov, V., & Entrepreneurs, V. (2002). *The Use of Force in the Making of Russian Capitalism*. Ithaca, NY: Cornell University Press, p. 18.

77. Frisby, T. (January 1998). The Rise of Organized Crime in Russia: Its Roots and Social Significance. *Europe-Asia Studies*, 50; Paoli, L. (July 2002). "The Price of Freedom: Illegal Drug Markets and Policies in Post-Soviet Russia. *The Annals of the American Academy of Political and Social Science*.

78. Rosner, L. (Winter 2000). Cracking Pandora's Box: The Soviet Breakup and the Onset of Buccaneer Capitalism. *Trends in Organized Crime*, 6, 141; Serio, J. D. (2008). *Investigating the Russian Mafia*. Durham, NC: Carolina Academic Press.

79. Chin, K.-l., & Gangs, C. (2000). *Extortion, Enterprise, Ethnicity*. New York: Oxford University Press, p. 4.

80. *Chinatown Gangs: Extortion, Enterprise, Ethnicity*, p. 5.

81. Godson, R., & Olson, W. J. (1993). *International Organized Crime: Emerging Threat to U.S. Security*. Washington, DC: National Strategy Information Center, p. iii.

82. Zhang, S., & Chin, K.-L. (November 2002). Enter the Dragon: Inside Chinese Human Smuggling Organizations. *Criminology*, 40, 737; Chin, K. L., Zhang, S., & Kelly, R. T. (1998). Transnational Chinese Organized Crime Activities. *Transnational Organized Crime*, 4, 127–154; Zhang, S., & Chin, K. L. (2008). Snakeheads, Mules and Protective Umbrellas: A Review of Current Research on Chinese Organized Crime. *Crime, Law and Social Change*, 50, 177–195.

83. English, T. J. (1995). *Born to Kill: America's Most Notorious Vietnamese Gang*. New York: William Morrow, pp. 234–235.

84. Katz, L., & Gains, I.-G. (1996). *Evasion, Blackmail, Fraud, and Kindred Puzzles of the Law*. Chicago, IL: University of Chicago Press.

85. Albanese, J. (2001). Blackmail and Extortion. In C. Bryant (Ed.), *Encyclopedia of Criminology and Deviant Behavior*. London: Taylor & Francis; Krauze, E. "Mexico's Vigilante's on the March," *The New York Times* (2004).

86. Kirby, C., & Renner, T. C. (1986). *Mafia Assassin*. Toronto: Methuen.

87. *The Impact: Organized Crime Today*, pp. 68–69.

88. Criminal Intelligence Service Canada. *Annual Report on Organized Crime in Canada*, www.cisc.gc.ca/annual_reports/annual_report_2010/document/report_oc_2010_e.pdf (2010).

89. U.S. Department of Justice Federal Bureau of Investigation Criminal Investigative Division (1985). *Oriental Organized Crime*. Washington, DC: Federal Bureau of Investigation, pp. 29–30.

90. Kaplan, D. E., & Dubro, A. (2003). *Yakuza: Japan's Criminal Underworld*. Berkeley: University of California Press.

91. Transcrime. (2012). *Study on Extortion Racketeering: the Need for an Instrument to Combat Activities of Organised Crime*. Trento: Joint Research Centre on Transnational Crime; Europol. (2013). *Threat Assessment: Italian Organized Crime*. The Hague: Europol.

92. Zarembo, A. "The Worst Job in the World," *Newsweek International* (December 4, 2000), 36.

93. "Policeman Fired for Corruption," *Africa News Service* (November 21, 2000); Eckholm, E. "Chinese Find Power Abuse Isn't Limited to the Cities," *The New York Times* (December 3, 2000), 5; Hadfield, P. "Japanese Shocked by Police Misdeeds," *U.S. News & World Report* (July 10, 2000), 32; Wang, P. (2013). The Rise of the Red Mafia in China: A Case Study of Organised Crime and Corruption in Chongqing. *Trends Organized Crime, 16,* 49–73.

94. U.S. Department of Justice (July 18, 2013). *Former U.S. Customs and Border Protection Officer and Four Associates Sentenced for Carrying out Bribery and Alien Smuggling Activities Along Mexican Border.* Office of Public Affairs; Muratayaa, R., Chaconb, S., & Gonzalezc, Z. (2013). The Relationship between Mexican Drug Trafficking Organizations and Corruption in the Mexican Criminal Justice and Political Systems: A Review Essay. *International Journal of Comparative and Applied Criminal Justice, 10,* 1–18.

95. United Nations Convention on Corruption (2005). www.unodc.org/unodc/en/treaties/CAC/index.html#UNCACfulltext (February 6, 2014).

96. Albini, J. (2001). Dealing with the Modern Terrorist: The Need for Changes in Strategies and Tactics in the New War on Terrorism. *Criminal Justice Policy Review, 12.*

97. Roig-Franzia, M. "Man Convicted of Using Smuggling to Fund Hezbollah," *The Washington Post* (2002).

98. Watson, R., et al., "Death on the Spot," *Newsweek* (December 23, 1993), 16; Gately, W., & Fernandez, Y. (1994). *Dead Ringer: An Insider's Account of the Mob's Colombian Connection.* New York: Donald I. Fine.

99. Dombroski, J. "Narco-Terrorism Menace World," *Richmond Times Dispatch* (May 18, 2003), E–6; Lupsha, P. A. (1998). The Role of Drugs and Drug Trafficking in the Invisible Wars. In R. H. Ward & H. E. Smith (Eds.), *International Terrorism: Operational Issues.* Chicago: University of Illinois Office of International, Criminal Justice, pp. 177–190.

100. Barnard, D. (Fall 2003). Narco-Terrorism Realities: The Connection between Drugs and Terror. *Journal of Counterterrorism & Homeland Security International, 9.*

101. Perl, R., Congressional Research Service (2003). *Testimony: Narco-Terrorism: International Drug Trafficking and Terrorism—A Dangerous Mix.* U.S. Senate Judiciary Committee, May 20.

102. U.S. Comptroller General (1999). *Combatting Terrorism: Issues to be Resolved to Improve Counterterrorism Operations.* Washington, DC: U.S. General Accounting Office; National Commission on Terrorism (2000). *Countering the Changing Threat of International Terrorism.* Washington, DC: U.S. Government Printing Office; Henry, V. E. (December 2002). The Need for a Coordinated and Strategic Local Police Approach to Terrorism: A Practitioner's Perspective. *Police Practice & Research, 3,* 319–336.

103. Santi, A. D. "SCI Says 'Nontraditional' Gangs Enter N.J. Organized Crime," *The Associated Press* (April 29, 2003).

104. Williams, P. (2009). Organized Crime and Corruption in Iraq. *International Peacekeeping, 16,* 115–135.

105. Shanker, T. "NATO Reduces Scope of Its Afghanistan Plans," *The New York Times* (2013).

106. Rich, J. E. (Spring 2002). They'll Make You an Offer You Can't Refuse: A Comparative Analysis of International Organized Crime. *Tulsa Journal of Comparative & International Law, 9,* 569.

107. Freeh, L. (1994). Russian Organized Crime Group Spreads in U.S., Europe. *Organized Crime Digest, 15,* 3–4.

108. President's Commission on Organized Crime (1984). *Organized Crime of Asian Origin, Hearings Part III*. Washington, DC: U.S. Government Printing Office, p. 401.

109. *Organized Crime of Asian Origin, Hearings Part III*, p. 402; Harfield, C. (2008). The Organisation of 'Organized Crime Policing' and Its International Context. *Criminology & Criminal Justice, 8*, 483–507.

110. The White House. *Strategy to Combat Transnational Organized Crime: Addressing Converging Threats to National Security* www.whitehouse.gov/sites/default/files/Strategy_to_Combat_Transnational_Organized_Crime_July_2011.pdf (July, 2011).

CHAPTER 9

Investigative Tools

Organized crimes involve infiltration and conspiracy, which require the investigator to be as sophisticated as the offender.

INVESTIGATORS OF ORGANIZED CRIME

Federal investigations of organized crime are usually conducted through the U.S. Department of Justice. The Department of Justice is located in Washington, DC, but is represented across the country by 94 U.S. attorneys located in every federal judicial district. Each U.S. attorney is assisted by a staff of assistants of up to 160 lawyers in the largest metropolitan areas to about 10 attorneys in less populated areas. Unfortunately, few of these offices have specialized units that deal specifically with organized crime.

Federal organized crime strike forces originally existed in 14 U.S. cities, with sub-offices in 12 other cities. However, a total of 122 strike force attorneys nationwide were reassigned and made assistant U.S. attorneys by Attorney General Dick Thornburgh in 1990.[1] His rationale was to give the U.S. attorney in each district greater control over organized crime prosecutions in his or her jurisdiction, although the former strike force attorneys were still to work organized crime cases. There was an outcry in Congress when the strike forces were abolished, arguing their independence was needed given the higher turnover of U.S. attorneys as appointed officials.[2] Many experienced strike force prosecutors resigned after this reassignment, including 11 of the 15 prosecutors in the Brooklyn office.[3]

Federal agencies that participated with the strike forces included the Bureau of Alcohol, Tobacco, Firearms, and Explosives (ATF), Customs Service, Internal Revenue Service (IRS), and U.S. Secret Service (all of these agencies are in the Department of Treasury, although the ATF moved into the Department of Justice as part of the Homeland Security Act of 2002); the Drug Enforcement Administration (DEA), Immigration and Naturalization Service, U.S. Marshals Service, and Federal Bureau of Investigation (FBI) (all in the Department of

Justice, except Immigration moved to the Department of Homeland Security (DHS) in 2003); and the Department of Labor, the U.S. Postal Service, and the Securities and Exchange Commission. The strike forces obtained about 83% of their cases from the investigations of only four agencies: the ATF, DEA, FBI, and IRS.[4] In the case of federal drug convictions, the vast majority of cases originate with the DEA, DHS, FBI, and ATF.[5]

Currently, organized crime investigations at the federal level are coordinated by the Organized Crime Section at FBI headquarters, which is divided into seven units: African Criminal Enterprises, Asian Criminal Enterprises, Balkan Criminal Enterprises, Eurasian Criminal Enterprises, Italian Organized Crime/Mafia, Middle Eastern Criminal Enterprises, and a Sports Bribery Program. Each of the FBI's 56 field offices investigates criminal enterprises in its area and relies on headquarters for support. The FBI also participates in joint task forces with other federal, state, and local law enforcement agencies. These task forces are not coordinated centrally as were the original organized crime strike forces, but they have generated significant cases over the years.

Figure 9.1 illustrates federal agencies involved primarily in organized crime cases today. The lead investigative agency for federal organized crime prosecutions that resulted in convictions in December 2013 was the FBI, which accounted for 50% of convictions, followed by the DHS (12%), ATF (4%), and DEA (4%). Federal agencies contributing fewer convictions include the IRS.

Federal prosecutions of organized crime cases usually develop in the following manner: once one of these law enforcement agencies has a reasonable belief about the existence of organized illegal activity in its jurisdiction, a case

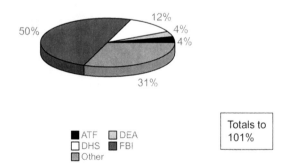

FIGURE 9.1 Federal investigative agencies that made organized crime cases (organized crime cases that resulted in convictions) Source: Transactional Records Clearinghouse at trac.syr.edu (December 2013)

initiation report is prepared by an assistant U.S. attorney (some U.S. attorney's offices have organized crime strike force units devoted to organized crime prosecutions). The case initiation report is forwarded to the Department of Justice Organized Crime and Racketeering Section. Once the investigation is completed, a prosecutive memorandum is written. The memorandum is reviewed by the U.S. attorney and the criminal division for approval. After approval is obtained, the attorney in charge of the case presents the evidence to a grand jury. If the citizens of the grand jury concur in a finding of probable cause of illegal conduct, they issue an indictment to formally accuse the suspect of a crime. The indictment is ultimately followed by a plea of guilt or a trial to determine guilt or innocence.

The enforcement of state laws against organized crime is not standardized. Some states have established specialized enforcement units to investigate only organized crime cases, whereas others have no distinct organized crime enforcement unit. About one-third of local police departments have one or more officers assigned to a multiagency drug enforcement task force, and there are additional specialized task forces in some areas focusing on human trafficking, financial crimes, cybercrimes, and related offenses that often involve organized crime.[6] In most states, local or state police obtain evidence of organized crime activity through surveillance or informants, and this evidence is referred to the county prosecutor or state attorney general's office for a decision to prosecute or to conduct further investigation.

INVESTIGATIVE TECHNIQUES AND INTELLIGENCE GATHERING

Unlike traditional police work, in which a crime is committed, someone calls the police, and the police begin a search for the offender, investigating organized crime requires a more sophisticated approach. Conventional policing for street crimes is primarily *reactive*: police generally respond to crimes after they have been committed. The investigation of organized crimes, however, must place more emphasis on *proactive* approaches. Because many organized crimes involving infiltration of business or conspiracy are not reported by the victim, investigations must often be initiated based only on reasonable suspicion of criminality or on informants' tips. Most investigations of organized crime activity, therefore, require long, and often tedious, searches through financial records; interviews of informants, criminals, and suspected victims; and surveillance activities. Only in this way can sufficient evidence be gathered to establish probable cause for arrest and indictment.

The unique nature of many types of organized crimes requires investigators to follow special rules. An example is obscenity cases. In Indiana, for example, police seized thousands of books and films from Fort Wayne Books based on a finding of probable cause. The U.S. Supreme Court held that such a pretrial seizure violated the First Amendment because there had been no judicial determination that the materials seized were, in fact, obscene. Therefore, materials believed to be obscene by police must be found to be obscene beyond a reasonable doubt at trial (or by plea) before police may seize the remaining stock. Prior cases "firmly hold that mere probable cause to believe a legal violation has transpired is not adequate to remove books or films from circulation."[7]

Determining probable cause in organized crime cases usually requires surveillance, and the extent of that surveillance was challenged in a case where the defendant claimed that law enforcement authorities violated the Fourth Amendment by conducting almost constant surveillance of his home using a video camera. Police had installed a fixed video camera on a utility pole across the street from the defendant's home and conducted surveillance of the front of his house for eight months. The U.S. Court of Appeals ruled that this did not violate the Fourth Amendment because the defendant does not have an expectation of privacy in the front of his home, as viewed by the camera. As there were no fences, gates, or shrubbery located in front of his home to obstruct the view from the street, the house was plainly visible.[8]

Determining probable cause can be difficult in organized crime cases because of the number of people involved in many schemes so the criminal activity is spread among multiple individuals who are involved in varying degrees. For example, John Gotti did not kill Paul Castellano; instead he had others do it at his behest, something that was difficult to investigate and prove conclusively. Judges review an investigator's determination of probable cause by assessing whether there is a "fair probability that contraband or evidence of a crime will be found."[9] For example, a warrant issued to Pittsburgh police to search a commercial building for illegal video poker machines was challenged in court. It was argued that it did not contain probable cause and was overly broad— violations of the Fourth Amendment of the U.S. Constitution. The U.S. Court of Appeals recognized that the supporting affidavit submitted by the police "must be read in its entirety and in a common sense and nontechnical manner."[10] Even though the warrant did not contain direct evidence of criminal wrongdoing, direct evidence is not required. "Instead, probable cause can be, and often is, inferred by 'considering the type of crime, the nature of the items sought, the suspect's opportunity for concealment and normal inferences about where a criminal might hide stolen property.'"[11] Indirect evidence, such as prior arrests and convictions for similar crimes, "is not only permissible, but is often helpful."[12]

A search warrant must also be specific in its statement of probable cause in order to protect a person's lawful privacy of personal property and effects.

In searches for specific papers, for example, "it is certain that some innocuous documents will be at least cursorily perused in order to determine whether they are among those papers to be seized." However, the Fourth Amendment does not prohibit a search "merely because it cannot be performed with surgical precision."[13] In one case, IRS agents searched a person's bank records for alleged failure to file currency transaction reports needed for large cash deposits (see "Bank Secrecy Act" in the next chapter). All financial records were seized, and the defendant argued on appeal that the seizure exceeded the stated purpose of the search (i.e., evidence of five instances of criminal behavior involving financial transactions). The U.S. Court of Appeals held that seizure of "every piece of paper or documents relating to a business is proper when probable cause exists that the enterprise is permeated by fraud."[14] The court held in the IRS case that the language of the warrant must be "sufficiently specific," although the police are not required to list the items in "elaborate detail" and the validity of the warrant was upheld.[15]

It can be seen from these examples that successful organized crime investigations require more training and perseverance than investigations of conventional street crimes. In some cases, evidence is sought not to build a case but to gather intelligence. This intelligence information is organized and used in building subsequent cases later on.[16] For example, it does not make sense to arrest every drug seller in a city if suppliers and higher level distributors remain untouched. Surveillance, interviews, informants, and searches can be used to establish the precise nature and scope of an enterprise so it may be defeated successfully on a larger scale. The remainder of this chapter explains five major kinds of investigative tools used most often in organized crime cases.

Financial Analysis

A common investigative technique in organized crime investigations is financial analysis. Financial analysis is an investigative assessment of income, expenditures, and/or net worth designed to determine the presence of illegal income. For example, if you drive a car worth $50,000, live in an apartment with a rent of $1,000 per month, have little money in the bank, yet earn $9 per hour working at McDonald's, financial analysis can determine precisely how far you are living beyond your means, and you can then be asked to account for this discrepancy. The IRS uses financial analysis in its tax investigations, especially where no records or books are kept. These methods are now used by investigators for other forms of organized crime and corruption, such as embezzlement, illegal kickbacks, and fraud.[17]

Three basic methods are used for financial analysis: net worth method, expenditures method, and bank deposits method. All three are designed to determine the total wealth or expenditures made by someone to compare with his or her reported income.

The net worth method examines changes in a person's net financial worth over time, looking at all sources of reported income, bank balances, and assets. Significant changes in net worth should be explained by changes in income, investments, gifts, or other means that can be documented. If a person cannot document the sources of these changes, the unreported income forms the basis for further investigation. A famous example of the net worth method was the case of Al Capone (see Figure 9.2). The IRS examined Capone's bank accounts and bills in Miami and Chicago over a period of time and found that he spent $7,000 for suits, $1,500 per week for hotel bills, $40,000 for his house on Palm Island, $39,000 worth of phone calls, and $20,000 worth of silverware, indicating an annual income of $165,000. He could not document this income over a period of years. Capone was ultimately tried and convicted for failing to pay taxes on $1 million of illegal income.[18]

The expenditures method measures funds by their flow during the year rather than by observing changes in net worth over time. It involves examination of weekly or monthly income reported by the employer and on tax forms and comparing it to expenditures of the individual (through credit card receipts, bank withdrawals, and items purchased with cash). Large discrepancies suggest the possibility of unlawful income. The expenditures method was used in a case

FIGURE 9.2 Alphonse Gabriel "Al" Capone was an American gangster who led a Prohibition-era crime syndicate. Capone was ultimately convicted on federal charges of tax evasion in 1931 for failing to pay taxes on his illegal income. *en.wikipedia.com*

at the University of Wisconsin when the state attorney general was notified about an employee suspected of embezzling funds from the university. The employee in question was in charge of collecting money, amounting to more than $100,000 per year, from students for copying documents and transcripts. Investigators from the state attorney general's corruption unit conducted an analysis of the employee's spending habits and found that she was spending far in excess of her earnings. When confronted with the facts, the employee could not explain the large discrepancy and confessed to a systematic embezzlement scheme conducted over a four-year period that netted $40,000-$50,000. The corruption unit discovered that the university's poor accounting and auditing practices permitted this to occur.[19]

The bank deposits method is based on the theory that a person engaged in an income-producing business or occupation deposits money in bank accounts under his or her control, and those bank deposits are taxable income. Any expenditure by the person from funds not deposited in any bank or from any other documented source also represents taxable income. The bank deposits method tries to reconcile receipts from bank deposits, cash purchases (money spent without going through banks), and money stored in other places (cash on hand), examining the money flow to look for unreported and unlawful sources of income. The bank deposits method was used in a Texas case in which a housing developer was charged with making a series of 46 cash bank deposits between $5,000 and $10,000 over a period of months, which could not be documented as part of his lawful business activity. He was charged as part of a conspiracy to import marijuana from Mexico.[20]

It can be seen, therefore, that financial records can be a fruitful technique for discovering organized criminal activity, such as the establishment of fictitious companies to launder funds, overpayment of employees or subcontractors to obtain kickbacks, and other fraudulent schemes to conceal income from unlawful sources.

Electronic Surveillance

Title III of the Omnibus Crime Control Act (1968) authorized federal law enforcement officials to eavesdrop on the conversations of crime suspects provided they obtain a warrant. The Title III warrant must show that there is "probable cause" to link a specific person to a particular crime.[21] Title III had two stated purposes: it was a weapon to fight organized crime and it was designed to safeguard the privacy of oral communications. The actual offenses for which Title III permits the use of electronic surveillance go beyond its stated purposes. It permits the use of wiretapping or electronic eavesdropping ("bugging") for most suspected federal offenses punishable by a year or more of imprisonment. The Uniting and Strengthening America by Providing Appropriate Tools Required to Intercept and Obstruct Terrorism Act of 2001, known as the

CRITICAL THINKING EXERCISE 9.1

Using the information provided in this chapter, respond to the following scenario. Employ current legal principles to justify your response.

The Case from Charlotte to Hezbollah

A deputy sheriff was moonlighting as a security officer at JR Discount, a tobacco wholesaler in North Carolina. He saw three men speaking Arabic, each buying 300 cartons of cigarettes, reaching into shopping bags and pulling out large wads of cash wrapped in rubber bands to pay for them. The men were regular customers buying cigarettes, loading them from pallets into waiting vans, and driving away. In a joint investigation with the Bureau of Alcohol, Tobacco, Firearms, and Explosives, surveillance revealed that the men drove these truckloads of cigarettes to Michigan where they were resold to others. A huge profit was made because cigarettes in North Carolina are much cheaper, taxed at 50 cents a carton, compared to Michigan where tax was $7.50 per carton. That's a $7 profit per carton—an illegal profit that violates tax laws regulating the distribution of cigarettes by unlicensed and untaxed dealers.

This was a tax fraud case that did not have much importance until the FBI caught wind of it and told other agents that they already had wiretaps on the phones of two of the three Arab men because they suspected them of being members of Hezbollah, the Lebanon-based terrorism organization. A total of six suspects were ultimately convicted and sentenced to 155 years in prison for racketeering and material support of Hezbollah. It turned out that the primary suspect,

Hammoud, was a quiet man in his mid-20s, who had been living in a middle-class neighborhood only 15 minutes from the deputy sheriff's home.

Hammoud was in the United States illegally. He originally was refused a visa from the U.S. Embassy in Syria so he went to Venezuela, bought a fake visa, and flew to New York where he demanded asylum and then disappeared while awaiting a hearing. He followed a member of his family to Charlotte and ended up delivering pizza for Domino's before he stumbled on tobacco smuggling, making about $13,000 per vanload of cigarettes. To avoid suspicion, he and his cohorts often hired white women to ride along, and they strapped bicycles to the back of their vans and trucks. Nearly all the suspects had bogus marriages in an effort to gain citizenship and stay in America.

Critical Thinking Questions

1. What were the clues that led to the original suspicion of criminal activity?
2. Did any of these clues suggest a possible connection to a larger criminal conspiracy?
3. What measures do you believe investigators should take to make sure they do not end an investigation too quickly and miss the connection to a larger crime?

Sources: David E. Kaplan, "Homegrown Terrorists," U.S. News & World Report (March 10, 2003), pp. 30-33; Manuel Roig-Franzia, "Man Convicted of Using Smuggling to Fund Hezbollah," The Washington Post (June 23, 2002), p. A17.

USA PATRIOT Act, passed a month after the September 11 terrorist attacks in New York and Washington, added crimes related to terrorism and computer trespass to the list of offenses for which electronic surveillance is permitted.[22] It also permits access to voice mail with a search warrant (a search warrant is easier to obtain than an order for electronic surveillance).

Unlike Title III, the Foreign Intelligence Surveillance Act (FISA) of 1978 permits wiretapping of aliens and U.S. citizens without probable cause of a crime if the government can show that the primary purpose of the electronic surveillance is intelligence gathering (rather than building a criminal case) and that the target is a member of a foreign terrorist group or is working for a foreign power. Also unlike Title III, FISA does not require the government to reveal the existence of the electronic surveillance to the target when it ends. Applications for FISA warrants are made by the U.S. Attorney General to a secret court for the purpose of collecting foreign intelligence information. The important difference between Title III and FISA surveillance is that the former is designed to develop criminal cases, whereas the latter is to collect intelligence information—so the standard of proof (i.e., the need for probable cause) is reduced. Under the USA PATRIOT Act, however, the FISA was amended to allow the evidence found to be used also in criminal cases, as long as intelligence gathering is also a significant purpose of the surveillance.[23]

The FISA historically has had little relation to organized crime, but since the events of September 11, 2001, terrorism investigations have overlapped to some degree with transnational organized crime investigations. In a report to Congress, the U.S. Justice Department indicated that in the year following September 11, 2001, 113 emergency authorizations for secret foreign intelligence warrants for electronic and physical surveillance were approved, compared to less than 50 during the previous 23 years. FISA surveillance became an issue in late 2005 when the *New York Times* revealed that President George Bush authorized interception of international electronic communications of al Qaeda operatives without authorization by the secret FISA court. The Bush administration defended its position because of the nature of the terrorism threat, but Attorney General Gonzalez relented in 2007, agreeing to bring its FISA surveillance requests before the court.[24]

The problem with Title III is that it never defines "organized crime." Case law provides little guidance for when generic felonies become eligible for eavesdropping. In a Maryland case, for example, a conspiracy among three people to distribute cocaine was found not to constitute organized crime, and electronic interceptions of conversations were suppressed.[25] But in an Ohio case, a conspiracy of three people to extort money from a bank occurred and the court concluded, "Extortion is a crime 'characteristic' of organized crime. That is all that is required." So eavesdropping was permitted.[26] In a Massachusetts case, a scheme by two local government officials to extort a kickback from a contractor "did not create reasonable suspicion" of organized crime involvement, and a consensual interception was suppressed.[27] A common legal definition of organized crime, such as that offered in Chapter 1, would go a long way in clarifying the precise acts for which electronic surveillance is appropriate.

A total of 29 states have adopted electronic surveillance laws similar to Title III for violations of state laws. States may not enact statutes more permissive than Title III, although they may restrict it more severely. Several states have done so. In Texas, for example, wiretapping is permitted only to investigate certain drug felonies (excluding marijuana possession). Illinois has a similar law.

Changes in technology since Title III was passed have created a need for changes in the scope of the law. If wire and oral communications are protected from interception without a Title III warrant, what about conversations over cellular or cordless telephones whose signals are carried primarily over radio waves? What expectation of privacy do you have in communicating via Internet? Is your e-mail private?

Questions like these required updating of Title III. The result was the Electronic Communications Privacy Act (ECPA).[28] It created a third legal category called "electronic communications" to be added to "wire" and "oral" communications covered by Title III. The ECPA protects electronic communications and also regulates pen registers and trap-and-trace devices not addressed by Title III. The act also permits "roving wiretaps" that allow investigators to intercept transmissions from multiple phones or locations employed by some criminal groups. Roving taps do not name a specific telephone line or e-mail account, but allow the government to tap any phone, cell phone, or Internet account that a particular suspect uses.

Prior to the ECPA, surreptitious or intentional interceptions of mobile radio-telephone conversations, ham radio broadcasts, cordless telephone conversations, and pager messages were allowable.[29] Title III suggested that if a radio communication "is susceptible to being overheard by the general public, then the participants to the communication lack a reasonable expectation of privacy."[30] The ECPA now protects most of these communications, making nonconsensual interception by private persons a crime. Police can intercept them with an "ECPA order," which is a special warrant that can be obtained by a wider range of officials and can be used for a broader range of offenses than a Title III warrant.[31] Radio communications not protected by the ECPA are those "transmitted by stations for the use of the general public" or those involving ships, aircraft, vehicles, citizen band radio, and electronic bulletin boards.[32] Personal e-mail is protected, however, due to its private nature (as a form of mail) and the need for passwords to access it. Likewise, remote communications from terminals or modems to computers is protected for similar reasons.

Pagers have varying degrees of protection from interception under the ECPA. Tone-only pagers can be intercepted without judicial approval of any kind. Those that display messages can be intercepted only with an ECPA order because they are electronic communications with a greater "expectation of privacy" than tone-only pagers. Tone and voice pagers require a Title III warrant that protects these "conversations" from interception without probable cause.

Cellular phones are unique in that they operate in a group of "service areas" with low-power transmitters. When you call a cellular phone, a transmitter sends the signal through the air over a radio frequency to a cell location. It travels over telephone lines or microwave systems to a telephone switching station, which transfers the call's frequency and switches it automatically as the person with the cellular phone moves from cell to cell. These calls can be intercepted with specially designed scanners. Under the ECPA, these calls are protected from interception without an ECPA order, even though they are carried, in part, over radio waves. Nevertheless, cordless telephone conversations are not protected by Title III or the ECPA. The cordless portion of these conversations "may be intercepted, and their contents used, without court authorization."[33]

The ECPA expands Title III in other ways as well. Electronic communications that are scrambled or encrypted are protected from unauthorized interception because they are not "readily accessible."[34] Law enforcement agencies have developed decoding software they would like to see adopted by the telecommunications industry to intercept these conversations in criminal investigations, but a Title III warrant is required for eavesdropping into the content of these communications.[35] In addition, "cloned" cellular phones have become a cottage industry for organized crime in recent years. A cloned phone has someone else's number programmed into it for billing purposes. This makes it extremely difficult for a tap or trace to be useful. Criminals use these phones for a few weeks and then throw them away. The telecommunications industry has worked to make it more difficult to clone or use cloned cellular phones, although cases have been discovered where drug dealers have used these clones because calls could not be traced to them.[36]

The ECPA provides both civil and criminal penalties for disclosure, as well as for interception, of communications when a person has reason to know the information was obtained unlawfully.[37] A growing number of states incorporated ECPA standards into their state electronic surveillance statutes.[38]

The ECPA also changed the law regarding pen registers and trap-and-trace devices. These devices are the converse of each other: trap-and-trace devices record the telephone numbers of incoming calls, whereas pen registers record the telephone numbers of outgoing calls. The ECPA changed the law regarding these devices in that they are now subject to a court authorization called an "ECPA order," although neither probable cause nor reasonable suspicion is required. Instead, the application must certify only "that the information likely to be obtained is relevant to an ongoing criminal investigation being conducted by that agency."[39] Under the ECPA, pen registers and trap-and-trace devices require court authorization when they are capable of converting to a monitoring device—even if the monitoring capability is disabled.[40]

The ECPA adds a "good faith" defense for police officers who eavesdrop using a warrant later found to be invalid. This follows on the trend begun in the U.S. Supreme Court in 1984 in creating exceptions to the exclusionary rule.[41] Ironically, there is no such defense for private citizens. A civilian defendant's "mistaken good faith belief" that it was lawful to intercept a communication does not constitute a defense.[42] Private citizens who violate Title III or the ECPA or police who engage in warrantless eavesdropping are subject to criminal penalties of up to five years' imprisonment and civil penalties up to $10,000 per day.

The USA PATRIOT Act expanded the scope of the ECPA in 2001 by permitting law enforcement to use pen registers and trap-and-trace devices on the Internet and other computer networks. Once a federal court approves the use of these devices, they can be used on communications nationwide to follow targeted numbers. However, law enforcement must file a special report with the court if "Carnivore" or a similar device is installed on the computer of a public provider. Carnivore is an electronic surveillance system that monitor's a person's e-mail and Internet activity, intercepting the address information and the contents of the communication. When used only as a "pen register," Carnivore collects electronic address information only. This distinction and the potential for invasions of private communications of innocent persons have caused much debate in Congress and among the general public.[43] As one observer put it, "New technology in law enforcement results in new challenges for the courts, not only in determining reliability of the evidence gathered, but also in balancing society's interest in law and order with an individual's constitutionally protected civil liberties."[44]

Another technological advance that the FBI has used is the Keystroke Logger System (KLS). The KLS monitors and records keystrokes entered into a computer, enabling access to passwords entered via the keystrokes, which are needed to decipher encrypted data. Consider the issues that arise in an actual case: Nicodemo Scarfo, a New Jersey organized crime figure and son of the imprisoned Nicodemo "Little Nicky" Scarfo Sr., kept encrypted computer records of alleged illegal gambling operations. The FBI obtained a search warrant and seized Scarfo's computer, but they could not decrypt the file. It was then that the FBI developed the KLS and obtained a warrant for a surreptitious entry into Scarfo's place of business, where they secretly placed the KLS on his computer. Over a 30-day period (the valid length of the warrant), the FBI entered Scarfo's business four times, recovering 27 pages of text and Scarfo's password. The password was used to decrypt data, revealing a record of gambling and loanshark operations. Scarfo was subsequently indicted and filed a motion for discovery, requesting technical details of the KLS.[45] The prosecution argued that revealing the technical specifications would damage national security. Scarfo, however, had the right to determine whether the KLS also intercepted the content of his communications without proper court authorization. (The KLS system records the communication between a person and the computer keyboard, whether or not it is stored, e-mailed, or otherwise communicated outside the computer or the home or office, raising the issue of electronically eavesdropped conversations and communications versus eavesdropping passwords and Internet addresses.) This case illustrates how sophisticated technology, which always engenders the possibility for abuse, causes problems for both prosecution (in preserving the utility of the technology for future cases) and the defense (in ensuring that unlawfully seized evidence is not being used).

The court ruled in this case that Scarfo would receive an unclassified summary of how the KLS operates. Scarfo ultimately pleaded guilty, ending his legal battle and postponing the resolution of this important question of law and technology.[44]

Table 9.1 provides a summary of this discussion of the complicated law of electronic surveillance. While these rules can seem overbearing, they all relate to a fundamental principle in interpreting the Fourth Amendment to the U.S. Constitution, which protects "the right of people to be secure in their persons, houses, papers, and effects against unreasonable searches and seizures." Courts and legislatures continue to struggle to apply this general rule to new methods of communication, technologies, and new crimes.

Since the passage of Title III and the ECPA, the U.S. Supreme Court has made many rulings in cases involving electronic surveillance. The net result has been a continuing expansion of the scope of electronic eavesdropping. Some of these court decisions have made it possible to use wiretap or eavesdropping evidence in court when (1) the evidence involves people who are third parties not named in the warrant who are implicated in intercepted conversations,[46] (2) names of suspects are inadvertently omitted from wiretap warrants,[47] (3) those whose dwellings are entered for placement of a bug without explicit court authorization,[48] and (4) a warrant is not required to conduct pen register surveillance (i.e., recording the numbers dialed from a telephone) or electronic "beeper" surveillance (i.e., surveillance through a radio transmitter).[49]

Table 9.1 Types of Communications and Judicial Approval Required

Type of Communication	Title III Warrant	ECPA Order	No Judicial Approval Required
Telephone conversation	X		
Conversation in rooms, cars	X		
Voice mail	X		
Cordless phone			X
Cell phone		X	
E-mail		X	
Internet account		X	
Remote communication to computers via modem or networks		X	
Pager—tone and voice	X		
Pager—message display		X	
Pager—tone only			X
Citizen band radio			X
Pen register (numbers dialed)		X	
Trap-and-trace device		X	

Each of these interpretations of Title III involved separate U.S. Supreme Court cases. Another case illustrates how technology is making the balance between privacy and law enforcement difficult.

Danny Kyllo lived in a multifamily home in Florence, Oregon, and federal agents suspected he was growing marijuana in his home. Such indoor cultivation of marijuana requires high-intensity heat lamps to simulate sunlight. The federal agents decided to scan Kyllo's house with a thermal imaging device, which registers the heat given off by objects from a distance. The agents used this device, without a warrant, from a parked car across the street from Kyllo's house at 3:00 A.M. They scanned other homes as well in order to compare heat readings and discovered that Kyllo's house generated more heat than neighboring homes. Using this information, Kyllo's high utility bills, and informants' tips, the agents obtained a search warrant, entered Kyllo's home, and found more than 100 marijuana plants. Kyllo challenged the use of the thermal imaging device in court, arguing it intruded into a constitutionally protected area— the interior of his home—without benefit of probable cause or a search warrant. The U.S. Supreme Court agreed with Kyllo that the agents' use of the thermal imaging device constituted an unlawful search, which they defined as "obtaining by sense-enhancing technology any information regarding the interior of a home that could not have been obtained without physical intrusion into a constitutionally protected area" in cases where the technology is not in general public use (as in this case).[50] The court held that the home has special protection under the constitution: "In the home, our cases show, all details are intimate details, because the entire area is held safe from prying government eyes" without a previous showing of probable cause of law violation.[51] As this case illustrates, the courts and legislatures will struggle in the coming years in reconciling privacy rights guaranteed in the Fourth Amendment with increasingly advanced surveillance technology.[52]

Table 9.2 provides a summary of authorized electronic surveillance by state and federal law enforcement agencies since 1970. It can be seen that the number of taps installed was nearly four times greater in 2010 than it was in 1970. Telephone taps have remained the most popular form of electronic surveillance, although cell phones and digital pagers are now more popular than fixed phones at homes or businesses. Currently, most intercepts are of cell phones and pagers (see Figure 9.3). This is a dramatic change from 20 years ago, when cellular phones accounted for only 10% of all telephone numbers in use and approximately one-third of telephone taps were of cell phones.[53]

Room bug installations are few because of their limited range and the need for a covert entry to place the microphone. This is both difficult and dangerous for police, although several of the most important organized crime prosecutions of recent decades, including that of Paul Castellano and John Gotti, relied on

Table 9.2 Court-Authorized Electronic Surveillance in the United States[a]

Devices	1970	1980	1990	2000	2010
Number installed	597	524	812	1139	2311
Telephone wiretaps (standard, cell, and mobile phones)	90%	91%	75%	81%	97%
Room microphones (fixed: homes and businesses)	4%	5%	4%	5%	1%
Electronic communications (roving tap, digital pagers, fax, computer)	NA[b]	NA[b]	13%	8%	1%
Number of extensions/per device	246	201	581	926	1925
	41%	38%	72%	81%	83%
Total days in use/days per device	11,200	11,939	28,782	47,729	93,078
	19 days	23 days	35 days	42 days	40 days

[a]Compiled from Administrative Office of the United States Courts, Reports on Applications for Orders Authorizing or Approving the Intercept of Wire or Oral Communications.

[b]Electronic communications not covered in Title III, only added after passage of Electronic Communications Privacy Act in 1987.

FIGURE 9.3 Communication towers, now ubiquitous across the landscape, provide radio coverage over a wide geographic area, enabling portable transceivers (e.g., mobile phones, pagers) to communicate with each other and with fixed transceivers and telephones anywhere in the network. *www.shutterstock.com*

room microphones.[54] In the case of Paul Castellano, a bug was placed in his kitchen, where he conducted business. In Gotti's case, bugs were placed in his social club, an apartment, and in hubcaps of cars on the street so conversations could be intercepted while he took walks. In Buffalo, the luxury boat and car of Benjamin "Sonny" Nicoletti were bugged in a gambling investigation.[55]

A small number (1%) of intercepts are "roving wiretaps." These are authorized when a judge is convinced that wiretapping a specific location or phone is not appropriate because the person under investigation moves from place to place, frequently using different phones or other means of communication. Roving wiretaps permit investigators to target a specific person rather than a particular telephone or location.

The proportion of intercept orders that entail extensions from the original 30-day approval period has increased significantly, as has total days per interception. Each extension must be approved by a judge who must be convinced of the need for continuation. One of the longest wiretaps was in a narcotics investigation by the New York State Organized Crime Task Force where the 30-day authorization was ultimately extended 28 times, for a total of 830 days. However, some wiretaps nationwide are in operation for less than one week. Defendants can challenge the extent of wiretap usage in later court proceedings, and in one case a New York city waterfront investigation of organized crime involved eavesdropping at three locations. One office was bugged for seven months and the telephone inside was tapped for four and one-half months. A second office was bugged for three months and the phone there was tapped for one month. A third telephone was tapped in another office for two months. The argument raised by the defendant at trial was that his privacy was violated due to the length and number of the intercepts, even though the telephone wiretaps and room microphones were placed with court authorization. The court held that the complexity of the criminal activity under investigation, and the nature of the premises under surveillance, must be considered in making such a judgment. The intercepted conversations were admitted in court.[56]

Table 9.3 presents suspected offenses for which court-authorized electronic surveillance was undertaken over 40 years. A significant shift in law enforcement priorities can clearly be seen. Gambling went from more than one-half of all intercepts in 1970 to only 1% of all intercepts in 2010. Conversely, drug

Table 9.3 Suspected Crimes in Authorized Electronic Surveillance (Percent of All Authorized Intercepts)[a]

Major Offenses	1970	1980	1990	2000	2010
Gambling (%)	55	35	13	4	1
Drugs	21	50	60	75	84
Racketeering	NA[b]	5	10	6	4
Homicide/assault	3	2	2	6	5
All others	21	8	15	9	6

[a]Compiled from Administrative Office of the United States Courts, Reports on Applications for Orders Authorizing or Approving the Intercept of Wire or Oral Communications.
[b]Racketeering not codified in law until 1970 as part of the Organized Crime Control Act.

investigations involving electronic surveillance have quadrupled over the same period, now accounting for 84% of all intercepts. This is a reflection of shifting public perceptions of the seriousness of these offenses, as well as shifts in organized crime activity itself. Chapter 7 explained how the President's Crime Commission in 1967 found gambling to be the largest source of revenue for organized crime. Gambling was replaced by illegal narcotics trafficking as the largest revenue source, as determined by the President's Commission on Organized Crime 20 years later. International drug trafficking that involves the United States accounts for many of the cases involving electronic surveillance in recent years.

Table 9.4 illustrates the results of electronic surveillance from 1970 forward. It can be seen that many more conversations are overheard now than was the case in earlier years. This may be due to increases in the size and complexity of organized crime activities and to the number and length of extensions granted to wiretap authorizations. However, the percentage of these conversations that are incriminating has dropped to less than 20%. This suggests that perhaps conspiracies are becoming "part-time" activity, resulting in fewer crime-related conversations during a given period, or that cases chosen for electronic surveillance are becoming less appropriate. Perhaps there also is a saturation point at which such surveillance ceases to be productive for investigative purposes. This is difficult to know without analysis of intercept characteristics in successful versus unsuccessful investigations, something that has not yet taken place.

Table 9.4 Results of Electronic Surveillance[a]

Averages per Intercept	1970	1980	1990	2000	2010
Persons intercepted	44	136	131	196	118
Intercepted conversations	655	1058	1487	1769	3199
Percent incriminating conversations (%)	45	30	22	35	19
Cost per tap ($)	5524	17,146	45,125	54,829	50,085
Total arrests/arrests per tap[b]	1874	1871	2057	3411	4711
	3.1	3.6	2.5	3.0	2.0
Total convictions/convictions per tap[b]	NR[c]	259	420	736	800
		0.50	0.52	0.62	0.35

[a]Compiled from Administrative Office of the United States Courts, Reports on Applications for Orders Authorizing or Approving the Intercept of Wire or Oral Communications.

[b]It is difficult to determine with precision year-to-year changes in arrests and convictions resulting from electronic surveillance. This is because arrests and convictions can occur a year or two following the surveillance, as more evidence is gathered.

[c]Court-authorized electronic surveillance began in 1969, after the passage of Title III a year earlier. No convictions were reported for 1970.

Given broad court authority to employ electronic surveillance, a limiting factor to its more widespread use is its prohibitive cost. The average cost per tap is almost 10 times higher than it was in 1970. Inflation has taken its toll over this period, but electronic surveillance is still one of the most expensive tools in the investigative repertoire. The high cost is largely due to the minimization requirement of Title III that mandates noncriminal conversations be excluded from interception to the extent possible. This means a police officer must be present 24 hours a day to listen to the beginning of each conversation, turn off the tape recorder audio if the conversation is not related to the eavesdropping warrant, and switch it back on every minute or so to determine whether the conversation has become related to the warrant. In addition, transcription of tapes, analysis of conversations, and directions of the conspiracy, as well as follow-up physical surveillance and other leads produced by the intercept, must be undertaken when conducting electronic surveillance. It is an intensive investigative tool that requires large amounts of dedicated time given the 30-day approval period.

The cost and effectiveness of electronic surveillance remain matters of debate. Electronic surveillance has formed the basis for many significant organized crime convictions in recent years, but some have questioned its cost-benefit. A "substantial minority" of the National Wiretap Commission concluded that even though it "has resulted in the conviction of a very small number of upper-echelon organized crime figures," in terms of cost, manpower, and convictions overall, it has been "generally unproductive."[57] Many significant organized crime convictions have occurred since that report was issued, casting doubt on that conclusion, although an objective assessment of the cost-benefit of electronic surveillance versus other competing investigative tools is needed. An analysis of wiretap transcripts, and other material, by Kip Schlegel found that electronic surveillance has problems because criminal conspiracies "often take an inordinate amount of time to complete." In addition, their planning generally takes place across "a variety of locations," working against the utility of electronic eavesdropping. In addition, there are problems of interpretation (e.g., is a "hit" a robbery, a murder, a monetary loss?) and validity (people often lie, brag, and mislead others in their conversations).[58]

The increasing utilization of electronic surveillance illustrates its growing acceptance as a law enforcement tool, although issues remain about the scope of the use of emerging technologies such as night-vision devices, thermal imagers, biometric devices, and encryption devices.[59] Legal, privacy, and practical usage issues will be resolved through legislation, public opinion, court decisions, and law enforcement agency rules. Whether electronic surveillance works best for certain types of cases, locations, suspects, or in conjunction with other investigative tools has not been studied objectively to help determine whether increased physical surveillance, use of informants, or other kinds of investigative tools are ultimately less expensive or more effective than electronic surveillance. After such an analysis is conducted, electronic surveillance may be carried out more profitably in terms of costs and convictions.

Informants

The use of informants in organized crime cases is common. It can be argued that use of confidential informants is the most cost-effective investigative tool in organized crime cases.

The typical informant is a criminal who chooses to cooperate with the police in exchange for a reduced charge, sentence, or immunity from prosecution. But this is not always the case. Some honest people simply wish to report wrongdoing.[60] Informants, whether criminal or not, wish anonymity. Courts have generally held that the government is entitled to keep secret the identity of an informant who has provided information about a possible law violation.[61] This is called the "informer's privilege." The privilege is not absolute, however, and can be overcome if the defense can show that the informant's identity is relevant to the defendant's case.[62]

Information obtained from the informant is commonly used to investigate more serious criminality. For example, an arrested street drug dealer can be used to determine who the suppliers in a given area are. An illegal waste disposer can provide information about the organizers of the illicit enterprise. Such informants are extremely cost-effective because there is usually little expense involved, unless the informant is paid for the information or is placed in the witness protection program (discussed in Chapter 10). In addition, informers can provide information that would require months of undercover investigation to obtain.

In recent years there has been a well-documented stream of organized crime figures who have become informants. Such high-level criminals as Nicky Barnes, Jimmy Fratianno, Sammy Gravano, Mickey Featherstone, Anthony Casso, Anthony Accetturo, Michael Franzese, and Peter Savino all became informants for the government and testified against their former cohorts in crime.[63] This has occurred for three reasons:

1. Extended sentences available under the racketeering and drug laws force criminals to consider prison as the "end of the line" rather than as merely a temporary cost of doing business.
2. The witness protection program (discussed in the following chapter) allows a potential informant a way to avoid the wrath of his co-conspirators if he testifies against them.
3. A diminished sense of "honor among thieves" and loyalty to an organization or heritage exists now than was the case in the past. Many

criminals are simply in it for the money, and when caught they look for the easiest way out, regardless of who might be "sacrificed" to accomplish it.

The decline of loyalty within Mafia-related groups is particularly notable because there had been a tradition of "omerta" for many years. Omerta is the code of silence, said to exist in Mafia culture, where speaking to others outside the group about Mafia operations is a violation punishable by death. Over the past 30 years, however, a series of Mafia members have testified against their former associates in court, weakening the meaning of this tradition in practice. Different observers place varying levels of weight on the three reasons just given for this trend, but certainly some combination of them has changed the stakes in creating criminal informants.[64]

The low cost of informants is offset to some degree by problems of reliability and credibility. As noted in Chapter 6, several of the mob trials of the 1980s and 1990s resulted in acquittals due to juries not believing the testimony of government informants. As a journalist reported after one of these acquittals, "The last piece of evidence requested by the jury for re-examination was a chart introduced by the defense that showed the criminal backgrounds of seven prosecution witnesses. It listed 69 crimes, including murder, drug possession and sales, and kidnapping."[65] An FBI report obtained by *USA Today* under the Freedom of Information Act revealed that the FBI gave its informants permission to break the law more than 5,600 times in a single year, pointing to the problem of sometimes looking past the crimes committed by informants in order to obtain information to convict higher-ups.[66] The concern here, of course, as defense attorney Alan Dershowitz has pointed out, is that "A bought witness may tell the truth—but only if it suits his interest to do so."[67]

This issue of the reliability of informants (in mob trials, many were admitted criminals) and credibility (many were forced to admit they had lied in the past) becomes a problem particularly when the witnesses have been, or are being, paid by the government. This situation appears, at least in some cases, to work against the credibility of the informant's testimony from the jury's perspective. For example, Sammy Gravano's testimony against former "boss" John Gotti was apparently believed by the jury, but his testimony against Pasquale Conte and other alleged crime figures in another trial was not. Two hours after it began deliberations, the jury sent out a note that said, "We believe that Sammy Gravano's testimony is essential to the government's case. We have already debated his credibility, and have reached an impasse."[68]

One factor that works against the development of noncriminal informants is the fear that their identities will eventually become known. The occasional body of a cooperating witness found slain "gangland style" may have some deterrent effect, although such incidents are rare when they involve people out-side the criminal organization itself.[69] The FBI thought the Freedom of Infor-mation Act would reduce the willingness of people to provide information or to become informants due to a fear their identity could ultimately become known. A review of the files of 7,000 FBI agents over 19 months documented only 19 instances of people refusing to provide information out of fear of discovery.[70] Noncriminals become informants, therefore, for other reasons. These reasons should be examined so that noncriminals from business, government, and neighborhoods can be found more often to develop criminal cases.

Informants must be managed properly to be useful in making significant crim-inal cases. In a well-known case in Boston, former FBI agent John Connolly was convicted of racketeering in 2002 for tipping off Whitey Bulger, Stephen Flemmi, and other Boston-area Irish-American organized crime figures that they were about to be indicted. Bulger had been working as an FBI informant (see Figure 9.4). It was shown in court that the FBI agent became too close to Bulger, protecting his criminal activities in an effort to build cases against other Mafia-linked Italian-American groups.[71] A separate judicial inquiry concluded that Connolly overstated the value of his informants in FBI files, minimized the extent of their criminal activities, and leaked information about other individ-uals who were serving as informants.[72] Stricter and better-enforced agency rules

FIGURE 9.4 Former FBI agent John J. Connolly Jr., center, is surrounded by cameramen as he leaves the Federal Courthouse in Boston after he was found guilty in his racketeering trial in 2002. *AP Photo/ Charles Krupa*

regarding the handling of informants would be helpful in preventing future situations of this kind, but as Amanda Schreiber observes, the FBI (and all other law enforcement agencies) "must ultimately rely on the good faith and professionalism of its individual agents."[73]

The generally low cost of informants, together with their ability to provide information more rapidly and with less risk than electronic surveillance or undercover investigations, ensures that they will remain an important investigative source in organized crime cases. A single informer in New York, for example, provided information that led to the indictments of 45 suspects of the Genovese crime group.[74] The merits and problems of witness immunity and the witness protection program, as they relate to government informants, are assessed in the next chapter.

Undercover Agents

Undercover investigations are not used as much as is commonly believed in organized crime cases due to the length of time required to gain acceptance and access to information about criminal organizations, as well as the constant danger to the undercover officer if his or her identity is discovered. Nevertheless, in recent years, there have been several extremely significant undercover agents whose work resulted in numerous convictions. The most well known is Joe Pistone, who worked undercover as "Donnie Brasco" inside the Bonanno crime group in New York for six years. His work resulted in more than 100 convictions of organized crime figures.[75] Other undercover agents have also produced significant cases over the years.[76]

The danger to undercover agents is apparent, as they are the last to know when their cover is blown, making serious injury or death difficult to foresee. In New York city, nearly 200 undercover officers (about two-thirds of New York's entire undercover force) were transferred to less dangerous duty following the killings of two undercover detectives and complaints regarding danger, outmoded equipment, and inadequate backup for officers involved in undercover operations.[77] In addition, nearly one in five undercover officers in the New York Police Department reported they had been in confrontations in which they were mistaken for suspects by fellow officers, finding themselves at gunpoint by officers who were unaware of who they were. This demonstrates that the danger to uncover officers lies in their uncertain status in the eyes of both criminals and other police.

Sting operations involve more officers, but they are also long-term and expensive investigations. A scam involving the exchange of drugs for green cards for immigrants was ended after a two-year sting operation in New York state. Fifty-seven drug suspects and 39 illegal immigrants were arrested.[78] The FBI charged 76 people with dealing in stolen furs, cars, and other property valued at $17 million from a boutique they had set up in New Jersey.[79] Other stings elsewhere in New Jersey, Florida, and Wisconsin enjoyed similar success, although they usually involved investigations lasting at least two years.[80]

In a variation of this technique, a two-year investigation of an Internet prostitution ring run by a resident of North Tampa resulted in a series of arrests for conspiracy, racketeering, and prostitution. A Web site contained message boards for prostitution in all 50 states and several countries, including Canada, Germany, and France. The owner claimed to make $18,000 a month from it. Most of the escort's clients were high-salaried, white-collar professionals. For $129.95 a year, the site offered detailed instructions to members on topics such as how to hire an "escort." Fees for the escort services ranged from $175 per hour to $17,000 for a date with a porn star. It was estimated that 50,000 people worldwide had used the Web site. Escorts paid the operators $129 per year to be listed on the Web site, with large ads costing as much as $900 per month. Tipped off about the site, investigators twice tried to use a decoy without success. They were finally successful when they managed to create a fictitious prostitute named Lia Nice. In 10 minutes the Web page received 3,000 hits. Potential customers who offered Lia Nice money for sex were persuaded to cooperate with the sheriff's office. More arrests were expected, and one police official said, "We'll be knocking on a lot of people's doors."[81] This case provides another example of the time-intensive nature of undercover investigations.

Sting operations are usually designed to infiltrate criminal markets, but these require multiple undercover officers over an extended period of time. In the "Fast and Furious" operation, ATF agents allowed illegal gun sales to occur so they could track and locate the ultimate destination of the guns. However, the tracking proved difficult, and thousands of guns ended up in Mexico in the hands of drug cartels. This dealt a blow to sting operations, and the FBI said it planned to investigate other ATF sting operations in several cities in which smoke shops were opened as a cover to make underworld buys of drugs and guns.[82] This situation illustrates the difficulty and complexity of successful undercover sting operations.

A study found that agents selected for undercover assignments tend to be the "newly recruited and inexperienced members" and that supervision of these agents in the field "may be lax." Interviews with undercover agents showed that these agents are exposed to great danger without adequate briefing or preparation.[83] The effectiveness of and consequences for undercover operatives have also not been evaluated.

> There is little information about how effective undercover investigations are, what they cost (economically, psychologically, or constitutionally), or why they fail. Similarly, the extent to which police departments use the strategy is unknown.[84]

Adjustment problems of undercover officers after completing their assignment have also not received enough attention from either police agencies or the public.[85] The FBI claims that its undercover agents were responsible for 680 convictions, $5.7 million in forfeitures, and $741.1 million in potential economic losses prevented in a single year. Although these figures were modified somewhat by a General Accounting Office audit, the benefits of undercover work have not yet been evaluated objectively against their costs in terms of time invested, risk, manpower, and their impact on the officer, the police agency, and on affected third parties.[86]

In the case of Joseph Pistone, he and his family had to move four times while he was testifying, he did not see his family for three months at a time over a six-year period while undercover, and he resigned from the FBI without serving long enough to earn a pension because of threats against him.[87] He believes there is a $500,000 contract on his life so his life undercover appears to have changed rather than ended.

Figure 9.5 illustrates some of the difficulties in investigative decision making in organized crime cases. In every suspected case, there is a need for information that sometimes cannot be provided by traditional means of physical surveillance or interrogation. The issue to be faced is a question of finding the proper balance between individual privacy and public safety. Each of the three methods of electronic surveillance, use of informants, and undercover operations has a distinct purpose: to find information not available by other means. At the same time, each of these methods poses certain risks to privacy of the suspect and surrounding others, as well as risks to informants and investigators.

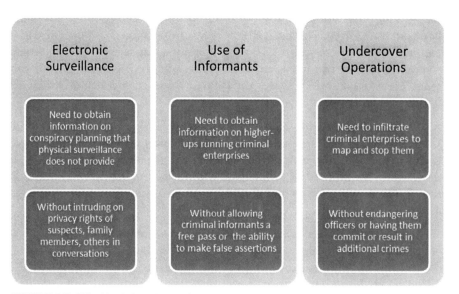

FIGURE 9.5 Difficulties in investigative decision making in organized crime cases.

The feasibility of each of these investigative techniques cannot be determined outside of a particular set of facts, but it is useful to outline the pros and cons of each decision in order to understand the difficulty and stakes involved in making the appropriate investigative decisions.

Citizens Commissions

An often overlooked investigative resource for organized crime is citizens commissions. These investigative commissions have been established from time to time throughout the history of the United States to examine the problems of crime in a specific locality. The Chicago Crime Commission and the Pennsylvania Crime Commission are among the oldest and most productive of the citizens crime commissions.[88] Over the years, these commissions have played a useful role in the investigation of organized crime. For example, the New Mexico special prosecutions division reported that when it first initiated operations, the information and intelligence it received from the Governor's Organized Crime Commission was useful in choosing areas for further investigation and developing cases for prosecution.[89]

There are essentially three types of crime commissions:

1. Government-funded, bipartisan groups—in which investigators have police status but no arrest authority (e.g., Pennsylvania Crime Commission)
2. Groups funded by the private sector—having no law enforcement authority (e.g., Chicago Crime Commission)
3. Government-sponsored, temporary groups—which investigate a specific incident or phenomenon (e.g., Knapp Commission, President's Commission on Organized Crime)[90]

These commissions are useful in developing information and also in focusing public concern on organized crime. Due to the consensual nature of the vices and the fact that many organized crime groups appear to kill within their group, the public is not as aroused about organized crime as it might be. Commission hearings, reports, and publicity about specific incidents and trends in the community serve as a way to galvanize community feeling and reduce tolerance for organized crime activities in a locality.

The legal authority of citizens commissions varies from state to state. In New Jersey, for example, the State Commission of Investigation may engage in electronic surveillance on approval of the state attorney general. In Oklahoma, the Citizens Crime Commission pays rewards for information leading to the arrests of suspects charged with crimes.[91] It has been found that witnesses feel freer to talk to these commissions because their main task is to gather information rather than build specific cases.[92] The National Association of Attorneys General concluded:

While it is true that most law enforcement agencies that do not have the benefit of a statewide grand jury or of electronic surveillance very much desire these tools, it also appears that anti-corruption efforts have been waged by states without them, using more traditional, less "easy" investigative tools.[93]

It is apparent, then, that the investigation of organized crime is not limited solely to the actions of law enforcement agencies and that commissions that rely heavily on private citizens can be a useful adjunct to traditional law enforcement tools.

Commissions usually are not empowered to make criminal cases, nor is that their interest. This enables them to take the long view and assess longer impacts of current trends. This distinguishes their role from traditional law enforcement. Of course, commissions formed by the government can also be dissolved by the government. The Pennsylvania Crime Commission was allowed to expire in 1994, two months after it issued a report linking the state attorney general to illegal video poker vendors.[94] The state police was to assume the duties of the commission, although no funding was provided to carry them out. It appears in the case of Pennsylvania as if the reason for the formation of a crime commission, that is, a neutral, objective examination of a serious problem, was forgotten in favor of political expediency. Nevertheless, ongoing citizens commissions, such as the Chicago Crime Commission, can do a great deal to educate the public, mobilize opinion, and influence enforcement and crime policy.[95]

CRITICAL THINKING EXERCISE 9.2

Using the information provided in this chapter, respond to the scenario that follows. Employ current legal principles to justify your response.

The Case of Standing Next to a Pay Phone
You are a police officer standing next to a prisoner at lockup. He is from Thailand and speaks little English. He communicates that he would like to make a telephone call. You consent and stand next to him, pursuant to department policy.

You believe the prisoner may be implicating himself in further illegal activity on the telephone so you turn on your pocket tape recorder and record his end of the telephone conversation without his knowledge. Although he spoke in Thai, you later bring the tape to a local college professor who speaks Thai. He transcribes the tape.

Your hunch was correct! The prisoner implicated himself in a crime while talking on the telephone.

Critical Thinking Questions
1. Is your tape recording admissible as evidence in court against the prisoner?
2. How would the case be different if the prisoner spoke in English on the telephone?
3. How would the case be different if you overheard the conversation without using a tape recorder?

SUMMARY

The investigation of organized crime involves strategies and techniques quite different from conventional crimes. Whereas traditional crimes of assault and theft involve force or stealth, organized crimes involve infiltration and conspiracy, which require the investigator to be as sophisticated as the offender. The five techniques described in this chapter characterized the difference between organized crime investigations and investigations for other crimes. These tools involve more planning, organization, and time-intensive effort than traditional law enforcement tools, but they are necessary to investigate criminal behavior that also is better planned and organized than traditional crimes. Each investigative technique was shown to have both strengths and weaknesses, and they continue to be used in a variety of cases.

ORGANIZED CRIME BIOGRAPHY

Biographies tell the life story of interesting people. In the world of criminal justice, biographies of organized crime figures offer insight into the background and motivations of the individuals who choose that lifestyle, the reasons for their choices, and their consequences. The following is a brief summary of an organized crime biography, followed by questions that ask you to reflect on the connections between that person's life and the content of this book.

Making Jack Falcone: An Undercover FBI Agent Takes Down a Mafia Family
Joaquin Garcia and Michael Levin (Pocket, 2009).

This book is an autobiographical account of a Cuban-American undercover FBI agent who tells of his infiltration of the Gambino family of the Mafia in New York (and several other undercover roles he played during his career). An excellent description is presented of the mob lifestyle, criminal activities, and the dangers of undercover work.

Garcia's biggest case was his undercover role in the Gambino crime family, ultimately rising to work directly under the group's leader, Greg DePalma. A variety of criminal enterprises were developed through a constant search for new ways to make money (illegally) and the need to threaten those who failed to pay their percentage of illicit profits to the boss. The scams involved gambling, weapons, diamonds, and drugs, among others.

The FBI pulled Garcia from his undercover role after he had been proposed by DePalma for membership into the Gambino family. Garcia believed this was a mistake because, as a "made" member, he would have access to higher level information about the criminal group's operations. However, working undercover for several years is both dangerous and exhausting work.

Questions
1. Why do you believe the FBI ended this case before Garcia was inducted into the Gambino crime group?
2. Do you believe there should be limits on the nature and time permitted for an undercover operation?

ORGANIZED CRIME AT THE MOVIES

Movies seek to entertain and inform the audience about a story, incident, or person. Many good movies also hit on important substantive themes relevant to understanding organized crime. Read the following movie summary (and watch the movie if you haven't already) and answer the questions that follow to make the organized crime subject matter connections.

Donnie Brasco
Mike Newell, Director (1997)

The film tells the true story of FBI agent Joe Pistone (Johnny Depp) who went undercover for six years as "Donnie Brasco," infiltrating the Bonanno crime family in New York city. The film focuses on Brasco's cover as a jewel thief and the friends he makes to get close to the crime family operations. Lefty Ruggiero (Al Pacino) is a hit man with a disastrous personal life, and Sonny Black (Michael Madsen) is the leader of the crime group.

Ruggiero is upset because he can't seem to get "promoted" within the crime family, even though he has killed 26 people in 30 years. He sees promise in Donnie Brasco, however, and introduces him to the other members of the crime group, teaching him how to talk, dress, and act as a mobster. Donnie is quickly accepted by the other members of the group, including Sonny Black.

As an undercover mobster, Brasco has little time for his real family (a wife and three children living in New Jersey), which is a source of tension as his wife (Anne Heche) declares, "You're becoming like them!" Brasco also realizes that any mistake he makes could cost him his and his family's lives. Family stress is combined with stress over rumors within the crime family that it has been infiltrated.

Instead of showing mob life to be fast and glamorous, the actual lifestyle is somewhat tedious and is a continuing struggle to find ways to make money. Over time, Brasco and Lefty become close friends, and Brasco realizes that when the FBI makes its arrests, Lefty will be killed by the mob for unwittingly allowing an undercover agent into the group. Brasco wrestles with the moral irony of that. *Donnie Brasco* was nominated for an Academy Award for Best Screenplay.

Questions
1. Joe Pistone was supposed to be undercover for a few months, but he ultimately did it for six years. What are the pros and cons of such an extended time undercover?
2. Given the success of Pistone's undercover operation, why do you think such a law enforcement strategy is not used more often?

References and Notes

1. Mayko, M. P. "Strike Force Retired," *Bridgeport Post-Telegram* (December 31, 1989), C1.
2. Ryan, P. J. (1994). A History of Organized Crime Control: Federal Strike Forces. In R. J. Kelly, K. Chin, & R. Schatzberg (Eds.), *Handbook of Organized Crime in the United States*. Westport, CT: Greenwood Press, pp. 333–358.
3. Jacobs, J. B. (1994). *Busting the Mob: United States v. Cosa Nostra*. New York: New York University Press, p. 15.
4. U.S. Comptroller General (1981). *Stronger Federal Effort Needed in Fight Against Organized Crime*. Washington, DC: U.S. General Accounting Office, p. 3.
5. Transactional Records Access Clearinghouse, trac.syr.edu.
6. Hickman, M. J., & Reaves, B. A. (2003). *Local Police Departments, 2000*. Washington, DC: Bureaus of Justice Statistics, see, for example, the task forces in Pennsylvania at www.justice.gov/usao/paw/task_forces.html (accessed February 24, 2014).
7. *Fort Wayne Books v. Indiana*, 109 S. Ct. 916 (1989) v at 929; *New York v. PJ Video*, 106 S. Ct. 1610 (1986).

8. *United States v. Bucci*, 582 F.3d 108 (2009).

9. *Jones v. United States*, 80 S. Ct. 725 (1960).

10. at 1206.

11. *United States v. Jackson*, 756 F.2d (9th Cir. 1985).

12. *United States v. Conley*, 4 F.3d 1200 (3d Cir. 1993) at 1207; *United States v. Golson*, No. 13-1416, F.3d, U.S. App. LEXIS 2537 (2014).

13. *United States v. Christine*, 687 F.2d 749 (3d Cir. 1982).

14. *United States v. Offices Known as 50 States Distributing*, 708 F.2d 1374 (9th Cir. 1983).

15. *United States v. Schmidt*, 947 F.2d 362 (9th Cir. 1991) at 373.

16. Peterson, M. B. (1994). Intelligence and Analysis within the Organized Crime Function. In R. J. Kelly, K. Chin, & R. Schatzberg (Eds.), *Handbook of Organized Crime in the United States*. Westport, CT: Greenwood Press, pp. 359–387.

17. Robert Blakey, G., Goldstock, R., & Rogovin, C. H. (1978). *Rackets Bureaus: Investigation and Prosecution of Organized Crime*. Washington, DC: U.S. Government Printing Office. Committee on the Office of the Attorney General (1978). *Attorney Generals' Corruption Control Units*. Raleigh, NC: National Association of Attorneys General. U.S. Department of Treasury. Financial Crimes Enforcement Network. *Combating Transnational Organized Crime*. www.fincen.gov/international/transnational/ (accessed February 24, 2014).

18. See Bergreen, L. (1994). *Capone: The Man and the Era*. New York: Simon and Schuster; Calder, J. D. (1992). Al Capone and the Internal Revenue Service: State-Sanctioned Criminology of Organized Crime. *Crime, Law and Social Change*, 17, 1–23.

19. *Attorney Generals' Corruption Control Units*, p. 10.

20. Welch, K. S. "Bushland Developer Indicted," *Amarillo Daily News (Texas)* (November 21, 2006).

21. P.L. 90–351 Sec. 801(c) 82 Stat. 211–2 (1968).

22. USA PATRIOT Act of 2001, Pub. L. No. 107–56 (October 26, 2001).

23. McCarthy, M. T. (2002). USA Patriot Act. *Harvard Journal on Legislation*, 39(Summer), 435.

24. Lichtblau, E. "Justice Department Lists Use of New Power to Fight Terror," *The New York Times* (May 21, 2003); Rivkin, D. B. Jr. "A Key Tool Salvaged?" *National Review* (February 2, 2007); Reyes, S. "Reality, Not Rhetoric on FISA," *The Washington Post* (May 30, 2007).

25. *Shingleton v. State*, 387 A.2d 1134 (1978).

26. *Nabozny v. Marshall*, 781 F.2d 83 (1986) cert. denied, 106 S. Ct. 2284.

27. *Commonwealth v. Jorabek*, 424 N.E. 2d 491 (1981).

28. P.L. 99–508 Sec. 111(a) effective 1987.

29. *United States v. Hoffa*, 436 F.2d 1246 (1970) cert. denied, 91 S. Ct. 455; *United States v. Rose*, 669 F.2d 23 (1982) cert. denied, 103 S. Ct. 63; *State v. Howard*, 679 P.2d 197 (1984); *Dorsey v. State*, 402 So.2d 1178 (1981).

30. *Wiretapping and Eavesdropping*, p. 76.

31. *Wiretapping and Eavesdropping*, p. 80.

32. 18 U.S.C. Sec. 2511 (g)(ii).

33. *Wiretapping and Eavesdropping*, p. 86.

34. Sec. 2510(16)(A).

35. Andrews, E. L. "U.S. Seeks Wiretap Software for Law Enforcement," *The New York Times* (February 12, 1994), 1.

36. Perez-Pena, R. "12 Charged in High-Tech Drug Deals," *The New York Times* (November 23, 1993), B1. "Secret Service Hits $250 Million Cell Phone Cloning Ring," *pursuitwire.com* (February 8, 2012).

37. Sec. 2511(1)(c).
38. These states include CO, FL, KS, MN, N Y, NJ, OR, PA, WI, and UT. Fishman, C. S. (1994). *Wiretapping and Eavesdropping, Cumulative Supplement.* New York: Clark, Boardman, Callaghan, p. 33; see also Stevens, G. M., & Doyle, C. (2009). *Privacy: An Overview of Federal Statutes Governing Wiretapping and Electronic Eavesdropping.* Washington, DC: Congressional Research Service.
39. Sec. 3122(b)(2).
40. *People v. Bialostok*, 80 N.Y.2d 738 (1993).
41. *United States v. Leon*, 104 S. Ct. 3405 (1984).
42. *Williams v. Poulos*, 11 F.3d 271 (1st Cir. 1993).
43. Schultz, C. D. H. (2001). Unrestricted Federal Agent: 'Carnivore' and the Need to Revise the Pen Register Statute. *Notre Dame Law Review, 76*(June), 1215–1259; Dunham, G. S. (2002). Carnivore: The FBI's E-mail Surveillance System: Devouring Criminals, Not Privacy. *Federal Communications Law Journal, 54*(May), 543; North, G. A. (2002). Carnivore in Cyberspace: Extending the Electronic Communications Privacy Act's Framework to Carnivore Surveillance. *Rutgers Computer and Technology Law Journal, 28*, 155.
44. Carrell, N. E. (2002). Spying on the Mob: United States v. Scarfo—A Constitutional Analysis. *University of Illinois Journal of Law, Technology, & Policy* (Spring), 193.
45. *United States v. Scarfo*, 180 F. Supp. 2d 572 (D.N.J. 2001).
46. *United States v. Kahn*, 415 U.S. 143 (1974).
47. *United States v. Donovan*, 97 S. Ct. 658 (1977).
48. *Dalia v. United States*, 99 S. Ct. 1682 (1979).
49. *Smith v. Maryland*, 99 S. Ct. 2577 (1979); *United States v. Knotts*, 103 S. Ct. 1081 (1983); *United States v. Karo*, 104 S. Ct. 3296 (1984).
50. *Kyllo v. United States*, 121 S. Ct. 2038 (2001).
51. at 1307.
52. Sullivan, D. A. (2002). A Bright Line in the Sky? Toward a New Fourth Amendment Search Standard for Advancing Surveillance Technology. *Arizona Law Review, 44*(Fall/Winter), 967; Horn, K. A. (2002). Privacy Versus Protection: Exploring the Boundaries of Electronic Surveillance in the Internet Age. *Fordham Urban Law Journal, 29*(August), 2233.
53. "Lack of Privacy Can Be Hindrance to Callers, Help to Law Enforcement Officials," *The Buffalo News* (June 26, 1994), 3.
54. O'Brien, J. F., & Kurins, A. (1991). *Boss of Bosses: The FBI and Paul Castellano.* New York: Simon and Schuster; Blum, H. (1993). *Gangland.* New York: Simon and Schuster; Blumenthal, R., & Miller, J. (1992). *The Gotti Tapes.* New York: Random House.
55. Herbeck, D. "Wired for Sound," *Buffalo Magazine* (September 29, 1991), 9.
56. *United States v. Clemente*, 482 F. Supp 102 (S.D.N.Y. 1989).
57. National Wiretap Commission (1976). *Electronic Surveillance Report.* Washington, DC: U.S. Government Printing Office, p. 3.
58. Schlegel, K. (1988). Life Imitating Art: Interpreting Information from Electronic Surveillance. In M. J. Palmiotto (Ed.), *Critical Issues in Criminal Investigation* (2nd ed.). Cincinnati, OH: Anderson Publishing, pp. 101–111.
59. Young, M. G. (2001). What Big Eyes and Ears You Have: A New Regime for Covert Governmental Surveillance. *Fordham Law Review, 70*(December), 1017; Roderman, W. "Is Someone Recording This? It's Harder to Find Out," *The New York Times* (April 7, 2013).
60. Salerno, J., & Rivele, S. J. (1991). *The Plumber.* New York: Knightsbridge.
61. *Lawmaster v. United States*, 114 S. Ct. 196 (1993).

62. *United States v. Foster*, 986 F.2d 541 (D.C. Cir. 1993).

63. Shawcross, T. (1995). *The War Against the Mafia*. New York: Harper; Franzese, M. (1993). *Quitting the Mob*. New York: Harper; Pryor, J. "Heroin King—Turned-Informer Hopes He Can Strike Deal," *The Buffalo News* (March 20, 1983) 13; Fried, J. P. "Ex-Mob Underboss Gets Lenient Term for Help as Witness," *The New York Times* (September 27, 1994), 1; Capeci, J. "Lucchese Crime Boss Sings," *The Daily News* (March 3, 1994) 8; Demaris, O. (1982). *The Last Mafioso*. New York: Bantam; English, T. J. (1991). *The Westies: The Irish Mob*. New York: St. Martin's; Raab, S. "Mafia Defector Says He Lost His Faith," *The New York Times* (March 2, 1994), B1.

64. Jacobs, J. B. (1994). *Busting the Mob: United States v. Cosa Nostra*. New York: New York University Press, p. 12; McShane, L. "Many in Mob Singing Like Canaries Lately," *The Buffalo News* (April 6, 1994), 3; Humphreys, A. "No Honour Among Thieves Anymore': Modern Gangsters Break Most Basic Rule of Organized Crime—Don't Be a Rat," *National Post* (Canada) (August 2, 2013).

65. Buder, L. "Gotti Is Acquitted in Conspiracy Case Involving the Mob," *The New York Times* (March 14, 1987), 1.

66. Heath, B. "FBI Allowed Informants to Commit 5,600 Crimes," *USA Today* (August 4, 2013).

67. Dershowitz, A. M. "Gotti Case Shows Flaws of Buying Witnesses," *The Buffalo News* (March 20, 1987), C3. see also Winston, A. "Cover of Darkness: S.F. Police Turned a Blind Eye to Some of the City's Most Dangerous Criminals—Who Were Also Some of Their Most Trusted Sources," *San Francisco Weekly* (May 8, 2013).

68. Bowles, P. "Brooklyn Jurors Gore Sammy the Bull," *New York Newsday* (January 6, 1993), 32.

69. Lyall, S. "Trash Hauler and Relative Killed on Long Island: Both Aided Investigators in Checking Mob Activities," *The New York Times* (August 11, 1989), B1.

70. Stern, C. "FBI Informants," *The New York Times* (February 10, 1982), 31.

71. Roane, K. R. "FBI's Glitches with Snitches in Boston," *US News & World Report* (January 31, 2000) 25, "Ex-FBI Agent Guilty of Racketeering," *CNN.com* (May 28, 2002).

72. Lehr, D., & O'Neill, G. (2000). *Black Mass: The Irish Mob, the FBI, and a Devil's Deal*. New York: Public Affairs, p. 315.

73. Schreiber, A. J. (2001). Dealing with the Devil: An Examination of the FBI's Troubled Relationship with Its Confidential Informants. *Columbia Journal of Law and Social Problems, 34*(Summer), 368.

74. Feuer, A. "A Mafia Informer Helps Investigators Charge 45," *The New York Times* (April 26, 2001). Simons, M. A. Retribution for Rats: Cooperation, Punishment, and Atonement. *Vanderbilt Law Review, 56*(January), 1.

75. Joseph, D. (1989). *Pistone, Donnie Brasco: My Undercover Life in the Mafia*. New York: Signet.

76. Wansley, L., & Stowers, C. (1989). *FBI Undercover*. New York: Pocket; McClintick, D. (1993). *Swordfish: A True Story of Ambition, Savagery and Betrayal*. New York: Pantheon.

77. McPhee, M. "192 Cops Undercover No Longer," *New York Daily News* (March 27, 2003) 22; Schmidt, M. S. "Report Highlights Special Risk of Undercover Police Work," *The New York Times* (December 1, 2009) 27.

78. Faison, S. "57 Dealers Are Seized after Sting Across U.S," *The New York Times* (December 1, 1993), B6.

79. "Union City," *USA Today* (September 27, 1990), 8.

80. DeQuine, J. "High-Tech Sting Zaps 93," *USA Today* (December 7, 1988), 3. "Car Ring Sting," *USA Today* (July 13, 1989), 3. Kertscher, T. "23 Internet Sex Arrests Made in County; Nearly One-Third of Men Caught in State's Sting Program Charged in Racine County," *Milwaukee Journal Sentinel* (December 22, 2002).

81. Herdy, A. "Web Prostitution Ring Called Global," *St Petersburg Times* (June 19, 2002).

82. U.S. Department of Justice. Office of the Inspector General (2012). A Review of ATF's Operation Fast and Furious and Related Matters. www.justice.gov/oig/reports/2012/s1209.pdf; Zaitz, L. "U.S. Justice Department to Probe ATF Sting Operations but Spares Oregon," *The Oregonian* (February 21, 2014).

83. Miller, G. I. (1987). Observations on Police Undercover Work. *Criminology, 25,* 27–46; Brown, M. F. (1985). Criminal Informants. *Journal of Police Science and Administration, 13,* 251–256.

84. "Observations on Police Undercover Work," p. 44.

85. Marx, G. T. (1982). Who Really Gets Stung? Some Issues Raised by the New Police Undercover Work. *Crime & Delinquency, 28*(April), 165–193.

86. U.S. Comptroller General (1984). *Accomplishments of FBI Undercover Operations.* Washington, DC: U.S. General Accounting Office.

87. Meddis, S. "Hunted by the Mob, He's Still Plugging Book," *USA Today* (January 17, 1989), 3.

88. Peterson, V. W. (1953). Citizens Crime Commissions. *Federal Probation Quarterly, 17*(March), 9–15; Landesco, J. (1929). *Organized Crime in Chicago Part III of the Illinois Crime Survey.* Chicago, IL: University of Chicago Press; (1991). *Pennsylvania Crime Commission, 1990 Report.* Conshohocken, PA: Pennsylvania Crime Commission.

89. *Attorney Generals' Corruption Control Units,* p. 59.

90. Rogovin, C. H., & Martens, F. T. (1994). The Role of Crime Commissions in Organized Crime Control. In R. J. Kelly, K. Chin, & R. Schatzberg (Eds.), *Handbook of Organized Crime in the United States.* Westport, CT: Greenwood Press, pp. 389–400.

91. "Police Seek Man Charged in Federal Drug Case," *Tulsa World* (June 13, 2002).

92. Knapp Commission (1973). *Report on Police Corruption.* New York: George Braziller, p. 42.

93. *Attorney Generals' Corruption Control Units,* p. 60.

94. Clark, J. "Pennsylvania Loses Its OC Watchdog: Crime Commission Is Scuttled," *Law Enforcement News* (June 30, 1994), 1.

95. www.chicagocrimecommission.org (accessed February 24, 2014).

CHAPTER 10

Prosecution Strategies

The prosecution of organized crime cases has come a long way in the last few decades.

TOOLS FOR THE PROSECUTION

The past four decades have witnessed a dramatic increase in the scope, power, and use of investigative tools to aid in the prosecution of organized crime. In fact, a primary reason behind the Valachi hearings during the 1960s was to convince Congress of the need for legislation to make it easier to investigate and prosecute organized criminals. The reason why the Department of Justice had Joseph Valachi testify publicly in 1963 was made clear by Attorney General Robert Kennedy at the beginning of the hearings:

> One major purpose in my appearing here is to seek the help of Congress in the form of additional legislation—the authority to provide immunity to witnesses in racketeering investigations; and reform and revision of the wiretapping law.[1]

Kennedy also pointed to the need for public support. "We have yet to exploit properly our most powerful asset in the battle against the rackets: an aroused, informed, and insistent public." These new laws were passed in 1968 and 1970, although it took years before they were employed to make significant organized crime cases, and before the federal prosecution response became more organized and systematic.[2]

The first law to be enacted in response to Valachi's testimony (and its repetition in the 1967 President's Crime Commission Report) was Title III of the Omnibus Crime Control and Safe Streets Act of 1968. Title III provided law enforcement agencies with the power to wiretap in a wide variety of suspected criminal activities, including organized crime. The provisions of Title III are detailed in Chapter 9. Two years later, the Organized Crime Control Act of 1970 was passed, establishing the power to "use" immunity from prosecution to compel witnesses to testify, special investigative grand juries, the witness protection program, and the ongoing criminal enterprise (RICO) statute with its special sentencing provisions for organized criminals. Both these laws had vehement defenders and critics: defenders pointing to the need for effective organized crime prosecutions and critics arguing the laws went too far and jeopardized innocent citizens.

According to the language of the Organized Crime Control Act,

> It is the purpose of this Act to seek the eradication of organized crime in the United States by strengthening the legal tools in the evidence-gathering process, by establishing new penal prohibitions, and by providing enhanced sanctions and new remedies to deal with the unlawful activities of those engaged in organized crime.[3]

The strengths and weaknesses of the provisions of these organized crime prosecution tools are examined in this chapter.

The precise method by which cases are prosecuted is generating increasing attention, as governments seek to obtain maximum output from their agencies. The traditional model dictates that police investigate, and when they are finished, the case is turned over to the prosecutor's office for adjudication. This system has never worked very well and the problems are exacerbated by the separate government hierarchies to which police and prosecutors must answer. The traditional model breeds distrust, suspicion, and poor work habits. Police feel that they work hard and are making "good" cases when they can. They become angry and frustrated when a number of their "good" cases are declined for prosecution or, if adjudicated, the police officers are treated poorly by the prosecution in court.

However, prosecutors often complain about the lack of "good" cases and what they consider to be shoddy police work. The result is each side blaming the other for the same problem. A failure to communicate at the beginning of an investigation—and while the investigation is in progress—is at the root of most of this mutual interagency distrust. The historical problem of parallel government bureaucracies for police and prosecutors does not help the situation, but a solution has been found. The establishment of police-prosecutor "teams" has been attempted in a number of jurisdictions and works extremely well. The reasons are obvious: investigative and prosecution priorities are agreed upon before the investigation begins, and police and prosecutors consult regularly with each other during the investigation about the types of evidence needed, use of informants, warrants, and other investigative issues. By the time a case is at the arrest stage, the prosecutor and investigator have been communicating daily for weeks or months, eliminating "surprises" in the courtroom later on. Examples of such police-prosecutor teams have included the Oriental Gang

Unit in the New York City Police Department and the Multnomah County Organized Crime/Narcotics Task Force in Oregon.[4] FBI agents and U.S. Attorney's offices often work cases in similar fashion. Keys to the success of these programs include the fact that the police and prosecutor work in "physical proximity" and have "daily access" to each other. Investigators always work with the same prosecutors, and "vertical prosecution is the general rule."[5] Developing a sense of ownership over a case from the start also breeds a greater sense of responsibility for the outcome from all parties involved. Indeed, much can be done in realigning the historical working relationships between law enforcement and prosecution.[6]

Six important prosecution tools created since 1970 are assessed in this chapter: the provision for special grand juries, use of immunity for witnesses, the witness protection program, the provision for extended penalties for crimes committed by continuing criminal enterprises, the Bank Secrecy Act, and money laundering provisions in organized crime prosecutions.

Special Grand Juries

Title I of the Organized Crime Control Act provided the first prosecution tool intended to increase the number and success of organized crime prosecutions. Provision for a "special grand jury" was designed to facilitate the investigation of organized crime across multiple jurisdictions.

According to the act, special grand juries are to be called at least every 18 months in federal judicial districts of four million or more population. In addition, these grand juries can be called by special request of the prosecutor. The life of these grand juries may be extended up to 36 months.

Similar to traditional grand juries, these special grand juries hold secret proceedings where the prosecutor presents evidence to establish probable cause for indictment. Special grand juries have the added powers of issuing a public report at the end of their term that describes organized crime conditions or official corruption in the area, and they also can conduct continuing investigations along with police. It is due to these added functions that special grand juries are sometimes called "investigating grand juries." Title I appears to guarantee citizens the right to have their allegations heard by a federal grand jury.[7] There have been very few court challenges to this notion, but Title I appears to remove the prosecutor's unfettered discretion in deciding whether to present information to a grand jury. Therefore, special grand jury provisions serve to encourage public participation and give them a degree of control over the prosecution process.[8]

Some states have since established investigating grand juries to deal with multicounty crimes in the same manner that special grand juries on the federal level are directed primarily at multistate crimes. The President's Commission on Organized Crime believed that all states should establish legal authority for statewide grand juries.[9] Although some states already have laws authorizing a statewide grand jury, others face resistance from local district attorneys who do not wish to relinquish prosecutorial authority for crimes committed in their jurisdictions.

There has been much debate over the merits of special grand juries. Proponents argue that such broad investigative powers are necessary to prosecute organized crime successfully when crimes often span several jurisdictions. In addition, special grand juries may be better insulated from local political pressures to avoid or go after certain targets, unlike county grand juries. Although there is little information publicly available on the actual workings of special grand juries due to the Federal Rules of Criminal Procedure (which require secrecy), a special grand jury was convened to investigate alleged energy and financial crimes by Enron Corporation in 2002, and these special grand juries could be used to investigate the often complex wrongdoing that occurs among public officials, organized crime, and sometimes legitimate businesses as well.[10]

Critics of special grand juries, however, cite the grand jury's potential for use as harassment against groups based on their political leanings and the potential for their use to "invent" a case rather than determining if one already exists. Both advocates and critics of special grand juries can cite case examples to demonstrate the productive use or, alternatively, the misuse of the broad powers of this prosecution tool.[11]

As a general rule, prosecutors are not required to present exculpatory evidence to a grand jury, and this has been criticized. Courts have held that "the function of a grand jury is investigative. Its proceedings are not adversary in nature, but rather consist of inquiries conducted by laymen without resort to the technicalities of trial procedure."[12] The failure to present evidence that "clearly negates the target's guilt" is abuse of a prosecutor's discretion.[13] In cases in which a defendant alleges prosecutorial abuse of the grand jury, the court reviews the evidence brought to light by the defendant to see if it directly negates "any inference of guilt."[14] In a Virginia drug paraphernalia case, the defendant argued that the prosecutor's failure to present testimony regarding the significantly less carcinogenic attributes of Syrian or Oriental water pipes constituted grand jury abuse by the prosecutor. The court found that this information "hardly serves to exculpate" the defendant. The efficacy of the water pipe in filtering tobacco smoke "bears little, if any, relationship to the question whether probable cause existed to believe that defendants were engaged in the manufacture, importation, distribution, or sale of drug paraphernalia."[15] Therefore, a claim of grand jury abuse must bear directly on the crime alleged and the suspect's responsibility for it.

Unfortunately, there has been no objective evaluation of benefits (in terms of multijurisdiction organized crime prosecutions) versus costs (in terms of any harassment, unwarranted privacy invasions, or Fifth Amendment abuses) of investigative grand juries. Such an evaluation would make the debate over special grand juries more than a matter of discussing anecdotal case examples and possibilities.

It is somewhat ironic, but it is interesting to note that the original purpose of grand juries was to protect citizens from arbitrary accusations by the government. Now, however, the reverse is true. Grand juries generally operate as a tool for the prosecution rather than as a protective device for the accused. This has come about primarily through the lack of representation of the accused before grand juries and the wide latitude given prosecutors in calling witnesses and in their use of evidence.[16] The grand jury was invented in England, where it has since been abolished. In the United States, preliminary hearings before a judge are often used to establish probable cause in place of a grand jury. Nevertheless, investigative grand juries can function much like the citizens commissions discussed in Chapter 9, with the added benefit of being able to prosecute those cases they discover.

Witness Immunity

The second prosecution tool, the ability to provide witnesses with immunity, was granted to federal law enforcement agencies by Title II of the Organized Crime Control Act of 1970. Witnesses to organized crime are often reluctant to testify about their knowledge either because of fear of becoming involved, or because of an unwillingness to incriminate themselves. The Organized Crime Control Act of 1970 permits federal prosecutors to grant witnesses immunity from prosecution in exchange for testimony. The purpose, of course, is to make it easier to prosecute higher echelon criminals through the testimony of less important figures.

The act provides for *use immunity*, which prohibits the use of evidence against a witness obtained through that witness's compelled testimony or any information derived directly or indirectly from such testimony. The only exception to this prohibition is prosecution for perjury or false statements given while under immunity. Despite these safeguards, use immunity does not protect a witness from being prosecuted based on evidence obtained independently of the compelled testimony. Prior to 1970, only transactional immunity was permitted at the federal level. Transactional immunity prohibited any prosecution of a witness, whether or not the evidence was derived from the immunized testimony. As a result, use immunity is a more powerful prosecution tool than transactional immunity. See Figure 10.1.

FIGURE 10.1 Reputed underworld financier Meyer Lansky was granted immunity by a grand jury in 1975, and permitted to testify for short periods of time due to health problems. Here Lansky is shown taking a break from giving a deposition in 1982. *AP Photo/Kathy Willens*

The allowance for independent evidence to be admitted in court through use immunity has caused concern among some observers that such an application of immunized testimony may violate the Fifth Amendment of the U.S. Constitution, which states, in part, "... nor shall [a person] be compelled in any criminal cases to be a witness against himself." This is especially important in cases in which testimony made under a federal grant of immunity exposes a person to prosecution under state laws. The U.S. Supreme Court dealt with this issue in *Malloy v. Hogan*, holding that the Fifth Amendment protection against self-incrimination is applicable to the states as a matter of due process for all citizens, guaranteed by the Fourteenth Amendment.[17] As a result, testimony given under a grant of immunity may not be used for criminal prosecution in another jurisdiction.

Use immunity has been criticized on other grounds as well. The extraction of forced testimony through the use of immunity has been questioned in the dissenting opinions of such U.S. Supreme Court cases as *Kastigar v. United States* and *Lefkowitz v. Cunningham*.[18] These criticisms include the fear that immunity may be provided by prosecutors as a mere "fishing expedition" to obtain information without any specific idea of the individuals or crimes suspected. In addition, independently derived evidence can be used against an immunized witness, and the burden to prove this independence from the compelled testimony is on the prosecutor. The problem remains that an overzealous prosecutor might use immunized testimony improperly in a subsequent case without any systematic oversight of his actions. As Block and Chambliss have pointed out, "one can easily imagine how difficult a time a defendant would have proving evidence was tainted.[19]

Third, immunity provides no protection from civil suits for witnesses who incriminate themselves. Therefore, a person may be held liable for damages and compensation from an injured party, even though no criminal prosecution can result. This might occur in cases in which an immunized witness reveals his involvement in infiltrating a legitimate business or harming a person, and the victim seeks compensation for losses suffered.

Fourth, the use of any testimony that is the result of "inducements" is suspect. Because immunized testimony is coerced, inasmuch as a defendant cannot refuse to testify after a grant of immunity without being held in contempt of court and imprisoned, such testimony is tainted, which makes it less convincing to judges or juries in criminal prosecutions. It can also lead to erroneous convictions of wrongfully accused defendants, when false testimony made by an immunized witness is taken as fact by prosecutors, judges, or juries.

However, witness immunity has many defenders in the criminal justice system. It has been argued that for conspiratorial crimes characteristic of organized crime, there are often few alternatives to obtaining evidence of a conspiracy from reluctant witnesses. As Robert Rhodes has observed, many prosecutors see immunity as a vital prosecution tool because "immunity forces testimony without forcing incriminating statements."[20]

It can also be argued that procedural safeguards exist to ensure that immunized testimony is not either self-serving to the witness or false. First, the rules of criminal procedure, which include such provisions as cross-examination of witnesses at trial and the corroboration of certain types of evidence, serve as a check on the accuracy of immunized testimony. Second, the Organized Crime Control Act requires that the need for immunity be demonstrated to the U.S. Attorney General prior to its being granted, indicating that the testimony is "necessary to the public interest" and that the information cannot be obtained voluntarily from the individual. Third, the law permits perjury prosecutions in cases in which the immunized witness is found to have lied.

It can be seen, therefore, that there are arguments on both sides regarding the provision of use immunity. However, there is no objective empirical evidence to offer an indication of relative costs (in terms of unprosecuted crimes and abuses of immunity) versus benefits (convictions of upper echelon organized crime figures). If such information were assembled, a more complete picture would emerge of the utility of witness immunity in balancing the interests of the public and the interests of the witness.

Witness Protection Program

A third significant prosecution tool included in the Organized Crime Control Act was Title V, which authorized the U.S. Attorney General to provide security to government witnesses in organized crime cases. This authorization led to the establishment of the witness protection program, also known as the Witness Security Program (WITSEC).

A prosecuting attorney who believes that a witness's life will be in danger due to testimony in an organized crime proceeding can request admission of the witness to WITSEC. This request is made to the U.S. Justice Department, which determines whether the witness will be protected based on recommendations of the FBI, the appropriate division of the Justice Department, and the U.S. Marshals Service. Once a witness is admitted to the program, a new identity is provided, complete with a new birth certificate and social security number. The witness is relocated to an area far from the target of the testimony, and he or she is provided a subsistence allowance and other help until the relocated witness can be self-supporting. These services and supervision are provided by the U.S. Marshals Service.

When the program first began, it was estimated that 25 to 50 witnesses would be relocated each year at a cost of less than $1 million. In its first 13 years, however, more than 4,400 witnesses and 8,000 family members entered the program. The annual cost exceeded $25 million.[21] Clearly, the program has been utilized frequently in organized crime prosecutions. As Gerald Shur, the founder of the program, indicated, one witness per week was sent to WITSEC in 1970, but this increased to nearly 500 per year within the next six years.[22]

Protecting witnesses is more difficult than it may appear. In some cases, the witness's parents or siblings are threatened or harmed in an effort to intimidate the protected witness. The wives and children who are relocated with the witness suffer because they must give up everything and move to a new place with a new identity without their extended family. As Gerald Shur observed from his experience running the WITSEC program for many years, "This was a program of last resort. No matter how much we tried to do to make the transition easy, being relocated was always a painful event—a move that you made only because you knew it was the only way to stay alive."[23] The three primary problems faced by those in the WITSEC program are money, secrecy, and home.

1. **Never enough money**—Many offenders were spendthrifts who made a lot of money and spent it quickly. They did not know how to budget money, have the discipline to work a 9 to 5 job, or save money for the long term. These skills had to be learned.

2. **Perpetual secrecy**—Even though offenders were told not to tell anyone where they were, there was a tendency to tell parents or a sibling, and this information eventually leaked and threatened the security of the person in the program.
3. **Never going home**—There was an overwhelming desire to return home at some point to see family, friends, and the old neighborhood. The risk of doing this is very high, and the WITSEC program must work very hard to convince offenders of the need to leave the past behind forever.

These three aspects of human nature make the WITSEC program very difficult to manage because of the need to be constantly vigilant in protecting witnesses and their families from retaliation and from their own desires to return to the "way things were," which can never happen.[24]

The U.S. General Accounting Office (GAO) conducted an evaluation of the performance of the witness protection program, comparing its costs (as measured by relocations and crimes committed by witnesses while in the program) to its benefits (successful prosecutions of high-level organized criminals). The benefits of the program were evaluated by reviewing 220 cases that involved the testimony of protected witnesses. This sample of 220 included all available cases involving witnesses admitted into the program during a single year. It was found that 75% of the defendants (965 of 1,283) who were subjects of the testimony of protected witnesses were found guilty; 84% of these were sentenced to prison for a median term of 4.4 years. Of those defendants identified as "ringleaders" ($N = 150$), 88% were convicted with a median sentence of 11.2 years. It was also discovered that nearly one-half of these cases involved narcotics (32%) or murder or murder conspiracy (13%) charges. The targets of these prosecutions were most often "various" organized criminal groups (43%), traditional organized crime groups (27%), or single criminal acts by an individual or group (15%). The remaining cases (15%) involved crimes by public officials, motorcycle gangs, union officials, prison gangs, or white-collar professionals. In recent years, the witness protection program has been used in terrorism cases as well.[25]

The relative importance of these prosecutions can be best judged when they are compared to federal prosecutions of organized crime cases that do not involve protected witnesses. The GAO found that twice as many defendants are sentenced to two years or more in prison in cases involving protected witnesses than in other organized crime prosecutions. In Canada, a more modest program led police officials to believe it was a factor in preventing insiders from coming forward.[26] As a result, many other countries have begun witness protection programs. The United Nations Convention against Transnational Organized Crime, now ratified by 179 countries, requires that each participating country "shall take appropriate measures within its means to provide effective protection from potential retaliation or intimidation of witnesses in criminal proceedings who give testimony (related to organized crime)."[27] This protection is to include their relatives and victims, and it must involve physical protection, relocation where feasible, and nondisclosure of identity information. The UN Convention has prompted many countries to begin their own versions of witness protection programs in order to become more effective in prosecuting cases of transnational organized crime.[28] In the United States, California established a modest witness protection program of its own in 1998 to help local police departments in cases involving gang intimidation. In a single year, the program spent $2 million to relocate more than 100 witnesses and family members, but it produced nearly 500 convictions.[29] Other jurisdictions have been encouraged to develop their own programs to prevent gang- and drug-related witness intimidation.[30]

Costs of the witness protection program involve both the cost of relocation and assistance provided to these witnesses and the possibility that protected witnesses who are criminals may commit new crimes after being relocated. The GAO evaluation found that the typical protected witness entering the program had been arrested more than seven times. More than half of these arrests were for violent crimes. After admission to the program, the typical protected witness was arrested twice, and less than one-third of these arrests were for violent crimes. It appears, therefore, that protected witnesses engage in fewer crimes and fewer serious crimes after entering the program. As the GAO observed, however, these before-and-after comparisons may be caused by differences in the length of time they have been in the program.

> The observation that protected witnesses were arrested more often and charged with more serious crimes before they entered the program when compared with post-program arrests data may be almost entirely caused by differences in the pre- and post-program observation periods. For example, many witnesses had criminal histories of 10 years or more before they entered the program, while the average post-program observation period for the witnesses sampled was only about 3.5 years.[31]

As a result, before-and-after differences may simply be due to the fact that the follow-up of witnesses in the program was not long enough to compare fairly with their previous criminal behavior. If one looks at the recidivism rate, however, it is possible to determine what percentage of protected witnesses are arrested for new crimes after their relocation.

The GAO examined the criminal activity of 365 protected witnesses admitted into the program. It was found that just over 21% were arrested within the next two years. A study conducted by the U.S. Marshals Service, which administers the program, found a 10% recidivism rate.[32] Therefore, benefits of the witness protection program in making possible significant organized crime prosecutions must be weighed against the more than $25 million annual cost of the program and the recidivism rate of protected witnesses. One woman sued the federal government after her brother was killed, apparently by a witness relocated to her city.[33] Others have complained of shoddy treatment by the government, problems with their new identities, and their continued safety.[34] As the GAO concluded, "program benefits do not come without costs." Today, there are more than 16,000 witnesses and family members in the WITSEC program. About 10 new witnesses enter every month.[32]

A comparison of similar cases, some employing protected witnesses with others that do not, would provide an objective indication of the cost-benefit of the witness protection program, but this has yet to be done. In pragmatic terms, the high cost of the program has brought more attention in recent years to "graduating" protected witnesses from the program once they are set up in a new community, new job, and new identity. A "significant problem" is how to "ease out" certain witnesses, "especially those who are older and who never held a legitimate job."[35] The large number of WITSEC informants who are career criminals makes this a daunting task. Job training and working for a living wage are not easy activities for people who have no experience of ever doing it before and whose youth has passed. As noted earlier, it is likewise difficult not to "go home again" when that is the only place you've ever lived. As a result, the witness protection program requires substantial motivation on the part of accepted witnesses to change their lives completely, a decision that is often difficult to carry out.

Racketeer Influenced and Corrupt Organizations (RICO)

A fourth important prosecution tool was included as part of the Organized Crime Control Act (1970). Title IX of the act, called "Racketeer Influenced and Corrupt Organizations," makes it unlawful to acquire, operate, or receive income from an enterprise through a pattern of racketeering activity. This means that any individual or group (an "enterprise") who commits two or more indictable offenses ("racketeering activity") within a 10-year period (a "pattern") is subject to 20 years' imprisonment, fines up to $25,000, and forfeiture of any interest in the enterprise, as well as civil damages and dissolution of the enterprise itself.[36]

Although this statute was designed to combat organized crime infiltration of legitimate businesses, it has since been employed to prosecute criminal activities by a county sheriff's department, the Philadelphia traffic court, abortion protesters, a state tax bureau, the Tennessee governor's office, schools, and the Louisiana Department of Agriculture.[37] Clearly, the use of RICO has been extended to encompass all forms of organized and white-collar crime.[38] The list of crimes that can be used as predicate offenses under RICO is expansive and includes most felonies, including immigration crimes, money laundering, and mailing obscene materials, among many others.[39] Each of the predicate offenses must have a relationship to, and a continuity of, the enterprise. Thus, they need not be related to each other as long as they each had a common purpose of furthering the enterprise.

Because RICO targets continuous activities that constitute a "pattern," sporadic activity or "two isolated acts of racketeering do not constitute a pattern."[40] Although the pattern requires at least two crimes within 10 years of each other, simply proving two acts may not be adequate for a RICO case if they cannot be connected as part of an ongoing operation or enterprise.[41]

A U.S. Supreme Court case, *United States v. Turkette*, made it clear that the provisions of RICO encompass the crimes of wholly illegitimate enterprises, as well as crimes committed by otherwise legitimate businesses or government agencies.[42] As a result, any enterprise committing two or more felonies within a 10-year period (excluding any period of imprisonment) is subject to prosecution under RICO. Civil penalties allow for any injured party to recover threefold the damages sustained. Upon conviction, the U.S. Attorney General can seize all property and assets of the illegal enterprise.

The application of RICO was extended further in *Sedima v. Imrex Co.*[40] The case arose from a civil suit between two corporations engaged in a joint venture. Sedima believed it was being cheated by Imrex through an overbilling scheme. Sedima sued Imrex for mail and wire fraud (as the two predicate acts required to establish a "pattern" of racketeering activity under RICO). Sedima claimed injury of at least $175,000 from the overbilling and sought treble damages and attorneys' fees.

The issues faced by the U.S. Supreme Court were two: (1) whether the predicate acts required for a RICO prosecution had to be prior (i.e., preexisting) criminal convictions and (2) whether simple monetary loss is sufficient to qualify as a "racketeering injury" to justify a RICO suit. In both cases, the court favored broad application of RICO provisions.

The court held that prior criminal convictions are not required for a RICO suit. According to the court, the "language of RICO gives no obvious indication that a civil action can proceed only after a criminal conviction." A five-justice majority held that "the word 'conviction' does not appear in any relevant portion of the statute" so predicate offenses need not be established prior to the suit filed under RICO.

> In sum, we can find no support in the statute's history, its language, or
> considerations of policy for a requirement that a private treble damages
> action under [RICO] can proceed only against a defendant who has already
> been criminally convicted. To the contrary, every indication is that no such
> requirement exists. Accordingly, the fact that Imrex and the individual
> defendants have not been convicted under RICO or the federal mail and wire
> fraud statutes does not bar Sedima's action.[43]

Therefore, as long as two criminal acts are proved in the current case, a prior
record is not required to establish the pattern required for RICO. The court also
held that monetary loss is sufficient "racketeering injury" to qualify for prosecution under RICO. "Racketeering activity" under the law's provisions "consists
of no more and no less than commission of a predicate act." The majority held,
therefore, that "we are initially doubtful about the requirement of a 'racketeering injury' separate from the harm from the predicate acts." The majority reading of the statute "belies any such requirement."

This case continued the broad application of RICO to all forms of organized
crime, whether committed by professional criminals or by corporations.
According to the U.S. Supreme Court,

> This less restrictive reading is amply supported by our prior cases and the
> general principles surrounding this statute. RICO is to be read broadly. This is
> the lesson not only of Congress' self-consciously expansive language and
> overall approach, but also of its express admonition that RICO is to "be
> liberally construed to effectuate its remedial purposes."[44]

It can be seen that the Supreme Court relied heavily on the legislative history of
the law to assess congressional intent behind it.

A four-justice dissent argued that Congress did not intend the RICO provisions
to apply to "garden variety frauds," such as those in the *Sedima* case. They
claimed that remedies under state law are adequate in such cases and that
the severe penalties available under RICO encourage spurious suits.

> [L]itigants, lured by the prospect of treble damages and attorney's fees, have
> a strong incentive to invoke RICO's provisions whenever they can allege in
> good faith two instances of mail or wire fraud. Then the defendant, facing
> tremendous financial exposure in addition to the threat of being labelled a
> "racketeer," will have a strong interest in settling the dispute.[45]

Given the findings in the *Turkette* and *Sedima* cases, court interpretation of the
RICO provisions is quite broad. Regardless of how one reads original congressional intent, the Supreme Court has found it to apply to both legitimate and
illegal organizations without predicate convictions and involving only monetary losses. Therefore, the scope of allowable prosecutions of organized crime

under RICO is expansive and is the most potent weapon in the prosecutor's organized crime control repertoire. In a 2009 case, the defendant was charged in connection with a series of bank thefts that were allegedly conducted by a group that was loosely organized and did not appear to have had a leader or hierarchy. The defendant argued that the RICO statute should not apply to him because there was no structural hierarchy distinct from the charged crimes. The U.S. Supreme Court held that although RICO requires an "enterprise," a "structure" is not required because RICO broadly encompasses any group of individuals who are associated, and it is not limited to "business-like entities." Three structural features are necessary for an enterprise under RICO: (1) a purpose, (2) relationships among those associated with the enterprise, and (3) sufficient longevity to permit pursuit of the purpose. However, additional structural features such as hierarchy or a chain of command are not required.[46]

Subsequent challenges at the U.S. Court of Appeals have upheld the broad use of RICO. In one case, a challenge was denied regarding the existence of a demonstrated pattern in the use of extortion and fraud to obtain money from a labor union, and in another case it was held that successive RICO prosecutions do not violate double jeopardy unless the racketeering enterprise and the pattern of racketeering elements were the same in both prosecutions. If the scope of the activities charged is different, a second RICO prosecution can occur.[47]

RICO laws that apply to "patterns" of "racketeering activity" that violate state laws have been passed in 24 states. The President's Commission on Organized Crime recommended that states pass RICO laws for violations that do not involve federal laws, such as state beverage control or tax laws. State-level RICO laws have been used infrequently thus far, much in the same way the federal RICO law was little used in its first 10 years of existence.[48] Reasons for nonusage of the federal RICO law for nearly a decade after it was passed were subjects of a historical study by James Calder. He found three primary reasons that had nothing to do with the complex and conceptual nature of the RICO statute compared to traditional criminal laws. Instead he found a declining interest in organized crime by Presidents Nixon, Ford, and Carter through the 1970s; a rapid turnover of attorneys general, allowing the FBI and U.S. attorneys to continue with their past patterns of handling gambling and drugs cases; and the changeover within the FBI when its director J. Edgar Hoover died in 1972, after heading the bureau since 1924.[49]

Since then, the application of the RICO statute has been expansive. Consider its use in the following cases:

- The former governor of Louisiana, Edwin Edwards, and several others were convicted under RICO for various schemes to make money from Louisiana's riverboat gambling licensing process by exploiting Edwards's ability to influence who would receive license approval.[50]

- The president of the Outlaws Motorcycle Club was convicted under RICO for conspiracy to distribute illegal drugs, assaulting members of another motorcycle club, and conspiring to kill members of the Hell's Angels. A Texas leader of the Latin Kings street gang was similarly convicted under RICO.[51]
- A member of a Charlestown-based group in Massachusetts was convicted under RICO for orchestrating a computer theft ring composed of UPS drivers and for receiving unauthorized health care benefits through a teamster's local union.[52]
- A federal judge ruled that the Los Angeles Police Department could be sued under RICO by people claiming that corrupt officers from the Rampart Station had violated their civil rights through unlawful beatings, shootings, and framing innocent people.[53]
- Members of the Aryan Brotherhood, a white supremacist gang that espouses separatism, were convicted on RICO charges for multiple crimes, including murder, committed as part of the group's activities.[54]

These cases illustrate the wide variety of situations in which RICO can be employed when a pattern of underlying criminal conduct can be proven. Indeed, it has been argued that RICO has extended beyond its original intended target, but at the same time there are calls for RICO to expand to cover even more crimes, such as cybercrime.[55]

Another racketeering statute available to federal prosecutors is the Continuing Criminal Enterprise (CCE) law (1987), which is limited to drug traffickers. CCE makes it a crime to engage in a conspiracy to commit at least three related violations of felony drug laws with five or more persons. To be convicted, the offender must be the organizer, manager, or supervisor of the continuing operation and receiving substantial income or property from it. The CCE law provides for mandatory minimum sentences of 20 years for first violations, fines up to $2 million, and forfeiture of profits and any interest in the enterprise. In many ways, the CCE statute resembles a RICO law for drug law violations.

Table 10.1 summarizes lead charges in federal organized crime prosecutions from 2005 to 2013. It can be seen from Table 10.1 that federal organized crime cases (with the seven different lead charges displayed) are dominated by drug cases. Racketeering (RICO) cases comprise only about 1% of prosecutions, extortion (3%), and money laundering (2%) of the nearly 25,000 lead charges reported annually. Drug offenses comprise the major portion of the federal organized crime prosecution effort in organized crime–related cases. Given the data presented from 2005 to 2013, there also appear to be only small differences in the nature of lead charges in the different years, although there has been a slight decline in the total number of prosecutions over years, with the exception of extortion. Extortion as a lead charge rose from 494 federal prosecutions in 2005 to 835 in 2013, a 90% increase over that period.

Table 10.1 Lead Charges in Federal Organized Crime Prosecutions

Lead Charges in Federal Prosecutions	2005	2010	2013
21 USC 0841—drugs/prohibited acts	15,302	14,449	11,829
21 USC 0846—drugs/conspiracy	10,919	9,490	10,784
18 USC 1951—interfere with commerce threats/violence (extortion)	494	655	835
18 USC 1956—laundering of monetary instrument (money laundering)	601	364	415
18 USC 1962—racketeering-prohibited acts (RICO cases)	258	287	221
21 USC 0963—drugs/conspiracy in export/import	401	258	192
21 USC 0848—drugs/continuing criminal enterprise	46	55	16
Total—all lead charges reported	28,021	25,608	24,292

Compiled from Transactional Records Clearinghouse at trac.syr.edu (lead charges in all cases are not reported by the federal government, so totals do not represent all federal cases brought under these statutes).

Because the evidence needed to prosecute a RICO or CCE case is greater, given the multiple elements that must be proven (i.e., multiple felonies and the need to show evidence of a continuing enterprise), comparatively fewer cases are prosecuted under these statutes. Instead, many more cases are brought under traditional conspiracy and other statutes that allege specific individual offenses (e.g., drugs, money laundering, extortion).

All federal organized crime prosecutions in the United States can be examined to assess trends over time. Table 10.2 presents data trends since 1995 to show how cases progress from referral for prosecution to conviction. These data indicate a drop in the number of prosecutions under the federal organized crime program filed between 1995 and 2013, as has the percentage of cases prosecuted (from all those cases referred from prosecution) from 66% to 56%. The percentage of convictions earned from prosecuted cases increased from 84% to 89%, as has the percentage of those convicted sentenced to prison, increasing substantially from 54% to 87% over the 18-year period. This suggests that potential cases are being more carefully reviewed at the prosecution stage, resulting in more serious cases being brought more successfully, reflected in higher conviction and imprisonment rates. Specific sentence lengths are discussed in Chapter 12.

Table 10.2 All Federal Organized Crime Prosecutions[a]

Organized Crime Cases	1995	2000	2005	2010	2013
Prosecutions filed	965	765	646	572	390
Percent prosecuted (of cases referred for prosecution)	66%	64%	68%	64%	56%
Percent of convictions (of cases prosecuted)	84%	86%	84%	87%	89%
Percent sentenced to prison (of those convicted)	54%	77%	72%	86%	87%

[a]Transactional Records Clearinghouse at trac.syr.edu. Includes violations of statutes relating to gambling, extortion, and alcoholic beverages; infiltration of legitimate business by organized crime; and related organized crime offenses under the federal organized crime program.

It is also possible to see locations where organized crime is the largest problem by looking at the locations of federal prosecutions over time. Figure 10.2 summarizes all federal organized crime prosecutions that resulted in convictions from 2008 to 2013 in the most active districts where these cases occurred. The bar graph shows the geographic location of where the most convictions occurred (in the federal judicial district where the crimes took place).

The top two locations, Brooklyn (including Queens and Long Island) and Manhattan in New York City, accounted for a total of 793 federal organized crime convictions during this period, a number almost as large as the next eight largest

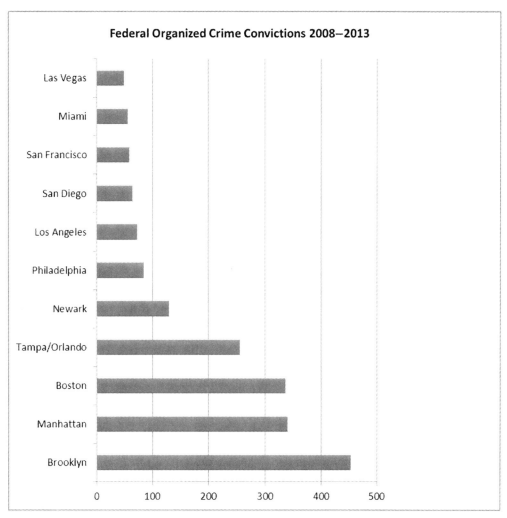

FIGURE 10.2 Top 11 locations for federal organized crime convictions (2008-2013). Compiled from Transactional Records Clearinghouse at trac.syr.edu.

locations combined. It can also be seen that traditional northeastern organized crime locations, such as Boston, Newark, and Philadelphia, have been matched by significant organized crime operations in Florida and California. Taken together, the top 11 locations accounted for nearly two-thirds of all the federal organized crime convictions in the United States during the five-year period from 2008 to 2013.

CRITICAL THINKING EXERCISE 10.1

Using the information provided in this chapter, read the following scenario and respond to the questions that follow. Explain your rationale, given your knowledge of current law and policy.

The Case of Enough Evidence

You are a federal prosecutor faced with the case of a career criminal named "Clyde." Clyde is charged with loansharking and threatening people who fall behind on their payments. One of his neighbors, "Fifi," has information about Clyde selling stolen property that might help convict Clyde, but she is afraid to testify given Clyde's reputation for threats. Fifi also has a checkered past, with a few arrests for receiving stolen property. The only other evidence against Clyde is from Vinnie, whom he threatened for nonpayment of a gambling debt, but Vinnie is a compulsive gambler with a prior record, he is nervous, and he could skip town before trial.

Critical Thinking Questions

1. Do you have enough facts to prove a RICO violation against Clyde?
2. If you had time to gather additional evidence, what would you look for?
3. If you were a juror, would you convict Clyde given the facts provided?

Bank Secrecy Act

The Bank Secrecy Act (1970) is a fifth prosecution tool, which is designed to make it difficult to "launder" illicitly obtained cash through legitimate channels. To accomplish this, the law established three primary requirements for banks and individuals.

First, the act requires that banks must file a Currency Transaction Report (CTR) for every deposit, withdrawal, or exchange of funds greater than $10,000. Second, a Currency or Monetary Instruments Report (CMIR) must be filed with the U.S. Customs Service if more than $10,000 in cash or other monetary instruments (e.g., personal or cashier's check, etc.) leaves or enters the United States. Third, a citizen holding bank accounts in foreign countries must declare them on his or her federal tax return. Violation of these provisions can result in criminal fines up to $500,000, as well as civil remedies by the Department of the Treasury. The U.S. Treasury Department is responsible for enforcing these provisions through the Internal Revenue Service, Customs Service, Comptroller of the Currency, Federal Reserve System, Federal Deposit Insurance Corporation,

Federal Home Loan Bank Board, National Credit Union Administration, and Securities and Exchange Commission.

The U.S. General Accounting Office conducted an examination of the effectiveness of this enforcement effort. The GAO found that the Treasury Department did not "play an active role" in administering the Bank Secrecy Act until the Bank of Boston pleaded guilty to criminal violations of the act. The number of civil reviews for compliance increased to 76 in that year, most resulting from "voluntary admission of possible noncompliance" by banks and other financial institutions. This is a dramatic increase in enforcement, as civil penalties totaling $800,000 from only seven financial institutions were imposed during the first 15 years of the act. By 1990, however, the IRS Criminal Investigation Division had conducted investigations that resulted in more than 1,000 convictions in only three years for crimes related to money laundering.[56] The Customs Service was similarly active in conducting investigations and making cases.

The GAO evaluation found that the potential of the Bank Secrecy Act to prevent laundering of illicit funds had not yet been realized. It found that the Treasury Department "lacks current and specific information about the way various reporting agencies are handling their duties."[56] One problem is the growing volume of CTRs being filed. In a single year, nine million CTRs were filed, reporting more than $417 billion in currency transactions.[57] Clearly, this intimidating volume of information works against its being used efficiently. Indeed, law enforcement agencies have been criticized for not exploiting CTR information. "The large volume of reports has made meaningful analysis difficult."[58]

The Financial Crime Enforcement Network (FinCEN) was established in 1990 in the Department of the Treasury to support law enforcement agencies in identifying money laundering activity. With a staff of 200, FinCEN provides strategic analysis and disseminates financial data to federal, state, local, and foreign law enforcement agencies.[59] This agency helps traditional law enforcement agencies to keep abreast of money laundering techniques and operations in their area.

The Bank Secrecy Act was subsequently amended to make it illegal to make multiple cash transactions just under $10,000 in an effort to "willfully" avoid the CTR requirement. The U.S. Supreme Court held that people who have multiple cash transactions with banks under $10,000 each cannot be convicted of violating the Bank Secrecy Act "without proof that they knew such action is illegal."[60]

The ability of the Bank Secrecy Act to detect illegal movement of cash has been demonstrated in actual cases where such detection was made a priority. For example, Maria Torres was stopped by Customs officers at the Los Angeles Airport prior to boarding a plane for Vancouver, Canada. She was interviewed as part of a routine "outbound currency program" because she appeared to be "weighted down" with bulky clothes and she was in a hurry. Torres told Customs she was carrying about $3,000. A search discovered over $146,000 in U.S. currency in the pockets of her jumpsuit, in her purse, and in a plastic bag she was carrying. She was convicted of failing to file a CMIR, fined $5,000, and given five years' probation. The currency she was carrying was forfeited to the government.[60]

At the same time vigilance is required, because cases continue to occur in which there is a failure to follow legal provisions. In one case, a New York Check Cashing Company and its owner pleaded guilty to a $19 million scheme in which checks to be cashed at the company were written on accounts of shell corporations that appeared to be health-care related, but in fact, the corporations did no legitimate business at all. The shell corporations and their bank accounts on which the checks were written were in the names of foreign nationals, many of whom were no longer in the United States. The check-cashing company never obtained any identification documents or information from those individuals, and it filed false currency transaction reports.[61] On a larger scale, major corporations have been subject to enforcement actions for similar conduct. Citigroup bank was subject to an enforcement action for failure to monitor cash transactions for potentially suspicious activity. HSBC bank agreed to a record $1.92 billion deal with authorities to settle accusations that it transferred billions of dollars for nations like Iran and enabled Mexican drug cartels to move money illegally through its American subsidiaries.[62] Therefore, careful monitoring and vigilance regarding the flow of money is required to discover illegally generated income.

The ability of the Bank Secrecy Act to inhibit the laundering of illegally obtained cash in legitimate financial institutions led the President's Commission on Organized Crime to suggest that similar laws on the state level may provide information for state prosecutions as well. Such state laws exist in about half the states and "reflect the critical need state law enforcement officials have for the information contained in the currency transaction reports." As the commission noted, however, "this need can also be met by greater cooperation between state and federal officials."[63] State and local money laundering awareness and training programs now exist in some jurisdictions around the United States.[64]

Money Laundering Control

A sixth prosecution tool relates to money laundering, the processing of criminal proceeds to disguise their illegal origin. A criminal might own a pizza parlor, for example, to make it look like her profits from the sale of illegal drugs actually came from selling pizzas. In this way, the drug profits are "laundered" through the pizza parlor to make the income look as if it was earned lawfully. Money laundering is crucial to organized crime operations because offenders would be discovered easily if they could not "merge" their illegal cash into a legal business. Another type of money laundering is "smurfing," by which illicitly obtained cash is exchanged for bank checks or money orders that are then deposited into the offender's account by a third party. Still other forms include using nonbank financial institutions, such as cashing in casino chips and airplane tickets that have been purchased with cash or depositing funds in offshore banks.[65] Some of these methods have been made more difficult with changes to U.S. legislation described later, but most other countries do not have similar regulations.

Congress passed the Money Laundering Control Act (1986), which punishes anyone who conducts a monetary transaction knowing that the funds were derived from unlawful activity. If a defendant is "willfully blind" to the source of the funds and does not exercise the reasonable care expected in a financial transaction, that suffices for knowledge.[66] A series of suspicious transfers were reported to the FBI by the Bank of New York in a well-known case. An investigation uncovered the fact that more than $10 billion had been laundered through the bank by a company called Benex Worldwide, run by Semion Mogilevitch, an alleged Russian organized crime figure. The FBI also uncovered a money laundering scheme that included skimming billions of dollars that had been loaned to Russia by the International Monetary Fund. The Bank of America was charged with failure to take adequate steps to verify the accuracy of information provided by its depositors to ensure that the money was not the product of criminal activity (hence "willfully blind" to accepting large deposits without verifying the source of the funds and the customer's background).[67] In response to this case, Congress introduced new legislation to strengthen money laundering laws, but new provisions were not adopted until the passage of the USA PATRIOT Act in 2001. The PATRIOT Act broadened the reach of money laundering laws by forcing nonbanks that handled money to conform to the reporting requirements of the Bank Secrecy Act. Therefore, check-cashing companies, money transmitters (e.g., Western Union), jewelers, pawnbrokers, casinos, credit card companies, and traveler's check and money order issuers are now subject to money laundering laws, just as are banks. To better control international money laundering and funds that might go to terrorists and transnational organized crime operations, the PATRIOT Act allows the U.S. Treasury to boycott financial institutions in countries that are uncooperative with the control of money laundering. This is enforceable by permitting the assets of foreign banks also operating in the United States to be seized, even if the actual accounts in question are located abroad.[68] This makes it possible to bring a money laundering case in the United States when a foreign bank or government is not cooperating.

In a case that made it to the U.S. Supreme Court, the defendant ran an illegal lottery and paid both lottery winners and his employees while a second defendant received a salary as a collector. In neither case was the money involved in the lottery's profits, but the court had to determine whether "proceeds" of the illegal gambling activity meant "receipts" or "profits" as stated in the statute. This is an important distinction because if "proceeds" meant "receipts," nearly every illegal lottery violation would also be money laundering because paying a winner involves receipts intended to promote the lottery. The court ruled that the prosecution need only show that a single instance of specified unlawful activity was profitable and gave rise to the money involved in the transaction being charged. "Proceeds" meant "profits" because there was no legislative history behind the statute stating otherwise.[69]

Table 10.3 provides an illustration of the persistence of money laundering. Although the number of federal convictions for money laundering has declined since 2008, there are still nearly 300 convictions each year with conviction and incarceration of offenders in more than 80% of the cases brought. It can also be seen that the prison terms for those convicted has increased over time to an average of more than four years.

The International Monetary Fund estimates that between 2% and 5% of the world's gross domestic product involves illegal income. A 2% rate is equivalent to the total economy of Spain.[70] The Financial Action Task Force (FATF) was created in 1989 as an international body to work toward the control of money laundering. Beginning in 2000, the FATF named countries that are "noncooperative in the world effort against money laundering," a list that included 23 nations by 2001, but was reduced to zero by 2006. The FATF's approach of identifying noncooperating countries and territories proved successful in forcing improvements in the anti–money laundering and counterterrorist financing systems of a number of countries.[71] Through financial incentives, sanctions, and monitoring, the FATF has successfully encouraged countries to create and enforce money laundering laws and to cooperate in international investigations.

In a Boston case, the head of a real estate firm was convicted of laundering the criminal proceeds of organized crime figure Stephen "The Rifleman" Flemmi by purchasing a condominium and buying equipment for a laundromat business with funds obtained via crime. The U.S. Attorney remarked, "If the red flags are there, the law does not permit you to turn a blind eye concerning the source of the money."[72] It is a crime to knowingly invest criminal proceeds, as well as to invest proceeds that a reasonable person should have known were obtained illegally. Common indicators of "red flags" of potential money laundering activity include

Table 10.3 Federal Money Laundering Prosecutions (18 U.S.C. Laundering of Monetary Instruments)

	2008	2010	2012
Convictions	347	286	275
Conviction rate	77%	73%	83%
Percent sentenced to prison	80%	77%	81%
Average prison term (months)	43	45	52

Compiled from Transactional Records Clearinghouse at trac.syr.edu

- Frequent high-dollar cash transactions.
- Use of large amounts of cash when checks would be expected and would be more convenient.
- Many wire transfers to or from known bank secrecy havens around the world.
- Immediate check or debit card withdrawals of large and frequent sums received by wire transfer.
- An account holder who pays undue attention to secrecy regarding personal or business identity.
- Lack of general knowledge about the customer's stated business.

These are the kinds of indicators that financial institutions and businesses dealing in cash transactions are expected to act on when unusual financial transactions occur.[73] Money laundering laws are enforceable with both criminal and civil penalties. As shown in Chapter 12, civil forfeiture of proceeds from organized crime can have a significant impact on organized crime operations.

Figure 10.3 illustrates the major prosecution tools and their purposes. This figure shows how the multiple tools discussed in this chapter have been created to make it more difficult to be involved in ongoing criminal enterprises.

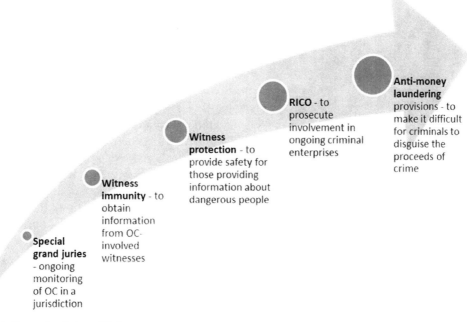

FIGURE 10.3 Prosecution tools and their uses.

CRITICAL THINKING EXERCISE 10.2

Using the information provided in this chapter, read the following scenario and respond to the questions that follow. Explain your rationale, given your knowledge of current law and policy.

The Case of Money Laundering and Terrorism

Many people have trouble understanding how Osama bin Laden was able to raise millions of dollars to support terrorist activities. No one handles cash in such large amounts, so why can't banks be monitored more effectively to look for large monetary transactions in suspect geographic locations and among targeted individuals?

Money laundering legislation is designed to make it more difficult to disguise illicitly obtained money, or money directed toward illicit individuals, and prevent it from traveling through banks around the world. But it is not so easy. More stringent money laundering legislation has been opposed by the banking industry because it will likely reduce profits by making it more difficult to accept large deposits from certain individuals or corporations. In addition, a business-friendly Congress and administration did not pursue new money laundering legislation until the September 11 terrorist attacks because they did not wish to stifle economic growth in any way. (Banks earn transaction fees and extra interest fees as money flows through them.)

A congressional proposal recommended barring U.S. banks from doing business with foreign "shell banks," which are financial institutions that have no physical offices but simply exist to move money from one place to another in secrecy. Although most banks avoid shell banks, a lobbying group attempted to create an exception for financial services companies (i.e., investment companies). It is easy to set up an unregulated financial service firm (Osama bin Laden was alleged to have established one called Taba Investments). If an exception were created for financial service companies, it is easy to see how money laundering prohibitions could be circumvented. Furthermore, some banks don't want to be in a position to "spy" on their clients by being forced to investigate the source of their deposits or transactions.

Critical Thinking Questions

1. New money laundering legislation could impact the American economy in some way. How would you propose to balance the competing demands of preventing further economic decline with the need to address the funding of terrorist organizations?
2. If you were the President, how would you explain your position to the banking industry?

SUMMARY

The prosecution of organized crime cases has come a long way in the past three decades. A large number of significant convictions were the result of successful use of the prosecution tools described in this chapter. The Witness Protection Program, RICO and CCE provisions, the Bank Secrecy Act, and money laundering provisions have been especially important in prosecuting criminal enterprises, not just individual organized crime leaders. Proper use of these prosecution strategies, together with an understanding of their strengths and weaknesses, bodes well for future efforts to contain organized crime in this manner.

ORGANIZED CRIME BIOGRAPHY

Biographies tell the life story of interesting people. In the world of criminal justice, biographies of organized crime figures offer insight into the background and motivations of the individuals who choose that lifestyle, the reasons for their choices, and *their consequences. The following is a brief summary of an organized crime biography, followed by questions that ask you to reflect on the connections between that person's life and the content of this book.*

Family Secrets: The Case That Crippled the Chicago Mob
Jeff Coen, (Chicago Review Press, 2010)

The "Family Secrets case" occurred in 2007 and involved the boss and other high-profile members of the Chicago Outfit, who were accused in a total of 18 gangland killings that occurred during the 1960s, 1970s, and 1980s. It was an unusual case because it sought to close murder cases that were long ago believed unsolvable.

The author, a reporter for the *Chicago Tribune*, brings to life many of the crime figures involved. The Chicago Syndicate, known as the Outfit, was led by Frank Calabrese Sr., and its members committed crimes of bribery, extortion, illegal gambling, loansharking, and murder. In the late 1990s, however, Calabrese's son, Frank Jr., decided to become an informant for the government in retaliation for his abusive father's failure to deliver on promises. Frank Jr. wore a wire to gather evidence against his father and other associates known for strangling their loansharking victims who failed to pay on time and for stabbing, shooting, and bombing those who challenged Frank Sr.'s authority. Frank Sr.'s brother, Nick, also became an informant in this case.

The ultimate trial contained testimony from all sides and demonstrated a series of murders, family loyalties, disloyalties, and confrontations within the Chicago Outfit. The trial was also notable for the colorful characters involved, including James "Jimmy Light" Marcello, the acting head of the Chicago mob; Joey "the Clown" Lombardo; Paul "the Indian" Schiro; and a former Chicago police officer, Anthony "Twan" Doyle, among others.

Questions
1. Why do you believe a prosecution was permitted for murders that occurred decades earlier?
2. Why do you believe that many traditional organized crime figures have such interesting nicknames?

ORGANIZED CRIME AT THE MOVIES

Movies seek to entertain and inform the audience about a story, incident, or person. Many good movies also hit upon important substantive themes relevant to understanding organized crime. Read the following movie summary (and watch the movie if you haven't already) and answer the questions that follow to make the organized crime subject matter connections.

The Untouchables
Brian de Palma, Director (1987)

The 1920s and early 1930s saw the expansion of organized crime in the United States in response to Prohibition. Criminal gangs fought for control over the illegal market in alcoholic beverages. The City of Chicago was a center for this activity, with a gang headed by Al Capone (Robert De Niro), which violently protected its territory from competitors and from the police.

The U.S. Treasury Department put agent Eliot Ness (Kevin Costner) in charge of disrupting these gangs, a problem aggravated by widespread corruption within the police. Ness obtains the help of an honest Irish-American police officer, Jim Malone (Sean Connery), and together they form a group of incorruptible police officers, including a sharp-shooting Italian cop (Andy Garcia) and also an accountant; hence, "the untouchables."

The new law enforcement group makes their first successful raid on a post office, where a back room was used to store liquor. Their accountant, Oscar Wallace (Charles Martin Smith), tells Ness that Capone has not filed an income tax return for years, making him a candidate for prosecution on tax evasion charges. Ness's efforts to get insiders within Capone's gang to testify against him are thwarted by their violent deaths.

Jim Malone is later ambushed and shot many times, but before he dies he tells Ness that one of Capone's accountants is about to leave Chicago by train. In a violent gun battle, Ness's group is able to capture Capone's accountant alive. He ultimately testifies against Capone in court; during the proceedings, Ness learns of Malone's killer and that the jury has been bribed by Capone. Ness convinces the judge to switch to a different jury, and Capone is found guilty and sentenced to 11 years in prison.

The film is based on actual events. *The Untouchables* was nominated for four Academy Awards, and Sean Connery won for Best Supporting Actor.

Questions
1. Why was police corruption so prevalent during this period of U.S. history?
2. If Prohibition strengthened American organized crime, why didn't organized crime groups weaken or dissolve after Prohibition was repealed?

References and Notes

1. U.S. Senate Committee on Government Operations Permanent Subcommittee on Investigations (1963). *Organized Crime and Illicit Traffic in Narcotics: Hearings Part I 88th Congress, 1st session.* Washington, DC: U.S. Government Printing Office, p. 15.

2. U.S. Senate Committee on Government Operations Permanent Subcommittee on Investigations (1963). *Organized Crime and Illicit Traffic in Narcotics: Hearings Part I 88th Congress, 1st session.* Washington, DC: U.S. Government Printing Office, p. 9; Calder, J.D., & Lynch, S. (2008). From Apalachin to the Buffalo Project: Obstacles on the Path to Effective Federal Responses to Organized Crime, 1957–1967. *Trends in Organized Crime, 11,* 207–269.

3. Pub. Law 91–452; 84 Stat. 922.

4. Buchanan, J. (1989). *Police Prosecutor Teams: Innovations in Several Jurisdictions.* Washington, DC: National Institute of Justice.

5. *Police Prosecutor Teams: Innovations in Several Jurisdictions*, p. 5.

6. Goldstock, R. (1994). The Prosecutor as Problem Solver. In R.J. Kelly, K. Chin, & R. Schatzberg (Eds.), *Handbook of Organized Crime in the United States.* Westport, CT: Greenwood Press, pp. 431–450.

7. *In re Grand Jury Application*, 617 F. Supp. 199 (S.D.N.Y. 1985).

8. Cohen, J.M. (October 24, 2002). People Power: Citizen Complaints before Federal Grand Juries. *New York Law Journal, 228,* 4.

9. President's Commission on Organized Crime (1987). *The Impact: Organized Crime Today.* Washington, DC: U.S. Government Printing Office, p. 163.

10. Buchwald, M.F. (Winter 2007). Of the People, By the People, For the People: The Role of Special Grand Juries in Investigating Wrongdoing by Public Officials. *The Georgetown Journal of Law & Public Policy, 5,* 79–112.

11. "Judging the Grand Jury," *Time* (February 7, 1992), 59–60; Lewin, N. "The Misuse of Grand Juries," *The Nation* (December 23, 1972), 18–20; Organized Crime: Crime Control versus Civil Liberties, ch. 4; Kuckes, N. (Winter 2004). The Useful, Dangerous Fiction of Grand Jury Independence. *American Criminal Law Review, 41,* 1–65.

12. *United States v. Ruyle*, 524 F.2d 1135 (6th Cir. 1975).

13. *United States v. Olin Corp.*, 465 F. Supp 1127 (W.D.N.Y. 1979); *United States v. Dorfman*, 532 F. Supp 118 (N.D. Ill. 1981).

14. *United States v. Dyer*, 750 F. Supp 1300 (E.D. Va. 1990).

15. at 1301.

16. Frankel, M.E., & Naftalis, G.P. (1977). *The Grand Jury: An Institution on Trial.* New York: Hill and Wang; Stashenko, J. "Pending Appeal Makes a Case for Redefining Grand Jury's Role," *The Buffalo News* (January 22, 1990), 3.

17. *Malloy v. Hogan*, 378 U.S. 1 (1964).

18. *Lefkowitz v. Cunningham*, 431 U.S. 801 (1977); *Kastigar v. United States*, 92 S. Ct. 1653 (1972).

19. Block, A.A., & Chambliss, W.J. (1981). *Organizing Crime.* New York: Elsevier North Holland, p. 205

20. Rhodes, R.P. (1984). *Organized Crime: Crime Control versus Civil Liberties.* New York: Random House, p. 194.

21. U.S. Comptroller General (1984). *Witness Security Program: Prosecutive Results and Participant Arrest Data.* Washington, DC: U.S. General Accounting Office.

22. Earley, P., & Shur, G. (2002). *WITSEC: Inside the Federal Witness Protection Program.* New York: Bantam Books, p. 131.

23. *WITSEC: Inside the Federal Witness Protection Program*, p. 91; see also Violet, A., & Partington, J. (2011). *The Mob and Me: Wiseguys and the Witness Protection Program*. New York: Pocket Star Books; Falcon, G. "Inside The Witness Protection Program," *CNN.com* (February 16, 2013).

24. *WITSEC: Inside the Federal Witness Protection Program*, pp. 226–227; McShane, L. "With No Fear of Mafia Retribution, Informants Quit Witness Protection Program," *The Buffalo News* (January 2, 2000).

25. Kash, D.A. (May 2004). Hiding in Plain Sight A Peek into the Witness Security Program. *FBI Law Enforcement Bulletin*, 73, 25–32; Knickerbocker, B. "U.S. Loses Track of Terrorists In Witness Protection: Poor Data Sharing Blamed," *The Christian Science Monitor* (May 16, 2013).

26. Edwards, P., & Brothers, B. (1990). *How Canada's Most Powerful Mafia Family Runs Its Business*. Toronto: Key Porter Books, p. 170.

27. *United Nations Convention against Transnational Organized Crime and the Protocols Thereto*. www.unodc.org/unodc/en/treaties/CTOC/index.html (March 4, 2014).

28. Fyfe, N.R., & McKay, H. (2000). Police Protection of Intimidated Witnesses: A Study of the Strathclyde Police Witness Protection. *Policing & Society*, 10, 277–300; Dandurand, Y., & Kristin, F. (2010). *A Review of Selected Witness Protection Programs*. Ottawa: Public Safety Canada; Trotter, A. (2012). Witness Intimidation In International Trials: Balancing the Need For Protection Against the Rights of the Accused. *George Washington International Law Review*, 44, 521–537.

29. "Standing Up to Street Gangs: Witness Protection Works," *Los Angeles Times* (July 15, 2002).

30. Finn, P., & Murphy Healey, K. (1996). *Preventing Gang- and Drug-Related Witness Intimidation*. Washington, DC: National Institute of Justice; Briscoe, D. (May 2, 2005). The New Face of Witness Protection. *Newsweek*, 145, 56.

31. *Preventing Gang- and Drug-Related Witness Intimidation*, p. 22; Elizabeth, B. (Fall 2007). The Scope of the Use Immunity Statute And Its Perjury Exception: Can Immunized Evidence Be Used to Prosecute Perjury or Crimes Committed After an Immunized Proceeding? *George Mason Law Review*, 15, 161–199.

32. www.usdoj.gov/marshals (2014).

33. (January 26, 1994). Suit Takes Fault with Federal Witness Protection Program. *Organized Crime Digest*, 15, 1.

34. Mathews, J. "One Witness' Experience Points Out Flaws in Protection Program," *The Buffalo News*. (August 23, 1990), 3; Montanino, F. (1990). Protecting Organized Crime Witnesses in the United States. *International Journal of Comparative and Applied Criminal Justice*, 14 (Spring-Winter), 123–132; Arena, S. "New York Liable in Witness Slays," *New York Daily News*, (January 3, 1997).

35. Kelly, R.J., Schatzberg, R., & Chin, K.-L. (1994). "Without Fear of Retribution: The Witness Protection Program. In: R.J. Kelly, K.-L. Chin, & R. Schatzberg (Eds.), *Handbook of Organized Crime in the United States*. Westport, CT: Greenwood Publishing, pp. 491–504.

36. Atkinson, J. (March 1978). Racketeer Influenced and Corrupt Organizations, 18 U.S.C.: Broadest of Federal Criminal Statutes. *Journal of Criminal Law and Criminology*, 69, 1–18; Blakey, R., & Robert Blakey, J. (1997). Civil and Criminal RICO: An Overview of the Statute and Its Operations. *Defense Counsel Journal*, 64, 36; Urbina, M.G., & Kreitzer, S. (September 2004). The Practical Utility and Ramifications of RICO: Thirty-Two Years after Its Implementation. *Criminal Justice Policy Review*, 15, 294–323; Blakey, R.G. (Summer 2006). RICO: The Genesis of an Idea. *Trends in Organized Crime*, 9, 8–34.

37. Jones, A., Satory, J., & Mace, T. (Spring 2002). Racketeer Influenced and Corrupt Organizations. *American Criminal Law Review*, 39, 989.

38. Poklemba, J., & Crusco, P. (May-June 1982). Public Enterprises and RICO: The Aftermath of United States v. Turkette. *Criminal Law Bulletin*, 18, 197–203,

39. Crimes were added as part of the Comprehensive Crime Control Act of 1984 and the Antiterrorism and Effective Death Penalty Act of 1996. See 18 U.S.C. Sec. 1962(a) (2000), and Luccaro, D., Mishelow, J., Snodgrass, B.N., & Suh, J.G. (Summer 2001). Racketeer Influenced and Corrupt Organizations. *American Criminal Law Review, 38,* 1213; Laxmidas Sawkar, A. (1999). From the Mafia to Milking Cows: State RICO Act Expansion. *Arizona Law Review, 41,* 1133.

40. *Sedima v. Imrex,* 105 S. Ct. 3275 (1985).

41. *H.J., Inc. v. Northwestern Bell Telephone,* 492 U.S. 229 (1989).

42. *United States v. Turkette,* 101 S. Ct. 2524 (1980); Neuenschwander, J. (December 1981). RICO Extended to Apply to Wholly Illegitimate Enterprises. *Journal of Criminal Law and Criminology, 72,* 1426–1443.

43. at 3284.

44. at 3286.

45. at 3294.

46. *Boyle v. United States,* 129 S. Ct. 2237 (2009).

47. *U.S. v. Coppola,* 671 F.3d 220 (2012) cert. denied *Coppola v. United States,* 2013 U.S. LEXIS 390 (2013); *U.S. v. Boyle,* 452 Fed. Appx. 55 (2011) cert. denied *Boyle v. United States,* 133 S. Ct. 373 (2012).

48. President's Commission on Organized Crime (1987). *The Impact: Organized Crime Today.* Washington, DC: U.S. Government Printing Office, p. 135; Rebovich, D.J., Coyle, K.R., & Schaaf, J.C. (1993). *Local Prosecution of Organized Crime: The Use of State RICO Statutes.* Washington, DC: National Institute of Justice.

49. Calder, J.D. (Spring 2000). RICO's 'Troubled. . .Transition': Organized Crime, Strategic Institutional Factors, and Implementation Delay, 1971–1981. *Criminal Justice Review, 25,* 31.

50. *United States v. Edwards,* 303 F.3d. 606 (2002).

51. *United States v. Bowman,* 303 F.3d 1228 (2002); U.S. Department of Justice. (2013). *Texas Leader of Latin Kings Street Gang Sentenced in Indiana to 262 Months in Prison for Racketeering Conspiracy.* Washington, DC: Office of Public Affairs, September 18.

52. "Charlestown Man Affiliated with the International Brotherhood of Teamsters Local 25 Sentenced for Racketeering and Extortion," *PR Newswire* (November 19, 2002).

53. "L.A.P.D. Can Be Sued for Racketeering," *The New York Times* (August 29, 2000).

54. U.S. Department of Justice (2013). *Aryan Brotherhood of Texas Gang Leader Sentenced in Houston for Role in Racketeering Conspiracy.* Washington, DC: Office of Public Affairs, September 26.

55. Rockwell, M. "DOJ Wants to Prosecute Cyber Criminal Activity under Racketeering Law," *Government Security News* (November 16, 2011); Coppola, L., & DeMarco, N. (Summer 2012). Civil RICO: How Ambiguity Allowed the Racketeer Influenced and Corrupt Organizations Act to Expand Beyond its Intended Purpose. *New England Journal on Criminal & Civil Confinement, 38,* 241–254.

56. U.S. Comptroller General (1986). *Bank Secrecy Act: Treasury Can Improve Implementation of the Act.* Washington, DC: U.S. General Accounting Office, pp. 15–19; U.S. Comptroller General (1991). *Money Laundering: The U.S. Government Is Responding to the Problem.* Washington, DC: U.S. General Accounting Office, p. 33.

57. U.S. Comptroller General (1993). *Money Laundering: Characteristics of Currency Transactions Reports.* Washington, DC: U.S. General Accounting Office, p. 2.

58. U.S. Comptroller General (1993). *Money Laundering: The Use of Bank Secrecy Act Reports by Law Enforcement Could Be Increased.* Washington, DC: U.S. General Accounting Office, p. 1.

59. U.S. Comptroller General (1993). *Money Laundering: Progress Report on Treasury's Financial Crimes Enforcement Network.* Washington, DC: U.S. Government Printing Office; U.S.

Comptroller General (1991). *Money Laundering: Treasury's Financial Crimes Enforcement Network*. Washington, DC: U.S. General Accounting Office.

60. *Ratzlaf v. United States*, 115 S. Ct. 1196 (1994).

61. U.S. Department of Justice (2013). *New York Check Cashing Company and Owner Plead Guilty for Roles in $19 Million Scheme*. Washington, DC: Office of Public Affairs, November 5.

62. Silver-Greenberg, J. "Citigroup Is Faulted Over Money Laundering Controls," *The New York Times*. (March 27, 2013).

63. *The Impact*, p. 169; see also Malm, A., & Bichler, G. (2013). Using Friends For Money: The Positional Importance of Money-Launderers In Organized Crime. *Trends in Organized Crime, 16,* 365–381.

64. Karchmer, C., & Ruch, D. (1992). *State and Local Money Laundering Control Strategies*. National Institute of Justice: Washington, DC; U.S. Comptroller General. *Money Laundering: State Efforts to Fight It Are Increasing but More Federal Help Is Needed*. Washington, DC: U.S. General Accounting Office; Reuter, P., & Truman, E.M. (2004). *Chasing Dirty Money: Progress on Anti-Money Laundering*. Washington, DC: Institute for International Economics.

65. Levi, M. (July 2002). Money Laundering and Its Regulation. *The Annals of the American Academy of Political and Social Science*, 181; Sharman, J.C. (2011). *The Money Laundry: Regulating Criminal Finance in the Global Economy*. Ithaca, NY: Cornell University Press.

66. April, D.H., & Grasso, A.M. (Summer 2001). Money Laundering. *American Criminal Law Review, 38,* 1051.

67. Allen, M. "Prosecution Faces Hurdles in Bank Case," *Wall Street Journal* (August 30, 1999), A3; "Bank of America Settles Money Laundering Probe," *North Country Gazette* (September 27, 2006).

68. Rueda, A. (Summer 2001). International Money Laundering Law Enforcement and the USA Patriot Act of 2001. *Michigan State University-DCL Journal of International Law, 10,* 141.

69. *U.S. v. Santos and Diaz*, 128 S.Ct. 2020 (2008).

70. Financial Action Task Force. "Financial Action Task Force on Money Laundering," www.l.oecd.org/fatf (2002).

71. (October 2006). Myanmar off Money Laundering List. *OECD Observer* (Organization for Economic Cooperation and Development), *257*, 4; "Appointment of UK President of the Financial Action Task Force," *M2 Presswire* (April 3, 2007).

72. "Boston Realtor Convicted of Money Laundering for Convicted Organized Crime Leader," *PR Newswire* (April 16, 2002).

73. Reed Edge, K. (December 2013). Bank On It: Money Laundering; It's a Dirty Business. *Tennessee Bar Journal, 49,* 27–31.

CHAPTER 11

Organizing a Criminal Defense

Justice is like a train that's nearly always late.

—Yevgeny Yevtushenko (1963)

Legal defenses to organized crimes are somewhat more complex than those for conventional crimes. Although the available defenses themselves do not change, the applicability of various defenses is an issue for some crimes more so than for others. As a result, accusations of organized crimes are generally met with more organized and complex defenses. Several examples of defenses that come up almost exclusively in cases of organized crime serve to illustrate the point: entrapment, duress, and other more offense-specific claims. The issue of "mob lawyers" is also addressed as an issue of consequence for the defense in organized crime cases.

ENTRAPMENT

Entrapment is a defense that was made popular in the Abscam political corruption (newly popularized in the 2013 movie *American Hustle*) and DeLorean drug cases, where several defendants felt that they were "tricked" or "trapped" into committing crimes they did not wish to commit. Unfortunately, the courts have not always agreed with this position.[1]

The purpose of the entrapment defense is to prevent the government from manufacturing crime by setting "traps" for the unwary citizen. In addition, the entrapment defense is aimed strictly at misconduct on the part of the government, that is if a private citizen, not associated with the government, entraps another into committing an offense, the defense is not available.

Two forms of the entrapment defense have been developed: the traditional (or "subjective") formulation looks at the defendant's conduct, and the defense applies if the defendant had no predisposition to commit the offense and only did so because government agents originated a criminal design, implanted it in the defendant's mind, and induced the defendant to commit the offense (which

315

the defendant would not otherwise have done). The "objective" formulation of the entrapment defense looks not at the defendant's conduct (his or her predisposition to commit the crime), but rather at the government agent's conduct: namely, the agent induced the defendant to commit the offense by creating a substantial risk that an innocent (i.e., unpredisposed) person would be induced (by persuasion) to commit it.

The traditional formulation of the defense of entrapment was established by the U.S. Supreme Court in 1932.[2] The case first recognized the defense of entrapment in the federal courts. In this case, which occurred during Prohibition, Sorrells was approached by an undercover police officer who had been in Sorrells's military unit during World War I. The two men got into a discussion of old times and, at several points in the conversation, the friend (now undercover police officer) asked Sorrells if he could obtain some liquor for him (which was illegal at the time). The first two times the police officer asked for liquor, Sorrells said no. But after the third request, and not knowing his friend was now a police officer, Sorrells left and brought back some liquor.

Sorrells was arrested by the police officer and tried for possession and sale of liquor. Sorrells was convicted, and he appealed all the way to the U.S. Supreme Court. The U.S. Supreme Court reversed his conviction. The court held that entrapment arises when "the criminal design originates with the officials of the government, and they implant in the mind of an innocent person the disposition to commit the alleged offense and induce its commission in order that they may prosecute."[3]

The U.S. Supreme Court held that the undercover officer's actions amounted to entrapment.

> Entrapment exists if the defendant was not predisposed to commit the crimes in question, and his intent originated with the officials of the government.

This 1932 finding in the Sorrells case is often called the *subjective formulation* of the entrapment defense because it focuses on the defendant's frame of mind.

The government's role in committing a crime can range from trivial to very influential. The precise role necessary for entrapment has been the subject of many subsequent court decisions. The U.S. Supreme Court heard another entrapment case in which two drug addicts were in a doctor's office for treatment of their addiction. One asked the defendant, Sherman, where he could obtain drugs. Sherman avoided the issue. They met for treatment at the same doctor's office three or four more times, however, and each time the same drug addict asked Sherman to get some drugs for him. Sherman finally acquiesced and obtained the illegal drugs.[4]

As it turned out, the drug addict was an informer for the government, and Sherman was arrested for selling drugs. Sherman raised the defense of entrapment at trial, but he was convicted and sentenced to 10 years' imprisonment.

The U.S. Supreme Court decided to review Sherman's case, and it used criteria for determining entrapment that was established in the Sorrells decision 26 years earlier. The U.S. Supreme Court looked at three criteria it felt important in considering the applicability of the entrapment defense. The fact that government agents "merely afford opportunities or facilities for the commission of the offense" does not constitute entrapment. Entrapment only occurs when the criminal conduct was "the product of creative activity" of law enforcement officials. The court went on to say the following:

> to determine whether entrapment has been established, a line must be drawn between a trap for the unwary innocent and the trap for the unwary criminal . . . . On the one hand, at trial the accused may examine the conduct of the government agent; on the other hand, the accused will be subjected to an "appropriate and searching inquiry into his own conduct and predisposition" as bearing on his claim of innocence.[5]

The court concluded that the police conduct in this case constitutes just what the entrapment defense is designed to prevent.

> The case at bar illustrates an evil which the defense of entrapment is designed to overcome. The government informer entices someone attempting to avoid narcotics not only into carrying out an illegal sale but also returning to the habit of use. Selecting the proper time, the informer then tells the government agent. The set-up is accepted by the agent without even a question as to the manner in which the informer encountered the seller. Thus the Government plays on the weaknesses of an innocent party and beguiles him into committing crimes which he otherwise would not have attempted. Law enforcement does not require such methods as this.

Four other justices on the U.S. Supreme Court concurred with the majority, but thought the decision ought to be arrived at using a different standard. These justices felt that

> in holding out inducements [government agents] should act in such a manner as is likely to induce to the commission of the crime—only these persons and not others who would normally avoid crime and through self-struggle resist ordinary temptations. This test shifts attention from the record and predisposition of the particular defendant to the conduct of the police and the likelihood, objectively considered, that it would entrap only those ready and willing to commit crime.[6]

This standard is called the *objective formulation* of the entrapment defense. It can be stated as follows:

> Entrapment occurs when government agents induce or encourage another person to engage in criminal behavior by knowingly making false representations about the lawfulness of the conduct or by employing methods that create a substantial risk that such an offense will be committed by innocent [i.e., unpredisposed] persons.

As this objective formulation suggests, it shifts attention away from prior conduct and predisposition of the defendant to the conduct of the government agent. Both subjective and objective formulations address only the dangers of inducement to crime by innocent persons but, under the objective standard, the predisposition of the defendant is irrelevant.

Tables 11.1 and 11.2 contain the elements of proof that must be established in order to defeat the government's prosecution of the case. Table 11.1 shows the traditional or "subjective" method, and Table 11.2 shows the "objective" method.

The importance of this difference between objective and subjective formulations of the defense was made clear in a subsequent case. An undercover police officer went to Russell's home, claiming he wanted to become involved in the manufacture of methamphetamine. The undercover officer offered to supply an essential ingredient of the illegal drug in return for one-half of the total amount manufactured. The officer's actual aim, however, was to locate

---

Table 11.1 Elements of Proof: Entrapment Defense "Subjective" Formulation

1. The defendant had no predisposition to commit the criminal offense.
2. Government agents originated a criminal design.
3. Government agents then implanted that criminal design in the defendant's mind.
4. Government agents then induced (by persuasion) the defendant to commit the criminal offense, which the defendant would not otherwise have done.

Table 11.2 Elements of Proof: Entrapment Defense "Objective" Formulation

1. Government agents induced the defendant to commit the offense.
2. Government agents' inducement, in an objective sense, created a substantial risk that an innocent person (one who normally would resist ordinary temptations and avoid crime) would commit the criminal offense.

the manufacturing laboratory, so he demanded to see where the drug was actually made. Russell took the officer to the factory, and the officer eventually supplied him with the necessary ingredient to manufacture the drug. Russell and his associates were later arrested for the manufacture and sale of a controlled dangerous substance. Russell claimed that he was entrapped.[7]

The U.S. Supreme Court adhered to the subjective standard of its earlier decisions in *Sorrells* and *Sherman*. Furthermore, the court rejected the argument that the constitutional requirement of due process mandated use of the objective standard. The result of the decision in *Russell* is that states are free to adopt either the subjective or the objective formulation of the entrapment defense. The court, therefore, upheld the conviction of Russell:

> It does not seem particularly desirable for the law to grant complete immunity from prosecution to one who himself planned to commit a crime, and then committed it, simply because government undercover agents subjected him to inducements which might have seduced a hypothetical individual who was not so predisposed.[8]

It is clear that this decision was reached according to the subjective standard due to its focus on the predisposition of the defendant rather than on the conduct of the government agent. Three justices dissented in this case, however, urging adoption of the objective standard for entrapment. They felt that a reasonable application of the objective standard in this case would result in a finding of entrapment. The dissent argued that "the agent's undertaking to supply this ingredient to the respondent, thus making it possible for the government to prosecute him for manufacturing an illicit drug with it, was, I think, precisely the type of governmental conduct that the entrapment defense is meant to prevent."[9] It is easy to see from the court's opinion in this case, as well as from the dissenting opinion, that use of the subjective or objective standard to establish entrapment can lead to very different conclusions based on the same set of facts.

In a more recent case, the U.S. Supreme Court had an opportunity to reevaluate the entrapment defense. Keith Jacobson ordered two magazines, titled *Bare Boys*, from a bookstore. The magazines contained photographs of nude preteen and teenage boys. Finding Jacobson's name on the bookstore mailing list, the postal service and the customs service sent mail to him using five different fictitious organizations and a bogus pen pal. The organizations claimed to represent those interested in sexual freedom and against censorship. The organizations were said to support lobbying efforts through sales of publications. Jacobson corresponded on occasion with these organizations, giving his views of censorship and the "hysteria" surrounding child pornography.

The correspondence to Jacobson was an attempt to see if he would violate the Child Protection Act of 1984 by receiving sexually explicit depictions of children through the mail.[10] After more than 2 years of receiving these mailings, Jacobson ordered a magazine depicting young boys engaged in sexual acts. He was arrested under the Child Protection Act, and a search of his house found no sexually oriented materials, except for the *Bare Boys* magazines and the government agencies' bogus mailings.

Jacobson was convicted at trial, although he claimed entrapment.[11] The appeal was heard by the U.S. Supreme Court, which recognized that the prosecution must show (using the subjective formulation) that the defendant was disposed to commit the criminal act prior to first being approached by government agents.

CRITICAL THINKING EXERCISE 11.1

Using the legal principles discussed in this chapter, respond to the scenario that follows. Be sure to indicate how and why the principles you select are appropriate.

The Case of the Informant, the Prostitute, and the Heroin Dealer

The FBI employed Helen as an informant to investigate Simpson, a suspected heroin dealer. Helen was a prostitute, heroin user, and a fugitive from Canada, but was used as an informant because of her knowledge of the drug market in the area. She ultimately became sexually intimate with Simpson (the man she was investigating), and she obtained drugs through requests she made of him. Simpson was arrested for distributing narcotics.

Critical Thinking Questions

1. Using the objective formulation of the entrapment defense, was Simpson entrapped?
2. Using the subjective formulation, was Simpson entrapped?

The court made several observations relevant to organized crime investigations. In the case of "sting" operations, for example, in which a government-sponsored stolen property "fence" is set up, a defendant is provided an opportunity to commit a crime. The entrapment defense "is of little use because the ready commission of the criminal act amply demonstrates the defendant's predisposition."[12] Likewise, an agent who offers the opportunity to buy or sell drugs may make an immediate arrest under federal law, if the offer is accepted.

In the case of Jacobson, the court conceded that if the government agents had simply offered him the opportunity to order child pornography by mail, and he promptly ordered it, the entrapment defense would not be applicable. But the facts in this case were different. By the time Jacobson violated the law, he had been the target of 26 months of repeated mailings. Jacobson's earlier order of the *Bare Boys* magazines cannot be used to show predisposition because they were legal at the time they were ordered and Jacobson's uncontradicted testimony stated he did not know the magazines would depict minors until they arrived in the mail.

The U.S. Supreme Court has previously held that a person's sexual inclinations, tastes, and "fantasies ... are his own and beyond the reach of the government."[13] It was held that in Jacobson's case the government "excited Jacobson's interest in illegal sexually explicit materials" and "exerted substantial pressure" to buy this material as part of a fight against censorship and infringement of individual privacy.[14]

The court concluded in a five-to-four vote that "when the government's quest for conviction leads to the apprehension of an otherwise law-abiding citizen who, if left to his own devices, likely would have never run afoul of the law, the courts should intervene."[15] The U.S. Supreme Court intervened in this case and reversed Jacobson's conviction.

Under federal law, therefore, government agents "in their zeal to enforce the law ... may not originate a criminal design," that entails creating the disposition to commit a criminal act in a person's mind, "and then induce commission of the crime so that the government may prosecute."[16] This is what the entrapment defense is designed to prevent.

The viability of a claim of entrapment is usually decided during pretrial motions before a judge; it is not decided by a jury. In order to invoke entrapment as a defense, the defendant must necessarily admit to engaging in the unlawful conduct, that is, if you claim you were entrapped, you are admitting that you did commit the crime. However, if the defendant can demonstrate government inducement to commit a crime (under the objective formulation) or that he or she was not predisposed to committing the crime and the government originated the criminal design (under the subjective formulation), he or she will be acquitted. Despite the perspective of the federal courts, the objective standard has been adopted in the Model Penal Code, in the proposed revised federal criminal code, as well as in a number of states.[17]

Aggressive "reverse stings" have been used increasingly by law enforcement to infiltrate stolen goods markets and drug rings. This tactic has been challenged for the same reasons raised in prior entrapment cases: creating a crime that would not have otherwise occurred. In one case, five targeted suspects were told that they should burst into a Baltimore hotel room with guns and grab $400,000 worth of cocaine stashed there by an out-of-town supplier. But as the suspects headed to the hotel, Baltimore police working with the Drug Enforcement Administration swooped in to arrest them for conspiracy to distribute drugs, robbery, and gun violations. The entire story—the coke, the supplier, and the hotel room—had been made up by law enforcement. Defense attorneys argue the government is luring petty criminals into imaginary crimes, and prosecutors are forced to defend the government's distinction between aggressive policing and entrapment.[18]

To summarize, first, the traditional ("subjective") formulation of the entrapment defense requires a showing that (1) government agents originated the criminal design (i.e., the defendant had no predisposition to commit the crime), (2) they implanted that design in the mind of the defendant (i.e., giving him or her the disposition to consider committing the crime), and (3) they induced the defendant to commit the crime (i.e., the defendant would not otherwise have committed the crime). Second, under the "objective" formulation of the entrapment defense, it must be shown that government agents employed methods ("inducements") that created a substantial risk that an innocent person (i.e., one who had no predisposition to commit the crime) would in fact commit the crime. Here, the focus is on the government agent's conduct rather than on the defendant's prior conduct and predisposition, which are irrelevant under the objective formulation.

DURESS

A defense that often arises in cases of organized crime is duress. Generally, three conditions must be met for a successful claim of duress as a defense. A person must engage in a criminal act (1) due to threat of serious bodily harm by another person, (2) the threat must be immediate, without reasonable possibility for escape, and (3) in most jurisdictions, the defense is disallowed where a person intentionally or recklessly places himself or herself in a situation subject to duress.

Therefore, if you join a gang of organized criminals who tell you to embezzle $1,000 from your employer, but you are caught, your attempt to claim a defense of duress (i.e., you were forced to do it against your will) would be denied in most states because you placed yourself in a situation subject to duress by joining the gang of criminals. The defense of duress is also called "coercion" or "compulsion" in some jurisdictions.

In a case in Carlsbad, California, Larry LaFleur claimed he was held at gunpoint by his co-felon Nick Holm and forced to shoot and kill their kidnapped victim. LaFleur argued that the murder charge against him should be reduced to voluntary manslaughter because of the duress placed upon him by Holm.

The U.S. Court of Appeals commented that the defense of duress "is based on the rationale that a person, when confronted with two evils, should not be punished for engaging in the lesser of the evils." The problem in LaFleur's case is that the two evils he was faced with (his own death and that of an innocent person) have the same degree of harm. The court held that "consistent with the common law rule, a defendant should not be excused from taking the life of an innocent third person because of the threat of harm to himself."[19] There is no rule of "human jettison," nor does duress "legally mitigate murder to manslaughter." It should also be added that LaFleur recklessly placed himself in a situation subject to duress by engaging in a violent felony.

In a case involving two prison escapees who claimed there had been "various threats and beatings directed at them" inside the prison, the U.S. Supreme Court ruled that duress was not applicable because no "bonafide effort" was made by the defendants "to surrender or return to custody as soon as the claimed duress or necessity had lost its coercive force."[20] The defendants were at large for a month or more.

Therefore, criminal acts committed while under immediate, serious, and non-reckless duress are excused only while the coercive threats are in force and the action taken results in less harm than the act avoided. Once the duress is ended, no further criminal conduct is excused under law.

The U.S. Supreme Court heard the appeal of Keshia Dixon who was convicted of purchasing firearms while under indictment and for making false statements while acquiring the firearms. Dixon suffered an escalating cycle of violence at the hands of her boyfriend; prior to the commission of these crimes, the boyfriend threatened her and her daughters with greater harm if she refused to purchase the firearms. She raised the defense of duress, arguing that she did not act willfully in the firearms crimes, given her situation. The U.S. Supreme Court held that a defendant has the burden to prove duress by a preponderance of the evidence and that Dixon failed to meet this burden. Dixon received the same punishment as a defendant who did not act under coercive circumstances, although it is left to individual states to determine how duress is established in court.[21] This is an important issue because it is reasonable to ask whether Dixon's sentence should have been reduced because of her circumstances, even if she did not meet the threshold for the defense of duress. Another case explains this in a related way—a defendant traveled from Nicaragua to the United States and became involved with smugglers in attempting to commit the crime of illegal reentry into the United States. While he suffered a terrible ordeal upon arriving in the United States, he placed himself in a dangerous situation by becoming involved with the smugglers for an illegal purpose.[22] So it is clear that the circumstances are crucial in applying the defense of duress.[23] Figure 11.1 illustrates the requirement for the three central elements of duress to be present in any circumstance.

CLAIMS THAT ARE POTENTIAL DEFENSES

Sometimes defendants make claims in an effort to avoid culpability and conviction. Most of these claims are not allowable defenses or else are permitted only in very limited circumstances. Those claims most common in organized crime cases include adequacy of representation, RICO participation, gambling while intoxicated, the consequences of extortion and perjury, and amnesia.

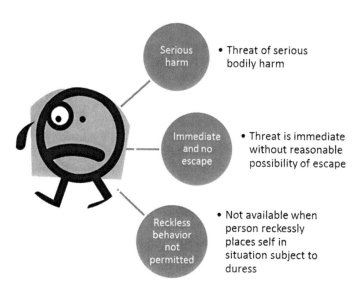

Serious harm
- Threat of serious bodily harm

Immediate and no escape
- Threat is immediate without reasonable possibility of escape

Reckless behavior not permitted
- Not available when person reckessly places self in situation subject to duress

FIGURE 11.1 Three central elements of the defense of duress.

Adequacy of Legal Representation

Sometimes a defendant will allege that he or she acted improperly under "advice of counsel." Mistaken advice on the part of counsel is not a defense, however. It may be shown where it would disprove the requisite intent needed for the crime, but it is not an absolute defense in itself. As a result, a man who was told by his lawyer that a prostitution ring disguised as a "dating service" was legal would have no defense in a criminal case. The best the defendant could do would be to show that the crime was committed without "willfulness" or not "knowingly" if this was an element of the crime. In these cases, the degree of crime charged might be reduced (e.g., from first- to second-degree prostitution charges), but only if the jury believed the defendant's claim that a reasonable person would not be aware of the act's illegal nature.

In a New York City case, Wong Chi Keung was convicted of conspiracy to distribute heroin. A lawyer who had represented her in an earlier case allegedly helped target her in the current case through his representation of a coconspirator.[24] The court recognized that "prejudice is presumed" when a defendant can "establish that an actual conflict of interest adversely affects [her] lawyer's performance."[25] However, the court found that in Keung's case there was "no showing of either such a conflict or such an effect." This is because it was apparent that her attorney "had no role in selecting Wong as a target" and no confidences were disclosed to the lawyer.[26]

Absent a conflict of interest, it might be claimed that the attorney's performance "fell below an objective standard of reasonableness" and that "but for his deficient conduct the result of the trial would have been different."[27] In determining competency of counsel, the court examines the lawyer's performance of his or her task of representation. It is obviously difficult to find incompetency so great as to cause a different result in a case, and defendants rarely prevail on these grounds. In the Keung case, for example, the court found her attorney "a skilled and persistent advocate," and there were no facts or circumstances in the case "to suggest a contrary result" in the outcome of the case was possible.[28]

RICO Participation

A person is not liable for prosecution for racketeering under RICO unless he or she has participated in the operation or management of the criminal enterprise itself. Therefore, an accounting firm, which audited the books of a business criminal enterprise and found them to be in order, did not "participate in management or operation" of the enterprise. As a result, it cannot be prosecuted under RICO for failing to inform the board of the business enterprise about its potential insolvency.[29]

Likewise, an attorney's sporadic involvement in a fraudulent scheme through the preparation of two letters, a partnership agreement, and assistance in a bankruptcy proceeding was "not sufficient" to meet the conduct or participation requirements for prosecution under RICO.[30] Therefore, RICO punishes the operation or *substantial participation* in the management of an enterprise, instead of those who might commit acts that directly or indirectly help the enterprise continue.

Gambling While Intoxicated

Voluntary, self-induced intoxication is not a defense in criminal cases, although it is sometimes relevant when the intoxication and act occur under certain circumstances. In Atlantic City, a casino was sued by a patron to recover gambling losses he incurred at the casino.[31] He was a "high roller," often betting $10,000 on a single hand of blackjack, and he would sometimes play five or more hands at the same time.

The nature of gambling is such that all gamblers will lose at least some of the time. Therefore, casinos "cause" people to lose money. The question in this case was the extent to which the casino is responsible to protect gamblers from financial loss if they gamble "while [their] mental facilities are impaired by alcohol." Any losses incurred while a casino patron is allowed to continue gambling while drunk "is proximately caused by the casino's negligence."[32] As a result, the patron would not be liable for losses under these circumstances. In criminal terms, however, any criminal conduct engaged in while voluntarily intoxicated would not be excused, because we are responsible for our voluntary actions.

Extortion, Perjury, and Consequences

It is a defense to extortion that the defendant reasonably believed a false allegation to be true and that his or her sole purpose was to compel or induce the victim to take reasonable action to make good a wrongful act. For example, the defendant (an employer) was charged with extortion against an employee who had stolen $50 from the defendant. Upon discovery of the theft, the employer demanded that the employee reimburse the employer, and stated that if the employee did not do so, the police would be notified. It is a defense to the charge of extortion if the defendant reasonably believed the theft to be true, and acted with the sole purpose of compelling or inducing the victim to take reasonable action to make good a wrongful act.

It is also a defense to a charge of perjury to retract a false statement during the course of a proceeding before it substantially affects the proceeding and before it becomes manifest that its falsity would be exposed. A woman who lied under oath about her whereabouts on a certain date could correct her statement, without penalty, as long as she did so before it became clear that she had lied. Such a defense is designed to encourage witnesses to tell the truth, even in cases where they began telling lies during sworn testimony.

It is sometimes claimed that an offense committed had an "unintended consequence" and, therefore, a person should not be held accountable for it. A person is legally responsible for all unintended consequences, however, of any unlawful act.[33] Unintended consequence is only an allowable defense where the act (that caused the unintended result) was lawful. Therefore, a person who shoots at you, but misses and kills someone else, is criminally liable for that person's death, even though it was an "unintended consequence" of his or her action.

Amnesia

Occasionally, a defendant will claim that he "cannot remember" whether he committed a particular offense. Unfortunately, amnesia is not a defense in itself. If it is shown that the defendant was suffering from severe mental disease or defect at the time of the crime and that this prevented him or her from understanding the nature of the act and that it was wrong, an insanity defense may be appropriate.[34] Amnesia, however, may only be considered in determining the penalty for a crime. Therefore, a judge can consider a valid claim of amnesia in sentencing, but it does not relieve the defendant of liability for the crime.

MOB LAWYERS

The President's Commission on Organized Crime drew attention to what it called "mob-connected" lawyers. It was claimed these individuals "are not criminal lawyers. They are lawyer-criminals."[35] Although "few in number," the commission believed they used their status to undermine the justice system. Five case studies of mob-connected lawyers were presented in the commission's report to show precisely how these attorneys represented the interests of organized crime groups rather than legal interests.

Martin Light was an attorney in New York who later served a 15-year sentence for heroin possession. In testimony before the commission, he said he represented a "crew" within a Cosa Nostra group. He stated that if a member of the crew was arrested and did not call him, Light would go to federal court and "see who he got as a lawyer. If he got [a] Legal Aid [attorney], that would be a tip-off that he might be cooperating." He said the penalty for a member who cooperated with the government was "death."[36]

Kevin Rankin was a lawyer for the Philadelphia Cosa Nostra group. He secured and utilized perjured affidavits and testimony on behalf of family members charged with crimes. He also paid off a corrections officer to perjure himself.[37] Rankin was ultimately convicted for his role as a participant in an organized crime narcotics conspiracy. He was sentenced to 54 years in prison.

Bruce Cutler was the attorney for John Gotti, and later for Gotti's son. Prosecutors successfully disqualified him from representing them in several cases, arguing he had a conflict of interest due to his friendship with his clients and participation in some of the events that would be raised at trial. Defense attorney Benjamin Brafman argues, "if you allow prosecutors to control who does or does not appear at the defense table, it's giving the government more power than it already has and more power than the criminal justice system should permit." The prosecution's view is "the reality is that attorneys are as integral a part of the Gambino family as any of its members," making their representation of Gotti a conflict of interest.[38]

A similar issue arose in the trial of Whitey Bulger, who was charged with being a leader of a criminal organization in Boston from 1972 to 1999. Bulger's case for trial was randomly assigned to a judge who, earlier in his career, had held a variety of managerial and supervisory appointments within the U.S. Attorney's Office in Boston that had engaged in investigations of Bulger. At issue was whether a reasonable person might question the judge's ability to remain impartial in hearing the case, because he had supervisory responsibility for prosecutorial activities during some of the time when Bulger was under investigation. This apparent conflict was challenged by the defense, and the case was reassigned to another judge.[39]

An interesting case is that of attorney Frank Ragano, who spent 30 years representing alleged organized crime figures such as Santo Trafficante of Florida, Carlos Marcello of New Orleans, and Jimmy Hoffa of the Teamster's Union.[40]

He recounts in a subsequent book how he was seduced by the power and influence of these individuals, and why he ultimately decided to leave that circle of clients. He told this story after the deaths of Trafficante in 1987 and Marcello in 1993. Ragano revealed that in his early association with Trafficante and Marcello, they "seemed incapable" of violence. Instead they appeared interested only in gambling enterprises, real estate deals, and "semi-legitimate" deals with politicians. Ragano says that an elderly Trafficante told him about his role in the assassination of President John Kennedy.[41]

In terms of his role as a "mob lawyer," Ragano confessed that "my gravest error as a lawyer was merging a professional life with a personal life. Ambition and aspiration for wealth, prestige, and recognition clouded my judgment. ... Representing Santo and Jimmy was a shortcut to success—too much of a shortcut."[42] He admitted that he "crossed the professional line" when he became intimate friends with his infamous clients. He "gradually began to think like them and to rationalize their aberrant behavior. Their enemies became my enemies; their friends, my friends; their values, my values; their interests, my interests."[43] Ironically, an IRS audit of his tax records was ordered soon after his successful defense of Trafficante in 1986. Ultimately, Ragano was sentenced to a year in prison.

In 2009, attorney Robert Simels, famous for representing mobsters such as Henry Hill, among others, was sentenced to 14 years in prison for plotting to bribe or hurt witnesses testifying against his client in a drug case (see Figure 11.2). He told the judge at sentencing, "Whatever self-esteem I had, whatever self-worth I had, is destroyed."[44]

The President's Commission concluded that reasons for this unethical and illegal activity on the part of mob-connected attorneys include friendship, drug addiction, greed, and excitement.[45] Remedies for the problem are less clear.

Under forfeiture laws the proceeds of organized crime-related activity may be forfeited to the government. Lawyers argue that if the fees paid to them by organized crime-linked defendants can be forfeited under this provision, attorneys will avoid representing this kind of client.[46] This impacts upon a defendant's right to counsel and due process. If defense attorneys are required to ask their clients about the source of their legal fees, it would set a poor precedent for "high-profile" defendants. Should their physicians, accountants, and pastors be required to ask the same question? This does not appear to be either workable or desirable. The legal profession places great significance on the privacy of dealings with clients and on the attorney-client privilege, which many see as threatened by efforts to make lawyers monitor the source of their clients' funds.[47]

However, defendants do not have a right to high-priced counsel, and the government maintains that they do not have the right to use funds obtained from crime for lawyer's fees or living expenses during court proceedings. Other countries

FIGURE 11.2 Attorney Robert Simels arrives at Brooklyn Federal Court in New York, fighting charges that he plotted with a drug dealing paramilitary leader to silence witnesses. Simels spent years cultivating an image as a hard-charging defense attorney with a client list that included mobsters, drug lords, and professional athletes. *AP Photo/Seth Wenig*

permit defendants to use suspected illegal funds to defend themselves and for living expenses during trials. The U.S. government view is characterized in this way:

> If a criminal robbed a bank and was caught holding the bags of cash taken from the vault, I think we would all agree that the money would be returned to the bank and the robber should not be entitled to use the proceeds of his crime to pay for lawyers to mount his defense. It should be no different for other types of crimes.[48]

The tension between a professional having to know the source of his client's funds and a defendant's use of alleged illegal funds for legal representation is a difficult dilemma that deters some attorneys from taking organized crime cases.

Finally, there is "no uniform or coordinated procedure" for federal, state, and local jurisdictions to exchange information regarding disciplinary problems with attorneys. Attorneys disciplined in one state, therefore, "are not automatically scrutinized in other states where they may also be licensed to practice." There is also "no formal arrangement" where state bar disciplinary committees are notified of disciplinary actions or convictions against attorneys in federal court within or outside their state.[49] Although the problem appears to be small, the issue of mob-connected lawyers will likely become larger without greater efforts toward apprehension and disciplinary actions against those who violate the law or the rules of professional responsibility. Concern has been expressed as well in other countries, such as France, Italy, and the United Kingdom, to find better ways to detect and prevent misconduct by legal counsel in organized crime cases. [50]

CRITICAL THINKING EXERCISE 11.2

Using the legal principles discussed in this chapter, respond to the scenario that follows. Be sure to indicate how and why the principles you select are appropriate.

The Case of Vincent "The Chin" and Mental Illness

Vincent "The Chin" Gigante is an anachronism in the history of organized crime. He was alleged to be the boss of the Genovese crime family in New York City for many years, but he avoided prosecution because he wandered around the streets in a bathrobe, unshaven, and muttering incoherently. Some called him "The Oddfather." He was evaluated by prosecution psychiatrists many times and found mentally incompetent. In 1997, however, prosecutors were successful in convicting Gigante under RICO, and he was sentenced to 12 years in prison.

In an unusual turn of events, prosecutors filed obstruction of justice charges against Gigante in 2002 (after he had been in prison for 5 years) for "pretending he was crazy." Prosecutors alleged he had faked mental illness for decades to avoid prosecution and that he was still running the Genovese crime family from prison. A federal judge ruled that Gigante was mentally fit to stand trial on these new charges, and Gigante's lawyer did not object. A year later, Gigante, now in frail physical condition, pled guilty to obstruction of justice at age 75 and was sentenced to an additional 3 years in prison. His plea indicated that in order to avoid prosecution, he had deceived psychiatrists evaluating his competency for at least 7 years before his conviction in 1997.

It is unclear why the prosecution brought these additional charges, although it has been alleged that it was part of a deal with the government to get a better deal for his son Andrew who faced a possible sentence of 10-20 years on racketeering charges. A further twist to the story occurred when a *New York Times* reporter asked the question "how could some of the most respected minds in forensic psychiatry ... get it wrong?" A total of 34 different doctors, including a number of prominent psychiatrists, had been called in over the years to evaluate Gigante. Excerpts from their statements include, "He is suffering from schizophrenia ... he was unable to discuss meaningfully any aspect of his case ... he manifests organic brain damage by his inability, for example, to subtract 7 from 100. His memory is impaired. He is sometimes very confused and doesn't know where he is or the time of day, or the year."[49] It appears that Vincent Gigante fooled some very good psychiatrists over many years and that he actually ran the Genovese family business from prison or else there were other reasons for his plea in 2003.

Critical Thinking Questions

1. What would Vincent Gigante have to prove to claim the insanity defense?
2. Why didn't he simply claim amnesia?
3. Why do you think other organized crime figures never copied Gigante's behaviors in an effort to avoid prosecution?

Sources: *William Glaberson, "Gigante Is Sane and Runs Mob, U.S. Charges," New York Times (January 24, 2002); William Glaberson, "Gigante Found Fit for Trial as Defense Shifts Strategy," New York Times (April 24, 2002); Andy Newman, "Analyze This: Vincent Gigante, Not Crazy After All Those Years," New York Times (April 13, 2003).*

SUMMARY

A number of defenses exist that often arise in cases of organized crime. Likewise, there are claims applicable only in certain situations or for particular types of crimes. There are, of course, other available defenses, but the ones presented here come up most often in organized crime cases. An understanding of how these defenses apply in principle will enable one to anticipate their relevance in actual cases in the future. The issue of "mob-connected" lawyers appears to be small, but a greater effort toward detection and disciplinary actions against violating attorneys appears necessary.

ORGANIZED CRIME BIOGRAPHY

Biographies tell the life story of interesting people. In the world of criminal justice, biographies of organized crime figures offer insight into the background and motivations of the individuals who choose that lifestyle, the reasons for their choices, and their consequences. The following is a brief summary of an organized crime biography, followed by questions that ask you to reflect on the connections between that person's life and the content of this book.

King of the Godfathers: Joseph Massino and the Fall of the Bonanno Crime Family
Anthony DeStefano (Pinnacle, 2007)

The book presents the life story, criminal acts, and ultimate downfall of Joey Massino, a boss of the Bonanno crime family in New York City. Massino was an eighth-grade dropout, weighed 300 pounds, and lived a low-key lifestyle centered in Queens, New York. Massino's underboss was also his brother-in-law, Sal Vitale, who later became an informant against Massino due to Massino's poor treatment of many around him.

Many other Bonanno associates also became informants against one another in a federal case against Massino. For more than 20 years, Joseph "Big Joey" Massino ran what was called the largest criminal network in the United States, employing more than 250 "made" men and numerous associates. The group was responsible for more than 30 murders, including a number of its own members in order to enforce its authority.

Massino bragged throughout his criminal career that there was never a rat (informant) in the Bonanno crime group, although this ended with the undercover work of Donnie Brasco (Joe Pistone), who Massino never met, but who compromised and ultimately convicted many Bonanno group members. Massino was always fearful of informants, and many of the murders he ordered were the result of this fear. Massino's case is notable for the large number of members who became informants in order to reduce their own sentences and as "payback" for their perceived mistreatment by others. One associate was still on the street when he came to police voluntarily to become an informant. When Massino ultimately became an informant himself (when facing murder charges), his family was angry and ashamed of his decision to cooperate with the government.

Questions
1. How would you explain the large number of criminals who became government informants in this case?
2. Why do you think Massino was so much in fear of informants, even before the infiltration of Donnie Brasco?

ORGANIZED CRIME AT THE MOVIES

Movies seek to entertain and inform the audience about a story, incident, or person. Many good movies also hit upon important substantive themes relevant to understanding organized crime. Read the following movie summary (and watch the movie if you haven't already) and answer the questions that follow to make the organized crime subject matter connections.

Road to Perdition
Sam Mendes, Director (2002)

Road to Perdition is a story about father-son relationships in the context of organized crime. Michael Sullivan (Tom Hanks) is an enforcer/hit man for John Rooney (Paul Newman), who is an Irish-American organized crime boss in Illinois during the 1930s. An orphan, Sullivan was raised by Rooney and worked for him his entire life. Sullivan's 12-year-old son, Michael Jr., follows them on one occasion and witnesses them commit a murder. His father swears him to secrecy.

John Rooney's son, Connor (Daniel Craig), is jealous of Sullivan's relationship with Rooney and plans to have him assassinated. He succeeds in murdering Sullivan's wife and other son, but Sullivan and Michael Jr. (Tyler Hoechlin) escape to Chicago.

Sullivan seeks revenge by planning to steal the syndicate's money with the assistance of Al Capone's gang, but Capone tries instead to have Sullivan and Michael Jr. killed. In the

Continued

ORGANIZED CRIME AT THE MOVIES—CONT'D

process, Sullivan is severely injured, although he wounds his attacker, Harlen Maguire (Jude Law), in the face. Sullivan is taken by his son to a farm where an elderly couple helps him recover. During this time, Sullivan finds ledgers indicating that Connor has embezzled money from his father using the names of gang members he murdered.

Upon his recovery, Sullivan meets with Rooney secretly and tells him what he knows about Connor, but Rooney will not let his son be harmed. Sullivan then turns on Rooney's gang, killing them and John Rooney. With Rooney gone, Capone's lieutenant tips Sullivan to Connor's location, where he is killed.

Now free from the gang, Sullivan and his son leave for the town of Perdition, Kansas. But a disfigured Maguire tracks them down. Michael Jr. gets the advantage on Maguire, but Sullivan tells him not to kill him. Instead, Sullivan kills Maguire, but is fatally wounded himself. As he dies, Sullivan tells Michael Jr. not to seek revenge, and Michael returns to live with the elderly couple who had helped them earlier. The film is based on the graphic novel of the same name, written by Max Allan Collins and illustrated by Richard Piers Rayner. *Road to Perdition* was nominated for six Academy Awards, including Paul Newman for Best Supporting Actor. It won for Best Cinematography.

Questions

1. The theme of a father wanting his son to have a better life than he did is a common one. Why do so many sons of organized crime figures in real life follow in their father's criminal footsteps, even though their fathers have been the targets of assault, prosecution, and betrayal by friends?

2. Revenge is also a common theme in books and films. Why is revenge "to make things even" not recognized as a defense in criminal cases?

References and Notes

1. Roiphe, R. (2003). The Serpent Beguiled Me: The History of the Entrapment Defense. *Seton Hall Law Review, 33,* 257; Greene, R. W. (1982). *The Sting Man: Inside Abscam.* New York: Ballantine.

2. *Sorrells v. United States,* 53 S. Ct. 210 (1932).

3. at 215.

4. *Sherman v. United States,* 78 S. Ct. 819 (1958).

5. at 827.

6. at 830.

7. *United States v. Russell,* 93 S. Ct. 1637 (1973).

8. at 1643.

9. at 1648.

10. 18 U.S.C. Sec. 2552(a)(2)(A).

11. *Jacobson v. United States,* 112 S. Ct. 1535 (1992).

12. at 1541.

13. *Paris Adult Theatre I v. Slaton,* 93 S. Ct. 2628 (1973).

14. *Jacobson v. United States,* at 1542.

15. at 1543.

16. *Sorrells v. United States,* at 212; *Sherman v. United States,* at 820.

17. Marcus, P. (1986). The Entrapment Defense. *Criminal Law Bulletin, 22*(May–June), 197–243; Frampton, W. (2013). Criminal Law: Predisposition and Positivism: The Forgotten

Foundations of the Entrapment Doctrine. *Journal of Criminal Law & Criminology, 103*(Winter), 111–145.

18. Duncan, I. "Federal Authorities Ensnare Criminals in "Reverse Stings": Lawyers for Men Caught in Drug Enforcement Agency Operation Say They Were Entrapped," *The Baltimore Sun* (June 28, 2013). See also Heath, B. "ATF Uses Fake Drugs, Big Bucks to Snare Suspects," *USA Today* (June 28, 2013).

19. *United States v. LaFleur*, 971 F.2d 200 (9th Cir. 1991) at 204, 206.

20. *United States v. Bailey*, 100 S. Ct. 624 (1980); *United States v. Caban*, 173 F.3d 89 (2d Cir. 1999).

21. *Dixon v. United States*, 126 S. Ct. 2437 (2006); Engel, M. (2008). Unweaving the Dixon Blanket Rule: Flexible Treatment to Protect the Morally Innocent. *Oregon Law Review, 87*, 1327–1356.

22. *United States v. Ramirez-Chavez*, U.S. District Court for the Western District of Texas, Del Rio Division, 2013 U.S. Dist. Lexis 92990 (July 2, 2013).

23. Bedi, M. (2011). Criminal Law: Excusing Behavior: Reclassifying the Federal Common Law Defenses of Duress and Necessity Relying on the Victim's Role. *Journal of Criminal Law & Criminology, 101*(Spring), 575–632.

24. *United States v. Keung*, 761 F. Supp (S.D.N.Y. 1991).

25. *United States v. Jones*, 900 F.2d 512 (2d Cir. 1990) cert. denied, 111 S. Ct. 131.

26. *United States v. Keung*, at 255–256.

27. *United States v. Jones*, at 519.

28. *United States v. Keung*, at 256; Gur-Arye, M. (2002). Reliance on a Layer's Mistaken Advice—Should It Be an Excuse from Criminal Liability? *American Criminal Law Review, 29*(Summer), 455.

29. *Reves v. Ernst and Young*, 113 S. Ct. 1163 (1993).

30. *Baumer v. Pachl*, 8 F.3d 1341 (9th Cir. 1993); Jones, A., Satory, J., & Mace, T. (2002). Racketeer Influenced and Corrupt Organizations. *American Criminal Law Review, 39*(Spring), 977.

31. *Tose v. Greate Bay Hotel and Casino*, 819 F. Supp 1312 (D.N.J. 1993).

32. at 1318, 1320; Drennan, M. (2003). Duty of Care to the Intoxicated: "The Irish Approach?" *San Diego International Law Journal, 4*, 423.

33. Dix, G. E., Michael Sharlot, M., & Newman, J. S. (2002). *Criminal Law: Cases and Materials* (5th ed.). St. Paul, MN: West Wadsworth, p. 213.

34. 18 U.S.C. Sec. 17 (2000); *United States v. Knott*, 894 F.2d. 1119 (9th Cir. 1990).

35. President's Commission on Organized Crime (1987). *The Impact: Organized Crime Today.* Washington, DC: U.S. Government Printing Office, p. 221.

36. President's Commission on Organized Crime (1986). *Transcript of Proceedings: Testimony of Martin Light.* Washington, DC: U.S. Government Printing Office, pp. 40, 74.

37. *The Impact: Organized Crime Today*, pp. 228–229.

38. Glaberson, W. "Effort to Oust Gotti Lawyer Reopens Debate on Tactics," *The New York Times* (May 4, 1998), B6; Groth, A. "The Don of Criminal Defense Attorneys: Gerald Shargel Defends Collars of Every Color . . . as well as the Mob," *New York Superlawyers.com* (September 2011).

39. *In re James L. Bulger*, 710 F.3d 42 (2013).

40. Ragano, F., & Raab, S. (1997). *Mob Lawyer.* New York: Simon & Schuster.

41. Ragano and Raab, *Mob Lawyer*, p. 357.

42. *Mob Lawyer*, p. 362.

43. *Mob Lawyer*.

44. Marzulli, J. "Mob Lawyer Gets 14 Years in Bribe Case," *Daily News* (New York) (December 5, 2009), 10.

45. *The Impact: Organized Crime Today*, p. 249.

46. *The Impact: Organized Crime Today*, p. 253.

47. Abendano, K. A. (2001). The Role of Lawyers in the Right against Money Laundering: Is a Reporting Requirement Appropriate? *Journal of Legislation, 27*, 463; Fine, A. J. (2013). Kaley V. United States: The Right to Counsel of Choice Caught in the Wide Net of Asset Forfeiture. *Duke Journal of Constitutional Law & Public Policy Sidebar, 9*, 59–80.

48. Samuel, L. M. (2002). Restraining the Global Threat. In R. Broadhurst (Ed.), *Transnational Organized Crime Conference: Proceedings*. Hong Kong Police Force.

49. *The Impact: Organized Crime Today*, p. 253; "Jacksonville Attorney Accused of Being Mastermind of $300 Million Gambling Scheme," *Jacksonville.com* (March 13, 2013).

50. Chevrier, E. (2004). The French Government's Will to Fight Organized Crime and Clean Up the Legal Professions: The Awkward Compromise between Professional Secrecy and Mandatory Reporting. *Crime, Law & Social Change, 42*, 184–200; Di Nicola, A., & Zoffi, P. (2004). Italian Lawyers and Criminal Clients: Risks and Countermeasures. *Crime, Law & Social Change, 42*, 201–225; Middleton, D. J., & Levi, M. (2004). The Role of Solicitors in Facilitating "Organized Crime": Situational Crime Opportunities and Their Regulation *Crime, Law & Social Change*, 123–161; U.S. Department of Justice (2013). *Defense Attorney Sentenced to Serve 63 Months in Prison for Obstruction of Justice*. Washington, DC: Office of Public Affairs, March 12.

CHAPTER 12

Sentencing and Prevention of Organized Crime

The only thing I have left is a few nice suits,
and I don't have any place to wear them.

—Larry Bronson (mob lawyer, upon being sentenced
for theft of client funds and tax evasion, 2008)

Nearly 40 years ago, an evaluation of the success of the federal effort in combating organized crime was critical of the effort. There was "no agreement on what organized crime is" and, predictably, the government had "not developed a strategy" for fighting organized crime.[1] Similar conclusions were drawn in an evaluation of state and county "rackets bureaus." That report found "no consensus" regarding the type of criminal activity to be targeted. A "variety of limitations" were found with agency jurisdictions, and training of police and prosecutors was found to be "woefully inadequate."[2] An analysis of gambling prosecutions in 17 cities found "no system of accountability" to guide the prosecution effort.[3] A follow-up investigation 4 years later found improvement but underutilization of the law. Only 50 RICO cases had been prosecuted since the earlier evaluation, and "no organized crime organizations" had been eliminated through prosecution.[4]

Since that time, things have changed. A series of significant prosecutions occurred beginning in the 1980s and continuing to the present (as outlined in Chapter 6). Existing laws, providing for extended penalties and asset forfeitures, were employed in many of these cases. This chapter examines sentences imposed in racketeering and drug trafficking cases as compared to other federal criminal sentences. The types of racketeering convictions achieved, the trends in assets forfeiture, and organized crime prevention alternatives for the future are assessed.

SENTENCES IMPOSED IN RACKETEERING AND DRUG CASES

Sentences imposed in organized crime cases can be evaluated by comparing them with past sentences, as well as sentences imposed for other,

Table 12.1 Sentences Imposed on Convicted Offenders

Organized Crime Sentencing	2003	2005	2010	2013
RICO case convictions after prosecution	195	232	188	228
Average RICO prison sentence (months)	67	88	135	138
Drugs—continuing criminal enterprise (CCE) convictions after prosecution	62	69	60	54
Average CCE prison sentence (months)	90	148	91	155
Drug trafficking conspiracy convictions after prosecution (non-CCE)	9,481	9,394	8,144	9,773
Average drug conspiracy sentence (months)	92	97	84	66
Total—all federal convictions after prosecution (all lead charges)	78,268	93,858	143,732	151,372
Average sentence (all federal convictions for all lead charges) (months)	45	40	27	25

non-organized crime-related federal offenses. Table 12.1 presents sentences of convicted federal offenders prosecuted by U.S. Attorneys' offices nationwide for selected offenses.

Table 12.1 indicates that prison sentences are quite long in organized crime cases and it illustrates trends over 10 years. In racketeering (RICO) cases, there are about 200 convictions each year, and the average sentence in those cases has increased over the years to 138 months in prison (11.5 years). Continuing criminal enterprise (CCE) drug conspiracy convictions are less common, averaging 54-69 convictions annually, but sentences increased to an average of 155 months in prison in 2013 (13 years). Other drug conspiracy offenders (non-CCE prosecutions) were sentenced to an average of 66 months (5.5 years) in prison in 2013, a number which has declined over the last decade. The last two rows in Table 12.1 show totals and averages for all federal prosecutions (for all lead charges). It can be seen that a very large number of convictions occur, which has been increasing dramatically in recent years to more than 151,000 nationwide in 2013. Average sentences for these offenses are 25 months (2.1 years). Therefore, racketeering and drug conspiracy offenses result in significantly longer prison sentences than other kinds of federal felony convictions. Although the RICO and CCE laws were enacted in 1970 and 1987, respectively, prosecutors did not utilize them immediately. These laws allow for prosecutions of ongoing conspiracies, as well as for individual crimes committed during the course of those conspiracies (i.e., predicate offenses) (see Chapter 10). They provide for extended penalties up to 20 years. These statutory changes, together with increasing usage of these laws by prosecutors in more serious cases, have resulted in a significant increase in the incarceration of offenders in organized crime-related cases.

Table 12.2 provides an indication of prosecution outcomes in all federal organized crime cases taken together. It shows moderate consistency in organized crime prosecutions over the years, with a decline in the number of convictions since the 1990s, but a rise in the percentage of offenders sentenced to prison.

Table 12.2 All Federal Organized Crime Prosecutions[a]

Organized Crime Cases	1995	2000	2005	2010	2013
Number convicted	582	468	468	396	290
Percent sentenced to prison	54	77	72	86	87
Average prison sentence (years)	4.8	4.5	4.8	8.3	6.3

[a]*Transactional Records Clearinghouse at trac.syr.edu. Includes violations of statutes relating to gambling, extortion, and alcoholic beverages; infiltration of legitimate business by organized crime; and related organized crime offenses.*

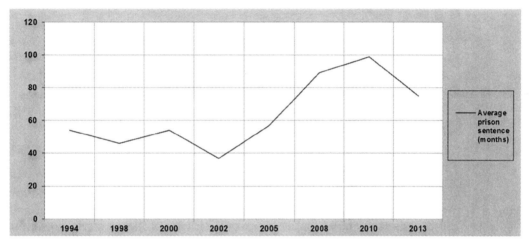

FIGURE 12.1 Average prison sentences imposed in federal organized crime cases (1994-2013). Source: Transactional Records Clearinghouse at http://trac.syr.edu

Convictions range from 582 to 290 each year with between 54% and 87% resulting in prison sentences. Since 1995, the average federal prison sentence in these cases has risen from 4.8 to 6.3 years in length.

A graphic depiction of trends in sentences in federal organized crime cases over a longer period is presented in Figure 12.1. It illustrates that over a 20-year period (1994-2013), sentences fluctuated but generally trended upward, averaging more than 5 years in prison (68 months). Sentences have increased in length in recent years, averaging more than 6 years in 2013. This fact also reinforces the high level of seriousness of sentences imposed in the mob trial cases (discussed in Chapter 6), which averaged sentences of 20 years in length.

TYPES OF RACKETEERING CONVICTIONS

Offenses that underlie a racketeering conspiracy provide an indication of the types of activities pursued by organized crime groups. A look at predicate

Table 12.3 Predicate Offenses in Racketeering Cases (18 USC 1962 RICO Prohibited Acts—Underlying Prosecution Target, Other Than the Racketeering Charge)

Predicate Target	Cases for Year 2013 (%)
Drug trafficking, conspiracy offenses	47
Organized crime—emerging groups	15
Organized crime—traditional groups	14
Organized crime—high-priority target group	8
Violent crime	7
Weapons offenses	4
Corruption	2
Fraud	1
Other	2

Based on 226 cases from 2013 for which predicate offense or target information was available.

offenses illustrates the nature of underlying racketeering organized crime activity, at least as it is reflected in criminal prosecutions.

Table 12.3 presents predicate (underlying) offenses or targets in organized crime racketeering convictions during 2013. It is important to understand that a racketeer must engage in a particular type of illegal activity to support an ongoing criminal enterprise. An understanding of these activities provides a clue as to which endeavors are at "high risk" of racketeer involvement.

It can be seen that drug trafficking cases dominated racketeering prosecutions for ongoing criminal conspiracies, comprising 47% of the total. Interestingly, cases involving specific organized crime groups dominate the remainder of the racketeering cases: those involving traditional (Italian-American) groups, emerging groups (other ethnicities and nationalities), and high-priority targets (a multi-agency target list of leadership elements of the most prolific international drug trafficking and money laundering organizations). Together, these three types of organized crime groups comprised 37% of all racketeering convictions in 2013. Smaller numbers of racketeering cases targeted violent crime, weapons offenses, corruption, and fraud.

The figures presented here may reflect law enforcement and prosecution priorities in making cases, or may provide a true indication of current racketeering conspiracies in the United States. It is likely that each of these possibilities has a degree of merit, depending on the geographic location under consideration and the specific case(s) one highlights. As the opportunities for organized crime continue to change with new technologies, communications, and travel possibilities, these trends are likely to shift again in the coming decade.

BACKGROUNDS OF CONVICTED OFFENDERS

The backgrounds of those convicted of organized crime-related offenses are quite different from those of street criminals. Offenders convicted in federal court of organized crime-related offenses are overwhelmingly male (90% on average), white (77%), and over 30 years old (72%). These numbers vary somewhat by type of offense, but the backgrounds of these offenders are remarkably consistent. The advanced age of some of the organized crime offenders is highlighted by the fact that 53% of RICO offenders are more than 40 years of age. Forty-two percent of both CCE and predicate offenders are older than 40.

When compared to "street" criminals serving time in state prisons, the differences are dramatic. With street criminals, the proportion of male versus female offenders is still overwhelming, but only half as many are white (35% versus 72%). The proportion of offenders under age 21 is four times that in organized crime cases (12% versus an average of 3% in organized crime cases).

Three-fourths of organized crime offenders have been incarcerated before, as compared to 61% of conventional criminals.[5] This is probably due to the younger ages of conventional criminals, who have not had as much life experience to break the law.

Another reason for differences between organized crime and conventional street criminals is that organized crimes often are carried out by career criminals with long-time relationships. Street criminals, however, most often commit crimes against property or crimes of violence that involve little planning or organization. Their apprehension for these street crimes may well be a function of their age and relative lack of sophistication, at least when it comes to law violation.

TRENDS IN ASSET FORFEITURE

In addition to longer prison sentences, another trend in sentencing has been forfeiture. The large revenues generated from narcotics trafficking and other organized crime activity can affect the legitimate banking system adversely, as well as the economy in general, through untaxed profits and illicitly funded investments. Asset forfeiture is seen as a way to undermine the fiscal structure and even the survival of an organized crime group or network by seizing illicitly obtained cash and any property involved in criminal activity. An actual case illustrates its importance: Several members of the North Carolina Almighty Latin King/Queen Nation (ALKQN) were sentenced to prison in federal court in North Carolina in 2013 for racketeering. ALKQN is a violent street gang that originated in Chicago in the 1960s and ultimately migrated to cities throughout the United States. ALKQN members met in North Carolina on a regular basis over several years to discuss criminal activity (including weapons distribution, robbery, fraud, and murder).[6] The proceeds of this criminal activity helped to finance the gang's illegal activities, so it can be seen how incarceration of leaders does not defeat ongoing activities of the group financed by past and future crimes. This is what asset forfeiture is designed to accomplish.

Congress enacted two major laws that provided the government with criminal forfeiture authority in organized crime cases. The RICO provisions of the Organized Crime Control Act state that an offender forfeits all interests in an enterprise when convicted for racketeering involvement. The Comprehensive Drug Prevention and Control Act allows for forfeiture of profits derived from a CCE that traffics in narcotics.

Civil forfeitures (i.e., those not requiring a criminal conviction) generally result from actions of the Drug Enforcement Administration (DEA) and U.S. Customs and Border Protection. Rather than attempting to seize the profits from illicit enterprises, civil forfeitures are usually directed against contraband (e.g., drugs or guns) and derivative contraband (e.g., vehicles and aircraft used to transport contraband).

Forfeiture laws were not used much when they were first available because their power to disrupt criminal enterprises was still unknown. Between 1970 and 1980, for example, the RICO and CCE provisions were applied in only 98 drug cases and assets forfeited amounted to only $2 million. This is extremely low usage of forfeiture when one considers that more than 5,000 class I violators (the most serious group) were arrested by the DEA during this period. Furthermore, these statutes were designed to combat the infiltration of organized crime into legitimate business, but a government evaluation found that during this period there was "no forfeiture of significant derivative proceeds or business interests acquired with illicit funds."[7]

The Organized Crime Drug Enforcement Task Force (OCDETF) program was established in 1983 by the federal government to "identify, investigate, and prosecute high-level members of drug trafficking enterprises and to destroy their operations." The program is composed of 13 task forces around the country. A national drug policy board, consisting of the directors of 10 federal agencies and departments, provides national oversight for the program. The board reviews national policy and interagency coordination required for OCDETF. Today, OCDETF member federal agencies include: the Drug Enforcement Administration (DEA), the Federal Bureau of Investigation (FBI), the Bureau of Immigration and Customs Enforcement (ICE), the Bureau of Alcohol, Tobacco, Firearms, and Explosives (ATF), the U.S. Marshals Service, the Internal Revenue Service (IRS), and the U.S. Coast Guard. These agencies work with the Department of Justice Criminal Division, the Tax Division, U.S. Attorney's Offices, and state and local law enforcement.

The OCDETF program seized $52 million in assets in 2 years in cases involving 1,408 offenders. Through 1990, federal law enforcement agencies had seized $1.4 billion in cash and property.[8] The program's effectiveness continues today as OCDETF agencies initiated 1,074 investigations, and seized $1.25 billion in cash and property in 2013 alone.[9] The GAO concluded that "the traditional law enforcement remedy, incarceration of drug dealers, has not made much of an impact on drug trafficking." Greater use of forfeiture offers the opportunity to disrupt continuing illicit enterprises and to curtail the effect of large amounts of illicitly obtained cash on the economy. A Presidential Executive Order was signed in 2011 as part of the *National Strategy to Combat Transnational Organized Crime* to block property and cash transactions of major transnational crime networks that threaten national security.[10] This action further elevated the role of asset forfeiture in addressing all forms of organized crime around the world that affect the United States.

In recent years, there has been a growing body of case law and policy regarding the seizure and disposition of property in asset forfeiture cases. These concerns generally fall into one of three categories:

1. Lawfulness of the assets seizure
2. Protecting the rights of third parties
3. Management and disposition of seized assets

CRITICAL THINKING EXERCISE 12.1

Read the following scenario and answer the questions that follow, applying principles from this chapter.

The Case of Deterring Terrorists Versus Organized Crime

One of the most frightening aspects of the terrorist incidents of September 11, 2001, was the fact that the perpetrators willingly killed themselves along with innocent people in the airplanes and on the ground. How can the violence of those willing to engage in suicide missions be deterred?

In October 2001, a judge in New York imposed life sentences on four men. One was convicted of carrying out the truck bomb attack at the U.S. Embassy in Tanzania in 1998 and murdering the 11 people who died there. Others were involved in the suicide truck bombing of the U.S. Embassy in Kenya on the same day as the Tanzania attack. They were convicted of murdering the 213 people killed in that blast.

That was the only U.S. trial against followers of Osama bin Laden to that point in time. U.S. Attorney General John Ashcroft said, "Today's sentence sends a message. The United States will hunt terrorists down and will make them pay the price for their evil acts of terrorism." At sentencing, one of the offenders, speaking Arabic, said: "To Allah we belong and to him we return. May God help me in my calamity and replace it with goodness. On God I rely and in him I put my trust." This illustrates the difficulty in preventing crimes committed by those who believe they are doing it for a "higher cause." In organized crime cases, the offenses are usually profit driven rather than ideologically or politically driven. When caught, because many organized crime figures see jail time as a cost of doing business rather than the "end of the line," prison sentences sometimes do not have the desired deterrent effect.

Critical Thinking Questions

1. In order for people to be deterred from committing crimes, what must be their state of mind and belief about criminal penalties?
2. Are there other ways (not involving the justice system) that can be employed to reduce the number of people who might believe that murder of innocents can be excused by appealing to a higher cause or rationale?
3. Compare the motivations of terrorists versus those involved in organized crime. Which type of criminal can be deterred more easily, and why?
4. Are there certain kinds of sentences that would serve as better deterrents to future crime than jail time?

Lawfulness of Asset Seizure

The legal principle behind forfeiture is that the government may take property without compensation to the owner if the property is acquired or used illegally. There are two methods of accomplishing this: civil and criminal.

In a criminal forfeiture, property can only be seized once the owner has been convicted of certain crimes (such as RICO). The forfeiture action in these cases is part of the criminal trial. A civil forfeiture occurs independently of any criminal proceeding and is directed at the property itself having been used or acquired illegally. Conviction of the property owner is not relevant in a civil forfeiture. In addition, there is a form of civil forfeiture called "administrative" forfeiture. In these cases, the seizing agency mails notices to all people known to have any ownership interest in the property, and a notice is also placed in the newspapers. If no one claims the property within 30 days, it is forfeited without court action.[11] This administrative procedure was designed to reduce the extent of processing and costs incurred if all seizures went through the courts. Civil forfeiture has been defended as an aid to law enforcement on the grounds that because it takes illegal property from those who purchased or owned it unlawfully, it may serve as a deterrent to criminal behavior, and it compensates the government for the cost of enforcing the law.[12] However, critics see a profit motive from some police agencies who seize assets in inappropriate cases in order to raise funds for the department.[13] (Police departments are permitted to keep most of the profits from property sold after it has been seized.)

The procedure for a civil forfeiture is different from other civil actions in that many forfeiture laws require only that the government show probable cause that the property was implicated in criminal activity. Originally, the burden then shifted to the property owner, who had to establish by a preponderance of the evidence that the law was not violated, probable cause does not exist, or he or she has an affirmative defense.[14] This provision was changed by the Civil Asset Forfeiture Reform Act (2000), which created an innocent owner defense and placed the burden of wrongdoing entirely on the government.[15] Government wrongdoing includes seizures made without probable cause, a law violation by government agents, or if an affirmative defense applies. Determination of probable cause is made by considering the "totality of circumstances" involved.[16] Certain types of circumstantial evidence can be used in evaluating these circumstances: "close proximity" between the asset and drugs, concealment efforts, extensive cash expenditures, and net worth analysis are examples.[17]

All "proceeds" of crime are subject to forfeiture, which has been interpreted to include interest, dividends, income, and real property. In North Carolina, for example, drug traffickers used their illicit profits to buy real estate there. Later, they sold it at a profit and bought other real estate in Florida with the proceeds. The government was able to seize that property as "derivative proceeds." The government was also able to keep, as part of that seizure, any appreciation earned on the investment (i.e., the increased value of the North Carolina property, as well as that of the Florida property).[18] On the other hand, the U.S. Supreme Court heard a case involving a person traveling with his family who failed to report that he was carrying more than $10,000 in cash on an international flight. The government sought forfeiture of the entire $357,144 he was carrying. Because the money was not connected to any crime (other than the failure to report it), the forfeiture was considered an excessive fine, violating the Eighth Amendment. The penalty was reduced to $20,000 and 3 years' probation.[19]

Protecting the Rights of Third Parties

A problem arises concerning the rights of individuals not involved in criminal activity, but whose property was used in, or derived from, the criminal activity of others. This might include uninformed lien holders and purchasers, joint tenants, or business partners.

However, a person who suspects his or her property is the target of a criminal or civil forfeiture investigation may sell the property, give ownership to family members, or otherwise dispose of it. The rule known as the "relation-back doctrine" holds that forfeiture occurs at the time that the property first becomes involved in an illegal act rather than at the later time when the government attempts to forfeit the property. Therefore, subsequent transfers to third parties are not dispositive in forfeiture proceedings.[20]

Third-party claims on seized property are delayed in criminal forfeitures because the claim cannot be litigated until the end of the criminal trial. As a result, third-party claims may not be heard until several years after the property is taken. The procedure is quicker in civil forfeitures because the forfeiture hearing usually occurs very soon after the forfeiture, usually within days. In criminal forfeitures, it is more difficult to make a successful third-party claim. A purchaser of an illegally used piece of property, for example, must have been "reasonably without knowledge" of any illegality. This has caused problems for defense attorneys whose fees may be subject to forfeiture, "since an attorney virtually always has reason to know that fees paid by an alleged narcotics dealer are proceeds of crime."[21] The U.S. Supreme Court has upheld pretrial freezing of a defendant's assets, even where the defendant seeks to use the assets to pay his or her attorney.[22] In subsequent cases, however, the court has held that the owner of the property must be notified before the property is seized and given some chance to challenge the seizure before it takes place.[23]

In civil forfeitures, third parties are protected under the "innocent owner" exception if the government fails to establish that they had "knowledge, consent, or willful blindness" regarding illegal usage of the property.[24] After John Gotti's racketeering conviction, for example, the federal government filed a civil forfeiture suit aimed at seizing seven buildings and three businesses it contended were used to conduct illegal gambling and racketeering operations. A hunt-and-fish club, a bar, a restaurant, a garment manufacturer, the Ravenite Social Club, and other properties were targeted.[25] It is the task of the government to demonstrate by a preponderance of the evidence that the property owners had knowledge, gave consent, or showed willful blindness in how their property was used.

Disposition of Seized Assets

The most commonly seized assets are cash and cars, followed by boats, planes, jewelry, and weapons. These items comprise 95% of all seized assets, although less commonly confiscated residential and commercial property has a higher monetary value.[26] Once an asset is seized, it must be appraised. This appraisal determines the property's value, less any liens against it. The item must be stored and maintained while ownership and third-party claims are heard in court. If the challenge to the seizure is not effective, the property is taken for government use or auctioned. Notices of these sales and lists of forfeited property are published each month (see Figure 12.2).

FIGURE 12.2 A media preview for an auction that includes jewelry and other personal items from convicted felon Bernard Madoff''s penthouse apartment on Manhattan's Upper East Side and a Montauk, New York, beach house will be sold as part of the auction of property seized under the federal Asset Forfeiture Program. *Brian Zak/Sipa Press/madoff_bz.004/0911131949 (Sipa via AP Images)*

Storage and maintenance can be both profitable and costly. Cash seizures are kept in interest-bearing accounts. An arrangement in Fort Lauderdale allows the bank to count and simultaneously photograph every bill before depositing it in the law enforcement agency's account.[27] Cars, boats, and planes must be stored so that they are preserved and do not suffer damage. Storage of these things can be costly, as can maintenance of real property, and disposal can be difficult to arrange.[28]

Due to the administrative issues posed by the management and disposition of seized property, the U.S. Marshal's Service has more than 200 full-time and part-time employees assigned to handling assets seized by federal agencies. The U.S. Customs and Border Protection has more than 100 full-time paralegals to handle seized property. Occasionally, it is hard to dispose of some piece of property. In Broward County, Florida, a load of hashish had been surrounded by a load of maple wood. They considered donating the wood or giving it away because they could not justify returning it to the owner. They eventually destroyed it.[29]

Controversy continues over the use of seized assets by some local police agencies. State laws often earmark specific uses for their seized assets, such as for education and health costs. There have been cases, however, in which local police seize property and then turn it over to the federal government, which allows the police department to keep 80% of the seized assets for its own use. This has been viewed by some as "profiteering" by police, in that they may be directing their operations to activities that will bring seizures rather than law enforcement for the primary purpose of public safety.[30] Evidence is unclear in trying to demonstrate profit making by police over law enforcement objectives, but there is an incentive to do so, especially when enforcement budgets are tight.[31]

CRITICAL THINKING EXERCISE 12.2

Read the following scenario and answer the questions that follow, applying principles from this chapter.

The Case of a Close Family Friend
You decide to go away to college, but you don't know what to do with your 2,000 Corvette. It won't fit in your family's garage, you are afraid to leave it parked on the street, and you can't bring yourself to sell it.

A close family friend, Elvis, offers a solution. He offers to care for the car and keep it in his garage in exchange for you allowing him to drive it while you are away at college. When you come home for vacations and summers, the car will be yours. It sounds like the only possible solution, and you only hope your friend treats your car gently.

After you are away to school for a month, you receive notification that your Corvette has been seized by the U.S. government. Elvis has been charged with using your car to transport illegal narcotics.

Critical Thinking Questions
1. What are the important factors on the judge should rely to make his or her decision?
2. What reason does the judge have to believe you innocently loaned your car to a close family friend?
3. How would this case be different if you were a car rental agency and merely rented a car to Elvis in which he was caught transporting drugs?

INNOVATIONS IN SENTENCING AND CRIME PREVENTION

In addition to forfeiture, new and imaginative prevention measures and sanctions have been used in organized crime cases with potentially significant long-term impacts. These include oversight of union activities, offender deterrence tactics, threat assessments, and the role of public education.

Oversight of Union Activities

Italian-American organized crime has been involved with the infiltration of legitimate business (i.e., industrial racketeering) for most of the twentieth century. It took the form of wielding significant power in labor unions and in the companies themselves by choosing the workers to be hired and demanding monetary kickbacks on earnings. Prominent examples include the New York City garment district, the Fulton Fish Market, John F. Kennedy Airport, the Javits Convention Center, the waste-hauling industry, and the construction industry in the New York City area. In each case, a Cosa Nostra group successfully infiltrated a business by providing a service (usually protection from worker or supply stoppages) in exchange for a piece of the business (usually no-show employees or monetary kickbacks on contracts or earnings).[32] Criminal penalties that resulted from convictions of Cosa Nostra figures involved in these illicit activities had little impact on the operation of these scams. Penalties were regarded as an inconvenience rather than a deterrent. The application of civil RICO provisions, however, enabled prosecutors to seek restraining orders, injunctions, and court-ordered monitoring of businesses. Because the burden of proof is lower in civil cases than in criminal cases, the presence of organized crime in an industry is easier to prove. Several unique settlements in these cases resulted in the establishment of inspector generals to monitor businesses and in new corruption controls that included the licensing of firms only after they were found to be free of organized crime influence.

After 23 trash-hauling companies and 4 trade associations were indicted in New York City for large-scale corruption, the Trade Waste Commission was created to review and license every waste service provider in order to keep out unsavory operators. This restructuring of the entire industry in New York "appears to have succeeded in eliminating the mob from New York City waste management."[33] A federal oversight of union activities was documented in a study commissioned by the Teamsters Union and was conducted by a team of former prosecutors and FBI agents. The 641-page study found that only a few pockets of organized crime influence remained. "By removing a critical mass of racketeers and their associates, the government-imposed monitoring destroyed the mob's political base in the union at the same time law enforcement successes were shattering the myth of mob invincibility."[34]

However, an analysis of all 21 civil RICO union trusteeships to date found that only 3 were completely successful and that several were failures. A continuing problem has been that it was assumed by the government that court-appointed trustees (often former government investigators and attorneys) would be welcomed by the union membership, but "two decades of experience have proven otherwise. There is far more rank-and-file suspicion of the government, the courts, and the trustees than public officials had anticipated or want to admit."[35] Nevertheless, careful evaluations of the reasons behind the successes and failures are needed to provide answers to the question of whether long government oversight must continue to keep union activities honest.[36]

Offender Deterrence Tactics

There are ways to deter offenders from future misconduct, even if they have not been formally adjudicated. A Red Carpet Inn in Houston, for example, was the subject of frequent police activity. There were narcotics arrests and narcotics seizures of more than $800,000 in only 2 years. The Houston city attorney sent numerous letters to the hotel owner and manager, and officers from the Houston antidrug task force held meetings with the hotel owner to discuss suggestions for controlling narcotics activity at the hotel. These requests were ignored for 3 years. Finally, the U.S. attorney began a civil legal action seeking forfeiture of the Red Carpet Inn. Faced with the prospect of forfeiture, the owner finally agreed to implement the steps recommended by the Houston police, which included installation of additional lighting, monitoring hotel security cameras 24 hours a day, and having a licensed security guard on the premise at all times. In return for these changes, the U.S. attorney agreed to drop the forfeiture suit.[37] The threat of civil forfeiture was enough in this case to change behavior that affected both crime and the conditions in the community. A "landlord training program" has been designed to contribute to the deterrence of criminal activity by teaching landlords the warning signs of drug activity, what to do about it, screening potential tenants, and setting up "apartment watch" programs.[38]

There is a New York City Business Integrity Commission that regulates the wholesale meat, seafood, and produce markets operating on city-owned land in Hunts Point (in the South Bronx). The commission was created in 2001 to consolidate earlier efforts to combat organized crime infiltration in the wholesale food markets, commercial garbage hauling, and shipboard gambling. It collects personal information about those working in the markets and, after a state court decision, started focusing on workers outside the public markets to look for possible organized crime influence among vendors and related companies. Since 2009, the agency has registered 54 companies in the area adjoining the markets and has collected applications for background checks and identification cards from their employees. Employers face heavy fines for noncompliance. This strategy is designed to deter organized crime involvement in a high-risk environment without placing excessive burdens on law-abiding companies and individuals.[39]

In a similar way, gang injunctions have been used in a number of jurisdictions. These injunctions are based on documentation of the involvement of specific gangs and their members in creating a public nuisance, affecting the neighborhood residents' right to live in peace and security. The injunctions target those who engage in trespass, intimidation, disturbances, alcohol and other drug consumption, and related activities impacting the local neighborhood on an ongoing basis. These injunctions, enforceable through court orders and contempt charges for violations, are a way to limit the ability of gangs to disrupt life in a local area. In a related way, the city of Los Angeles won its first civil suit in 2009 against the 18th Street Gang under a state law that targeted the assets of gang leaders. The successful suit collected damages for property damage, personal injury, denying residents access to public parks, and emotional distress. [40]

These efforts show that criminal convictions are not needed to intervene in a meaningful way in criminal activity. Without proof of criminal wrongdoing, civil actions and threatened civil actions can be taken to encourage behavior that does not support organized crime activity.

Threat Assessment

It is not possible to prosecute our way out of the organized crime problem. Although enforcement will always be an important component of the repertoire, it addresses only part of the problem. A UN assessment of organized crime in West Africa characterized the problem in this way: "unless the flows of contraband are addressed, instability and lawlessness will persist … Each of these flows requires a tailored response, because the commodities involved respond to distinct sources of supply and demand (e.g., drugs, arms, counterfeit medicine, smuggled migrants)." Similarly the World Bank reported on the "ease with which corrupt actors hide their interests behind a corporate veil and the difficulties investigators face in trying to lift that veil."[41] Because organized crime is a "community of practice populated by individuals in ever mutating networks of relationality seeking to profit from illegal capitalism" there must be ways to identify and prevent these networks from forming.[42]

For example, Finland, Hungary, Italy, and the Netherlands reported an in-depth analysis of 15 cases of organized crime, looking for "red flags" that suggested possible preventive measures. These cases involved trafficking in women, smuggling of illegal immigrants, and drug trafficking. The analysis found three factors in common in these cases: demand for illegal products and services from the legal environment, abuse of facilitators in the legal environment (e.g., public officials, landlords, taxi drivers), and the availability of legal "tools" (e.g., forged documents, money laundering).[43] Both European Union (EU) and North American countries have examined individual and structural measures associated with organized crime, including money laundering control measures; forged document prevention; and making more difficult the manufacture of synthetic drugs, the smuggling of stolen art, restricted timber, and contraband cigarettes.[44] In addition, there have been efforts to exclude certain individuals and organizations from participating in different markets, such as construction and public works, due to past associations with organized crime activity.[45] These efforts are noteworthy because they are not primarily aimed at the perpetrators of organized crime, but rather at the circumstances that facilitate organized crime activity. In this way, enforcement efforts can become prevention efforts when they aim at goals beyond development of a single case.

Organized crime can be seen as the product of market forces, similar to those that cause legitimate businesses to flourish or die in the legal sector of the economy. When divided into its component parts, it is clear that "business" influences affect organized crime activity. All enterprises, both legal and illegal, exist to survive and make a profit. Whether the product is drugs, stolen property, sexual services, counterfeiting, or other crimes, the criminals must account for supply (of materials needed), the nature and location of demand (by potential customers), the regulators who might put them out of business (e.g., law, police), and competitors (comprised of other criminal groups and products) which might reduce their profitability or even survival in the market.

The enterprise and situational crime prevention perspectives (discussed in Chapter 4) can be combined in the case of organized crime to develop crime prevention measures best suited to the *entrepreneurial* aspects of organized crime. For example, the best methods for "increasing the risks" are much easier to develop, when you consider how these risks are distributed among the influences of suppliers, customers, regulators, and competitors when organized crime is seen as a form of enterprise. The same is true for "increasing the effort" needed by offenders to carry out crimes, and the other aspects of the situational crime prevention perspective (reducing rewards, provocation, and removing excuses). Therefore, the elements of enterprise theory help to target the precise types of efforts likely to impact ongoing organized crime activity. Efforts to prevent organized crime, using the principles of situational crime prevention, are more likely to be accurately-focused and comprehensive when applied through the lens of enterprise theory.

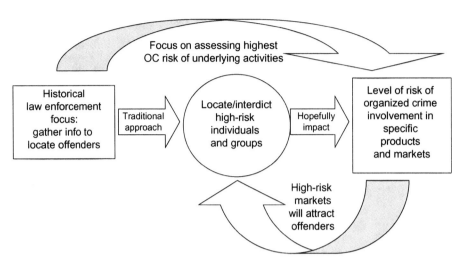

FIGURE 12.3 An illustration of how focusing on high-risk products and markets for organized crime involvement can lead to apprehension of individual offenders and groups.

If we properly assess and rank these illicit markets and activities, our targeting of these activities will lead us, in turn, to the high-risk people (organized crime groups) involved in them. Another way to illustrate this objective is presented in Figure 12.3.

Figure 12.3 compares traditional approaches to organized crime risk assessment. Historically, the focus of risk assessment has been to gather information on offenders to locate and interdict high-risk individuals and groups involved in organized crime. The long-term goal is that prosecution of these individuals will hopefully have an impact on the illicit activities involved (the straight arrows from left to right in Figure 12.3). The alternative prevention approach (following the large, curved arrows in Figure 12.3), looks to assessment of high risk in specific products and markets, knowing that these markets will attract the offenders that law enforcement seeks. The difference in the two approaches is that the traditional approach focuses on high-risk *offenders* (with impacts on illicit markets and activities a secondary concern), whereas the alternative approach focuses on identification of high-risk *products and markets* (knowing that targeting these will have a more substantial impact and also yield the offenders involved). Put another way, if you correctly identify the high-risk products and markets, you will know where to look for the offenders. This is an important distinction because even markets with no prior history of organized crime can be identified through this process, providing information for investigators beyond what might be obtained from targeting assessments to those individuals and groups with known ties to organized crime.

Efforts to address organized crime in this way have begun in several parts of the world. The Europol Scanning, Analysis, and Notification System provides EU governments with strategic early warning notices regarding new organized crime threats based on early assessments. Research-to-practice efforts in the United Kingdom and Canada also have focused on the reduction of organized crime rather than merely prosecution of known offenders. In addition, efforts by the World Economic Forum and others are now focusing on precursors and enablers of organized crime in order to better assess threats and target prevention efforts.[46]

Role of Public Education

A central problem to the persistence of organized crime is the public's tolerance for it. Organized crime profits are derived largely from the vices of the citizenry, whether it is drugs, gambling, prostitution, services of human trafficking victims, or stolen property of some kind. David Rocci pled guilty to conspiracy to violate the Digital Millennium Copyright Act. Rocci was the owner and operator of an Internet site dedicated to providing information about copyright infringement (www.iSONEWS.com). Rocci used this Web site to sell circumvention devices known as Amod chips, which defeat the security protections in Microsoft Xbox—allowing unlimited play of pirated games on the Xbox gaming console. As a condition of his guilty plea, Rocci transferred his domain name and Web site to the U.S. government. In an imaginative move, the government replaced iSONEWS.com with a new Web page providing information about the case *United States v. Rocci*, as well as a general antipiracy message outlining potential criminal consequences for engaging in illegal piracy. The case was the first time the United States assumed control of an active domain name in an intellectual property case. After 2 weeks, the site received more than 550,000 hits. The educational and deterrent value of this effort might exceed that of any alternative criminal sentence.

In a related vein, the Organized Crime Task Force in Northern Ireland was launched in 2002 to educate the public about the dangers of organized crime. It is also designed to make public the high priority given by the government to organized crime cases and to serve as a deterrent to potential offenders.[47] Similarly, the National Crime Agency was established in the United Kingdom in 2013, which consolidated it efforts in the areas of organized crime, border policing, economic crime, the Child Exploitation and Online Protection

Centre, and the National Cyber Crime Unit.[48] This new agency has partnership law enforcement that works with private industry, local and national governments, the charity and voluntary sectors, think tanks, and academia.

Efforts in the United States include a Transnational Organized Crime Rewards Program, established in 2013, which complements the existing Narcotics Rewards Program, by authorizing rewards for information on members of transnational criminal organizations involved in activities beyond drug trafficking that threaten national security, such as human trafficking, money laundering, and trafficking in arms and other illicit goods. A *National Strategy for Combating Wildlife Trafficking* was issued by President Obama in 2014 to strengthen enforcement in the illegal elephant ivory and rhino horn trade, but also to reduce demand for illegally traded wildlife by raising public awareness of the harm done by wildlife trafficking through outreach in the United States and public diplomacy abroad to dissuade consumers from purchasing illegally traded wildlife. A MafiaLeaks Web site was launched in Italy so victims can anonymously report corruption to police and journalists. It is aimed at shopkeepers or business owners forced to pay protection money, as well as members of the public who suspect mafia activity in their communities. These are examples of engaging the civil sector (individuals, schools, media, churches, civic associations) to reduce tolerance for organized crime and assist law enforcement in confronting it.[49]

The participation of so many "average citizens" in the market for stolen goods and illicit services frustrates efforts to weaken the grip of organized crime groups. When fewer people step over the line between innocence and the consumption of illicit goods, the influence of organized crime will be reduced.

SUMMARY

This chapter presented a review of the problems posed by unsuccessful organized crime prosecutions in the past. In recent years, a significant effort has been made, through legislation, law enforcement, and prosecution initiatives, to target organized crime operations more successfully. This effort has produced profound results. Prison sentences in organized crime cases now occur more often and are longer in duration than for virtually any other kind of crime. In the long term, however, the use of asset forfeiture may do more to destroy ongoing criminal enterprises than the incarceration of its current members. Innovative approaches to sentencing involving government monitoring and public education also show promise in making long-term contributions to the prevention of ongoing organized crime activity.

ORGANIZED CRIME BIOGRAPHY

Biographies tell the life story of interesting people. In the world of criminal justice, biographies of organized crime figures offer insight into the background and motivations of the individuals who choose that lifestyle, the reasons for their choices, and their consequences. The following is a brief summary of an organized crime biography, followed by questions that ask you to reflect on the connections between that person's life and the content of this book.

Breakshot: A Life in the 21st Century American Mafia
Kenny Gallo and Matthew Randazzo (Pocket, 2011)

Breakshot tells the story of Kenny "Kenji" Gallo, a Japanese-American youth from the suburbs of Orange County, California, who grew up to become an infamous criminal in the cocaine trade and pornography industry. Gallo led a double life as a suburban youth, leading a drug trafficking group, running a nightclub, producing pornographic movies, and being arrested for murder all before he was 21 years old.

After police had success against his drug trafficking, Gallo abandoned the cocaine trade and married a porn star, while making money in prostitution, credit card fraud, "pump-and-dump" stock fraud, gambling, and extortion. It was his involvement in the pornography industry that introduced him to members of the Mafia in Los Angeles. After years of criminal success, Gallo was ultimately caught and became an informant, wearing a wire against associates in New York's Colombo and Lucchese Mafia families. Given the code name "Breakshot" by the FBI, Gallo's undercover work resulted in jail sentences for several important mobsters, and contracts were put on his life by organized crime figures. Gallo is portrayed in the book as ultimately becoming a legitimate businessman, living in the witness protection program with a new identity, and rejecting his former life in organized crime.

Questions
1. Why do many organized crime figures begin their criminal conduct early in life?
2. Why do you believe it is so difficult for organized crime figures to go straight when given a second chance at life?

ORGANIZED CRIME AT THE MOVIES

Movies seek to entertain and inform the audience about a story, incident, or person. Many good movies also hit upon important substantive themes relevant to understanding organized crime. Read the following movie summary (and watch the movie if you haven't already) and answer the questions that follow to make the organized crime subject matter connections.

Traffic
Steven Soderbergh, Director (2001)

Traffic considers America's war on drugs using three interconnected story lines. The first plot involves a police officer in Mexico, Javier Rodriguez (Benicio Del Toro), who attempts to disrupt a cocaine shipment in the desert with a corrupt partner, Manolo Sanchez (Jacob Vargas). Working in this highly corrupt environment, Rodriguez is himself investigated by a suspect Mexican General who happens to be the U.S. drug enforcement liaison between Mexico and the United States.

A second story line occurs in Ohio and Washington, DC, where a newly appointed conservative federal drug czar, Ohio Judge Robert Wakefield (Michael Douglas), has his antidrug fervor dampened when he discovers that his 16-year-old daughter is a habitual drug user, a situation his wife has tried to keep secret.

A third plot line tells the story of Carlos Alaya (Steven Bauer), a drug kingpin in San Diego who is caught in a DEA sting operation by agents Montel Gordon (Don Cheadle) and Ray Castro (Luis Guzman), leaving behind his pregnant and clueless wife, Helena (Catharine Zeta-Jones). Carlos' shady

Continued

ORGANIZED CRIME AT THE MOVIES—CONT'D

lawyer, Arnie Metzger (Dennis Quaid), encourages Helena to carry on the "family business," which she does with tragic results.

Each of these stories plays out and overlaps with one another, and *Traffic* shows the complexity, frustration, and consequences of the war on drugs without taking a position on the issue. The Michael Douglas character expresses frustration when he says it is hard fighting a war on drugs when the enemy is ourselves.

Based on the 1980s British television miniseries *Traffik*, the film was nominated for five Academy Awards, including Best Picture. It won for Best Director, Best Supporting Actor (Benicio Del Toro), Best Editing, and Best Screenplay.

Questions

1. It can be said that the current "war on drugs" has forced organized crime groups to become more sophisticated, as they did during Prohibition, in order to avoid apprehension and keep making money. If better law enforcement produces fewer, but more highly developed, drug networks, what would you propose as a solution to this problem?

2. *Traffic* shows the interplay among supply, demand, traffickers, and law enforcement in dealing with illicit drugs. Explain which of these four factors you believe requires the most attention in dealing with illegal drugs more effectively.

References and Notes

1. U.S. Comptroller General (1977). *War on Organized Crime Faltering: Federal Strike Forces Not Getting the Job Done.* Washington, DC: U.S. General Accounting Office.

2. Blakey, G. R., Goldstock, R., & Rogovin, C. H. (1978). *Rackets Bureaus: Investigation and Prosecution of Organized Crime.* Washington, DC: U.S. Government Printing Office.

3. Fowler, F. J., Mangione, T. W., & Pratter, F. E. (1978). *Gambling Law Enforcement in Major American Cities.* Washington, DC: U.S. Government Printing Office.

4. U.S. Comptroller General (1981). *Stronger Federal Effort Needed in Fight Against Organized Crime.* Washington, DC: U.S. General Accounting Office.

5. Carlson, K., & Finn, P. (1993). *Prosecuting Criminal Enterprises.* Washington, DC: Bureau of Justice Statistics; Beck, A., et al. (2000). *Survey of State Prison Inmates.* Washington, DC: Bureau of Justice Statistics; Beck, A., et al. (2000). *Prisoners.* Washington, DC: Bureau of Justice Statistics.

6. Goodwin, B. (2002). Civil Versus Criminal RICO and the "Eradication" of La Cosa Nostra *New England Journal of Criminal and Civil Confinement, 28*(Summer), 279; U.S. Department of Justice (2013). *Three Members and One Associate of Violent North Carolina Latin Kings Gang Sentenced to Prison.* Washington, DC: Office of Public Affairs, August 15.

7. U.S. Comptroller General (1981). *Assets Forfeiture—A Seldom Used Tool in Combatting Drug Trafficking.* Washington, DC: U.S. General Accounting Office, p. 11.

8. U.S. Comptroller General (1987). *Drug Investigations: Organized Crime Drug Enforcement Task Force Program's Accomplishments.* Washington, DC: U.S. General Accounting Office; U.S. Comptroller General (1991). *Asset Forfeiture: Need for Stronger Marshals Service Oversight of Commercial Real Property.* Washington, DC: U.S. General Accounting Office, p. 3.

9. U.S. Department of Justice Organized Crime Drug Enforcement Task Forces (2014). *FY 2015. Interagency Crime and Drug Enforcement Congressional Budget Submission.* www.justice.gov/jmd/2015justification/pdf/ocdetf-justification.pdf.

10. President of the United States (2011). *Strategy to Combat Transnational Organized Crime.* www.whitehouse.gov/sites/default/files/Strategy_to_Combat_Transnational_Organized_Crime_July_2011.pdf; see also Smith, D. E., Clancy, M. T., & Peters, S. J. (2013). Combating

Transnational Organized Crime: Is the Department of Defense Doing Enough? *Small Wars Journal*, August 1.

11. Executive Office for Asset Forfeiture (1990). *Federal Forfeiture of the Instruments and Proceeds of Crime: The Program in a Nutshell.* Washington, DC: U.S. Department of Justice, p. 4.

12. *United States v. One Tintoretto Painting*, 692 F.2d 603 (2d Cir. 1982); McCaw, C. E. (2011). Asset Forfeiture as a Form of Punishment: A Case for Integrating Asset Forfeiture into Criminal Sentencing. *American Journal of Criminal Law*, *38*(Spring), 181–220.

13. O'Meara, K. P. (2000). When Feds Say Seize and Desist. *Insight*, 19, August 7; Gibson, D. T. (2012). Spreading the Wealth: Is Asset Forfeiture the Key to Enticing Local Agencies to Enforce Federal Drug Laws? *Hastings Constitutional Law Quarterly*, *39*(Winter), 569–591; Dodd, B. M. (2014). Commentary: Georgia's Dirty Secret: Asset Forfeiture. *Savannah Morning News*, 2, March 2.

14. Aylesworth, G. N. (1991). *Forfeiture of Real Property: An Overview.* Washington, DC: Bureau of Justice Assistance, p. 8; *United States v. $250,000 in Currency*, 808 F.2d 897 (1st Cir. 1987).

15. Civil Asset Forfeiture Is Law. *Journal of Property Management*, *65*(July), 12; Ramaswamy, J. (2013). Overview of Asset Forfeiture and Money Laundering Program. *United States Attorneys' Bulletin*, *61*(September).

16. *United States v. Thomas*, 913 F.2d 1111 (4th Cir. 1990).

17. Goldsmith, M. (1992). *Civil Forfeiture: Tracing the Proceeds of Narcotics Trafficking.* Washington, DC: U.S. General Accounting Office, p. 20; U.S. Comptroller General (1996). *Historical Perspective on Asset Forfeiture Issues.* Washington, DC: U.S. General Accounting Office.

18. *United States v. One Parcel of Real Estate*, 675 F. Supp 645 (D.Fla. 1987); *United States v. Ursery*, 116 S. Ct. 2135 (1996).

19. *United States v. Bajakajian*, 524 U.S. 321 (1998).

20. Goldsmith, M., & Lenck, W. (1990). *Protection of Third-Party Rights.* Washington, DC: Bureau of Justice Assistance, p. 8; Friedler, E. (2013). Protecting the Innocent—The Need to Adapt Federal Asset Forfeiture Laws to Protect the Interests of Third Parties in Digital Asset Seizures. *Cardozo Arts & Entertainment Law Journal*, *42*, 283–315.

21. *Protection of Third-Party Rights*, p. 28.

22. *United States v. Monsanto*, 109 S. Ct. 2657 (1989).

23. Mauro, T. "High Court Says Suspect Must Be Warned of Seizure," *USA Today* (December 14, 1993), 1; Skorup, B. Ensuring Eighth Amendment Protection from Excessive Fines in Civil Asset Forfeiture Cases. *George Mason University Civil Rights Law Journal*, *22*(Summer), 427–458.

24. 21 U.S.C. 881(a)(4)(C), effective 1988.

25. Fried, J. P. "Government Sues to Seize Gotti's Ill-Gotten Assets," *The New York Times* (January 15, 1993), B1.

26. Gallagher, G. P. (1988). *The Management and Disposition of Seized Assets.* Washington, DC: Bureau of Justice Assistance, p. 2.

27. *The Management and Disposition of Seized Assets*, p. 4.

28. U.S. Comptroller General (1991). *Asset Forfeiture: Need for Stronger Marshals Service Oversight of Commercial Real Property.* Washington, DC: U.S. General Accounting Office; U.S. Comptroller General (1991). *Asset Forfeiture: Noncash Property Should Be Consolidated Under the Marshals Service.* Washington, DC: U.S. General Accounting Office; U.S. Comptroller General (1991). *Asset Forfeiture: Customs Reports over Sales of Forfeited Property.* Washington, DC: U.S. General Accounting Office.

29. Ibid., p. 8.

30. Kaplan, D. E. "A Case Study in Policing for Profit," *US News & World Report* (July 10, 2000), 22–23; Thompson, I. "Law to Clean Up "Nuisances" Costs Innocent People Their Homes,"

ProPublica (August 5, 2013); Connect, Z. E. Asset Forfeiture Gets a Close Look in Nevada: Official Review Follows Allegations of Unlawful Seizure of Thousands of Dollars. *The Wall Street Journal*, March 16.

31. Worrall, J. L., & Koyandzic, T. V. (2008). Is Policing for Profit? Answers from Asset Forfeiture. *Criminology & Public Policy*, 7(May), 219–244; Baumer, E. P. (2008). Evaluating the Balance Sheet of Asset Forfeiture Laws: Toward Evidence-Based Policy Assessments. *Criminology & Public Policy*, 7(May), 245–255; Skolnick, J. H. (2008). Policing Should Not Be for Profit. *Criminology & Public Policy*, 7(May), 257–261; Geis, G. (2008). Asset Forfeiture and Policing. *Criminology & Public Policy*, 7(May), 215–218.

32. Jacobs, J. B., Friel, C., & Radick, R. (1999). *Gotham Unbound: How New York City Was Liberated from the Grip of Organized Crime*. New York: New York University Press.

33. Gerlat, A. "Mob Mentality—NYC Breaks Longtime Grip," *Waste News* (April 15, 2002), 12.

34. Greenhouse, S. "Teamsters Have Cleaner Union, Study Finds," *The New York Times* (October 3, 2002), A20.

35. Jacobs, J. B. (2006). *Mobsters, Unions, and Feds: The Mafia and the American Labor Movement*. NewYork: New York University Press, p. 261.

36. Jacobs, J. R., & Cooperman, K. T. (2011). *Breaking the Devil's Pact: The Battle to Free the Teamsters from the Mob*. New York: New York University Press.

37. Federal Bureau of Investigation (1999). *Hearings: Oversight of Federal Asset Forfeiture: Its Role in Fighting Crime*. U.S. Senate Committee on the Judiciary. Subcommittee on Criminal Justice Oversight, July 21.

38. Campbell, J. H. (2000). *Keeping Illegal Activity out of Rental Property: A Police Guide for Establishing Landlord Training Programs*. Washington, DC: Bureau of Justice Assistance.

39. Hu, W. "Food Workers in Hunts Point Criticize a Commission's Scrutiny," *The New York Times* (September 20, 2013).

40. Shiner, M. (2009). *Civil Gang Injunctions: A Guide for Prosecutors, National District Attorneys Association*. Washington, DC: U.S. Bureau of Justice Assistance; Wood, D. B. "In New Tactic, L.A. Goes After Gangs' Money," *The Christian Science Monitor* (January 15, 2009).

41. United Nations Office (2013). *Transnational Organized Crime in West Africa: A Threat Assessment*. Vienna: UNODC; van der Does de Willebois, E., Halter, E. M., Harrison, R. A., Park, J. W., & Sharman, J. C. (2011). *The Puppet Masters: How the Corrupt Use Legal Structures to Hide Stolen Assets and What to Do About It*. Washington, DC: The Word Bank and UNODC.

42. Hobbs, D. (2013). *Lush Life: Constructing Organized Crime in the UK*. Oxford, UK: Oxford University Press.

43. Van de Bunt, H. G., & van der Schoot, C. R. A. (2003). *Prevention of Organised Crime: A Situational Approach*. The Netherlands: WODC.

44. Abele, G. (2004). Synthetic Drugs: Trafficking in Three European Cities: Major Trends and the Involvement of Organized Crime. *Trends in Organized Crime*, 8(Fall), 24–37; Boorsma, J. (2003). Forged Official Documents. In H. G. van de Bunt, & C. R. A. van der Schoot (Eds.), *The Identification and Prevention of Opportunities That Facilitate Organised Crime*. The Hague: WODC; Bowman, B. A. (2008). Transnational Crimes against Culture: Looting at Archeological Sites and the "Grey" Market in Antiquities. *Journal of Contemporary Criminal Justice*, 24(August), 225–242; Graycar, A., & Felson, M. (2010). Situational Prevention of Organized Timber Theft and Related Corruption. In K. Bullock, R. V. Clarke, & N. Tilley (Eds.), *Situational Prevention of Organised Crimes*. Devon, UK: Willan Publishing; Reuter, P., & Truman, E. (2004). *Chasing Dirty Money: The Fight Against Money Laundering*. Institute for International Economics; Lampe, K. V. (2010). Preventing Organised Crime: The Case of Contraband Cigarettes. In K. Bullock, R. V. Clarke, & N. Tilley (Eds.), *Situational Prevention of Organised Crimes*. Devon, UK: Willan Publishing.

45. Goldstock, R., Marcus, M., Thacher, T., & Jacobs, J. (1991). *Corruption and Racketeering in the New York City Construction Industry: The Final Report of the New York State Organized Crime*

Taskforce. New York: New York University Press; Nelen, H. (2010). Situational Organised Crime Prevention in Amsterdam: The Administrative Approach. In K. Bullock, R. V. Clarke, & N. Tilley (Eds.), *Situational Prevention of Organised Crimes.* Devon, UK: Willan Publishing; Rashbaum, W. K. "Use of Mob-Linked Firm Shows M.T.A. Problem Vetting Subcontractors," *The New York Times* (May 19, 2010); Savona, E. U. (2010). Infiltration of the Public Construction Industry by Italian Organised Crime. In K. Bullock, R. V. Clarke, & N. Tilley (Eds.), *Situational Prevention of Organised Crimes.* Devon, UK: Willan Publishing.

46. Europol (2010). *Europol Launches Scan System for Strategic Notices on Newly Identified Organised Crime Threats.* www.europol.europa.eu/, January 10; Kirby, S., & Nailer, L. (2013). Reducing the Offending of a UK Organized Crime Group Using an Opportunity-Reducing Framework—A Three Year Case Study. *Trends in Organized Crime, 16,* 397–412; Europol (2010). *Organised Crime & Energy Supply: Scenarios to 2020.* The Hague: Europol, August 10; Caneppele, S., Riccardi, M., & Standridge, P. (2013). Green Energy and Black Economy: Mafia Investments in the Wind Power Sector in Italy. *Crime, Law and Social Change, 59,* 319–339; Mackenzie, S., & Hamilton-Smith, N. (2011). Measuring Police Impact on Organized Crime: Performance Management and Harm Reduction. *Policing: An International Journal of Police Strategies & Management, 34*(1), 7–30; Savona, E., Calderine, F., & Remmerswaal, A. M. (2011). *Understudied Organized Crime Offending: A Discussion of the Canadian Situation in International Context.* Ottawa: Public Safety Canada, August; William, C. J., & Bell, P. (2011). The Role of Strategic Intelligence in Anticipating Transnational Crime: A Literary Review. *International Journal of Law, Crime and Justice, 39,* 60–78; World Economic Forum. (2012). *Organized Crime Enablers.* Washington, DC, July.

47. "Website to Fight Organised Crime," *Belfast Newsletter* (September 25, 2002), 13.

48. www.nationalcrimeagency.gov.uk/ (accessed March 12, 2014).

49. Finckenauer, J. (2012). Organized Crime. In M. Tonry (Ed.), *The Oxford Handbook of Crime and Public Policy.* Oxford, UK: Oxford University Press; *Transnational Organized Crime Rewards Program: Targeting Global Criminal Networks.* www.state.gov/TOCrewards (October 31, 2013); U.S. Department of State (2013). *First Reward Offer for Transnational Organized Crime Information.* www.state.gov/j/inl/tocrewards/index.htm; "MafiaLeaks Website," *Daily Mail Reporter* (November 5, 2013); President of the United States (2014). *National Strategy for Combating Wildlife Trafficking.* www.whitehouse.gov/sites/default/files/docs/nationalstrategywildlifetrafficking.pdf, February.

Glossary

Apalachin Incident (1957) A meeting of 65 men (including 58 Italians, some with criminal records) gathered at Joseph Barbera's home in Apalachin, New York; hearings by a committee of the New York State legislature caused a great deal of publicity (like the Kefauver hearings years before) and went a long way toward cementing people's attitudes about the nature of organized crime, despite the absence of hard evidence about its structure.

arms trafficking Trafficking in firearms. See *trafficking*. Unlawful sale and movement of nuclear components, mines, grenades, missile launchers, counterfeit guns, and ammunition in violation of national and international laws. Arms trafficking has grown with the steady supply of overstock, low-cost, secondhand, and counterfeit weapons, which are difficult to control. These weapons supply an increasingly armed group of insurgents, conflict zones, private groups, and free agents.

associate Person who associates with "made" (induced) members of Mafia groups in order to conduct a (usually illegal) business without harassment. Such a person may have aspirations of being invited to join a Mafia group.

ATF Acronym for Bureau of Alcohol, Tobacco, and Firearms (now called the Bureau of Alcohol, Tobacco, Firearms, and Explosives) within the U.S. Department of Homeland Security.

bank deposit method One of three methods of investigative financial analysis. It is based on the theory that a person engaged in an income-producing business or occupation deposits money in bank accounts under his or her control, and those bank deposits are taxable income. Any expenditure by the person from funds not deposited in any bank or from any other documented source also represents taxable income. The bank deposit method tries to reconcile receipts from bank deposits, cash purchases (money spent without going through banks), and money stored in other places (cash on hand), examining the money flow to look for unreported and unlawful sources of income.

Bank Secrecy Act (1970) Federal law enacted as a tool to make it difficult to "launder" illicitly obtained cash and other monetary instruments (e.g., personal or cashier check) through legitimate means; requires banks to file a Currency Transaction Report (CTR); requires individuals to file with the U.S. Customs Service a Currency or Monetary Instruments Report (CMIR); requires citizens holding bank accounts in foreign countries to declare them on their federal income tax returns; illegal for an individual to make multiple under-$10,000 cash transactions to willfully avoid the CTR requirement.

beeper A radio transmitter that, when attached to a car or object, discloses its location via radio signals. It is used by law enforcement for surveillance.

bid-rigging of contracts Bidders on a contract (e.g., for construction of a building, or supplies for a large business or government customer) secretly agree prior to the bid on who will be the low bidder. The bidders take turns on "winning" low bids for different contracts without any company having to bid too low. Bid-rigging keeps profit margins artificially high.

black market Condition in which scarce or illegal goods are in public demand, and criminal groups supply that demand by stealing those goods and selling them to a knowing and willing public.

blackmail Former term for extortion; obtaining property from another due to threats of future physical injury, property damage, or threatened exposure to ridicule or criminal charges.

bookmaking Form of gambling, in which a "bookie" takes bets (usually on sports contests) based on a "point spread" to equalize the number of bettors on either side of the contest to avoid too many winners on any given bet.

boss Head of a crime family or group who oversees the activity of "family" members.

bribery When a person voluntarily solicits or accepts any benefit in exchange for influencing an official act. Both the giver and the receiver are liable under the law.

Brickman, Arlyne Mistress to a number of prominent organized crime figures from the 1940s to 1970s who eventually became a government informant; her biography is *Mob Girl* (1992).

"bug" Slang term for an electronic listening device secretly hidden inside a room, a car, or building in order to overhear conversations from a remote location; for example, a "room bug" or "to bug a room," as authorized by a search warrant.

Cali Cartel See *Medellin Cartel and Cali Cartel.*

capo or caporegima Term used in Mafia groups for a high-ranking member of a crime family who heads a crew (or group) of soldiers and has social status and influence in the group. Sometimes is called a lieutenant or captain.

captain One of the supervisory ranks (after the boss, the underboss, and the consigliere) held by members of a Mafia crime family.

Castellammarese War A gangland war (according to Joseph Valachi) in New York City during the early 1930s, lasting for 14 months, after which gang leaders of Italian lineage established the "Cosa Nostra."

chain conspiracy Consists of several parties acting as links in a continuing criminal enterprise that requires multiple tasks to be carried out. Each party is legally accountable and responsible for the actions of everyone else in the chain, even if they never met each other.

charging grand jury Name sometimes used for traditional grand juries.

Child Online Protection Act (2000) A federal law passed with the intent to prohibit transmissions of objectionable material to minors via the Internet; declared unconstitutional by lower federal courts, ruling that it was impossible to enforce.

Child Pornography Act See *Protection of Children against Sexual Exploitation Act (1977).*

Child Protection Act (1984) Federal law prohibiting the receiving through the mail of sexually explicit depictions of children.

chop shop Location where stolen cars are brought and disassembled so that parts can be sold.

Citizens commissions See *crime commissions.*

Civil Asset Forfeiture Reform Act (2000) Federal law that created an innocent owner defense in a civil forfeiture of property action; also placed the burden of proof on the government to show, by a preponderance of evidence, that the law was violated (i.e., the property was implicated in criminal activity).

civil forfeiture action One of two types of civil forfeitures of property by which the government files suit against property (rather than against the owner of it) seeking a judgment of forfeiture; usually directed against contraband (e.g., drugs or guns) and derivative contraband (e.g., vehicles, aircraft, and boats used to transport contraband).

civil forfeiture (of property) Independent of a criminal proceeding (i.e., conviction of the property owner is immaterial), the government can forfeit an owner's property that has been acquired or used illegally. See *forfeiture (of property).*

Classicism theory A perspective on criminal behavior that sees crime as the free-will decision to choose crime rather than as the result of factors such as social and economic influences; it sees criminal decision making as the result of a simple weighing of pain versus pleasure involved in carrying out the act and considering the probability of apprehension.

cloned phone A cell phone that has someone else's cell phone number programmed into it for billing purposes; used by criminals for several weeks before discarding, thus making it extremely difficult for law enforcement to tap or trap and trace those phones.

CMIR Acronym for Currency or Monetary Instruments Report.

code of silence See *omerta*.

coercion Force or threat used to compel another person to engage in an action (or avoid an action) involuntarily.

Commission, The A group of crime bosses that handles intercrime family relations and disputes; example: bosses of the five reputed crime families in New York City.

Commission trial Held in 1986 involving alleged "bosses" of the five New York City "crime families" of the "Cosa Nostra"; the debate over the existence of the Mafia became moot because bosses conceded that the Mafia exists, has members, and there is a commission.

Communications Decency Act A federal law, as Title V of the Telecommunications Act (1966), passed with the intent to protect minors from pornographic images and messages on the Internet; declared unconstitutional by the U.S. Supreme Court, ruling that it was void for vagueness.

Comprehensive Drug Abuse Prevention and Control Act (1970) One of two federal laws providing to the government criminal forfeiture authority in organized crime cases; it specifically applies to forfeiture of profits derived from a continuing criminal enterprise (CCE), which is one that traffics in narcotics in violation of the Continuing Criminal Enterprise (CCE) law (1987). See *RICO statute*.

conducting an illegal gambling business Federal law that prohibits a person from participating in (i.e., conducting, financing, managing, supervising, directing, or owning) all or part of a gambling business that is illegal under state law, that involves five or more persons (excluding mere bettors), and that remains in substantially continuous operation for more than 30 days or grosses more than $2,000 in a single day.

consigliere Advisor in a Mafia crime family, ranking below the boss and the underboss.

conspiracy Planning with another person to commit a crime; thus, a written, oral, or tacit agreement between two or more persons to commit a criminal act or to achieve by unlawful means an act not in itself criminal; no formal agreement is required among the coconspirators; participation need only be slight; a running of the conspiracy is not required and the mere furtherance of its illegal objectives is sufficient; whether the planned crime takes place is immaterial; a person can be convicted of not only the planning of the crime, but also the commission of it; generally requires, also, an overt act in furtherance of the conspiracy as an element of the offense.

conspiracy to possess drugs with intent to distribute A crime for knowing of the conspiracy and participating in it voluntarily; membership in the conspiracy is not established by the mere purchase of drugs from the conspiracy, but it is sufficient when the purchaser knows of the conspiracy's general aims and purchases the drugs for resale.

Continuing Criminal Enterprise (CCE) Law (1987) Federal law applicable only to a drug trafficker (a person who is the organizer, manager, or supervisor of the continuing operation and receives substantial income or property from it); makes it a crime for a drug trafficker to commit at least three related violations of felony drug laws with five or more persons; provides for a mandatory minimum 20-year prison sentence for a first offense, as well as for fines up to $2 million, and for the forfeiture of the profits and any interest in the enterprise.

cooperating witness See *informant.*

corruption Misuse of public office or abuse of power for private gain; implies some combination of the offenses of embezzlement, fraud, nepotism, bribery, extortion, and influence peddling.

Cosa Nostra See *Mafia.*

crack cocaine Made by mixing powdered cocaine with baking soda or ammonia and water, which, when dried, is broken down into small "rocks" that are sold inexpensively.

crackhouse statute (1986) Federal law prohibiting landlords from knowingly maintaining any place for the purpose of manufacturing, distributing, or using controlled drug and from knowingly and intentionally renting, leasing, or making available for use with or without compensation a property to manufacture, distribute, or use drugs.

crime commissions Established from time to time to examine the problems of organized crime in a specific locality (e.g., Chicago Crime Commission; Pennsylvania Crime Commission); a way to develop information on organized crime, as well as to focus public concern about it; these commissions are generally not empowered to make criminal cases, but to assess the current situation and make recommendations for change.

crime family The Cosa Nostra is structured into groups (families) located in major cities; each group is run by a boss and has an underboss, consigliere, captains, and soldiers.

crime syndicate Name given by the media to loosely connected organized crime groups in major cities around the United States, primarily of Italian and Jewish heritage. This term is often used interchangeably with the "mob."

criminal enterprise See *enterprise.*

criminal forfeiture (of property) As part of a criminal proceeding, the government can forfeit an owner's property that has been acquired or used illegally once the owner has been convicted of certain offenses (e.g., RICO) related to that property. A third party who was a transferee of the property may have a successful claim on the property if the party was reasonably without any knowledge of the illegality. See *forfeiture (of property).*

CTR Acronym for currency transaction report.

Currency or monetary instruments report (CMIR) Filed by individuals if more than $10,000 in cash or other monetary instruments (e.g., personal or cashier's check) leaves or enters the United States.

Currency transaction report (CTR) Filed by banks for every deposit, withdrawal, or exchange of funds of more than $10,000.

DEA Acronym for Drug Enforcement Administration.

Depression, The See *Great Depression, The.*

derivative proceeds The government not only can forfeit property that is connected to criminal activity, but also can forfeit all proceeds of that property, including interest, dividends, income, and real property.

digital piracy See *online piracy or digital piracy.*

drug "mule" Person whose job is to carry illegal drugs as part of a larger drug distribution conspiracy.

drug "mule protector" Person whose job is to protect the mule from being robbed, ensure that the mule did not abscond with the drugs, and divert police attention from the mule.

drug trafficking Trafficking in drugs. See *trafficking.*

ECPA Acronym for the Electronic Communications Privacy Act (1987).

ECPA order A special warrant that allows police to intercept certain electronic communications (e.g., personal e-mail, cellular telephones) and to install pen registers and trap-and-trace devices; less proof is required to obtain the order than to obtain a search warrant (proof: a likelihood of information relevant to a criminal investigation rather than probable cause of criminal activity). See *Electronic Communications Privacy Act (1987)*.

Electronic Communications Privacy Act (ECPA) (1987) Federal law enacted because of changes in technology and decisions of the U.S. Supreme Court, expands the scope of Title III of the Omnibus Crime Control Act (1968)—which protects against warrantless interceptions of wire communications and oral communications—to include a third category, electronic communications (e.g., personal e-mail and cellular telephones); however, in contrast to wire and oral communications, ECPA allows a broader range of officials than just police to get a warrant (see *ECPA order*) and applies to a broader range of offenses than just specified felonies; also regulates pen registers and trap-and-trace devices; further, it provides both civil and criminal penalties for a person (private citizen or law enforcement officer) who either unlawfully intercepts communications or discloses communications when having reason to know that the information was obtained unlawfully.

electronic surveillance Use of electronic devices to intercept wire, oral, and electronic communications dealing with a wide variety of suspected criminal activities, including organized crime.

ensuring labor peace Guaranteeing that there will be no violence, strikes, or vandalism at the job site (usually involving labor union activity).

enterprise Defined under the RICO statute as an individual, partnership, corporation, association, or group of individuals engaged in ongoing activity, although not a legal entity.

Enterprise model Paradigm used to study the nature and structure of organized crime by focusing on the influences of suppliers, customers, regulators, and competitors on organized crime activity.

entrapment A defense to criminal liability when a government agent's actions induced ("tricked" or "trapped") a person into committing a crime (traditional or "subjective" form of the defense) or the agent's actions would likely have, from an objective standpoint, induced an innocent person into committing a crime that the person otherwise would not have committed ("objective" form of the defense).

entrapment—"objective" form In order to prosecute the defendant, a government agent subjected the defendant to inducements that—from an objective standpoint—would have caused a hypothetical innocent person (i.e., the hypothetical person was not predisposed to commit the offense) to commit the offense; the defendant's predisposition is immaterial. Also see *entrapment*.

entrapment—traditional or "subjective" form In order to prosecute the defendant, a government agent originated a criminal design, implanted that design in the defendant's innocent mind (i.e., defendant was not predisposed to commit the offense), and induced the defendant to commit the offense. Also see *entrapment*.

Ethical theory Theory of criminal behavior that emphasizes the lack of moral virtue, where the person makes criminal choices because of a failure to appreciate the wrongfulness of the acts and their impact on the victim, and where crime brings pleasure, not guilt; it deals with ethics and morality rather than social and economic conditions, or threat of police and criminal penalties, or political and economic reasons.

ethnic insularity Barriers of language, culture, and tradition of Asian organized crime groups, even more formidable than those of Cosa Nostra, which make it difficult for law enforcement officers seeking to understand and infiltrate the groups.

ethnicity Culture of a particular group of people, most often based on common genealogy or ancestry.

expenditure method One of three methods of financial analysis used primarily when no records or books are kept. The expenditures method measures funds by their flow during the year rather than by observing changes in net worth over time. It involves examination of weekly or monthly income reported by the employer and on tax forms and comparing it to expenditures of the individual (through credit cards receipts, bank withdrawals, and items purchased with cash). Large discrepancies suggest the possibility of unlawful income.

extortion Act of obtaining money or property from another person by use of force or threat of future harm, which can be in the form of physical injury, property damage, or exposure to ridicule or criminal charges; formerly called blackmail.

extraterritoriality Enforcing a U.S. criminal law for acts done outside the United States; this is legally permissible if the U.S. Congress intended that law to apply to the criminal acts at issue and if that law conformed to international law: namely, criminal acts produced detrimental effects within the United States (objective territorial principle) and criminal acts impinged upon the territorial integrity, security, or political independence of the United States (protective principle).

FBI Acronym for Federal Bureau of Investigation.

fence Person who knowingly buys and sells stolen property as an illicit business.

fencing Buying stolen property, which is then distributed (sold) to customers who don't care where it came from.

feudalism Social, economic, political system of Europe in the Middle Ages (from the ninth to about the fifteenth centuries); vassals gave military and other service to their lord in return for his protection and use of his land.

Financial Crime Enforcement Network (FinCEN) Established by the Department of Treasury in 1990 to alleviate the problem of the growing number of CTRs filed by banks; supports law enforcement agencies in identifying money laundering activity: that is, disseminates strategic analysis to law enforcement agencies in the United States and abroad.

FinCEN Acronym for Financial Crime Enforcement Network.

firearms trafficking Trafficking in firearms. See *arms trafficking*.

forfeiture (of property) Government's lawful seizure of a person's property (including derivative proceeds) without compensation in situations in which the person acquired or used the property illegally; two types of forfeitures are civil forfeiture (of property) and criminal forfeiture (of property); however, the seizure is subject to the rights of innocent individuals (i.e., those—such as lien holders or uninformed purchasers or joint tenants or business partners—who were not involved in criminal activity, but whose property was used in, or derived from, the criminal activity of others).

Fratianno, Jimmy Criminal turned government informer. See *Tieri trial*.

Fuk Ching Chinese organized crime group active in New York City, regarded as one of the most powerful and also most active transnationally, Chinese organized crime groups in the United States. They operate extortion and protection rackets among businesses in New York's Chinatown.

gabellotto See *mafioso*.

gambling Games of chance in which the outcome is determined more by luck than skill; examples: card games, dice games, casino games (e.g., slot machines), lotteries (e.g., bingo; policy games, also called "numbers"), sporting contests betting, horse race betting, and dog race betting. See *illegal gambling*.

Gravano, Salavatore "Sammy the Bull" Organized crime participant who testified as a government witness in its successful prosecution in the 1992 John Gotti trial and described the "administration" (under which are the captains and the soldiers), the induction ceremony into Cosa Nostra, and the "commission" (made up of leaders of the various "families").

Great Depression, The (1930s) Worldwide business slump, ranked as the worst and longest period of high unemployment and low business activity in modern times; businesses (banks, factories, stores, etc.) closed, leaving millions of Americans jobless and without funds, thereby relying on government or charities for subsistence; began in October 1929, when stock values dropped rapidly, and ended about 10 years later at the beginning of World War II.

gun running See *arms trafficking*.

Hennessey murder Interest in the "Mafia" in the United States can be traced to the murder of David Hennessey, the New Orleans Superintendent of Police in 1890; fatally shot by unknown assassins, he said, "Sicilians have done for me" or "Dagoes"—interpreted to mean an Italian connection.

Hierarchical model Paradigm used by government investigators to study the nature and structure of organized crime; there is a "family" structure with a military type of graded ranks of authority (from boss down to soldiers).

Hobbs Act (1946) Federal law prohibiting extortion by a government official: that is, from improperly inducing a payment from another in return for the official's explicit act or promise; its "under color of official right" provision also covers private citizens who aid or conspire with public officials to commit extortion.

human trafficking Trafficking in human beings. See *trafficking*. Recruitment, transportation, transfer, harboring, or receipt of persons by use of force, threat, fraud, or coercion for the purpose of exploitation (most often sexual exploitation or forced labor).

illegal gambling Games of chance not approved by the state (e.g., numbers gambling, sports betting outside Nevada, unlicensed casino games).

immunity (or immunity from prosecution) Prosecutor's promise to refrain from prosecuting a witness in exchange for the witness's testimony; a way to present the testimony of lower level organized crime figures in order to make it easier for the government to prosecute higher echelon organized crime figures. See *transactional immunity* and *use immunity*.

infiltration of business One of three primary categories of organized crime; includes coercive use of legal businesses for purposes of exploitation. Example: an organized crime group infiltrated a business successfully by providing a service (in the form of protection from worker or supply stoppages) in exchange for a piece of the business (in the form of no-show employees or monetary kickbacks on contracts or earnings). See *protection*.

informant Typically, a criminal who chooses to cooperate with the police in exchange for a reduced charge, recommended sentence, or immunity from prosecution; can be a cooperating witness (an honest person simply wishing to report wrongdoing).

informer's privilege Generally, the government is entitled to keep secret the identity of an informant who has provided information about a possible law violation; the privilege can be overcome if the identity is relevant to the defendant's case.

innocent owner defense Applicable to a third party in a civil forfeiture of property action when a person can show that he or she lacked knowledge, consent, or was not willfully blind regarding illegal usage of the property.

investigating grand jury Name sometimes used for special grand juries allowed by the Organized Crime Control Act (1970), Title I.

IRS Acronym for Internal Revenue Service.

Italian Connection Contrary to popular belief, and according to numerous authors, there appears to be no *formal* (i.e., centralized) organization in Italy (or Sicily) called the "Mafia" nor does it appear that a Mafia organization was imported to the United States. Instead there are numerous loosely connected and unconnected groups of Italians and Italian-Americans that, taken together, are called the Mafia.

Jamaican posses See *posses*.

Kefauver Hearings (1950) Held before a committee of the U.S. Senate and chaired by Senator Estes Kefauver, resulting in the assumption, but not any proof, that there is a sinister criminal organization known as the Mafia operating throughout the United States with ties to other countries.

kickbacks Payments or other types of compensation made in order to influence and gain profit from an individual or company. Kickbacks are a form of bribe or extortion payment for an unearned advantage, benefit, or opportunity by the payer.

labor peace Absence of violence, strikes, insufficient workers, or vandalism at the job site (usually involving labor union activity).

labor racketeering Using force or threats to obtain money for ensuring jobs or labor peace (if money is not paid, there will be no job for the worker or the company or there will be violence, strikes, and/or vandalism at the company).

labor union control Crime groups gained control of labor unions in various industries and thereby were able to engage systematically in extortion of businesses that relied on union workers by demanding kickbacks on contracts, guaranteeing labor peace, and providing uninterrupted shipment of supplies.

La Cosa Nostra See *Mafia*.

LCN Acronym for La Cosa Nostra. See *Mafia*.

loanshark One who engages in loansharking, that is, lending money at a usurious rate to a person who has no other way to obtain money to pay a gambling debt or other debts that lack legal standing (and therefore make bank loans impossible).

loansharking See *usury*.

Local/Ethnic model Paradigm used by social scientists to study the nature and structure of organized crime, which sees it as the product of locally based groups often connected and insulated by ethnic ties.

lottery Scheme for distributing prizes by lot or chance (based on a selection of numbers) in which a large number of tickets are sold, a few of which draw prizes.

Mafia The term is synonymous with LCN (La Cosa Nostra), referring primarily to groups of organized crime "families" in the United States and Italy. Members of these groups are of Italian descent and often are unrelated to each other; hence, the term "family" is not descriptive. Nevertheless, the group exists for noncriminal socializing as well as for carrying out criminal acts, and they are connected by both their ethnicity and by their sworn allegiance to each other (which in recent years has eroded with numerous cases of Mafia members testifying against each other).

mafioso Middleman who emerged during the 1800s in Sicily after feudalism was legally abolished—and a class of landowners and a class of peasants resulted—who provided protection to landowners that the government could not provide and ensured that peasants paid rent in return for the opportunity to cultivate the land.

Mann Act (1910) Also called the *White-Slave Traffic Act*, it prohibits the interstate transport of females for "immoral purposes"—with the intent to prevent prostitution. This federal law makes it illegal for anyone to knowingly persuade, induce, entice, or coerce any woman or girl to travel between states or countries for the purpose of prostitution or debauchery with or without her consent.

marriages of convenience Alliances formed, especially in narcotics trafficking, to overcome problems posed by the manufacture, transportation, shipping, smuggling, and distribution of narcotics between criminal groups and customers (e.g., some Sicilian groups and the Medellin cartel in Colombia, South America) who work together, albeit warily, to make a profit.

McClellan (Valachi) hearings (1963) Held before a committee of the U.S. Senate, chaired by Senator McClellan, and where Joseph Valachi testified; the first time an "insider" ever admitted belonging to a "Mafia" or talked about a criminal conspiracy in the country.

Medellin Cartel and Cali Cartel Two organized crime groups in Colombia, South America, that enjoyed a great deal of success because of high worldwide demand for cocaine; Colombia is a poor nation with a weak government, and the cartels were wealthier than anyone else, thus making corruption rather easy and mobilization of public opinion (against the cartels) very difficult.

mob tax Slang term for extortionate demands of organized crime groups on businesses for "protection" from violence and vandalism.

mob trials Held in the 1980s and 1990s; remembered as a period when the U.S. Justice Department took new initiative and began the largest organized crime prosecution effort in U.S. history, resulting in convictions of a large number of organized crime figures around the country and weakening the influence of Mafia-related organized crime in the United States. See *Commission trial*.

money laundering Obtaining money from an illicit business (such as drug trafficking), funneling it through a legitimate business, especially one that has a large number of cash transactions (such as a restaurant), and then reporting it as income of that legitimate business; thus, the processing of criminal proceeds to disguise their illegal origin (i.e., to make the income appear to be earned lawfully; examples: depositing illicitly obtained cash in offshore banks or in nonbank situations or purchasing casino chips or airplane tickets and then returning them for refund of cash; offenders would easily be discovered if they could not "merge" their illegal cash into a legal business.

Money Laundering Control Act (1986) Federal law prohibiting anyone from conducting a monetary transaction knowing that funds were derived from unlawful activity; "knowledge" includes a person who is "willfully blind" to the source of the funds and does not exercise the reasonable care expected in a financial transaction.

mule Person who transports drugs as part of the larger drug trafficking conspiracy.

mule protector Person who protects the mule, ensures that the mule does not abscond with the drugs, and diverts police attention from the mule.

narcoterrorism Term used in connection with drugs and organized crime; it includes drug traffickers who are terrorists, terrorist-type tactics used by drug organizations to intimidate governments (e.g., Medellin cartel in Colombia, South America), and interactions between drug traffickers and revolutionary organizations against an incumbent regime (e.g., in some South American and Asian nations).

net worth method One of three methods of financial analysis, it involves examining changes in a person's net financial worth over time, looking at all sources of reported income, bank balances, and assets. If a person cannot document sources of changes in net worth, the unreported income forms the basis for further investigation.

no-show jobs Jobs arranged through organized crime connections where businesses issue paychecks for a job that does not exist or for which no one ever shows up for work. These jobs are usually a form of *kickback* or payment by the employer for organized crime "protection."

numbers gambling Lottery that operates without the approval of the state.

obscene material Material that an average person, by applying contemporary community standards, would find (1) when taken as a whole, appeals to a prurient (i.e., lascivious; lewd; lustful) interest in sex, (2) portrays sexual conduct in a patently (i.e., obviously) offensive way, and (3) when taken as a whole, lacks serious literary, artistic, political, or scientific value.

OCDETF Acronym for the Organized Crime Drug Enforcement Task Force Program.

Organized Crime Drug Enforcement Task Force Program (OCDETF) Established in 1983 by the federal government to identify, investigate, and prosecute high-level members of drug trafficking enterprises and to destroy their operations; agencies that participate in the 13 task forces around the country include not only federal agencies (U.S. Attorney's Offices, DEA, FBI, U.S. Customs Service, ATF, IRS, U.S. Marshals Service, Immigration and Naturalization Service, and U.S. Coast Guard), but also local agencies.

omerta Code of silence said to exist in Mafia culture, where speaking to others outside the group about Mafia operations is a violation of omerta and punishable by death. Over the past 25 years, however, there have been a series of Mafia members who have testified against their former associates in court, weakening the meaning of this tradition.

Omnibus Crime Control and Safe Streets Act (1968) Federal law conferring power to the government to wiretap conversations in a wide variety of suspected criminal activities, including organized crime; includes Title III on electronic surveillance.

online piracy or digital piracy Theft of intellectual property, a new variation of stolen property crimes, occurs where unauthorized copies of pirated music CDs, movies, software, and video games are manufactured and distributed around the world without payment to the holders of the copyright or licensed distributors.

Organized Crime Control Act (1970) Federal law with the stated purpose of seeking the eradication of organized crime in the United States; Title I establishes special grand juries (investigating grand juries); Title II establishes "use" immunity from prosecution (i.e., the power to compel witnesses to testify); Title V establishes the witness security program (WITSEC); Title IX establishes the ongoing criminal enterprise (RICO) offense with its special sentencing provisions for organized crime convicted offenders. See *use immunity; Witness Security Program (WITSEC); special grand jury; RICO offense.*

organized prostitution Offering of sex for pay on a systematic basis.

outlaw motorcycle club Refers to members of the Hells Angels, Outlaws, Pagans, Banditos, Satan's Choice, and so on who engage in drug trafficking, robbery, and extortion; gangs are generally composed of criminal members and noncriminal members, which makes it difficult to distinguish criminal members from others.

oversight of union activities Use of civil RICO provisions to address pervasive organized crime problems that have not been solved through criminal prosecutions. Continuing oversight is provided through a "trusteeship," which permits the government to manage a union over a period of years to root out corruption and racketeer involvement in union activities and finances.

overt act in furtherance of the conspiracy An act to achieve the object of a conspiracy; required for a conviction under most federal statutes (except the drug conspiracy statute) and virtually all state statutes.

paradigms of organized crime Model or explanation that is developed in order to better understand the nature and structure of organized crime.

pattern Defined under the RICO statute as two or more criminal offenses that are designated as "racketeering activity," committed within a 10-year period, and which even if not related to each other are each related to a continuing criminal enterprise.

pen register Electronic equipment that records the telephone numbers of *outgoing* calls. See *trap-and-trace device; ECPA Order*.

pornographic material Generic term, carrying no legal significance, which refers to sexually explicit material. Such material is only considered illegal when it is "obscene" under the law. See *obscene material*.

pornography Manufacturing and marketing of illicit depictions of sex in the form of photographs, films, and videos to a segment of the population that desires them. See *obscene material*.

Positivism theory A perspective on criminal behavior that looks to internal (psychological or biological) or external (social or economic) influences as the cause of criminal behavior. Positivism assumes that changes in these conditions will reduce or prevent criminal behavior.

posses Jamaican gangs involved in both narcotics (primarily crack cocaine) and firearms trafficking by either stealing or illegally buying guns in the United States and then smuggling them back to Jamaica, where they are sold to local gangs at inflated prices.

possession of stolen property offense Distribution, possession, or sale of property "knowing" that it was stolen (i.e., a "reasonable person" should have known it was stolen).

predicate offenses Those individual crimes defined as "racketeering activity" under the RICO statute. See *racketeering activity*.

President's Commission on Organized Crime Reporting in 1987, as part of 2 years of hearings, this Commission placed a great deal of emphasis on organized crime activity apart from the traditional focus on Italian-American organized crime: namely, on outlaw motorcycle gangs and prison gangs, as well as on Chinese, Vietnamese, Japanese, Cuban, Colombian, Irish, Russian, and Canadian criminal groups; in contrast to the Task Force Report on Organized Crime (TFR), it found drug (narcotics) trafficking to be the most widespread and lucrative organized crime activity in the United States, and it devoted more attention to labor-management racketeering and money laundering.

Prohibition Period between 1920 and 1933 in the United States when laws, passed pursuant to the 18th Amendment to the U.S. Constitution (1920), prohibited the making or selling of alcoholic liquors; that amendment was repealed by the 21st Amendment to the U.S. Constitution (1933); this era was probably responsible more than any other single event for the emergence of strong organized crime groups who controlled the illegal distribution of liquor.

prostitution See *organized prostitution*.

protection Organized crime's guarantee to protect a business from harm, either potential or actual, and for which a business pays money. This occurs most often because government and police are unable to provide the services or the business obtains an unfair advantage in the marketplace. See *infiltration of business*.

Protection of Children against Sexual Exploitation Act (1977) Federal law prohibiting knowingly manufacturing, distributing, or receiving a visual depiction of a minor engaged in sexually explicit material, knowing that the person is a minor; also referred to as the Child Pornography Act.

protection racket A form of extortion, long associated with organized crime groups and used as a source of their income, by which money is extracted from a victim in exchange for not doing damage to the victim's business, construction site, or employees; if the victim refuses, damage is done and then the victim often relents and pays under duress.

provision of illicit goods One of three primary categories for describing the typology of organized crime (i.e., types of illicit criminal behaviors); includes narcotics and stolen property.

provision of illicit services One of three primary categories for describing the typology of organized crime (i.e., types of illicit criminal behavior); includes gambling, lending (loansharking), and sex.

racketeering Engaging in ongoing criminal conspiracies or enterprises.

racketeering activity Defined under the RICO statute in broad terms as specified indictable offenses (i.e., most state felonies—those that are punishable by imprisonment of more than 1 year—and specified federal felony offenses); those offenses include prior offenses not resulting in charges or convictions (i.e., they need not be preexisting convictions).

reasonable knowledge Required for liability for nearly all crimes; thus, actual knowledge of a crime is not necessary if a reasonable person should have known of it.

receiving stolen property Offense of obtaining stolen property, knowing that the property was stolen.

relation-back doctrine Forfeiture of property occurs at the time that the property became involved with illegal activity (rather than at the later time when the government seizes it); therefore, the owner's subsequent transfer of the property to someone else will not defeat the forfeiture unless the transferee was reasonably without knowledge of any illegality.

RICO Acronym for Racketeer Influenced and Corrupt Organizations. See *RICO statute*.

RICO offense Under federal law it is unlawful for a person to acquire, operate, or receive income from an enterprise through a pattern of racketeering activity; law provides for extended penalties (up to $25,000 fine and 20 years in prison). See *enterprise; pattern; predicate offenses; racketeering activity; RICO statute*.

RICO statute Federal law as part of the Organized Crime Control Act (1970), Title IX; the "Racketeer Influenced and Corrupt Organizations" section; established to attack organized crime groups and their organizations; it is applied broadly; provides for the RICO offense; is one of two federal laws providing to the government criminal forfeiture authority in organized crime cases; specifies that a convicted RICO offender forfeits all interests in the enterprise; it provides for civil damages and dissolution of the enterprise itself; many states have their own RICO statues with predicate offenses not involving federal law. See *Comprehensive Drug Abuse Prevention and Control Act (1970); RICO offense*.

robbery Act of obtaining of property from another by using threats of *immediate* harm.

roving wiretaps (or roving taps) Allows government agents to intercept transmissions from multiple locations or devices (phones, cell phones, e-mail, Internet accounts) that a particular suspect uses; a specific telephone line or e-mail or location is not named because the suspect moves from place to place frequently and uses different phones or other means of communicating.

runner Person who would sell policy tickets (in the illicit lottery business) or anyone involved in delivering messages among organized crime members.

search warrant Court order used to search a particular place for particular things based on an affidavit (sworn statement) containing sufficient information to show probable cause (a reasonable probability) to believe that those things are at that place and that they are linked to a particular crime (e.g., contraband, evidence of crime), or, in regard to communication (e.g., to bug a room or tap a telephone), probable cause to believe that a particular person is linked to a particular crime (this includes most suspected federal offenses punishable by a year or more imprisonment: i.e., felonies); it is an investigative tool (to seek evidence), not a prosecutorial tool (to present evidence in court).

SEC Acronym for Securities and Exchange Commission.

shadow economy See *black market*.

shylock Person who lends money at exorbitant interest rates. See *loanshark*.

smuggling Illegal and secretive transportation of goods or people, usually across a border.

smurfing Type of money laundering by which illicitly obtained cash is exchanged for bank checks or money orders, which a third party then deposits into the offender's account.

soldiers Lowest ranking members of a crime family, broken into units headed by a lieutenant or captain.

speakeasy Establishment used for selling and drinking alcoholic beverages during the Prohibition era (1920-1933) when the sale, manufacture, and transportation of alcohol were illegal.

special grand jury Sometimes called an "investigating grand jury"; authorized by the Organized Crime Control Act (1970), Title I; has the same powers as a traditional grand jury; however, also has additional special powers: it is called every 18 months or by special request of the prosecutor; can meet for a long term (up to 36 months); thereafter, may issue a public report (describing organized crime conditions or official corruption); can conduct continuing investigations along with police; deals primarily with statewide investigations, in contrast to those that are local investigations. See *traditional grand jury*.

sting or sting operation Operation in which police officers work undercover as purported criminals in order to entice, but not entrap, criminals to reveal their criminal operations.

street tax Ongoing payments that an organized crime group extorts from a licit or illicit business as payment for protection from harm to that business that the group would otherwise inflict. See *protection racket*.

strike force Group of agents from various law enforcement agencies (e.g., ATF, DEA, FBI, and IRS) in various cities to investigate and prosecute organized crime activities and groups.

Structuralist theory Theory of criminal behavior that focuses on how acts come to be defined as criminal, such as arbitrary laws, which encourage people to disregard the rights of others and are created to control the working class; it deals with inconsistencies in the criminal law and its enforcement.

subterranean economy See *black market*.

syndicate (or crime syndicate) takeover Use of coercion to intimidate legitimate business owners either to sell their businesses or to have their businesses operated by an outsider.

"tap" An electronic listening device secretly connected to a telephone line in order to overhear conversations from a remote location; for example, a "telephone tap" or "to tap a telephone," as authorized by a search warrant.

Task Force on Organized Crime (TFR) As part of the President's Commission on Law Enforcement and Administration of Justice, the TFR issued its report in 1967. Through hearings and research over a 2-year period, it recognized difficulties in obtaining proof in organized crime investigations and recommended a federal witness protection program, a federal wiretapping law, and a federal special grand jury law—all of which became law within the next 3 years; among other things, it recommended that for felonies committed as part of a continuing enterprise, the law should provide for extended prison sentences, which resulted in the RICO statute.

territory Area (e.g., of a city) under control of an organized crime group.

Tieri trial Criminal turned government informer Jimmy Fratianno (a high-ranking member of an organized crime group) testified about the organization of LCN families; the significance of this case is in the government's attempt to prove in court the existence of the Cosa Nostra as a continuing criminal enterprise (in violation of RICO provisions).

Title III of the Omnibus Crime Control Act (1968) Authorizes federal law enforcement officials—when having a search warrant—to eavesdrop on the conversations of crime suspects; its two stated purposes are safeguarding the privacy of wire and oral communications and providing law enforcement with a weapon to fight organized crime. Also see *search warrant*; *Electronic Communications Privacy Act (1987)*.

Tong Chinese secret society originally created for mutual support and protection, but now its activities are often criminal as a form of organized crime.

traditional grand jury Sometimes called a "charging grand jury"; holds secret proceedings in which the prosecutor presents evidence to establish probable cause for an indictment, which it then issues; if probable cause is not established, it issues a "no bill."

trafficking Smuggling of commodities (e.g., cigarettes, drugs, weapons) or people (e.g., illegal immigrants) as an illicit business activity or enterprise. See *smuggling*.

transactional immunity Authorized by case law for centuries, this is a witness's full immunity from prosecution in exchange for being compelled (under penalty of contempt) to give up the Fifth Amendment to remain silent. The government may not prosecute the witness at all in regard to the subject matter of the witness's immunized testimony; thus, this type of immunity is a weaker prosecution tool than use immunity.

trap-and-trace device Equipment that records the telephone numbers of *incoming* calls. See *pen register; ECPA order*.

Travel Act (1961) Federal law prohibiting use of interstate or foreign commerce in promotion of an illegal activity (including prostitution).

Triads Branches of Chinese underground society that consist of decentralized entrepreneurs who engage in organized crime activity for profit. Size and scale of Triad membership are unknown because the groups act independently in their illicit activities.

tribute Percentage of illicit profits that one organized crime group has to pay another organized crime group for operating in the latter's territory.

typology Study of, or analysis or classification based on, types.

underboss Second in charge of a crime family, ranking just below the boss.

undercover agent Police officer whose identity is concealed and who uses a cover (a fictitious biography) to pose as a person in the criminal element.

United Bamboo A Chinese organized crime group with headquarters in Taiwan. It has a number of branches, mostly in China's urban areas, as well as in some cities in the United States, Canada, and Asia. It has been involved in drug trafficking, prostitution, human smuggling, and related crimes.

unlawful debt Under federal law, a debt incurred during illegal gambling activity (thus, because the illegal gambling activity is unlawful, any debts incurred from it are also unlawful).

use immunity Authorized by the Organized Crime Control Act (1970), Title II; this is a witness's partial immunity from prosecution in exchange for being compelled (under penalty of contempt) to give up the Fifth Amendment right to remain silent. The government may prosecute the witness in regard to the subject matter of the witness's immunized testimony, but is prohibited from using the information in that testimony, as well as any information that is derived directly or indirectly from that testimony; thus, this type of immunity is a more powerful prosecution tool than transactional immunity.

U.S. PATRIOT Act (2001) The Uniting and Strengthening America by Providing Appropriate Tools Required to Intercept and Obstruct Terrorism Act of 2001. Federal law that extended the Bank Secrecy Act to nonbanks: check-cashing companies, money transmitters (e.g., Western Union), jewelers, pawnbrokers, casinos, credit card companies, and traveler's check and money order issuers.

U.S. Presidential Commissions There have been two U.S. presidential commissions that focused specifically on organized crime. See *Task Force on Organized Crime* and *President's Commission on Organized Crime*.

usurious loan Loan that violates the usury law because the interest rate charged is above the legal limit.

usury Lending money at a rate of interest in excess of the legal rate that may be charged to a borrower for the use of money. See *loanshark*.

Valachi, Joseph Testified in the McClellan hearings (1963), wherein he revealed the existence of the Castellammarese War and described the workings of the "Cosa Nostra" in terms that fit the hierarchical model of organized crime.

withdrawal from a conspiracy Requires a coconspirator to take some affirmative action that defeats the purpose of the conspiracy; mere cessation of activity in the conspiracy is not enough.

witness immunity See *immunity; transactional immunity; use immunity.*

witness protection See *Witness Security Program (WITSEC).*

Witness Security Program (WITSEC) Authorized by the Organized Crime Control Act (1970), Title V; a government witness, whose life is in danger, is provided security at the request of a prosecutor and approval of the U.S. Attorney General, and under the supervision and service of the U.S. Marshals Service; a new identity (including a new birth certificate and social security number), relocation to an area far from the target of the witness's testimony, and provision of a subsistence allowance and other help are provided until the witness is self-supporting.

WITSEC Acronym for Witness Security Program.

work stoppages Workers—without good cause—walking off the job site or not coming to it.

Timeline of Organized Crime in the United States

Event and Its Significance	
1890	**Hennessey murder in New Orleans.** Interest in the Mafia in the United States is traced to the murder of a police superintendent, whose dying words were "Sicilians have done for me" or "Dagoes"—*interpreted as an Italian connection to his death.*
1920-1933	**Prohibition.** Laws passed pursuant to the 18th Amendment to the U.S. Constitution (later repealed by the 21st Amendment) prohibited the making and selling of alcoholic beverages. Gangs started illegal manufacturing, smuggling, and speakeasy operations. *This era was probably responsible more than any other event for the emergence of strong organized crime groups*, with much public/official corruption among police and politicians so organized crime groups maintained a degree of immunity from prosecution.
1930s	**The Great Depression.** A worldwide business slump, ranked as the worst and longest period of high unemployment and low business activity in modern times. Businesses (banks, stores, factories) closed, leaving millions of Americans jobless and without money, thereby relying on government or charities for subsistence. It began in October 1929, when stock values dropped rapidly, and ended about 10 years later at the beginning of World War II (1939). *The Great Depression hurt organized crime by reducing the money available to spend on liquor and the vices, but organized crime groups survived on illicit gambling as desperate bettors sought a change in their luck.*
1950	**Kefauver Hearings.** Live television coverage of public hearings—conducted by U.S. Senator Estes Kefauver—*brought the concept of "Mafia" to the forefront of public concern*. Law enforcement officials claimed that a Mafia existed, but criminal offenders denied membership in, or knowledge of, a Mafia. The committee concluded that "there is a sinister criminal organization known as the Mafia operating throughout the country with ties in other nations." *Others have since concluded that the committee did not prove, but merely assumed, its existence.*
1957	**Apalachin Incident.** Sixty-five men (including 58 Italians, some with criminal records)—meeting in a home in upstate Apalachin, New York—fled and were stopped and detained temporarily by police. Hearings by a committee of the New York State legislature *caused a great deal of publicity (like the Kefauver hearings years before) and went a long way toward cementing people's attitudes about the nature of organized crime,* despite the lack of hard evidence.

Continued

Event and Its Significance—cont'd	
1963	**McClellan (Valachi) Hearings.** Joseph Valachi, a lower level member of the Genovese crime family in New York City, testified before a U.S. senate subcommittee (headed by Senator McClellan) about the power struggles among Italian-American gangs during the early 1930s (the Castellammarese War) and *the existence of a structured (hierarchical) organization (the Cosa Nostra) whose principal activity was to engage in criminal activity as an ongoing criminal conspiracy.* His testimony led to legislation permitting widespread use of wiretaps, special grand juries, witness immunity, and other prosecution tools.
1967	**President's Crime Commission: The Task Force on Organized Crime (1967) ("TFR").** After hearings and Joe Valachi's testimony, TFR *proposed a witness protection program, a federal wiretapping law, a special grand jury, and a RICO law (i.e., one with extended prison terms for felonies committed as part of a continuing enterprise). The TFR concluded that the largest source of organized crime revenue was gambling, followed by loansharking.*
1968	**Title III of Omnibus Crime Control and Safe Street Act (1968).** Enacted in response to the Valachi testimony and the President's Commission Report, it *authorized federal law enforcement officials to wiretap conversations in a wide variety of suspected criminal activities as evidence for use in court.*
1970	**Organized Crime Control Act (1970).** Enacted in response to the Valachi testimony and TFR report, it *established the power of "use" immunity from prosecution to compel witnesses to testify; special investigative grand juries; the witness protection program; and RICO with its special sentencing provisions for criminal enterprises.*
1970	**Bank Secrecy Act (1970).** Federal law enacted to *deter criminals from "laundering" illicitly obtained cash through legitimate businesses and banks.*
1980	**Tieri Trial (1980).** Jimmy Fratianno, a high-ranking member of an organized crime group and a criminal turned government informant, testified against Frank Tieri, who was charged with racketeering (RICO) and conspiracy. *This was the first time the government proved in court that (1) the Cosa Nostra existed and that (2) a defendant was a "boss" of a Cosa Nostra "family."* A massive U.S. prosecution effort against organized crime followed in a series of significant cases.
1986	**Commission Trial (1986).** The five "bosses" of the New York City crime "families" were charged with numerous offenses. *They admitted that the "Mafia exists and has members, and that it has a commission" to handle disputes. This finally ended the debate over the existence and structure of the Mafia.* Result: all were convicted and sentenced to 100 years in prison.
1986	**Money Laundering Control Act (1986).** This act *punishes anyone (i.e., an insider) who conducts a monetary transaction knowing that funds were derived from unlawful activity.* "Knowledge" includes "being willfully blind" to the source of the funds.
1987	**President's Commission on Organized Crime (1987).** After 2 years of hearings, the commission *proposed the enactment of state law versions of federal laws (wiretapping, witness immunity, special grand juries, and RICO). It also concluded that the largest source of revenue for organized crime was narcotics.*

Event and Its Significance—cont'd	
2001	**U.S. PATRIOT Act (2001).** *Extended the Bank Secrecy Act to nonbanks*: check-cashing companies, money transmitters (e.g., Western Union, jewelers, pawnbrokers, casinos, credit card companies, and traveler's check and money order issuers).
2003	**The New York Times (2003).** After a new round of mob indictments in New York, the paper concluded that "reports of its death have been greatly exaggerated".
2008	**Bonanno Crime Group (2008).** Acting boss and members of the Bonanno crime group in New York are sentenced to 15-30 years in prison for murder conspiracy.
2009	**The Chicago Outfit (2009).** Longtime leaders of Chicago's organized crime scene are convicted and sentenced to life in prison for their involvement in a 16-year wave of murders to silence witnesses and settle disputes.
2010	**John A. "Junior" Gotti (2010).** Alleged one-time boss of Gambino crime group in New York City is tried four times with hung juries in each case (2005-2009) on racketeering charges, and the government ends its Gotti prosecution effort in 2010.
2011	**Vincent "Vinnie Gorgeous" Basciano (2011).** Former acting boss of Bonanno crime group in New York City convicted of murder conspiracy and received sentence of life in prison.
2013	**James "Whitey" Bulger (2013).** After 16 years as a fugitive, Bulger was captured and convicted of racketeering and his roles in 11 killings during his years as leader of the Winter Hill gang in Boston during the 1970s and 1980s. He was sentenced to two life prison terms at age 84.

Index